Mary Queen of Scots and French 1
1542–1600

Mary Queen of Scots and French Public Opinion, 1542–1600

Alexander S. Wilkinson

First published 2004 by
PALGRAVE MACMILLAN
Houndmills, Basingstoke, Hampshire RG21 6XS and 175 Fifth Avenue, New York, N. Y. 10010
Companies and representatives throughout the world

PALGRAVE MACMILLAN is the global academic imprint of the Palgrave Macmillan division of St. Martin's Press, LLC and of Palgrave Macmillan Ltd. Macmillan® is a registered trademark in the United States, United Kingdom and other countries. Palgrave is a registered trademark in the European Union and other countries.

ISBN 1–4039–2039–7

This book is printed on paper suitable for recycling and made from fully managed and sustained forest sources.

A catalogue record for this book is available from the British Library.

Library of Congress Cataloging-in-Publication Data
Wilkinson, Alexander S., 1975–
    Mary, Queen of Scots and French public opinion, 1542-1600 / Alexander S. Wilkinson.
        p. cm.
    Includes bibliographical references (p.) and index.
    ISBN 1–4039–2039–7
        1. Mary, Queen of Scots, 1542–1587.   2. Mary, Queen of Scots, 1542–1587 – Homes and haunts – France.   3. Scotland – History – Mary Stuart, 1542–1567 – Historiography.   4. Public opinion – France – History – 16th century.   5. Scotland – Foreign public opinion, French.   6. Scotland – Foreign relations – France.   7. France – Foreign relations – Scotland.   8. Queens – Scotland – Biography.   9. Scotland – Relations – France.   10. France – Relations – Scotland.   I. Title.
DA787.A1W55 2004
941.105'092 – dc22   2004041508

10 9 8 7 6 5 4 3 2 1
13 12 11 10 09 08 07 06 05 04

Printed and bound in Great Britain by
Antony Rowe Ltd, Chippenham and Eastbourne

To my parents Jannette and Alex Wilkinson, my grandfather David Farmer, and to the memory of my grandmother Emma Farmer

Contents

List of Figures and Tables

Figures

Tables

ix

Acknowledgements

'If you are lucky enough to have lived in Paris as a young man, then wherever you go for the rest of your life, it stays with you, for Paris is a moveable feast.' — Ernest Hemingway to a friend, 1950

It is easy to become sentimental when coming to the end of a piece of research that has taken almost four years to complete. Around half of this time was spent in libraries and archives in France. I will never forget the year I spent in Paris: the rich archival and library collections, the city, the memorable personalities and the feasts – moveable and otherwise.

The study that follows is a revised version of my doctoral thesis, completed at the University of St Andrews in September 2001. The research for this project was financed largely by the Carnegie Trust for the Universities of Scotland, for whose generosity I will always be grateful. The Trust not only consented to pay my way through three years of the PhD, but also provided a considerable sum of money to defray the costs of undertaking research in France. The School of History at the University of St Andrews, moreover, very kindly provided me with several grants to cover the costs of visiting several French provincial libraries and archives. Few scholars have the luxury of moving beyond the principal collections in Paris. I would like also to acknowledge the generosity of Dr Anthony Pollock who provided accommodation in Paris in August 2003, where most of the revisions to transform the thesis into this book were carried out.

This study has benefited immeasurably from conversations with a number of scholars, for whose time, advice and in many cases friendship, I thank them. In particular, I am grateful to Kenneth Austin, Margaret Beckett, Jennifer Britnell, Thomas Brochard, Michael Bruening, Fiona Campbell, Philip Conner, Mirko Fischer, Stuart Foster, Julian Goodare, Bruce Gordon, Max von Habsburg, Matthew Hall, David Hartley, Jeff Jaynes, Augustine Kelly, Karin Maag, Roy McCullough, Roger Mason, Matthew McLean, Terry Murphy, Geoffrey Parker, Luc Racaut, Jonathon Reid, Ben Sanders, James Supple and Malcolm Walsby.

My fiancée, Melissa Pollock, has lived with this project almost as long as I have. For her patience, support and insight, I would like to say a huge 'thank you'.

Above all, however, the study that follows owes an enormous amount to my PhD supervisor, Andrew Pettegree. No student wishing to enter the academic world could have a better role model.

St Andrews   ALEXANDER S. WILKINSON

List of Abbreviations

AAC	Angers Archives Communales
AAD	Angers Archives Départementales de Maine–et–Loire
ADC	Archives Départementales du Calvados, Caen
AHR	*American Historical Review*
AN	Archives Nationale, Paris
ADSM	Archives Départementales de la Seine–Maritime
AS	Archivo de Simancas
BHR	*Bibliothèque d'Humanisme et Renaissance*
BL	British Library
BNF	Bibliothèque Nationale de France, Paris
CAD	Caen, Archives Départementales du Calvados
CHR	*Catholic Historical Review*
CSPF	*Calendar of State Papers Foreign Series*
CSP Scot.	*Calendar of State Papers. Scottish Series*
CSP Venetian	*Calendar of State Papers. Venetian Series*
DNB	*Dictionary of National Biography*
EAL	Edinburgh Advocates Library
EHR	*English Historical Review*
ENL	Edinburgh National Library
FH	*French History*
FHS	*French Historical Studies*
FVB	St Andrews Sixteenth–Century French Vernacular Book Project
HS	*Historical Society*
JMH	*Journal of Modern History*
NAC	Nantes Archives Communales
P&P	*Past and Present*
RFHL	*Revue français d'histoire du Livre*
RMS	*Renaissance and Modern Studies*
SCJ	*Sixteenth Century Journal*
SHR	*Scottish Historical Review*
SLJ	*Scottish Literary Journal*

Introduction

The French Wars of Religion were a series of conflicts of bitter and often desperate struggle fought for over forty years. It was a war characterised by massacres, sieges and heroic resistance, but also by a high level of participation amongst ordinary people. For this was a war as much fought for hearts and minds as for outright military victory. The conflict began with an upsurge of Protestant sentiment born on a wave of aggressive published print. But Protestantism was soon turned back by a Catholic polemical assault of even greater ferocity. Far less than is casually assumed, largely on the basis of German evidence, was the book the exclusive property of evangelicals.[1] In France, Catholics outpublished and eventually outthought their Protestant opponents. Then, in the last decade of the conflict, Catholics turned the power of the printed word against the crown. While they had initially fought to save the monarchy for their faith, in 1588, on the Day of the Barricades, they turned decisively against the royal leadership that they felt had betrayed them.

In this bitter and, even by the standards of the age, unusually bloody struggle, the printed book played a remarkably active role. Protestants propagated their beliefs and pleaded for toleration in numerous printed works. Once the fighting was under way, the Protestant nobility justified their resistance in printed manifestos. Meanwhile, and right from the beginning of the conflict, those prepared to defend the old faith made their case in theological and polemical works which conceded nothing to their Protestant opponents either in polemical fervour or literary skill. These books were then brought to their market by willing allies in the Parisian book world. Paris was the centre of the French book trade, and indeed one of Europe's principal centres of book production. Its complete and unmistakable allegiance to the Catholic cause was an

1

important and perhaps decisive advantage for the supporters of the traditional religion. Yet even the zealous publishers of Paris could not have sustained their efforts had their work not found resonance in the market. From an early point in the conflict, the debate over the settlement of the religious question in France commanded the interest and engagement of a remarkably wide public. This was the case in the first years of the conflict when the Protestant threat was most pressing, in the wake of the massacre of St Bartholomew, when the reading public eagerly consumed repeated editions gloating at the misfortune of the Huguenots, and most of all in the period that forms the climax of this study, the struggle between Henri III and the Catholic League.

Those who wrote for the market clearly believed that there were reasons to engage the attention of the urban public. And events bore them out. Frequently during the Wars of Religion, populations of city and countryside turned out to sustain the beliefs in which they had been tutored by religious writers. Yet, an understanding of this public engagement, and how it was created, has hardly even begun to be integrated into the standard literature. Building on an older tradition, many general studies of the Wars of Religion continue to treat the conflict as fundamentally a struggle between elites, an opportunist assault on a weakened monarchy by aristocratic factions.[2] This specific tradition meshes with an influential historiographical trend, emanating from scholars of eighteenth-century political culture, which doubts the existence of an active public opinion as early as the sixteenth century.

If several influential historians of eighteenth-century political culture have expressed profound scepticism at the existence of 'public opinion' before the middle of the 1800s, it is because of their very particular definition of that concept. Modern usage of the term 'public opinion', as the view of the majority of people on a given issue, is rejected by these scholars. They seek to reclaim the phrase for how it would have been understood by certain enlightened thinkers of the second half of the eighteenth century. The seminal study of eighteenth-century 'public opinion', the impetus of this approach, was Jürgen Habermas' *The Structural Transformation of the Public Sphere*.[3] Analysing the rise of an active and informed bourgeois public, Habermas posited that 'public opinion' was something that developed in Great Britain only at the turn of the eighteenth century and in France 'not before roughly the middle of the eighteenth century'.[4] The public sphere could not have existed before the mid–eighteenth century in France, because the socio-economic conditions for the emergence of a civil society, including the institutional structures such as cafés and salons necessary to support rational debate, were not yet in place. The public sphere in his discussion is defined as a theoretical space which exists between, and is insulated from, the 'private realm' on the one hand and the 'sphere of public authority' on the other.[5] Within this idealised space, away from vested socio-economic influences, private individuals could come together and engage in rational-critical debate. The product of these discussions within the 'public sphere' was 'public opinion'. Initially confined to the 'world of letters', the public sphere soon began to engage in political debate. In consequence, 'a political consciousness developed in the public sphere of civil society which, in opposition to absolute sovereignty, articulated the concept of and demand for general and abstract laws which ultimately came to assert itself (i.e. public opinion) as the only legitimate source of this law'.[6] While Habermas' central thesis has undergone some significant modifications, neo-revisionist historians such as Keith Baker, have tended to follow tenaciously the notion of the rationality of 'public opinion'.[7]

While this model does highlight a changing understanding of the relationship between the bourgeoisie and the state during the late eighteenth century, it remains a highly problematic and idealised thesis. It assumes that rational-critical debate can take place within a vacuum, while its understanding of the 'public sphere' is, in consequence, profoundly restrictive. In attempting to visualise how society functioned, these scholars have over-emphasised the congruence between political philosophy and political reality.

Simply because there was no understanding of public opinion as a legitimising force in sixteenth-century discourse, does not mean it did not exist or that it was unimportant. The word 'opinion' itself may indeed have been used pejoratively by contemporary authors who saw it as a negative and dangerous force. Yet, paradoxically, such authors, writing in the vernacular to reach as broad an audience as possible, recognised that this public voice mattered.[8] Whether fully recognised in political rhetoric or not, public opinion was influential long before the late eighteenth century. On an everyday level even those who were excluded from directly participating in the political process could feel some sense of involvement in the world around them. The populace, especially the urban population, paid considerable attention to current affairs. It was one way, as today, in which men and women could feel a sense of involvement in politics, despite in practical terms being excluded from it. Yet as a public, from the humblest members of society to the most prominent nobles, their voice was more difficult to ignore.

The state, and groups within the state, could disregard the opinions of the public at its peril. The public had several ways of making their feelings known on issues that were important to them. The recourse to riots and massacres always remained a menacing possibility for local and national authorities.[9]

This study will seek to reconstruct as far as is possible the opinions of the public, broadly defined, whether those opinions were 'rational' or not. It will seek to do so, primarily, through an examination of printed books and pamphlets. Recent research into the communications process in early modern Europe has indicated that there is compelling evidence to force a readjustment in the emphasis traditionally placed on the printed book in cementing, forming or reforming attitudes. The importance of other media such as the sermon, the theatre, the visual image and the song in what was predominantly an oral culture, has now been broadly acknowledged.[10] Such research highlights that print was by no means the only or even the most important form of communication in this period. Yet, an examination of the printed word remains a vital indicator of public opinion for a number of reasons.

Firstly, the majority of printed books from this period have survived, whereas evidence for other media is at best fragmentary and at worst non-existent.[11] Secondly, while other media, including sermons, visual images and songs were the most important way in which ideas were transmitted in an oral society, the book was by no means the preserve of the literate. Several important studies have probed the boundaries between oral and literate cultures and found them to be highly porous. The printed broadside ballads in England, for instance, discussed so masterfully by Tessa Watt in *Cheap Print and Popular Piety*, were marketed at the humblest members of the literate public. These ballads were then sung to traditional or recently composed melodies. Moreover, Robert Scribner in his seminal study, *For the Sake of Simple Folk*, highlights the vital importance of visual media in Germany, principally woodcut images as a means of spreading the message of the Reformation to the illiterate majority. Such studies continue to remind us of the complexity and hybridisation of the communications process. While there were important national cultural divergences (for instance there was no real equivalent to the broadside ballad in France), one critical point remains salient. While it is estimated that only around 30 per cent of the adult urban population could read, books were read aloud.[12] The ideas contained within them were circulated through discussions and meetings – though this, it must be said, is an argument more often asserted than demonstrated. This study, however, will provide important evidence to show that there was a significant if not overwhelming overlap between the ideas circulated in the printed word and those circulated through other media (see chapter 4).[1] For instance, printed works repeated ideas that could first be heard on the street and vice versa. The general public were both creators and consumers of opinion. Printed books, particularly the smaller vernacular pamphlets which reached almost every level of society, are the single most important indicator of public opinion available to historians. In the words of Peter Matheson, who has studied the pamphlet literature of the German Reformation, such works are 'like a periscope sticking out of the ocean, of that vast, submarine force of discussion and dissent, which we call public opinion'.[13]

The warfare waged to win the hearts and minds of the French public during the Religious Wars in France involved an assault against ideological opponents on several fronts. Yet, scholars have paid too little attention to the fact that the polemical attack on Catholicism and Protestantism consisted of far more than learned discourses. In fact a larger stratum of works, more often than not small octavo pamphlets, touched on immediate political issues, reporting for instance the details of battles or attacking or defending prominent noble figures. Such publications have suffered from comparative neglect: seen perhaps as being irrational, unrestrained, violent and of no intrinsic intellectual merit.[14] Over the past two decades, however, with the exemplary work of scholars such as Barbara Diefendorf, Wylie Sypher and Luc Racaut, there are encouraging signs that this fundamental imbalance in the literature is slowly beginning to be redressed.[15]

This study deals not only with works of literary, theological and intellectual sophistication aimed primarily at the bourgeois and nobility, but also with other types of printed literature which would have reached every level of society. It seeks to make a contribution to understanding the political and polemical works published during the Wars of Religion, and therefore to what motivated religious activism during this period, by examining one theme. Even apparently peripheral or collateral issues could be engaged to make partisan points, and this was certainly the case with the polemic relating to Mary Queen of Scots. Mary was a complex figure, difficult to present as an unambiguous symbol of Catholicism or, following her execution by Elizabeth in February 1587, as an unambiguous martyr of the Catholic cause. Mary was also, as the opening chapter of this study intends to demonstrate, a very French figure. She spent her formative years in France. In 1558 she married the dauphin François and, on the death of Henri II in 1560, the couple unified the crowns of France and Scotland. Although Mary returned to Scotland following the death of her husband, she continued to possess and manage considerable French estates, the legacy of the dowry settled upon her as a consequence of her brief marriage. In Scotland, and even during the period of her English imprisonment, Mary maintained a predominantly French household and a pronounced interest in French affairs. French was her first language; she employed a significant number of French personnel in her own household and was an avid reader of French literature.

This study will seek to analyse the extent and nature of French public interest in the career of Mary Queen of Scots. It may seem surprising that, to date, it is a subject that has attracted so little historical interest, especially given the voluminous body of scholarship that has examined and re-examined the life of the Scottish Queen. In fact, only two studies have attempted to tackle the subject in any detail. Georges Ascoli's *La Grande–Bretagne devant l'opinion française depuis la Guerre de Cent Ans jusqu'à la fin du XVIe siècle*, published in 1927, discussed the place of Britain in French public opinion by examining a number of works in Latin and in French.[16] With a literary rather than historical focus, Ascoli paid useful but very circumscribed attention to the representation of Mary. The second study is far better known – James Emerson Phillips' *Images of a Queen. Mary Stuart in Sixteenth–Century Literature*, published in 1964.[17] It is an ambitious monograph, examining the image of Mary in sixteenth-century Latin, English and French literature. Its broad scope, however, and the author's decision to adopt a chronological rather than geographic approach, has tended to blur the specificity of national approaches to Mary. The evolution of Mary's image in France and elsewhere in Europe is often subsumed by Phillips' concentration on the English literature.

The critical problem that faced both these scholars was that they had at their disposal very incomplete bibliographical information. A major obstacle facing any historian wishing to embark on research based on French printed polemic has been the lack of a comprehensive bibliography of sixteenth-century French books. From the 1920s onwards, scholars of British history have had at their disposal the *Short Title Catalogue of Books Printed in England, Scotland and Ireland, and of English Books Printed Abroad, 1475–1640*.[18] Yet, there has been no comparable project to catalogue texts published in France or in French. With printing in France far more dispersed than in Britain, with over thirty significant centres of book production, bibliographical studies have tended to concentrate on individual centres of production or on particular themes or authors.[19] For bibliographical information, Ascoli could turn to John Scott's useful *Bibliography of Works Relating to Mary Queen of Scots, 1544–1700*, published in 1896.[20] Meanwhile Phillips, in addition to his own investigations, was also able to consult a bibliography produced by the Bibliothèque Nationale in 1931,[21] together with a bibliography published in 1944. This was Samuel and Dorothy Tannenbaum's *Marie Stuart, Queen of Scots. A Concise Bibliography*, a bibliography that historians might have wished had never been published at all.[22] It offers a selection of abridged records that are too often misleading and inaccurate.

An advantage enjoyed by the present study over previous assessments of the French public response to Mary Queen of Scots is that it has been able to draw on a major new bibliographical project based within the Reformation Studies Institute at the University of St Andrews and directed by Professor Andrew Pettegree.[23] The St Andrews Sixteenth-Century French Vernacular Book Project (FVB), which began work in 1997 initially as the Religious Book Project, now aims to catalogue and provide detailed bibliographical descriptions for all books published in the French language before 1601. Indeed, the project is now well on its way to achieving this objective. It is expected that by the time a short-title catalogue is published in 2007, it will contain approximately 50,000 bibliographically distinct items which exist in over 150,000 copies.

Access to this unique resource has meant that, for the first time, it has been possible to survey with accuracy sixteenth-century French publications relative to Mary Queen of Scots and the British Isles and, of course, to situate this corpus within its broader bibliographical context.[24] The compilation of a reliable bibliography of works relating to the Scottish Queen has formed the crucial backbone to this study.[25] Comprising no fewer than four hundred and twenty distinct items, it was compiled in two principal stages. The first was to prepare an initial list of editions to be consulted from existing bibliographical sources and from references in the secondary literature. This was an important task given that many editions containing references to Mary cannot be readily identified as such from their titles alone. These references were then checked against the files of FVB; additional copies and editions were noted, together with a list of suspected ghost editions. The second stage in the process of compiling the bibliography involved consulting these books in libraries in France and elsewhere, examining those noted in the initial list prepared in St Andrews and examining as many others as possible in the hope of finding previously unknown references to the Scottish Queen. Libraries with major collections were visited, including the National Library of Scotland in Edinburgh and the libraries of Paris:

La Bibliothèque Nationale de France, La Bibliothèque Historique de la Ville de Paris, La Bibliothèque du Protestantisme, La Bibliothèque de Saint-Geneviève, the Mazarine and the Arsenal. But by no means all the books relative to Mary could be found in these libraries. Visits were also undertaken to numerous French provincial libraries, whose rich collections are all too often overlooked by historians such as Angers, Avignon, Beaune, Besançon, Bordeaux, Caen, Dijon, La Rochelle, Lyon, Montpellier, Le Mans, Nantes, Nîmes, Niort, Rouen, Saintes and Valognes. The confiscations of monastic and noble collections which accompanied the French Revolution in 1789 and the lack of any subsequent systematic centralisation of patrimonial collections has resulted in the continued existence of truly exceptional provincial collections.[26]

The bibliographical work which underpins this study is not without its limitations. Clearly, there will be editions relating to Mary which have escaped the notice of this study. For instance, it was simply by chance that a book such as *Apologie contre certaines calomnies mises sus, à la desfaveur & desavantage de l'estat des affaires de ce royaume* was ever included.[27] This particular work, supporting the crown's policy of pragmatic toleration in the early 1560s, contains a small reference to Mary towards the end of this quarto pamphlet. But there is no indication from the title or even from a brief reading of the text that this should have been so. Despite this caveat, from the compilation of an updated bibliography and from reading a significant proportion of these texts, it is now possible to trace more accurately than has been possible before, the contours of French public interest in the Queen of Scots.

Figure I.1 illustrates the chronological distribution of publications relating to Mary Queen of Scots and the British Isles. There was a peak of interest in Mary around the time of her marriage to the dauphin, 1558–61, followed by a steady stream of interest in the Queen from 1562 to 1586. The most significant interest in Mary, however, occurred in the period 1587–9, when the presses responded to the execution of the imprisoned Queen. The study that follows, arranged in five chapters, will attempt to examine the development of French public interest in the Queen of Scots. The first will sketch the historical relationship between Mary and France, demonstrating the extent to which the Queen of Scots was a figure deeply embedded in French Catholic culture. The remaining four chapters will deal directly with her treatment in French printed polemic. Chapter 2 will focus on how Mary was represented by Catholic propagandists from around 1548 when she was promised in marriage to the dauphin, to the period just before her execution when she had spent seventeen years languishing in an English

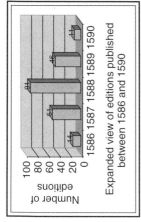

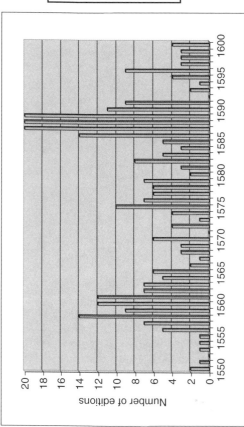

Figure 1.1 Chronological overview of editions relative to Mary Queen of Scots and the British Isles published in French during the second half of the sixteenth century

prison. Chapter 3 will focus on the evolution of the Huguenot portrait of the Queen. However, the climax of this long and turbulent engagement can be found in chapters 4 and 5, which deal with the polemical literature that poured off the presses in response to Mary's execution from 1587. This 'tragic' event became one of the most prominent and radical themes in the campaign of the Catholic League, a revolutionary party which came to challenge the authority of the French King, Henri III. Chapter 4 examines the way in which the printed image of the martyred Queen interfaced with other media such as sermons and rumour to rally popular opinion against Henri III. Chapter 5 analyses the printed literature in more detail, especially how the extraordinarily emotive account of Mary's final moments was reported in the Catholic press.

1
Mary Queen of Scots: A French Life

On 21 September 1548, Mary Stuart, Queen of Scotland and fiancée to the dauphin François, arrived in Angers.[1] A spectacular *entrée* festival greeted her arrival. A rich display of tapestries produced a flow of colour, draping neatly from almost every building that lined the streets of the city.[2] On arrival, the royal party and, most likely, representative groups from the various social strata of the city, processed from the gate of Saint-Nicholas to the church of Angers.[3] Guillaume Lerat, sieur de Beauchamp, then in his final year as mayor delivered the official *harangue* 'as if to the King' and a number of gifts were presented to Mary.[4] Among these offerings from the citizens of Angers were luxury foods intended to symbolise the fertility of the Loire region such as sugared almonds, jams and a selection of ripe fruits including pears, prunes, plums and grapes. The Queen's governors, Lord Erskine and Lord Livingston, who had accompanied Mary on her stormy voyage from Scotland, were given a fine selection of red and white wine.[5]

High on the festival programme came a gun salute and a military parade.[6] However, another event would have particularly amazed the gathered crowds. This was the rather unconventional performance of a foreign monarch, a young girl aged five, granting letters of remission to a number of carefully chosen, presumably high profile prisoners.[7] The message that the *entrée* was attempting to transmit was very clear. It was an articulation, in ceremony, of Mary's royal status in France. The deliberate parallels between the events of 21 September 1548 and royal *entrées*, spectacles that welcomed newly anointed kings of France on their first visit to a city, would not have been lost on the population of Angers.[8]

That Mary's relationship with France should have taken such a course could not have been foreseen at the time of her birth in 1542. Certainly,

Mary's attractive dynastic position had always warranted serious political consideration. Her mother was none other than Marie de Guise, the daughter of Claude de Lorraine Duc de Guise and Antoinette de Bourbon-Vendôme, and thus a member of one of the most powerful noble families in Europe. More importantly, the tragic death of her father, James V, only six days after her birth at Linlithgow Palace near Edinburgh on 8 December 1542, brought Mary the crown of Scotland in her infancy, and with it a clear if strongly contested claim to the English throne.[9] François I's broader foreign policy conditioned the French response to Mary's position. Preoccupied as he was throughout his reign by the conflict with Charles V, François I always remained far more attentive to events in Italy than in the British Isles. Nevertheless, he could ill afford to ignore the political situation across the channel. Of critical importance to French interests was Henry VIII's attempt to secure Mary's hand in marriage for his son, the future Edward VI, thereby subjugating Scotland to the will of the English crown. Uppermost in French policy towards Scotland, then, was the French desire to preserve the sovereignty of this country in order to maintain the option of a second front against England. To this end, François aimed to thwart any prospect of an English marriage for Mary, but did not yet cultivate any notion of securing her for France. In fact, in 1543, the French even attempted to unite the Scottish Queen with one of her own noble subjects.[10] Three years later, in 1546, in order to cement a triple alliance between France, Denmark and Scotland, François I instructed his ambassador to offer Mary in marriage to the son of King Christian of Denmark.[11] There was no attempt made to capitalise on Marie de Guise's advantageous position in Scotland, and while the French did send significant military aid to the Scots to combat an aggressive and protracted English assault that historians have dryly labelled the 'Rough Wooing',[12] periods of expedition remained remarkably brief.[13]

The convergence of two events brought about a reorientation of French foreign policy and consequently a transformation in France's relationship with Mary. The first of these was the accession of Henri II to the throne of France following the death of François I in 1547. Henri favoured intervening in Scotland and England. In particular, such ambitions were reinforced and informed by the continuing rise of the Guise family at court, demonstrated by the appointment to the Privy Council of such favourites as the youthful Cardinal Charles de Guise, Mary Stuart's uncle.[14] The second event that spurred the French into adopting a new attitude to the British Isles was the crushing defeat of the

Scots at the battle of Pinkie, near Musselburgh, on 10 September 1547. Pinkie was a triumph for Protector Edward Seymour, Duke of Somerset, representing the climax of the English policy of Rough Wooing. But while the battle brought defeat for the Scots, it proved to be little more than a Pyrrhic victory for the English – the standard outcome of Anglo-Scottish hostilities since the late thirteenth century. As the Constable of France, Anne de Montmorency reported, 'the [French] court could not have received a greater displeasure if the said loss had been inflicted on themselves'.[15] For the Scots to withstand such abrasive English assaults, significant and timely French aid was imperative. It was in recognition of this that the Treaty of Haddington was signed in July 1548. In return for military and financial aid, the Scots were prepared to grant Henri certain Scottish strongholds and, more significantly, approved the marriage of their young Queen to the dauphin.

French investment in strengthening the Scots' military defence against England was considerable and has been estimated at around two million livres tournois between June 1548 and April 1550.[16] The war was protracted, due to the exigencies of a conflict characterised by the need to hold territory by the erection or occupation of strong points, such as at Inveresk, Luffness, Dunglass, Eyemouth, Home Castle, Lauder, Jedburgh and Old Roxburgh.[17] For the French, the benefits of this policy were not immediately evident. In particular, the investment of money and troops was domestically unpopular. As the Spanish ambassador to France reported, Scotland came to be known in France as 'the tomb of Frenchmen'.[18] Despite this unpopularity, Henri's pursuance of his bold dynastic policy led to significant gains, which came to be enshrined in the Peace of Boulogne signed on the 25 March 1550. English pretensions to the hand of Mary were abandoned, while England had little choice but to offer tacit recognition of an ever-increasing French presence in Scottish affairs.

It was within the context of this volatile political and military geography that Marie de Guise sent her daughter to be educated in France. Mary departed from Dumbarton on 29 July 1548, bound for the continent. Brest was the intended landing place for the fleet, but, following severe weather, it reached instead St Pol in Brittany on 15 August.[19] From the moment of her arrival, Mary was treated with lavish honour. Elaborate *entrées* were organised for her as she crossed by land and by river barge from St Pol to Saint-Germain-en-Laye. In this, Henri II made it very clear that he wished Mary to be treated as 'my own daughter', and nowhere is this intention highlighted more dramatically than in the preparations for the Angers *entrée*. A series of letters and council minutes, uncovered recently in the communal archives in Angers, reveal the preparations for this event.[20]

The *entrée* was almost wholly orchestrated by the office of Henri II through his *valet de chambre* the Sieur de La Cabassoles. A standard letter written by Henri II to the various cities that were to receive the Queen's party illustrates his insistence on directing these festivals.[21] In the following instance, the letter is addressed to the mayor, council and inhabitants of Angers and is dated from Mascon 23 July 1548:

> As our very dear and beloved daughter and cousin the Queen of Scotland will shortly be arriving in our kingdom, we wish that by the towns and places where she will pass, that she should be well honoured and well treated as if she were our own daughter. And for this cause, we command and expressly entreat you that when the said Queen passes by our town of Angers you will come before her with the best company of high-ranking men that can be assembled in order to receive and honour her and make gifts of wines, fruits and other offerings as you will hear more about from our representative the Sieur de Cabassoles – the present carrier of this letter, our *valet de chambre*, whom you should trust as if you were dealing with me in person as such is our pleasure. He will also inform you of everything else that we wish to be carried out.[22]

But while Angers had been informed that it would be on the route that Mary Stuart would take on her journey from the end of July 1548, the level of municipal participation in the organisation of the *entrée* was limited to dealing with practical detail, not with the grand political vision the event was intended to project. Such details included organising various painting projects, blocking plans to renovate the Hôtel de Ville lest the work remain incomplete on the arrival of the Queen, and planning the logistics of when and where the guards were to take their breaks.[23] One might suspect that even these smaller practical details were monitored very carefully by the King's representative La Cabassoles. The records even reveal that the speech the mayor of Angers was to deliver to the Queen was carefully crafted on his behalf.[24]

This elaborate projection of Mary's regal status reflected a conscious campaign by Henri II to identify his reign with an ambitious foreign policy. Perhaps a better known example of the dramatisation of this identity came with Henri II's *entrée* into Rouen on 1 October 1550. The publication of a printed text celebrating this festival in 1551, filled with magnificent woodcut illustrations of the celebrations, reveals an event ripe with symbolism and imagery.[25] The reconquest of Boulogne and the salvation of the Scots were the principal themes. But also, the *entrée* included the construction of a Brazilian camp replete with genuine natives; there was a mock sea battle, in which the French vessel triumphed over the Portuguese, while numerous classical representations were displayed including that of Hercules fighting the Hydra.[26] Henri's global ambitions were symbolised by his motto *Donec totum impleat orbem* (until it may fill the whole world), and his European ambitions by the image of the three crescents, taken to represent France, Scotland and England.[27] The presence of Marie de Guise, Mary's mother and Queen Dowager of Scotland lent additional weight to Henri's claims.[28] The more modest Angers festivities two years before anticipated the unity of France and Scotland; Mary Stuart was empowered with the authority of the French monarch to release prisoners. In addition, it was no coincidence that Mary's initial *entrée* festivities in 1548 took place at a time when Henri was himself making his initial royal *entrées* such as into Lyon on 23 September 1548 and into Paris in June 1549.[29]

In the years that followed these celebrations, Mary enjoyed a lifestyle that exceeded other members of the royal family.[30] In a letter written by Henri II in 1548, he indicated that he wished Mary to 'march before my daughters, on account of the marriage to my son and because she is a crowned Queen, and as such I desire that she will be honoured and well served'.[31] This period was to be one of the happiest in Mary's life, a time indeed that she was later to remember with great affection. Mary took precedence among the other royal and noble children, and shared 'the best room' with princess Elizabeth, who was to be the future wife of Philip II of Spain.[32] Also among her playmates was her future husband, François, for whom, despite his sickly disposition, she held a genuine affection from an early age.[33] A sense of the conspicuous magnificence of the environment in which Mary was nurtured can be gained from accounts of the expenditure of the nursery. For 1551, a massive 18,321 livres tournois was required for the nursery.[34] Thirty–seven children belonging to noble families were brought up with the dauphin François and his sisters. To staff this household, there were one hundred and fifty officials, fifty-seven cooks and assistants, five to twelve purveyors of wine and one water carrier. Among the manuscripts in the British Library, there are some food bills for 1551. For just one day, 1 December 1551, the household required two calves, sixteen sheep, five pigs, seven geese, a selection of choice beef, chickens, pigeons, hares and one pheasant. Also ordered were 36 pounds of cutlets, calves feet, partridges and larks, and no less than 72 dozen loaves. Five separate merchants provided the wine.[35] The accounts of Nicolas du Moncel, 'tailor to the Queen of Scots' for 1551 provide additional evidence, if any is required, of the luxurious lifestyle enjoyed by Mary. Among the many items listed, are 'a bodice of purple satin intricately sewn, cost 7 sols, a surcoat and a pair of sleeves slashed from white satin, 15 sols. A head-dress of crimson satin, 7 sols 6 deniers. A dress of damask gold, bordered with braids of gold, banded with crimson satin, with the top of the sleeves embroidered, 46 sols'.[36] No less than three brass cases were required to store Mary's jewellery.[37]

As to Mary's education, this was rooted firmly in the culture of the French Renaissance. The Scottish entourage that had accompanied Mary to France was quickly uncoupled from the young queen. According to Diane de Poitiers, various rivalries and tensions had built up from 1548 between the Scots and the staff of the royal nursery. Only the Queen's famous 'four Maries' who had accompanied her from Scotland remained.[38] These were Mary Stuart's maids of honour. Mary Beaton, Seaton, Fleming, and Livingstone were all of noble birth.[39] Even Mary's governess Lady Fleming was forced to return to Scotland in October 1551, following a brief affair with Henri II.[40] She was replaced by a French governess, Françoise d'Estampville, known as Madame de Parois. It was, however, to be another mistress of Henri II, Diane de Poitiers, who was eventually given principal responsibility for Mary's early education in France.[41] William Bryce has suggested tentatively, probably correctly, that it was Poitiers' corrosive influence that poisoned the previously amicable relationship between Mary and Catherine de Medici.[42] Alongside Diane de Poitiers, the Cardinal de Lorraine and Mary's grandmother, Antoinette de Bourbon-Vendôme Duchesse de Guise, also had an important role in Mary's upbringing. From around 1552, for example, when his niece was around ten, the Cardinal acted as *gouvernant*, chaperoning her at various celebrations organised by the citizens of Paris to honour the royal family.[43] Mary was presented to the French public with a triple identity; a Stuart Queen, a Valois and a Guise.

An accurate account of Mary's early life is only partially possible, due to the genre of source material on which historians and biographers are forced to rely. It is often difficult to separate reality from fiction in accounts marked more by eulogistic hyperbole than historical accuracy. Despite this caution, there does seem to be a genuine sense in which Mary impressed the French King, the Queen, the dauphin and all those who knew her at court. Henri II wrote on seeing Mary at Saint-Germain in 1549, that she was 'the most perfect child that I have ever seen'.[44] In a letter from the Cardinal de Lorraine to his sister, Marie de Guise, written at Saint-Germain on 25 February 1552, he wrote that:

> Your daughter is growing so much every day in grandeur, kindness, beauty, wisdom and virtue that she is as perfect and accomplished in all honest and virtuous affairs as is possible. There are none in this kingdom, not a noble's daughter or another of lower or middling birth of any condition or quality, that can match her.[45]

Besides a small body of court correspondence, often to Mary's mother Marie de Guise or between various ambassadors at court, the other principal source for this period of Mary's life are the remarks made by Pierre de Bourdeille, abbot of Brantôme. Beginning his career as a courtier in the clientele of the Guises, Brantôme was to be part of the group led by François de Lorraine, Duc de Guise, who accompanied Mary on her journey back to Scotland in 1561.[46] According to these sources, Mary had a 'very good and sweet voice' and enjoyed singing the songs of Clement Marot.[47] She played well on the cittern, the harp and the harpsichord. She danced with agility and grace, and learned needlework. Mary was proficient in several languages including French, Spanish, Italian and could understand Latin better than she could speak it. In fact, French was to be her 'natural' language – the language in which she would conduct the majority of her correspondence for the rest of her life. One incident noted by Brantôme occurred during this early stage in Mary's career. This was her assertion of the right of women, presumably noble women, to an education. This she delivered in a Latin oration in 1555 to Henri II and the French court in the great hall of the Louvre. Brantôme informs us 'that she did sustain and defend, against the common opinion, that it is very fitting for women to have knowledge of letters and the liberal arts'.[48] In fairness to Mary, she did her best to meet the demanding agenda that she had set forth. She developed, for instance, strong literary interests, 'she put aside for herself two hours a day to study and read. Above all, she liked poetry and the poets, especially Monsieur de Ronsard, Monsieur du Bellay and Monsieur de Maisonfleur'.[49]

Mary's beauty was praised repeatedly. It was reported, for example, that at fifteen, 'her beauty shone out in the midday light so that it would outshine the sun itself as its zenith; such was the beauty of her body. As for her soul, it was just as beautiful'.[50] Particularly, admiration of Mary's charm was directed towards her maturing 'cultured' femininity;

it was an eroticisation consciously and unconsciously interwoven with a more masculine Scottish identity. Brantôme described Mary thus:

> When she conversed with others, she used a very soft, sweet and agreeable speech, with a good majesty yet mixed with a very unobtrusive modest privacy and much grace. Even though her native tongue is in itself very rural, barbarous, ill sounding and unbefitting, she spoke it with such grace and fashioned it so that she made it seem very beautiful and agreeable when spoken by her – though not when spoken by others. Marvel at such virtue, such beauty and such grace, that can turn a language so crude and barbaric into something so elegant and fashionable. Even more astonishingly, even dressed as a savage (as I have seen her) and in the barbaric fashion of the savages of her country, she shines as a true Goddess beyond her mortal body and her barbarous and crude dress.[51]

On occasion – to impress the French court – Mary wore Scottish national dress. Even if this was for her, as her best known biographer Antonia Fraser has remarked, 'definitely a form of fancy dress', she recognised the advantages of its manipulation.[52] Cleverly, Mary played on the sixteenth–century stereotype of the Scots.

From a broad examination of sixteenth–century French literature, we can reconstruct the contours of this stereotype. One fascinating account, written around 1558 by Estienne Perlin, entitled *Description des royaumes d'Angleterre et d'Escosse*, found that the Scots drank too much and were only hospitable in so far as they expected to receive some profit.[53] The French perception of the Scots was one that moved seamlessly between cultural condescension and admiration. This perception applied also to the Lowland Scots, even though they were considered far more humane than those who, resembling the Irish, lived to the north of the 'rugged and terrible mountains'.[54]

Admiration of Mary lay, at least in part, in the space between lavish court culture and humanity untamed; she was, albeit in the best possible sense, something of a curiosity. The French perception of Scottish wildness is best summarised by the section on Scotland to be found in François de Belleforest's considerably revised edition of Sebastian Münster's *Cosmographie*, published in Paris in 1575. This Highland wildness was closely associated with a proud warrior spirit. Belleforest commented that:

> They have wit ... and when they apply themselves to something, they profit from it easily. They are proud and quick to vengeance.

Strong in war, they endure hunger, thirst and lack of sleep. Those who inhabit the central part are the best. They are well brought up and more human than the others, and they use the English language. Because there are hardly any forests, they make fire from black stone [coal] which they mine out of the ground. In the other part of the country, in the mountainous north, live a type of very hard and fierce people, which can be called savage. Those who live there are dressed in a cassock, with shirts dyed with saffron like those worn by the Irish and they walk with bare legs up to their knees. Their weapons are the bow and arrow, with a very broad sword and dagger, which cuts only on one side.[55]

The next significant stage in Mary's French career came with her marriage to the dauphin François on 24 April 1558 in the magnificent cathedral of Notre Dame in Paris. François was granted the crown matrimonial by the Scottish Parliament, a great tribute indeed to the political acumen of Marie de Guise, who had acted as regent of Scotland since 1554.[56] The marriage was an integral part of Henri II's foreign policy. In part, it was the culmination of a plan that had been ten years in the making. It was also the consequence of short–term domestic and international considerations which will be discussed further in the following chapter. By the terms of the less than secret marriage contract drawn up on 4 April 1558, if Mary died without heirs, Scotland would revert by Mary's 'pure and free gift' to France, as would 'all and such rights which do already or will appertain to the kingdom of England'.[57] Such an arrangement contrasts starkly with the fate of Philip in England. The contract made in November 1553 for his marriage to Mary Tudor indicated that under no circumstances could his heirs put forward any claim to the English throne.[58] The treaty bound Philip to uphold the laws of England, forbade him to promote foreigners to office or to possess any executive office of his own right.

With the marriage of Mary Queen of Scots to François, came a formal solidification of relations between Scotland and France. The Scottish Parliament in 1558 granted French subjects in Scotland the same privileges as native Scots; the reverse also held true across the channel.[59] This marriage, together with the death of the Catholic English monarch Mary Tudor in November 1558, marked an acceleration of Franco-Scottish pretensions to the crown of England.[60] Mary's coat of arms was quartered with that of England and displayed publicly. It is hardly surprising that Elizabeth I and her government viewed these developments with increasing alarm, seeing behind Mary's pretensions the ambitious designs of the house of Guise.[61]

Nevertheless, despite the formal symbols of unity between France and Scotland, the relationship between the two countries was by no means firm. While concern for defence made some form of alliance with France welcome, increasing nationalistic reaction had already occurred during the 1550s against France's ever-increasing encroachment into Scottish government. The political efforts of Marie de Guise had managed, through patronage, to build a cross-confessional pro-French basis of support in Scotland. However, as early as 1555, some signs of friction could be discerned, primarily in the French garrisons in Scotland. This tension was exacerbated by frequent delays in the payment of military wages, resulting in relaxed discipline. In 1555, an Act was passed which made it an offence to 'speak evil of the queen's grace and of Frenchmen'.[62] However, there was a subtle but important change in this act when compared with that of 1424, repeated in 1540, which indicated a strong shift in Scottish feeling. The 1555 Act was punishable only 'according to the quality of the fault in their bodies and goods at the Queen's Grace's pleasure', not, as before, by death.[63] While we should be careful not to overplay Scottish antagonism towards the French, it is clear that there was a significant degree of resentment during the 1550s directed against the presence of Frenchmen in the Scottish government. For whilst the highest secular office was granted to a Scottish magnate, the Earl of Huntly, the man closest to the figure of central authority and power, Marie de Guise, was a Frenchman named Yves de Rubay.[64]

Certain feelings of resentment towards the French, a growing movement in Scotland towards Protestant reform and developing sympathetic connections with the English shifted Scotland away from its 'auld alliance' with France into an albeit shaky and hesitant political orbit with its traditional enemy.[65] Marie de Guise had attempted to pursue a policy of religious toleration, but fears soon developed that she had changed this policy under pressure from France. The Reformers revolted against the regency of Marie, expelled her from the capital Edinburgh and deposed her on 21 October 1559. France sent troops to Scotland to combat the rebels. An unsuccessful expedition launched from Normandy directed by Marie's Guisard relatives in 1559–60 eager to ensure their family interests abroad, served simply to push the Scots further towards the English. The Scots appealed to England for support in March 1560. Despite English involvement, the failure of the French expedition to regain control over Scotland and suppress the rebels might also be explained by internal problems.[66] This failure sealed the fate of French interests in Britain, a fate reinforced by the eclipse of Guise power at court, and the death of the regent from dropsy in June. By the

Treaty of Edinburgh of July 1560, a victory indeed for Scottish Protestantism, France agreed to put an end to its influence in Scotland. The French also consented to the English demand to stop using English armorial bearings, although Mary herself refused to agree to this. For her, as one of her sternest critics, Jenny Wormald, has observed, undoubtedly correctly in this instance, 'political reality waited upon empty gesture'.[67] With the death of François II in December 1560, soon after his succession to the throne, came the formal end to the military alliance between France and Scotland. With hindsight, 1560 signalled a decisive change in Scotland's political relationship with France, even if in social, cultural, architectural, commercial, artistic, literary and educational terms, the two countries were to continue to develop close links.[68]

1560 was to be a year of grief and transition for Mary. Mary left the court and made her way to Rheims, the archiepiscopal city of her uncle, the Cardinal de Lorraine, where she retired to the monastery of Saint-Pierre-les-Dames. Renée de Lorraine, her aunt, was abbess there.[69] Respecting the traditional forty days of mourning for her husband François II and grieving also for her mother, Marie de Guise, Mary was encouraged to return to Scotland in 1561. As Brantôme later recounted, at this point

> She wished a hundred times more to reside in France a simple dowager, and to be content with Touraine and Poitou that were given to her as her dowry, than to go reign there in those savage lands. But Messieurs her uncles . . . advised her to do so, even pressed her (I will not say for what reasons), a decision they nevertheless thoroughly repented of afterwards.[70]

This comment cannot be seen entirely as artistic flourish. However, the situation was not as clear–cut as this source suggests. Mary must have recognised for herself, even in this sad period of her life, the broad opportunities available to her in Scotland. Remaining in France was not necessarily the most attractive option, in part due to the limited political opportunities available to a Queen Dowager. Moreover, Mary's position in France, had she remained, would have been further compromised by her strained personal relationship with Catherine de Medici, her powerful mother in law. On one occasion, Mary humiliated Catherine by calling her a 'merchant's daughter'; it was a remark that Catherine was not to forgive.[71] Despite the many positive factors encouraging Mary's return to a land where she could rule, albeit a land in political and religious crisis, there can be little doubt of the essence of truth in Brantôme's touching comment that, 'the Queen broke down in tears and said that she would miss the pomp, the attentions, the magnificence and the superb mounts of France that she had enjoyed for so long, but that she would be patient now that her paradise was to be exchanged for a hell'.[72] On her arrival in Scotland, Mary may well have felt a longing for the country she knew best, and which had treated her with such conspicuous magnificence.

Mary attempted to take a great deal of France back with her on her return to Scotland. It did not impress an ostensibly Protestant country weary of French influence that Mary chose to surround herself with Frenchmen. The records of Mary's household are incomplete, but from Mary's correspondence and a series of lists drafted in 1548–53,[73] 1560–1,[74] 13 February 1566–7 and an *état* drawn up five years after her imprisonment by Elizabeth I in 31 July 1573,[75] we can trace the personnel attached to the Scottish Queen.

Among those who accompanied Mary back to Scotland from France were Mary Seaton, Mary Beaton and Mary Livingston. Also accompanying her were members of the Beaucaire family, also called Peguillen.[76] Marie de Beaucaire had been in Mary's household since at least 1553. Perhaps it was her daughter that is referred to in the list of her Scottish household for 1566 and 1573 as 'Mademoiselle de Pinguillon'. Gilbert de Beaucaire, sieur de Peguillen, is mentioned from 1553 onwards as acting as Mary's master of the household. Another member of the Beaucaire family, François de Beaucaire was to function in Mary's Parisian council. Other individuals who accompanied Mary to Scotland included Léonard de Chaumont, seigneur d'Esguilly, another master of the household paid by Mary from at least 1560, Philibert du Crocq, an 'Eschoincons', and Claude de Parcheminier, who acted as one of Mary's secretaries. In addition, Mary was to retain several members of Marie de Guise's household, including her *comptroller* Bartholomew de Villemore, her master of the household Jean de Bussot, and also her apothecary, several *valets de chambre*, and a secretary, all of whom were French.[77] The high incidence of French names on the 1566–7 and 1573 lists is notable, both in terms of those in active service and those receiving pensions. These lists highlight Mary's refusal to be ruled by public opinion in Scotland on an issue so close to her heart. In many respects she was more prepared to compromise on the issue of her religion than deny her French tastes and connections.

These lists also highlight the decline in Mary's fortunes over the course of her career. From around 140 members in her employ in 1568,

Mary paid only 60 staff by 5 February 1569 following her imprisonment by Elizabeth, 16 by 1571, and a mere nine in 1572 following the symbolic retribution exacted by Elizabeth on Mary for the St. Bartholomew's Day Massacre.[78] While the *état* of 1573 lists expenditure for the household at 15,000 *livres tournois*, the majority of this was paid as pensions. Besides Mary's general munificence, another aspect worth noting about these lists is the particular pension paid in 1566–7 and in 1573 to her grandmother, the Dowager Duchesse de Guise, who was to receive 800 *livres tournois* per year.[79] Other links to the Guise–Lorraine household included her doctor, [Jacques] de Lugerie who received 300 *livres tournois* per annum. A one time priest in the diocese of Mans, Lugerie was also a doctor of medicine and acted, at various times, as vicar to the Cardinal de Lorraine.

Among the personnel that joined Mary in Scotland around 1561 but which cannot be found in the later *états*, was the famous Catholic preacher and prolific author, René Benoist who acted as Mary's confessor.[80] An oasis of Catholicism, Mary's household maintained the right to hear mass in what was a Protestant nation, and a Protestant country legitimised by Mary. The boundaries were quickly drawn, though, when Réné Benoist and Nicolas Winzet[81] were encouraged to leave the country after the alleged discovery of Catholic printing emanating from Mary's household in Edinburgh.[82] The nature of these offences, if real, remain opaque. Certainly no copies of any such books have survived and indeed one might doubt whether the resources of the primitive Scottish printing houses of the day would have permitted the easy dissemination of such writings in printed form.[83] It seems equally likely that Benoist and Winzet had been circulating Catholic writings in manuscript or perhaps even texts brought with them from France. That is, if the charges had not been trumped up simply to force their departure.

In Scotland, Mary continued to cultivate her interest in literature, revealed by the albeit incomplete records of her library.[84] While Italian, German, Spanish, Greek and Latin books can be found among her collection, English books of any genre are rare. Mary's predominant interest appears to have been in French literature, including The '*Epistles of Ovid in Frenche Meter*',[85] and '*Elegie upoun the Deid of Joachim de Bellay*'.[86] Pierre de Ronsard, the celebrated 'prince of poets' of the Pléiade school, seems to have been Mary's favourite French poet, and amongst her collection could be found *The First Buik of the Novallis of Ronsard*,[87] two editions or copies of *The Misereis of the Tyme Present be Ronsard*,[88] alongside *Ane Ansuer to Ronsard* – one of several pieces put into circulation by the Huguenots in opposition to Ronsard's *Discours*.[89] While Ronsard's interest in Mary was transitory, reflecting the political realities of the period, Mary's interest in Ronsard remained firm. An edition of his poetry was to reach Mary in captivity at Sheffield, at which time Mary promised to send via her secretary to England, Claude Nau, two thousand écus and 'a vase which was decorated with a rock representing Parnassus and Pegasus. Above it read: To Ronsard, the Apollo from the spring of the Muses.'[90]

While Mary maintained a pronounced affection for France, politically her relationship was to become strained and remained so from the moment of her arrival in Scotland in 1561 until her death in 1587. In the two years that followed Mary's return, 1561–3, relations with France were particularly tense. Thomas Randolph, the English ambassador, remarked that there were no closer relations between Scotland and France than between Scotland and Moscow.[91] In fact, this was a gross exaggeration, yet it did reflect just how strained relations had become between the two countries. Mary continued to maintain close contact with her Guisard relatives. However, Paul de Foix, the French ambassador in London, showed grave concern that the ancient alliance between Scotland and France was no longer a priority for the Queen, who inclined more towards forging surer relations with Elizabeth, from whom she sought guarantees as to her succession.[92]

The primary issue of contention between France and Mary during this period was the choice of her second marriage partner. Between 1561 and 1563, her Guisard relatives, particularly the Cardinal de Lorraine, had hoped to renew the family's fortunes, and reanimate the hopes of British Catholics by marrying Mary to Don Carlos, the son of Philip II. A Spanish ambassador, don Alvaro de la Quadra, was sent to Scotland in 1563 to begin the negotiations. Catherine de Medici opposed such a marriage, and presented instead two alternatives – either Charles IX or his brother, Henri Duc d'Anjou. Mary refused both, and it is perhaps worthwhile to pause and speculate why. Marriage would have enabled Mary to return to France and a life of considerably greater comfort. Certainly, as the Queen consort of the King of France, she would have enjoyed a position of far greater international prominence. Was the decision to refuse personal or political? If political, it may well be that Mary had calculated that the Scottish nobility would simply not stomach a second French alliance. If one takes into account that the revolution of 1559 was at least in part a war of liberation against French domination, then retreat to France may well have been, in effect, an abdication. Mary was growing in confidence, and may well have felt that her position as an effective ruling monarch in Scotland outweighed the attractions and comforts of France. There were also personal feelings. Mary had not wished to return to the tutelage of Catherine de Medici, and the proposed husbands were at this point still children. By this stage, moreover, Mary was also beginning to fall for the charms of Henry Lord Darnley, eldest son and heir of the Earl of Lennox, who himself had a strong claim to the English throne. Mary's decision does show the extent to which her relationship with France had changed in the years since her return.

Mary's choice of marriage partner was to backfire badly, for the subsequent history of her marriage is one of calamity. Darnley's jealous and unbalanced nature led to the murder of Mary's advisor, David Riccio, while his failure to attend the baptism of his son, the future James VI, swung Mary's anger against him. While no firm evidence exists to link Mary to the events at Kirk o'Field in Edinburgh, which saw the death by strangulation of Darnley on the evening of 9 February 1567, her subsequent marriage to James Hepburn, earl of Bothwell, implicated in the assassination, did much to provoke widespread anger. The French government sent Nicolas de Neuville, sieur de Villeroi, Secretary of State under Charles IX, Henri III, Henri IV and Louis XIII, to Scotland with instructions from Charles IX. These instructions leave little doubt that Charles IX recognised Mary's complicity – tacit or otherwise – in the events at Kirk o'Field. Charles's path was a delicate one, however. He wished neither the alienation of Scotland nor of Mary, as shown by the following letter:

> The King wishes the sieur du Croc to know that the desire and principal intention of His Majesty is to keep the kingdom of Scotland under his obedience, without allowing it, under the pretext of certain follies which have arisen, to retract from his rule or to seek a master other than himself. He is willing to do favours and help the Queen of Scots, but nothing which would result in the loss and ruin of his kingdom or damage the allegiance to the King and his affairs.[93]

Following Mary's deposition by the Scots and subsequent military defeat at the Battle of Langside in 1568, she fled on 16 May to England in the miscalculated hope that Elizabeth would aid her restoration. Considered a threat to national security, Mary remained incarcerated in a number of secure locations, mainly at Sheffield but also in places such as Tutbury and Chartley. During the period of Mary's imprisonment, from 1568 to 1587, the French were caught in a difficult diplomatic situation. On the one hand, they had some desire and obligation to help

Mary, Queen Dowager of France. On the other, they had to consider very carefully the more overwhelming need to preserve the international balance of power. Following Mary's imprisonment, Charles IX sent an embassy to London led by the sieur de Poigny, with the aim of negotiating a treaty between the two queens and the restoration of Mary to the throne. While this embassy was unsuccessful, Charles declared formally that 'the King of France will stop at nothing in order to preserve the rights of the Queen his sister in law'.[94] Catherine de Medici spoke with Henry Norris, saying that, 'the Queen of England had promised to see her restored, but if she delayed the matter the King would send 3,000 footmen thither'.[95] That no more decisive action was undertaken against Elizabeth, despite such threats, can be explained primarily by their fear of Spanish power, especially in the Netherlands. It was this fear of universal monarchy that convinced Charles IX to sign the Treaty of Blois with England in April 1572, confirmed in London in 1575. It omitted all references to the imprisoned Queen of Scots, to her considerable and understandable annoyance.[96] Charles IX and Henry III both recognised that the opportunity for any alliance against England was conditioned by political and economic circumstances. France was debilitated by civil war, there was a need to circumscribe the power of Spain, and in any case, the political climate in Scotland was such that, as a Protestant country developing ever–closer links with England, it hardly encouraged conditions for a successful alliance with France. The result was, of course, a complicated and difficult situation. One curious diplomatic conundrum involved the need to open relations with Scotland, despite the fact that the monarch was, technically, an usurper of the throne. The need for a permanent embassy, established from early 1582, was solved only by the approval of Mary herself for its existence.

But if formal relations with Mary were those of, in Professor Greengrass's well-turned phrase 'benevolent inactivity', what of the reaction of the house of Guise?[97] The often hysterical attitude to the Guise affinity found in English diplomatic correspondence was not entirely unjustified. While they could ill afford to act as patrons and employers to gentry outside France, they did involve themselves closely with seminary activists. It was their favour that allowed Cardinal Allen to establish the seminary at Reims, and had permitted the establishment of the Jesuit college at Eu, in Normandy, to which the Duc de Guise provided an annual pension. Moreover, as Greengrass notes, 'Guise patronage came to dominate the geography of the Catholic migration from the British Isles to France'. Nevertheless, after 1560, Guise assistance and finance for plots which sought to secure Mary's release was limited to the period between April 1578 and January 1585. In 1583, in opposition to the diplomatic policies of the crown, an invasion of England supported by the Spanish and the Guise faction had only just failed to set sail from the ports of Upper Normandy.[98] For the most part, however, Scotland and England were subordinated to France in the priorities of the Guise.[99]

During the period of her imprisonment, Mary was eager to remain informed of affairs in France. An extensive network of correspondence relayed information on all manner of matters, both domestic and foreign. The principal channels of communication can be established from her correspondence. James Beaton, archbishop of Glasgow, ambassador in Paris to the court of France and head of her council, was Mary's principal source of information. Beaton received by far the largest salary and in addition was rewarded with ecclesiastical benefices.[100] Other figures responsible for informing Mary of events in France include Henry Kir, Monsieur de Courcelles, Michel de Castelnau and his successor as French ambassador in Scotland from September 1585, Monsieur de L'Aubespine de Chateauneuf. On 31 March 1586, Mary wrote a letter to Monsieur de Mauvissière in which she thanked him 'affectionately for the trouble that you have taken since your departure from this kingdom in conveying to me news from France. I have taken singular pleasure in the few communications that I have received from there. It will always be the case that I will feel in my heart and affection the good and ill that befalls the crown there, following the strict obligation that I have towards it'.[101] This was, of course, something of an understatement. For despite her captivity, Mary was undoubtedly more fully aware of developments in France than 'most provincial governors'.[102] This constant stream of information between Mary and the continent, despite the use of cipher, was closely monitored by the English intelligence service, and was, with hindsight, to be the source of her undoing.[103]

Central to Mary's interests in France was her dowry. By the terms of her marriage contract ratified on 19 April 1558, Mary was assured an annual dowry of 60,000 *livres tournois* in the event of François's death without heirs.[104] This was to be 'located and assigned in and on the duchy, county, lands and lordships of Touraine and Poitou' – those same lands that had previously provided the dowry for Eleonor of Austria.[105] Besides the remuneration that such lands provided, Mary was entitled to appoint royal offices in areas under her control. This revenue and influence was to be a source of ever-increasing problems and frustrations for Mary; she was never to realise the full amount promised to her by the contract of 1558. The initial evaluation of revenues from these lands in 1561 revealed a shortfall which resulted in the further allocation of land in Champagne in partial compensation.[106] As Champagne was a frontier region, the Paris *parlement* did not permit Mary to nominate offices in this territory, as was her right in the other areas under her control.[107] Despite these shortcomings, until 1568, while Mary remained the reigning monarch in Scotland, the revenues provided by her dowry proved more than sufficient to finance a large household of 174 salaried posts. Some of Mary's personnel resided in France, where Mary maintained a prominent council to manage her dowry.

The deteriorating conditions that Mary was to endure during her English captivity, particularly at Tutbury, were mirrored by increasing difficulties in securing the revenue from her dowry in France. Various factors contributed to a dwindling in the real value of Mary's dowry. These included the past over-forestation of her lands in Epernay and St. Ménéhoud, the negative economic impact of periods of depression exacerbated by the Wars of Religion,[108] and alienations of land particularly during the reign of Henry III. In 1576, for example, the county of Touraine – part of the lands given to Mary – was granted to François duc d'Alençon in 1576, a grant naturally opposed by the Scottish Queen.[109] Moreover, attempts to compensate Mary for her deteriorating dowry did not go uncontested. Madame de Montpensier, for example, disputed Mary's rights in Senlis and Vitry, royal domains to the north of Paris granted in compensation for lands allocated to François duc d'Alençon.[110] Another alienation relating to a part of the duchy of Poitou, which came to be known as the Secondigny affair, cost Mary around 6,000 *livres* in legal costs by 1574.[111] This affair was not settled by the time of Mary's execution in February 1587. Even in her will, Mary referred to the law suit and even allocated, optimistically, the monies which would result from its successful resolution in her favour, including setting aside 'five hundred francs for the relief of the poor of Reims'.[112] Towards the end of her life, Mary made constant complaints of her impecunity. On 6 February 1585, for instance, she wrote to Monsieur de Mauvissière, 'I have written to you presently as I find myself in very great need of money. This forces me to disturb you at this time so that you can do everything in your power to pay promptly what my treasurer asks of you, by letter of credit or any other means, the terms of which I have duly made clear to him and enclosed in this present dispatch. I urge you to pay this to him and send him back to me at your earliest convenience'.[113] The imprisoned Queen of Scotland was even obliged to raise loans in London, and borrow from the earl of Arundel and from her secretary.[114] A statement of revenues owed by Henri III to the Scottish Queen, drawn up after her execution in 1587, outlined a debt of 164,595 *écus* 27 *sous* and 1 *denier*, an amount that equalled eight years of revenues of her original allocation of 60,000 *livres tournois* per annum.[115] Mary's council based in Paris managed her French interests. Evidence relating to this council is frustratingly sparse. Working from Mary's correspondence and the various *états* of Mary's household, Mark Greengrass has largely succeeded in reconstructing the composition of this council. At its head was Mary's 'protector', Charles Cardinal de Lorraine, to December 1574, succeeded by Louis I Cardinal de Guise to March 1578. Following the death of the cardinal, it is likely that this position rested unofficially with the Guise family. The position of protectorship was one with formal authority, including primacy in Mary's council, the right to dispose of the seals of the chancellor and dispense revenues of the council in the form of pensions.[116] The Parisian council was, at least in part, an extension of the Guise patronage network, often to Mary's anxiety if tacit resignation. That the position of protector was not just one of title is clear from Mary's request that her trusted ambassador in France and convener of her Council, the Archbishop of Glasgow, James Beaton,[117] approach the Cardinal to allocate certain posts in her duchy.[118]

Until 1574, Mary's Council based in Paris was marked by its professionalism and influence in French political life. An analysis of the composition of the Council reveals that its personnel were both prominent and well connected. Of the nineteen members of the Council in 1566, two were also members of the *chambre des comptes* in Paris, while three were senior lawyers in the Parisian courts. François de L'Aubespine, Mary's chancellor, was *président* of the grand *conseil* and a senior figure in the French legal hierarchy; he also served on the queen mother's council.[119] Mary's treasurer, René Dolu, was also well-connected: he had relatives in such high-ranking positions as president in the *chambre des comptes* and *secrétaire des finances*. The Council maintained strong connections with the Guise family – François de Beaucaire, sieur de Puyguillon was a servant in the clientele of the Guise, used by the Guise as the 'straw' bishop of Metz. His brother was Jean Beaucaire from a long line of royal servants; Jean himself served under François I. Another member of the Council, Pierre Hotman, was also the treasurer for the Cardinal de Lorraine. His son, Charles Hotman, who succeeded him in 1585, became one of the founder members of the League in Paris, and member of the Paris *Sixteen* until his death in 1587.[120]

1574 seemed however to mark a revolution in the calibre and policy of this council. As Mark Greengrass has noted, it can be characterised from this date less as a body of skilled administrators and more as a group of domestic servants enjoying contacts with the exile Catholic community in France.[121] François de Beaucaire de Puyguillon retired and François de L'Aubespine was replaced by Gilles du Verger, president of the *présidial* at Tours, who was himself later replaced by Jean de Champhuan, sieur de Ruisseau brother–in–law of Claude Nau, Mary's secretary in England. Mary's suspicions of mismanagement in her Council mounted, undoubtedly fuelled by the restless frustrations of imprisonment and the deteriorating ability of her council in Paris to realise the full extent of her promised dowry. In September 1574, for instance, Mary urged James Beaton to investigate the loss of 5,000 francs under the suspicion that either Hotman or M. Ferrarius, her treasurer, had embezzled.[122] Mary also became annoyed at the continued reluctance of her council to pursue new objectives. One can follow in her correspondence developing conflict with her treasurer René Dolu over the way in which her income should be spent, with Dolu preferring to save and invest while Mary advocated spending more on the exiles.[123] Mary, eager to secure the assistance of the Catholic exiles to bring about her release, accused Dolu of acting more in the interests of Henri III than her own, and he was finally dismissed in 1581.[124] He was replaced by M. de Chérelles, whose brother was an agent for the French ambassador in England from 1585 and in contact with Mary at Tutbury.

There is no clearer symbol of the new direction Mary wished her Council to adopt than the appointment in 1574 of Thomas Morgan, a Welsh exile and conspirator, closely followed by the appearance of the equally notorious Charles Paget. Thomas Morgan himself became a target of Protestant polemic.[125] A good sense of the man's aims can be gained from the confession of Guy Fawkes following the Gunpowder plot, when he mentioned Morgan's name as one who had proposed exactly the same thing in Queen Elizabeth's time.[126] Mary's council had, in effect, become a nest of conspiracy.

The example of David Chalmers demonstrates equally clearly why the threat posed to Elizabeth and the English government by this council was minimal, and ironically worked to their ultimate advantage.[127] James Beaton and Mary Stuart were both enthusiastic advocates of the Scots College in Paris.[128] Whether cultural advancement or image-making was on their mind when they provided David Chalmers with a pension is difficult to ascertain.[129] Certainly, Chalmers was a grateful recipient of monies given, and was undoubtedly closely associated with members of Mary's council. In 1579, he produced a trio of works – the *Histoire abbregée*, a second text entitled *La Recherche des singularitez*, and finally *Discours de la legitime succession des femmes.*[130] All three texts reinforced, albeit at tiresome length, Mary's legitimacy and right to the throne of England. What James Beaton, Mary Stuart or her Council did not recognise, however, was that from around 1573 until his return to Scotland in 1582, Chalmers also operated as a double agent for Sir Francis Walsingham, the head of the most advanced intelligence service in the early modern world.[131] The necessarily concealed nature of intelligence operations, combined with the deliberate destruction of sensitive documents, makes a full assessment of the penetration of Mary's council difficult to establish. That this council was a focus for dissent ironically served the better interests of the Elizabethan regime. Through their deep penetration of this council, they were aware of the most serious conspiracies against their Queen.

From a detailed list contained in the Calendar of State Papers for 1580, it is clear that Walsingham maintained an alert eye on the composition and activities of the *émigré* community in Paris, and in France more generally. This document may also have been used to target recruitment, no doubt with some success. The names on this list are divided into various categories, including 'great practisers'. Although this phrase suggests that the figures were well known to English intelligence, their reputation has not survived to this day, with the exception of Thomas Morgan whom we will discuss below. Such names include Brackford (a pensioner of the Queen of Scots), Clitherowe, Thomas Evans (a companion of David Chambers [sic for Chalmers]), Hiliard, Orton, Sudgrave, Warbutton and Watson.[132] As well as being kept informed from an administrative level of events in Mary's council through such agents as David Chalmers (to 1582), Walsingham may well have maintained agents in more prominent and influential positions.

Mary's council operated as a hub for various conspiracies directed against Elizabeth, drawing together exiled Catholics and the Guise family. For reasons discussed above, the French monarchy under Charles IX and Henri III sought to distance itself tactfully but firmly from association with the plotting element among the dissident exile communities in France. It was in this context that Thomas Morgan, the practical head of Mary's council in Paris, was, in an effort to appease Elizabeth in the aftermath of the Parry conspiracy, arrested by Henri III in 1585 and placed in the Bastille.[133] Nevertheless, until 1585, plotting did take place of which the French crown was undoubtedly aware. As an imprisoned Catholic sovereign, whom many in England and abroad considered to be the legitimate monarch of England on account of Elizabeth's illegitimacy, Mary became the willing focal point of conspiracies that sought to secure her release and place her on the throne in Elizabeth's place.

Mary had plotted against Elizabeth almost from the moment of her imprisonment. Three unsuccessful conspiracies against Elizabeth in the 1580s were to form the basis for Elizabeth's decision to execute Mary. The first of these was the Francis Throckmorton plot, a conspiracy that boasted a celebrity cast, including figures such as the Pope and Philip II, who underwrote the total cost of the enterprise, Henri, Duc de Guise, the Duke of Norfolk and Lord Henry Howard. On discovering this plot, Francis Walsingham was so shocked by the extent of Mary's contact with the outside world that he demanded her removal to a more secure location – Tutbury. A second plot named after its prime mover, William Parry, was uncovered in 1585 by the ever-vigilant intelligence service. In this particular case, Mary was not directly implicated, though Parry was quick to name Thomas Morgan as his partner in crime.

Decisive retribution followed the English government's discovery of yet another plot against the English Protestant state. The scene had been set by Mary's removal to Tutbury. Here, she had been starved of correspondence from the outside world from December 1584. When contact was offered via a brewer by way of a water–tight container in a beer cask, Mary, with eager naivety, was understandably overjoyed. However, this service was one engineered by Walsingham. From the moment Gilbert Gifford landed on English soil with the nascent plan in 1585, the intelligence services were fully aware of the evolving Babington conspiracy. Also functioning as *agents provocateurs*, the service influenced the conspirators by overestimating Spanish preparations for invasion, spurring them to even more treasonous designs – principally the assassination of Elizabeth. The information amassed during these conspiracies, and possibly others that have not come to light, provided a rich seam of evidence necessary to bring Mary to trial, and gave Elizabeth the upper hand against militant Catholic nobles in England who had corresponded with Mary during this period.

Other factors that motivated or encouraged the English government's decision to execute Mary in February 1587 included the potential consequences of her various illnesses. A document recently acquired by Cambridge University Library outlined a reply to Henri III, who had interceded unsuccessfully to urge that the sentence of execution be commuted on the grounds that Mary had little time left. The document retorted 'the shorter time the Scots Quene hath to live heare in this world the more hast hir complices will thinke they have to achive to her wicked intencons'.[134] The converse possibility was, of course, equally galling; that if Mary should outlive Elizabeth, then a Catholic would by rights succeed to the throne of England. Internationally, increasing brinkmanship between Spain and England from 1585 intensified the need to eliminate the Queen of Scots, who remained a focus for division and conspiracy in the kingdom.

On 14 and 15 October, therefore, under the Act of Association, Mary was indicted. Ten days later, on 25 October, the Star Chamber at Westminster declared Mary guilty of complicity to assassinate Elizabeth. Predictably, Parliament placed pressure on Elizabeth to pronounce the sentence of death, which with some hesitation was decreed on 4 December 1586. Two months later, on 1 February 1587 following the old style calendar, Elizabeth signed the death warrant, and even then she was to claim, in a display of professional dramatics, that her last minute decision to stay the execution had been countermanded. Through intelligence and Henri's established pattern of behaviour towards Mary, Elizabeth undertook the execution of a legitimate Catholic sovereign with strong ties to France in the knowledge that the action would not result in war.

Elizabeth had carefully prepared the ground. In 1586, she had sent extraordinary embassies to both Henri III and James VI following the Babington conspiracy. She did this in order that they might exhibit proof of the conspiracy and place before their eyes other evidence to sway the monarchs against Mary, such as her correspondence with Spain promising her rights to England and Scotland should James fail to convert to Catholicism.[135] Mary could not simply be deserted. When news reached the French King of the likelihood of Mary's execution, Henri sent Pomponne de Bellièvre, his most experienced politician and diplomat, on an embassy to negotiate a reduction in Mary's sentence. Bellièvre had three audiences with Elizabeth, on 7 December, 15 December 1586, and on 6 January 1587.[136] His rhetorical talents, however, proved insufficient to prevent the execution. Bellièvre departed London on 13 January; Mary was executed the following month at Fotheringhay castle in Northamptonshire. To a large extent Pomponne de Bellièvre's failure had been due to the terrible cards he had been authorised to bring to the diplomatic table. In promising only 20–30,000 écus to come from Mary's own dowry, alongside a pledge from the Duc de Guise not to involve himself further in conspiracies against the English Queen, Henri III had to all intents and purposes distanced both himself and the French state from Mary's plight.[137] Henri III was even willing to tolerate an abusive letter written by Elizabeth on 18 January 1587 which accused the French King of attempting to protect a murderess; it ended: 'Your estates, my good brother, do not allow you to have too many enemies'.[138] The English understood and were perhaps made to understand the French position. Leicester, for example, writing to his brother in law, the count of Bedford, remarked that while the French publicly protested against the indignity with which Mary was treated, this stemmed from propriety. Leicester assured Bedford that no action would follow from French words.[139]

That Henri failed to save the life of Mary Stuart, Queen of Scots, and Queen Dowager of France, diminished him in the eyes of the French public. That he did not adopt a stronger stance is even more surprising given the rumours circulating in France about his relationship with Elizabeth. On 25 November 1586, the head of the League wrote to the Spanish ambassador, 'you have seen the departure of Bellièvre for England to strengthen the offensive and defensive alliance with the Queen of England, and provide the means to advance it'.[140] This opinion was furthered by Bernardino de Mendoza. Writing on 22 December 1586 to Alexandre Farnese, he indicated that the deliverance of Mary Stuart was the 'moindre souci de la cour de France' – the least of the French court's worries.[141]

Henri recognised well the diplomatic situation with which he was faced. Bellièvre indicated to Elizabeth the position of the French monarchy, that 'if the Queen of England does not give these arguments any consideration, but wishes to proceed with such a harsh and extraordinary judgement, the French crown could do nothing other than resent it as a particularly serious offence'.[142] There is no evidence to suggest that Henri gave his tacit agreement to the execution of Mary; in fact, quite the contrary.[143] Yet, Henri simply did not have enough diplomatic currency to alter the English judgement, nor was he in a position to go to war over Mary Stuart. Henri and Elizabeth both knew it. According to one sympathetic account, following the execution, Henri suffered 'mortelles inquiétudes' in deciding how to react to the situation.[144] His reaction was to freeze French diplomatic links with England. Yet only three months later, and in defiance of French public opinion, normal diplomatic relations were quietly restored.

Until the very moment of Mary Stuart's execution at Fotheringhay on 18 February 1587, following the continental calendar,[145] Mary focused her attentions on France. The first request contained in Mary's last will and testament, drawn up according to the printed version 'the morning of my death, this Wednesday 20 February',[146] was that services be conducted for her soul in the *basilique* of Saint Denis to the north of Paris, the traditional resting place of the French kings, and at Saint Pierre in Reims, closely associated with the Guise family.[147] Mary asked that she be buried in Reims, a symbolically defiant gesture. Elizabeth refused this last request. After all, it would have been too risky to send Mary's body back to France, lest it intensify efforts to make the Scottish Queen a martyr or inflame French public sentiment against England. Mary was instead buried in Peterborough Cathedral. To Reims, Mary also requested that a contribution be given from her funds 'for the relief of the poor of Reims'.[148] Land at Trepigny was to be given to her cousin Guise for use by one of his daughters,[149] and the principal executor of her will was to be none other than the Duc de Guise.[150] Mary's intentions, as expressed in her last will and testament, remained largely unfulfilled. In contravention of her final wishes and despite the considerable monies owed to her by Henri III discussed earlier and her request that her dowry should continue to be paid a year after her death, by a royal edict of March 1587 in which Mary was respectively referred to as his 'late sister in law', all of Mary's dowry lands reverted to the crown.[151] In her final letter, written at 2.00am on the morning before her execution, Mary wrote to Henri III:

> It remains for me to beg you as Most Christian King, my brother in law and old ally, you who have always protested your love for me, to give proof in all these points of your virtue as much out of pity – to relieve me – as to free my conscience, and help me in something I cannot resolve without you, that is to reward my grieving servants and pay their wages.[152]

Henri dismissed his obligation to recompense Mary's servants, and it was left to Philip II, through his ambassador Bernardino Mendoza, to pay the wages and pensions that were due.

The sentiments and problems that marked the nature and execution of Mary's final wishes were indeed a fitting final tribute to her troubled relationship with France. Personally, of course, Mary considered herself French. She continued to cultivate this attachment, born from her years as the golden child at Henri II's court, after her return to Scotland in 1561, surrounding herself with Frenchmen and news from France. Politically, Mary's relations with France took rather more surprising turns. From 1561 to her execution in 1587, Mary presented persistent and thorny problems for France, largely of her own making. The French response to these problems was, effectively, to cast the Queen of Scots and Dowager Queen of France into the political wilderness. The French could ill afford to too closely associate themselves with Mary, for to do so would complicate even further their relationship with the Scots and more importantly exacerbate tensions with the English at a time when the Spanish threat demanded the need for a powerful ally, albeit an unfamiliar one. The demands of international politics short-circuited the call of international Catholicism.

2
The Public Face of France's Relationship with the Queen, 1548–85

During the dancing which accompanied the wedding celebrations for Mary Stuart and the Dauphin François in April 1558, Antoine de Bourbon, King of Navarre, spoke briefly to the Venetian ambassador, Giovanni Michiel. 'Ambassador', he whispered, 'thou this day seeist the conclusion of a fact, which very few persons credited until now'.[1] Michiel then related this conversation and another with the Cardinal de Lorraine to the Doge and Senate of Venice. From his report, the Venetian government learned of the powerful political opposition that had formed against the marriage. The report also revealed the identity of the principal opponent of this union: the Constable of France and Henri II's closest advisor, Anne de Montmorency.

Ten years earlier, the political capital to be realised from the engagement of the Dauphin to the Queen of Scots had been substantial, though a political promise of marriage did not necessarily imply an unbendable commitment to it. The Treaty of Haddington in 1548 had established a permanent though ill–defined protectoral relationship between France and Scotland that had enabled Henri II to assume control over Scottish foreign policy and diplomacy, while maintaining a military presence in Scotland after the cessation of hostilities with England.[2] French power grew in strength during the 1550s, evinced by the appointment of Marie de Guise as regent in 1554. While Henri's direct personal involvement in Scotland was restricted by his pre-occupation with more pressing international and domestic problems, especially his conflict with Charles V, Marie de Guise was able, through the effective use of patronage, to build a cross-confessional base of pro–French support. Nevertheless, there was nothing inevitable in the marriage of Mary to the Dauphin. Henri's final decision to agree to the union in April 1558 was taken after careful consideration of a number of inter-related international and domestic pressures.

Of immediate concern was England's entry into the Habsburg–Valois conflict against France. Such involvement was a consequence not only of the constant pleas of Philip II to his wife Mary Tudor to enter the war, but also the covert activity of France in England. Decisive was the French aid given to Thomas Stafford's invasion and capture of Scarborough castle in April 1557.[3] In order to limit the impact of any involvement on the continent, the French followed the proven device of using the Scots to occupy the English at home. However, there were problems weakening the Scottish front. While the Scots were willing to organise guerrilla warfare in the borders, they were reluctant to risk mounting any serious invasion, not least because they lacked adequate resources or the resolve to engage the English army in open battle. The fresh memories of Flodden in 1513, Solway Moss in 1542 and Pinkie in 1547 still haunted the Scots. In 1557, to strengthen Scottish resolve, France had planned to send four thousand foot soldiers to Scotland and 'to raise for that purpose [the invasion of England] 15,000 Scottish infantry to be paid by his most Christian Majesty [Henri II]'.[4] Conflict with the Habsburgs scuttled these designs, specifically the Habsburg victory at St Quentin in July 1557 led by Emmanuel Philibert, the exiled Duke of Savoy. In October 1557, moreover, Marie de Guise experienced serious problems in convincing the Scots to fight beyond their own borders.[5] While a Franco-Scottish army had marched down to Kelso and Marie had delivered an inspiring speech to the troops, the Scots nobility decided against invading and withdrew. The decision was taken not because of hostility towards France. Rather, it was primarily a consequence of bad weather combined with a logical analysis of their military position relative to the English, especially the fact that the English had been well informed of the Scots' arrival. It was also the consequence of the 'degenerative effect on Scottish morale' caused by the Habsburg victory at St Quentin.[6] Scotland's 'unofficial' incursions into England continued. Whatever the explanation for the Scots' decision, October 1557 must have brought home to Henri II that if the power of England was to be circumscribed, more effort and most importantly dynastic union would be needed to strengthen its back door and ensure Scotland's continuing commitment to alliance with France.

Such considerations were compounded by a significant shift in domestic politics in France. A strong faction had existed at the French court that sought the abandonment of the projected marriage between the Scottish Queen and the Dauphin. Some, including Anne de Montmorency, felt that such a union would bind France to a protracted conflict in Britain that would serve ultimately to increase the power and prestige of the house of Guise at home and abroad. This lobby did not argue for the complete abandonment of French interests in Scotland, but more subtly that it would be more suitable for Mary to marry a French nobleman, not the heir to the French throne. This would give the French greater room for manoeuvre. The imprisonment of the Constable by the Spanish following St Quentin in 1557 weakened the influence of this faction, despite the support of the Bourbon family and despite the fact that even from his prison in Ghent, the Constable continued to exert some influence on the decision-making of Henri II. This included dispatching an embassy to Henri, with the intention of thwarting the union. Nevertheless, Montmorency succeeded in doing little more than postponing the marriage, whilst the King considered the alternative proposal that François marry the sister of Philip II of Spain.[7] Montmorency's diminished credit and physical exclusion from affairs of state had left the Guise ascendant at court, a position amplified by the military victory of the Duc at Calais in January 1558.

It was for these reasons that in December 1557, the Scots were invited to send a delegation to negotiate a contract of marriage between their Queen and the heir to the throne of France.

A courtly portrait of Mary Queen of Scots

From the moment that she disembarked at St Pol in Britanny in 1548, the French crown publicly proclaimed the importance of the union between Mary and the Dauphin François. Throughout the 1550s, these imperial interests were furthered in an entirely positive fashion. The political machinations at court took place entirely behind closed doors. There was no attempt to engage public opinion in the debate.

In festival, the initial *entrée* ceremonies welcomed the impending unification of the crowns of France and Scotland. A symbolic beginning to this process came when Mary, in a scene carefully crafted by the office of Henri II, released a handful of prisoners at Angers, and was seen thereby to possess legitimate powers of royalty within France. At the *entrée* staged in Rouen in 1550, and the pageant of 1554 that celebrated Henri's triumphant return to Paris after a tour of the kingdom, France's intention to control England in addition to Scotland was publicly announced.[8] The elaborate projection of these imperial ambitions, in addition to others in the New World, exhibited and exaggerated the prestige and power of the French crown and commonwealth in an age of dynastic rivalry.

The printing press also offered a means of propagating the reputation, prestige and power of the French court. A few authors and poets praised the court because they had been engaged by the crown or other nobles to do so, whilst others composed their works with the hope of securing patronage. Before 1558, there was a gentle stream of mentions of Mary usually embedded within larger works which extolled the merits of other prominent French nobles. Mary was very much seen as an integral part of the French court.

Mary Queen of Scots made her first appearance in vernacular print in 1554 with the publication in Poitiers of *Les Poésies de Jacques Tahureau*.[9] In a volume dedicated to Louis Cardinal de Guise, and possibly sponsored by him, Mary was mentioned in one verse. In this, the poet congratulated the Dauphin François on acquiring a goddess of 'such beauty' and 'heavenly courage'.[10] Praise of Mary's beauty was not inseparable from the poetic conventions of political rhetoric. In 1556, another laudatory poem was addressed to the Queen of Scots. It was published in Paris and composed by none other than Pierre de Ronsard, who had followed Princess Madeleine, the daughter of François I, to Edinburgh in 1537, albeit for a brief time, following her marriage to James V of Scotland.[11] Now Ronsard acted as court poet to Henri II and 1556 witnessed the first of several verses that he was to compose to Mary over the course of his career.[12] It was printed within a collection entitled *Nouvelle continuation des amours*.[13] Ronsard, like Tahureau, focused tenderly on Mary's personal and political attractions:

> O beautiful and more than beautiful and pleasant dawn,
> You who have left your Scottish land,
> To come and live in the French region,
> Which is now adorned with your light.
> I have had the honour of leaving France,
> Sailing on the sea to follow your father,
> So far from my country, my brothers & my mother,
> I spent three years of my childhood in your country.[14]
> Take these verses kindly, Queen, that I give to you,
> To avoid the pitiful vice of being ungrateful,
> I was born to make humble service,
> To you, to your land, and to your crown.[15]

Such accolades carried with them strong undertones of possession; Mary was a prize sought and won by France. The following short poem printed in Lyon in 1557 and written by the Parisian Charles Fontaine, expressed this theme explicitly:[16]

> Here is the pearl of such lustre,
> That the East will be jealous of her,
> A pearl upon an illustrious diamond,
> Brilliant in natural splendour.[17]

These four lines, dedicated to the Queen of Scots, appeared in a section headed 'Princesses of France'. The verse is typical of the character of much of the courtly verse relating to Mary in this period. It is brief, embedded in a large volume of laudatory verse to the notables of the day, it has undertones of possession and it manipulates the rhetorical convention for noble women, by praising their political value through describing their personal beauty.

Praise of Mary was not confined to courtly verse. A quite different form of tribute came with Antoine Fouquelin's prose study, *La Rhétorique françoise*, published in Paris in 1555.[18] Fouquelin's work was designed to develop sophistication in the use of the vernacular. To illustrate his points, he drew his examples not only from classical authors such as Cicero, whom he translated, but also from his contemporaries, most particularly Pierre de Ronsard and Joachim du Bellay.[19] Fouquelin chose to dedicate his guidebook to rhetoric and the vernacular to Mary Queen of Scots, perhaps seeking to cultivate continued courtly support for the work of the Pléiade. In his dedication, uniquely amongst the eulogists of this early period, he focused his attentions on the intellectual qualities of the young Queen. In a humanist treatise, Fouquelin was perhaps less firmly constrained in how he might praise a woman and a Queen, than if he were writing within the established rhetorical conventions of courtly verse. In his dedication, Fouquelin drew particular attention to Mary's education and specifically to her oration in the Louvre held in the presence of Henri II. Here, against what the author derisively termed the common opinion, Mary argued 'that it is very fitting for women to have knowledge of letters and the liberal arts'.[20]

While Fouquelin chose to praise Mary's intellectual prowess, another work focused on her dynastic potential. This was Jean Le Féron's heraldic study *Le Symbol armorial des armoires de France, & d'Escosse, & de Lorraine*, published in September 1555.[21] The work was almost certainly sponsored by Mary's Guisard relations. It contained numerous dedications, primarily to Marie de Guise-Lorraine, since April 1554 regent of Scotland, and to the future 'royale preeminence', Mary Stuart. Other dedications included those to François Comte d'Aumale and duc de Guise, Charles Cardinal de Lorraine, Claude de Lorraine, Loïs de Lorraine, François de Lorraine and René de Lorraine.[22] Le Féron's work reflected the rising political ascendancy and pretensions of the house of Guise-Lorraine both within France and abroad. It was prefaced by the images of three coats of arms. Through an examination of these arms, Le Féron underlined the importance of Mary Queen of Scots and the firm historical connection between France, Scotland and the Guise.[23]

Jean de Beaugué's *Histoire de la guerre d'Escosse*, [24] published in 1556, was dedicated to the great political rivals of the Guise and specifically to François, eldest son of Anne de Montmorency.[25] It is difficult to determine the extent of Montmorency opposition to the union between Mary and François. Certainly over the next year, they would bring together a powerful force against the marriage. It seems unlikely that de Beaugué's work, which showed itself favourable to the union, should have been dedicated consciously to François de Montmorency to convince him of the error. More likely, given the discrete nature of political debate at court, de Beaugué was ignorant of the Montmorency position.

The work focused on the recent relationship between France and Scotland, and encapsulated well French attitudes to Mary and Scotland during the 1550s. Based on the author's personal experiences as a member of the French forces sent to Scotland in 1548 during the Rough Wooing, the book provided an expansive and detailed historical account of the successful military campaign, outlining major operations and recounting inspirational speeches to the troops. An air of imperial superiority permeated de Beaugué's analysis; the French were portrayed, not without some cause, as having rescued the Scots from certain destruction and ruin.[26] The war and French control over Scotland were seen within a framework of an evolving relationship that was both inevitable and positive.

The history singled out the prudence and virtue of Marie de Guise. Mary Queen of Scots herself, whose betrothal to François would secure her country for France, was mentioned only briefly. But de Beaugué did narrate the story of how Mary had been taken out of Scotland for her own safety and brought to France on the vessel Réal captained by the Sieur de Brézé, protected by four galleys.[27] Drawing from the conventions of courtly verse, Jean de Beaugué commented, not without an understanding of the current political promotion of the relationship between the two nations, that:

This Princess, perhaps then around five or six years old, was one of the most perfect creatures that has ever been seen. She has proven from such an early age to be of such promise, having made such a wonderful and laudable beginning, paying so great attention to herself that it is not possible to hope for more in any Princess on this earth.[28]

The celebration of the union between François and Mary in 1558

Ten years after her arrival in France, Henri II and the Scots agreed that the marriage between Mary and François should take place. A magnificent Renaissance celebration was held on 24 April 1558, to accompany the ceremony at Notre Dame cathedral in Paris. While some of the nation's élite may have had their reservations about the marriage, in print at least the union was welcomed as enthusiastically as would have been expected. A printed account of the celebration was written and rushed off the press just one week after the event itself.[29] It was published in Paris in two editions, as well as in Lyon and Rouen.[30] From 1550, with Henri's initial *entrées* around France, the crown had become increasingly conscious of the value of festival literature.[31] The printed word prolonged and expanded the impact of the event;[32] it reflected its order and claimed to be its final monument.[33] While there is no direct evidence to suggest that this was an officially commissioned account, the speed with which it appeared, and with a royal privilege, would seem to suggest that this was the case.

An abridged account of this official printed description of the festival is given below to provide an insight into how Mary was represented to the French public at what was certainly one of the high points of her career in France. In addition, this account offers a flavour of sixteenth–century festival and its reconstruction in print.

The text, possibly partly constructed beforehand from plans of the event with the addition of details from the day, evokes a sense of the energy and excitement of the unfolding drama. The *Discours* begins by describing the preparations. Theatres were constructed before the marriage ceremony, in the great room in the Palais de Justice in Paris, 'of such grandeur, beauty and excellent, that those who saw it marvelled at such artifice'.[34] Such rhetorical devices abound in the text. Another scaffold was erected in the square in front of Notre Dame cathedral itself. It stood 12 feet high, with a gallery constructed as an arch, going from the Bishop's Palace to the great door of the church and to the choir.[35]

On Sunday 24 April, the day of the wedding between the 'King-Dauphin & Queen-Dauphine', as François and Mary were now styled in the text, a royal ceiling was constructed, covered in *fleur de lys*.[36] Then between 10.00 am and 11.00 am came the procession, in strictly ordered hierarchy. The first to arrive at the scaffold outside Notre Dame were the Swiss guards, followed by Monsieur de Guise, who greeted Eustace du Bellay, the Bishop of Paris. Guise, observing that notables who accompanied du Bellay impeded the view of the throng of people, asked them to move. The text evoked the colour of the occasion, describing in turn each of the major group's clothes as they made their way in procession.

Also evoked in the *Discours* was sound, a key element in the festivities. Following the Guise were a 'great number of players of musical instruments, such as trumpets, clarions, oboes, flageolets, violas, violins, guitars and others, sounding and playing so melodiously that it was extremely delightful'.[37] After these musicians followed the King's household, princes, abbots, bishops, archbishops, and then the cardinals, the 'King-Dauphin', led by Antoine Roi de Navarre, Charles Duc d'Orléans and Henri Duc d'Angoulême.[38] Accompanying the 'Queen-Dauphine' were Henri II and the Duc de Lorraine.

Described in all its magnificence was Mary's white dress and the crown which was garnished with pearls, diamonds, rubies, sapphires, emeralds and other precious stones, and in its centre, an orb valued at 500,000 écus.[39] After the bride, came the Queen of France, accompanied by Louis Prince de Condé, then Margaret Queen of Navarre, the Duchesse de Berry and other princesses and ladies. The marriage ceremony and Mass were then celebrated. On two occasions, all manner of coins were thrown, no doubt to incite the energy of the crowd.[40]

After these festivities, a dinner was held. At 4.00 p.m. or 5.00 p.m, Henri II and his entourage processed to the royal palace along streets teeming with onlookers. Then came the royal ball which included 'masquerades, ballads, mimes and other games and pastimes'.[41] Among the attractions were twelve artificial horses, 'decked out with gold tapestries and silver cloth, guided and driven artificially'.[42] Afterwards, six artificial ships appeared with sails of silver covered in golden cloth, 'so ingeniously made and controlled with such dexterity that one could say that they floated on water'.[43] Each of the six ships appeared to be driven by the winds and had a capacity for one passenger in addition to a prince that guided the vessels. Henri II accompanied Mary Queen of Scots, while François accompanied his mother.[44]

The very final paragraph of the *Discours* recorded the marriage of another couple in that same week, between the son of the Count of

Tanda and the daughter of Marshal Pierre Strozzi. Strozzi was one of Guise's right-hand men during the Italian campaigns and was described by Giovanni Michiel as 'the mouth-piece of the Cardinal [de Lorraine].'[45] This week was a celebration indeed of Guise ascendancy.

While this printed account does omit certain details of the event,[46] noteworthy is the fact that none of the sources that we possess for the celebrations reveal any marked emphasis on the union's political significance. The political element was undoubtedly implicit with the heralds styling François and Mary respectively as 'Roy–Dauphin' and 'Royne–Dauphine'. But several opportunities for a broader projection of this union were not employed. One might have expected, for instance, more to have been made of the formal solidification of the auld alliance that had stretched back part-fictionally and part-historically for centuries, particularly with the presence of the Scottish ambassadors and the considerable number of Scots who were attending the ceremony.[47] Also absent from public view, as it was in the printed literature of the pre–1558 period, was Mary's claim to England.

Jacques Grévin's *Hymne à Monseigneur le Dauphin sur le mariage dudict Seigneur*, composed in Alexandrine verse, also sidelined the political importance of the match.[48] It was a work permeated by classical allusion. Despite its title, it spoke of the wedding very indirectly, seeing the newly–weds as the new Peleus and Thetis. According to Ovid, Thetis, a Nereid, was commanded to marry a mortal by Zeus and Poseidon. Reluctant, she resisted Peleus' advances by changing into various shapes. Nevertheless, assisted by the centaur Chiron, Peleus, King of the Myrmidons won her over.[49] Following this mythology, though not mentioned by Grévin, was the fact that the son issuing from this marriage was the mighty but flawed Achilles. Each Muse was invoked in turn, and from each Peleus learned something. Grévin had chosen this imagery from the festival itself. Though not mentioned in the printed account of the ceremony, the wedding celebrations had included a chariot pulled by six horses. In this chariot sat the Muses who sang and played in praise of Mary.[50] Grévin's work also echoed the celebrations by evoking a sense of Renaissance grandeur and majesty without dealing explicitly with the political implications of the union. It would be tempting to find some veiled Protestant critique of the marriage, given the growing attraction to Calvinism around this period of Grévin and the printer of this work Martin L'Homme. This, however, seems unlikely. If it was the case, the work disguised any such agenda well enough that it was to receive a royal privilege for no less than six years.[51]

Nevertheless, other works published in 1558 reveal a very different view of the public image of the marriage. The conservatism of the ceremony or of Grévin's *Hymne* was not evident in five other publications that appeared in 1558 to celebrate the union. Among these was Joachim du Bellay's *Hymne au Roy sur la prinse de Callais* [sic] published several months before the marriage itself.[52] This work represented a reinvigoration of the mentality of the Roman golden age; the imperialist mentality so prevalent at the festivals at Rouen in 1550 and Paris in 1554.[53] Henri II, who will make the world French, it reported, managed to recapture Calais, which for two hundred years had lain impregnable.[54] England, of course, was France's old enemy.[55] At the end of du Bellay's *Hymne* came a sonnet to Mary, in which, so the poet informs us, this Queen, whose beauty of spirit is prized as much as her physical beauty, will crush Spanish pride and bring France and England together.[56] Jean Antoine de Baïf's *Chant de joie* echoed many of these themes.[57] He mentioned French territorial ambitions to Britain, emphasising that the acquisition of England would take place without murder and without war. It was a fantasy that would nonetheless have been appealing to a readership and audience burdened by the costs of successive foreign wars.

> O happy marriage, that God wishes to bind,
> To make two kingdoms bow to one King,
> And not only two, but without murder and without war,
> For France and Scotland to be allied with England,
> O François, may your wife one day with friendly consent
> Submit the English to your laws.[58]

Such imperial sentiment can also be found in Jean de La Tapie d'Aurillac's *Chantz royale sur les triumphes* which identified François de Lorraine as the son of Mars, the god of war.[59] It drew attention to his taking of Calais, and emphasised the strategic importance of the control of Scotland and its waters to the taming of the English.[60] Mary's beauty was stressed, as was her 'holy deity' and 'eternal virtue'.[61]

La Tapie's *Chantz royale* bathed luxuriantly in classical allusion and drew on the theme of the Muses. Jehan de la Maison's *L'Adieu des neuf Muses*, which was granted a privilege at the end of May 1558, developed this theme further. The scene Berruyer constructed for the reader unfolded as follows. The nine Muses arrived from their divine land of Parnassus to witness the wedding of the Dauphin to Mary Stuart.[62] Just before their return, they delivered a poetic farewell to France, the King, the princes and princesses.[63] Calliope, the first and oldest of the nine Muses, provided the poet's *dramatis personae*. Firstly, she addressed Henri

II and Catherine de Medici the Queen, emphasising Henri's immortal fame and magnanimity and Catherine's wisdom and mildness.[64] Calliope then shifted her attention to the other nobles. Among these were Marguerite, only sister to Henri II,[65] Marguerite de Bourbon,[66] the Prince de Condé,[67] and Monsieur and Madame de Guise; the Duc was described as 'Le Chrestien Mars' having recently subdued Calais.[68] Interspersed with such laudatory versification was Calliopes' adieu to the 'King–Dauphin, & to the Queen of Scots his wife' in which France's hopes for their future King were articulated.[69] Calliope hoped that François would embody the same morality as his grandfather, François I – 'very Christian, learned and just'.[70] François, through whom Scotland and France had been united, was described as mature despite his young years. Mary, taking something of a backseat position behind the Dauphin, was portrayed largely in terms of her dynastic importance.[71]

Estienne Perlin's *Description des royaulmes d'Angleterre et d'Escosse*, published in May 1558, was essentially a guidebook to the kingdoms of Scotland and England.[72] Undoubtedly Perlin felt that a guidebook was necessary for the latter nation, as it would surely fall under the control of France in the near future. It is no coincidence that the *Description* was published only months after the union between Mary and the Dauphin. The imperialism of this work is striking. Perlin described Henri as the 'future monarch and emperor of the whole world'[73] while recalling the spirit of his *entrée* festivals of 1549 and 1550 through the inclusion of, for instance, the phrase *donec totum impleat orbem*, 'so he might complete the world'.[74] The *Description des royaulmes* is a colourful text offering valuable insights into contemporary French perceptions of the English and Scots. It observed, for example, that 'the people of this nation [England] hate the French to death', calling them dogs and sons of whores.[75] Particularly offensive to Perlin was what he saw as the indignity of the English coronation ceremony. Edward, he narrated, was quite improperly styled 'Edouart of grace lorde god the quin and Angleterre, and France, and Irelande'.[76] Despite the arrogance of the English, Perlin did nevertheless appreciate the charms of England. After Paris, he described London as one of the most beautiful cities in the world.[77]

Perlin wrote at length about the Scots, much of which was far from complimentary. We have already touched on some of these comments in chapter one.[78] Politically, the importance of this nation rested on the fact that they had been 'perpetual allies of the French crown and remained faithful to the noble fleur de lys. So much so that they have been protected until today from their only enemy who is worse than a dragon snake, crocodile and adder'.[79] Without the help of the kings of

France, however, the Scots would have lost their country. Therefore, Perlin saw France's relationship with Scotland as 'an infant sucking on the breasts of the very powerful and magnanimous King of France'.[80] Without Henri's assistance 'You [Scotland]', Perlin wrote, 'would have been put to the torch, your country spoilt and ruined by the English, the accursed of all Creation'.[81]

The bold foreign policy claims of many of the editions published to celebrate the marriage were echoed in the diplomatic relationship between France and Britain. As we have seen in chapter one, with Mary's marriage there came a formal strengthening of relations between France and Scotland. Just over a month after the wedding on 5 May 1558, charters were issued from France styling Mary and François as 'Rex et Regina Scotorum', 'King and Queen of Scotland'.[82] François, of course, largely due to the political acumen of Marie de Guise, had also been offered the crown matrimonial by the Scottish Parliament. The wedding medallion minted that year along with other coins, carried the message 'FECIT UTRAMQUE UNUM', he has made them one.[83] Efforts to incorporate Scotland into the French realm took another step forward on 8 July 1558 with the registration of an edict granting all Scots French citizenship; a parallel edict was passed in Scotland.[84]

Mary also held a strong claim to the English throne and with the death of Mary Tudor in November 1558, French claims to that realm, so prevalent in the literature written to accompany Mary's wedding a few months earlier, were pressed strongly. By birth and by religion, Elizabeth was believed incapable of rule and the opportunity was seized. A whole catalogue of official activity witnessed the vigour with which this claim was pursued. Such efforts were more than idle threats designed to counteract England's own claims to be the rightful rulers of France. If France was too weak at this moment to make good Mary's claim, it was sufficient to iterate and reiterate any claim that might be used to justify any future military engagement. Following Mary Tudor's death Mary Stuart dressed in white, a custom of French princesses mourning the death of their predecessor.[85] At the end of December 1558, the French involved themselves in negotiations with the Pope in an effort to declare Elizabeth illegitimate.[86] From the beginning of 1559, François and Mary declared themselves openly in various correspondence as 'King and Queen Dauphins of Scotland, England and Ireland', while during festivals such as the wedding to celebrate the marriage of Henri's daughter Claude with Duc Charles de Lorraine on 22 January, the arms of England could be seen quartered with those of France and 'their seals were engraved in like manner, to show their claim publicly'.[87]

When Antoine Perrenot de Granvelle received the Dauphin François's formal ratification of the Treaty of Cateau-Cambresis on 28 May 1559, it was signed, 'François by the grace of God King of Scotland, England and Ireland'.[88] During the tournament in July 1559 at which Henri II was fatally wounded, the arms of England were suspended on the stage where the judges sat. Following Henri II's death, François II and Mary persisted in styling themselves 'King and Queen of France, Scotland, England and Ireland' and quartered their arms with those of England, displaying them in their chambers, chapels, and wardrobes. Nicholas Throckmorton, the English ambassador in France, reported that the Great Seal that had lately been sent into Scotland had the arms of England, France and Scotland quartered upon it, carrying the inscription 'François and Mary, by the grace of God, King and Queen of Scotland, England and Ireland'.[89]

The peace of 1559, the death of Henri II and the reign of François II

The English may have hoped that the Treaty signed at Cateau-Cambresis in 1559 would dampen these potentially explosive claims. The Treaty brought peace between France, Spain, England and Scotland. It was a peace of exhaustion. Henri had been driven to conclude the treaty primarily by financial difficulties and by the pressing need for him to turn to the problems developing in his own kingdom, specifically the growth of organised Calvinism. In the literature that surrounded the publication of the peace, Mary, as Dauphine, rated a significant if technical appearance. As Queen of Scotland, she was a necessary signatory to a peace treaty that was well received. In a printed letter from Henri II, he stated that after the long and 'unfortunate' wars, it pleased him to take pity on his people and sign a sincere and perpetual peace with the King of Spain, the Queen of England and 'our children the King and Queen of Scotland'.[90]

Initially at least, the response to the treaty in French print would have been encouraging news for the English. The verse celebration *Discours moral de la paix* was followed by a short account of its publication in Paris on 17 April 1559. This emphasised the religious character of the celebrations. A *te deum* was held in Notre Dame, there was a religious procession and a relic from the True Cross was shown, all to demonstrate gratitude to God for the good peace.[91] In Lyon, two editions reported the festivities.[92] Between 16 and 18 April there was a general procession through the town. A 'Pyramid' dedicated to Mars, the god of war, was constructed with vases 'to receive the ashes of the bodies of noble and valiant captains' and put up on the bridge over the Saone.[93] There was an artillery salute at the Place des Cordeliers, while up the steep Rue St Sebastien played a great band full of violins and trumpets.[94] On Monday 17 April, thirteen inmates of the Lyon prison, the Rouanne, were given away in marriage to thirteen poor girls.[95] Two days later, bread was given to the poor. One intriguing celebration involved the printers of Lyon who put on 'a brave spectacle in the large square, the Place de Confort'. Here, a marvellously well–proportioned figure of Mars was constructed. It stood thirty feet high and was dressed for battle.[96] This impressive figure concealed a smaller image of Minerva, goddess of wisdom and the liberal arts; she was accompanied by the nine Muses. The use of the Muses may have been a conscious device to evoke the marriage of François and Mary a year earlier. Shots were fired and flames gradually consumed Mars. As the figure grew smaller, Minerva became visible 'which demonstrates that from Mars' death came the resurrection and the life of Minerva'.[97] Contrary to the anxieties of opposition elements before Mary's marriage, for the time being at least, Mary Stuart, the 'Scottish nymph' as she was described in one edition, was associated with peace.[98]

The publication of Jerome La Rouere's *Deux sermons funèbres* on the death of Henri II also reflected a mood that was less hostile to England.[99] La Rouere identified the securing of Mary, and through her the kingdom of Scotland, to be one of Henri's crowning glories. Not least, France had acquired in Mary a Queen who exhibited all virtues and graces in both beauty and spirit that one could ever wish for in a Princess.[100] But most significantly, La Rouere celebrated the state of good peace and alliance that Henri wisely maintained, particularly with Edward VI. Mary's claims to England were not mentioned.

Nevertheless, neither the attitudes of La Rouere nor those of the accounts of the peace existed in a vacuum. Existing side by side with these editions were more abrasive works. The republication of Joachim du Bellay's *Hymne au Roy sur la prinse de Calais* reenforced the atmosphere of the celebratory literature printed in 1558 in honour of Mary's marriage.[101] While du Bellay's hopes for the incorporation of England were not mentioned directly in his *Tumulus Henrici Secundi Gallorum Regis Christianis* published following the death of Henri II in July 1559,[102] Henri II was portrayed as a Hercules, a Hannibal, having won Boulogne and also having secured the sceptre of Scotland by defeating the English.[103] The omission of direct claims to England was a small concession indeed to the state of peace inaugurated by the Treaty of Cateau-Cambresis.

Intriguingly, the image that seems here to be suggested, and which directly parallels the situation before 1558, is of a certain cautiousness in print over antagonising Elizabeth. But this seems to be an anomaly rather than a significant trend. In other media, Mary's claims to England were conspicuously proclaimed. At the coronation ceremony at Reims on September 1559, the arms of England appeared alongside those of France and Scotland on the entrance gate.[104] It was not just that the English ambassadors were being overly sensitive. Even the French ambassador, Michel de Castelnau, looking back on these years, noted that the arms of England were joined flagrantly with those of the Scottish Queen and were placed 'publicly in Paris in several places and gates by the heralds of the Dauphin of France'.[105] At the royal *entrée* at Châtellerault on 23 November 1559, a triumphal arch greeted François II and Mary Stuart. Inscriptions were placed on either side of the gates, just underneath the portraits of the royal couple.[106] On the right side of the gateway appeared a portrait and the arms of François as King of France, and on the left, Mary as Queen of England, France and Scotland.[107] The following inscription was placed in golden lettering:

> Gallia perpetuis pugnaxq, Britannia bellis.
> Olim odio inter se dimicuere part.
> Nunc gallos totq. remotos orbe Britannos.
> Vnum dos Mariae cogit in Imperium.[108]

Only two printed accounts of the royal *entrées* were published, or have survived. These recorded the events at Orléans in December 1559 and at Chenonceau in March 1560. These printed accounts were less sensitive to the issue of armorial bearings and did not mention their presence, though such styling – at least at Chenonceau – certainly did take place.[109] Instead, they focused their attentions solely on conveying a sense of the power and magnificence of François II. There is a beautiful description of the *château* and of the gardens at Chenonceau,[110] and of particular attractions at the Orléans *entrée* which included a procession of the personnel of the university, a harangue delivered by the rector of the university to François and Mary, a triumphal arch and the presentation of the keys of the city to the new King.[111] Also emphasised were various devices in the festival that conveyed advice to the new monarch, for instance 'the health of the prince is the union of the people'.[112] Four cardinal virtues were extolled: the need for justice, prudence, force and temperance.[113] At Chenonceau, Mary Queen of Scots followed behind François, accompanied by Madame de Guise and several other ladies.[114] The text spoke of the 'arms of the King, queen,

queen mother, Monsieur d'Orléans and the governor of Orléans were displayed', without stating explicitly whether or not these arms included the bearings of England and Ireland.[115]

The war in Scotland, 1559–60

The deliberate styling of François and Mary as the legitimate rulers of England was worrying enough to Elizabeth's ambassadors. But far more threatening was France's direct involvement in a military campaign in Scotland in 1559–60.

Despite the leniency shown by the regent Marie de Guise towards Protestantism, increasing Scottish resentment towards French influence in government blended with the fear that Marie might soon attempt to eradicate the new faith. Open revolt broke out. To maintain their interests in Scotland, France sent an expeditionary force to quash the rebellion. Concerned by France's public claim to their realm, the English responded by sending forces north of the border to aid the rebels. For France, the expedition was to be disastrous. It was not the strength of the rebel forces that was responsible for the French defeat, but rather a series of critical problems that prevented them from being able to conduct a sustained military operation. These included: the effects on commerce and morale of the continuous English threat to shipping; war-weariness; the logistical and financial problems involved in refitting storm–damaged ships and in supplying and equipping relief operations.[116] The French were forced into signing the Treaty of Edinburgh on 6 July 1560.

The military engagement of 1559–60, which could so easily have escalated into a full–scale conflict, stimulated an impassioned debate in print between the courts of France and England. We will deal in the following chapter with the Huguenot image of Mary, Queen of Scots. For the moment, it is sufficient to note that the opening sally in the 1560 debate came from Elizabeth.[117] In reply to this, the French crown commissioned the publication of a protestation on behalf of François II which was delivered to Elizabeth and her court by the French ambassador to London, the Sieur de Seure. This text was given to at least two printers, Benoist Rigaud in Lyon and Jean Rousset in Tours. Both printers were awarded a privilege to publish the work, noting in the colophon of both works the phrase 'humble and obedient to His Majesty'. The editions appeared simultaneously around 20 May 1560.[118] A third edition of this *Protestation*, this time of much poorer quality, was also printed – on the Eloy Gibier press in Orléans. This edition carried

neither a privilege nor a similar message of humble obedience to
François II. Despite the indication of place of publication and the name
of the printer, this was undoubtedly a pirated copy. Gibier would not
have been too concerned about any reprisal for this infringement of
privilege. After all, Rigaud and Rousset would have been concerned only
with protecting their local markets, while the crown would have been
only too eager to see this work published elsewhere, particularly if
favours were not expected in return.

The *Protestation* was designed to ensure support for the military campaign, attempting to justify the action to the public and insulate French
opinion against the arguments put forward by Elizabeth. At the centre
of the *Protestation's* argument was a refutation of English claims that
involvement in Scotland had only been undertaken in the interests of
national security. Elizabeth's involvement in Scotland was designed
entirely, argued the French ambassador, to serve her own expansionist
ends.[119] Elizabeth's true objective was to deprive François and Mary of
their rightful kingdom. The pamphlet emphasised that the French were
intervening in Scotland solely to quash the rebels, and that they had
absolutely no intention of invading England.[120] Claims to that realm
were not only omitted, but assertions that François II and Mary had ever
styled themselves as King and Queen of that country were vehemently
denied.[121] The text referred to Elizabeth throughout as the Queen of
England, Mary's 'good sister and cousin',[122] and pointed to François II's
inheritance not only of the kingdom of France from his father and his
zeal for 'Christianity' but also his desire for a good and sure peace with
the English realm.[123] The seemingly conciliatory tone soon descended
into sarcastic rhetoric attacking England and Protestantism for their
support of the Scottish rebels. This contributed to a maturing theme
in Catholic polemic, the association between Protestantism and
rebellion.[124] In supporting rebels, Elizabeth had set a bad example for
Christian princes everywhere.

The French attitude to Mary and England following the death of François II, 1561–8

1560 was to be an *annus horribilis* for Mary. The Treaty of Edinburgh
signed in July 1560 was a bruising humiliation for the French and a
significant victory for Scottish Protestantism. While Mary refused
stubbornly to ratify the treaty, France agreed to all of its conditions
including the withdrawal of its troops from Scotland and a commitment
to end its practice of displaying English armorial bearings in France. In

August, only one month after the conclusion of the treaty, Mary's mother, Marie de Guise, died. Four months later, on 5 December, François II died and so Mary was no longer Queen of two kingdoms. Charles IX aged ten acceded to the throne. The political vacuum left by the death of her mother, in addition to the far more limited opportunities available to her if she were to stay in France under the regency of Catherine de Medici, convinced Mary to return to Scotland in August 1561.

Mary's eclipse from power in France was not immediately reflected by diminishing interest in the French press. 1561 saw a number of editions relating to her and her claim to the English throne. In January, Claude d'Espence's funeral oration for Marie de Guise was published. D'Espence had probably been encouraged to transpose his oration delivered on 12 August 1560 into a written form by a member of the Guise family.[125] The published version contained a touching dedication consoling Mary Stuart on the loss of her mother and husband.[126] In his dedication, d'Espence urged Mary Stuart to rest in the assurance of God's love, citing numerous Biblical references for her consolation. The text appears to have been published as much out of sympathy and affection for Mary Stuart as for her mother. This is suggested not only by the dedication, but also by the addition of a short piece at the end of the oration entitled 'the justice that God renders to the widow and the orphan'.[127] Mary, of course, was both a widow and an orphan.

The oration praised the many virtues of Marie de Guise. In particular, it spoke of Marie's commitment to maintaining and fostering the auld alliance between France and Scotland. To d'Espence, it was a bond that was 'impregnable' and such that one could not find a bond so long lasting, solid and sincere between two peoples in the world'.[128] The *fleur de lys*, the oration commented, augmented the King of Scotland's arms in recognition of this alliance, an alliance that was cemented continually by cultural links between the two countries. Religiously sincere, Marie had maintained her people in peace, unity and devotion to the crown of France.[129] With hindsight, the Treaty of Edinburgh marked the end of Scotland's military alliance with France. But such realisation dawned neither on d'Espence nor his contemporaries who, in 1561, looked forward to witnessing the development of the auld alliance during the reign of Marie's daughter, Mary Queen of Scots.

Other editions, exploiting anti-English feeling in France at this moment, proved to be far more controversial. Both the *Brief discours de la tempeste et foudre advenue en la cité de Londres en Angleterre, sur le grand temple et clocher nommé de Sainct Paul, le quatriesme juin, 1561* and the *Récit véritable du grand temple et clocher de la cité de Londres, nommé S.*

Paul, ruiné par la foudre, dealt with the significance of a bolt of lightning which had struck St Paul's cathedral on 4 June 1561.[130] By means of such apparently natural phenomena, the wisdom of God could be discerned; He had pronounced his judgement on the need for religious unity. The English example was a warning of the dangers of the divisive sect of Protestantism.

Other works were to voice even more aggressive criticisms of the situation in England, accenting the need for immediate action against Protestantism in France. October 1561 saw the publication of the *Histoire des scismes et hérésies des Albigeois*.[131] Written by the *procureur* of the Toulouse Parlement, Jean Gay, it urged in its preface that the Constable, Anne de Montmorency should continue the battle against heresy as his family had done in the past. This preface was clearly a response to Montmorency's decision in the spring of 1561 to join with François Duc de Guise, the marshal St André and later with Antoine Roi de Navarre who styled themselves as the defenders of French Catholicism.[132]

The text generated robust protests from the English government. Throckmorton wrote to Elizabeth:

> Lately a lewd book came to his hands, printed at Paris, wherein the author speaks slanderously of Kings Henry VIII and Edward VI. It is dedicated to the Constable, to whom he addressed his complaint to have reformation of the matter, who procured order to be addressed to his son, Marshal Montmorency, to have all the books suppressed, and the author is likely enough to be punished.[133]

At Elizabeth's request, Catherine de Medici intervened quickly and effectively to curb Gay's work and other editions that slandered the English Queen.[134] Catherine's involvement in censoring such works was no isolated incident. A month earlier, in September 1561, Catherine and notably François de Lorraine, Duc de Guise, had ordered the seizure of eight hundred copies of a work in Latin that carried a preface by Gabriel de Sacconay, an ultra-catholic ecclesiastical censor in Lyon.[135] This text defended Mary's right to the English crown and cast considerable doubt on the characters of Henry VIII and Anne Boleyn, whom Sacconay called a 'Jezebel', thereby denying the legitimacy of Elizabeth. Elizabeth demanded that such a lewd work be suppressed. Cecil had considered composing a reply to the work, but Throckmorton advised that any reply would be counter-productive, giving greater credence to its arguments.[136] In the end, demanding the suppression of the work proved to be successful. Offensive portions of the work were rewritten, with all attacks against the change in religion under Henry VIII suppressed.[137] It is surely a mark of how successful such seizures were that there is no known surviving copy of the original edition.

The single most important question that is raised by this series of events is why did the crown, together with the Guise, Montmorency and other Catholics who pursued a hard line against Protestantism in France, support the censorship of those editions which questioned Elizabeth's legitimacy and by implication favoured Mary's claim to the crown?

The crown acted principally because such editions represented a danger to its delicate relationship with England. The Treaty of Edinburgh had been a humiliation for the French, but one for the time being they were willing to nurse, particularly given the explosive growth of organised Calvinism at home attracting considerable noble support. No matter how committed the conservative element was to eliminating the cancerous sect of Protestantism within France, neither the Guise affinity nor Montmorency were willing to exacerbate tensions with England at this moment. Financial problems, internal discord and the fear that these might be exploited to Elizabeth's advantage made conciliation necessary in foreign if not domestic politics.

Catherine de Medici, nevertheless, was soon to realise the boundaries of this fragile internal consensus when she attempted to exploit it to the advantage of her domestic agenda of cross-confessional dialogue and moderation. Catherine had taken the tentative step of signalling concessions to the Huguenot movement by legitimising in December 1561 one of their core texts, the Psalter.[138] Politique works were also published, undoubtedly with the consent of the crown, which promoted the cause of the middle way, including one by Catherine's own advisor Jean de Monluc, Bishop of Valence. The *Apologie contre certaines calomnies mises sus à la desfaveur & desvantage de l'estat des affaires de ce roiaume*, published in 1562, was even to pay tribute to the religious moderation adopted by Mary on her return to Scotland, describing her as a 'wise, virtuous and Catholic Princess, counselled by wise advisors'.[139] However, one of the fundamental obstacles to the effective promotion of the moderate objectives of the crown was the tide of inflammatory anti-Protestant polemic. Catherine attempted to eradicate such polemic by tightening controls over privilege granting.[140] Texts could be granted authorisation by the crown or by the conservative parlement and faculty of theology, the Sorbonne. Catherine withdrew the right to award privilege from all but the crown and attempted to use the consensus gained on editions hostile to England to support this legislation.

Thus, in January 1562, François de Montmorency, the governor of Paris and politically moderate eldest son of Anne, passed legislation forbidding the printing of works without the authorisation of either the King or his council.[141] In so doing, he directly cited the scandal generated by the granting of a privilege by the Parlement of Paris to Jean Gay's *Histoire des Albigeois*. The crown was attempting to use censorship to curb Catholic works which were critical of crown policy and not only, as before, exclusively on works designated as heretical.

Of their own volition, the Catholic press demonstrated restraint over the issue of England. Neither the French crown nor the hard line Catholic leadership wished to antagonise Elizabeth unnecessarily. Only a single work printed in the period 1562 to 1571 made any hostile remarks against the English state. The English secretary, William Cecil, may have been so outraged at this work that he wished to pen a reply to such a 'slanderous epistle', but in fact the text was a remarkably restrained piece of prose to emerge from a Catholic country.[142] The offending work took the form of a letter to Elizabeth written by a Portugese historian, prelate and humanist named Jêrome Osorius. Osorius' letter was appended to Ferdinand I's *Les Graves et sainctes remonstrances de l'Empereur Ferdinand*, printed in 1563 originally in Latin and translated into French the same year.[143] Despite attempts by the crown to limit anti-English works printed in France, this work received a privilege. Undoubtedly, this was a defiant gesture against Elizabeth's involvement during the first civil war on the side of the Huguenots.[144]

Osorius' text offered advice to Elizabeth. She was portrayed as the lieutenant general of God on earth and such a position, Osorius pointed out, carried with it a celestial function.[145] A far more polemical tone was then developed; Osorius began to rail against the perverse sect of Protestantism. Founded on the multitude, he argued, this new religion sought to abolish differences in dignity and grandeur.[146] It was, consequently, a threat both to public order and public morality and would be the ruin of Kingdoms.[147] To avoid this, Osorius encouraged Elizabeth to work towards the eradication of the works of Satan, to embrace the true cross and to hate 'the wretched spreaders of this new plague, who so hate the said cross'.[148]

What is striking about Osorius' work, is the way in which it distanced Elizabeth from criticism, adopting instead the convention of blaming her evil counsellors. A wise monarch should not heed flatterers, he argued; no King should be esteemed by wealth but by the number of prudent and good men in his service.[149] Criticising the monarch's advisors was, of course, a conventional rhetorical device of attacking the monarch. But such restraint is in itself striking. It is, of course, difficult to take Osorius' rhetoric wholly at face value. Just how seriously, for instance, are we expected to believe his stated hope that Elizabeth would restore Catholicism to England? At one point, he even argued that the partial survival of Catholicism in England was due to the efforts of Elizabeth working against her counsellors.[150] Despite some degree of what was probably sarcasm, it is clear that throughout the work Elizabeth was always presented as the rightful monarch of England. There was not the slightest inkling that Mary Stuart should replace her as Queen. In fact, after 1560, no printed work was to assert Mary's claim to the English throne in place of Elizabeth.

Despite English involvement during the first religious war, the 1560s witnessed a developing alliance between England and France. A symbol of warming relations came in April 1564 with the signing of the Treaty of Troyes. In the printed account of the *Proclamation de la paix*, there was a recognition that Elizabeth was Queen of England 'by the same grace of God' as Charles IX was King of France.[151] The stated aim of the accord was to assure a 'good, firm, sincere, stable and perpetual peace, friendship and reconciliation' between the two sovereigns, their vassals and subjects. In fact, the critical catalyst for the treaty was trade, 'to go, to come and to stay, return, converse, to haggle, communicate and negotiate with each other in their respective countries, freely and securely'.[152] Relations improved but had their difficulties. Tensions, for instance, were reflected in a letter from Charles IX, dated 17 [sic for 12] September 1564 to the Bureau de la Ville de Paris.[153] Talking of the recent peace with England, Charles discussed the commerce between the two nations, and in particular the recent memo sent by the Bureau complaining of unfair subsidies favouring the English. The memo complained that on English goods Elizabeth charged 12 *deniers*, while on French goods, a 15 *deniers* tax was levied.[154] There were also complaints about favouritism in Normandy, where the French paid 20 *deniers tournois* per *livre*, while the English paid only 16 *deniers* per *livre*.[155] Obviously there were still problems, but trade did flow. Relations between the two countries did thaw, even if between January and May 1565, Elizabeth refused the hand of the young Charles IX in marriage.[156]

The fledgling relationship with England was celebrated in the publication in 1565 of a piece of court propaganda by the celebrated prince of poets, Pierre de Ronsard, entitled *Elegies, mascarades et bergeries*.[157] There can be little doubt that Ronsard's verse was a piece of official propaganda. In his dedicatory letter, Ronsard stated that it was on Catherine's instructions that the *Elegies* contained a substantial opening elegy dedicated to the English Queen.[158] In this, Ronsard focused on Elizabeth's beauty, which he compared to Mary's, saying that there were now 'two suns' on one island.[159] The verse celebrated the friendship between the two queens, their fame and their beauty. From the moment that Mary arrived in Scotland, she had maintained a conscious political distance from France, partly to appease a nobility tired of French influence over Scottish affairs, partly as a consequence of her acerbic personal relationship with Catherine. In spite of these tensions, Mary was treated in Ronsard's work with the respect and honour due to a Queen. The 'Bergerie' was dedicated to her, together with a small elegy.[160] The focus, however, was overwhelmingly on Elizabeth and on her key advisors. Laudatory poems were addressed to Robert Dudley, Earl of Leicester and William Cecil, Elizabeth's Secretary.[161]

As anxious as the French court would have been not to exacerbate diplomatic tensions with Scotland, the impetus for mentioning the Scottish Queen may not have come entirely, if at all, from Catherine de Medici. Ronsard would also have had his own interests at the forefront of his mind. As well as looking for patronage, often in vain, from the Guise-Lorraine family, he also cast his eye to Mary for favour. A copy of the *Mascarades* was sent to Mary and bound with it was an 'Elegy to the Queen' written by Ronsard, later published in the 1567 edition of his *Oeuvres*.[162] This mentioned idealistically that under her hand her Scottish subjects had been tamed.[163] His flattery did not go unrewarded; in 1566 he received a pension from Mary.[164]

Mary had attracted Ronsard's interest four years earlier. He commemorated her departure from France in August 1561 with an elegy published in Lyon that year.[165] Mary was presented within an idealistic and conventionalised framework, embodying beauty, majesty, grace and chastity. Her skin was made of alabaster, her hair was golden, and her radiant eyes had the effect of turning night into day.

The overall picture for the 1560s, however, reveals that Mary attracted very meagre attention in the French press. There was little interest in following her career when she returned to Scotland. In this respect, one edition was very much the exception. *La Harangue de Marie d'Estuart*, published in 1563, was the text of Mary's opening speech to the Scottish Parliament in May 1562. While this speech was not published at all in Scotland, it was printed in two editions at Lyon and Reims.[166] If not commissioned by one of Mary's Guise uncles, it was designed certainly to flatter their noble house. Jean de Foigny, printer to the Cardinal, printed the Reims edition while the *Harangue* itself was bound with a funeral oration to François de Lorraine, Duc de Guise who had been assassinated that year during the first religious war. Even if, as we have seen in the previous chapter, official political relations between France and Scotland were rather raw, at this moment at least, the Guise were eager to stress their relationship with the Scottish Queen.

In the *Harangue*, Mary addressed the Parliament of Scotland 'of which it pleased God to make me Queen and sovereign'.[167] The tone of the work was conciliatory and diplomatic but it did not lack resolve. Mary pointed to her own youthfulness and inexperience and raised an issue of obvious concern in Scotland, that of her affinity with France.[168] She did not deny her French education and connections, but indicated clearly that she had been sent to France by the common consent of the nobility in 1548 and had in any case left Scotland in the sure hands of her mother, Marie de Guise.[169] The speech demonstrated clearly the way in which Mary manipulated her perceived weaknesses to her own advantage, attempting to assure the Scottish nobility of her commitment to listen to their needs. For transparency and to uphold convention and tradition, Mary indicated her willingness to accept and act on the advice of the Parliament.[170] Her principal desire was, she said, to 'reign among you' as a father rules his children, and 'not as a tyrant'.[171] Mary assured her subjects that she would preserve their liberties and privileges just as her predecessors had done.[172] Thanking her subjects for their obedience, Mary nevertheless issued a thorny caution. She would rule in such a way that 'the virtuous are recompensed and the evil–doers chastised, often mixing justice with forgiveness, which is more appropriate for me than for anyone else, as a Queen and a woman'.[173] Mary would not be dictated to, but in deliberately and cleverly evoking her gender, she reassured the Scottish Parliament in a gentle fashion.

There were also a few less substantial mentions of Mary in the period before 1568. René Benoist, Mary's former confessor mentioned Mary in a theological work published in 1564 entitled *Traité du sacrifice évangélique*.[174] The book was dedicated to Mary and in the dedication, Benoist recalled how he had accompanied her back to Scotland in August 1561 and had stood by her in opposing the enemies of God.[175] He had remained with her for the agreed time and then returned to the troubles afflicting France [August 1562].[176] Benoist as a Doctor of Theology undertook 'reading, preaching and writing' in an attempt to expose to all 'how dangerous it is to leave the faith and Christian religion to follow the false and new doctrines'.[177] This was his task and he urged Mary to fulfil her responsibilities by continuing the promotion of the Catholic faith in Scotland and not to grant concessions to the heretics. Resolving to remain a firm servant to Mary, he congratulated the Queen on her constancy, 'I have been so bold as to protest that on no account would you ever wish to leave the Christian religion and Catholic profession of it, dedicating to you this little work on the evangelical sacrifice'.[178]

There were also a few incidental mentions of Mary in republished editions.[179] But any mention of Mary's personal reign proved to be the exception rather than the rule. There was no contemporary use of Mary for polemical purposes in the battle against Protestantism, despite her position as a Catholic monarch in a Protestant country. This quandary can be explained by three factors. Firstly, her political currency had become devalued by distancing herself from France, refusing for example Catherine's proposal that she should marry Charles IX. Secondly, it can also be explained by the growing amity between France and England. In such a situation, pronounced praise for Mary might be misinterpreted. However, perhaps the most significant explanation for the lack of interest in the Scottish Queen was her chequered career. She ill suited the role of hero of the Catholic cause, not least because of her policy of toleration towards the new faith. Benoist may have praised Mary's religious constancy, but this was difficult to reconcile with her toleration of the Protestant status quo in Scotland.

The imprisonment of Mary

The French presses did not report her marriage to Henry, Lord Darnley, nor the murder of her secretary David Rizzio – allegedly whilst Mary stood in horror, pregnant with the future James VI. Perhaps most remarkably, however, at a time when the printing presses found an avid audience for many types of sensational literature, even such an event as the bombing of the King of Scotland passed unmentioned. There may be both technical and political reasons for this. Much of the sensational literature emanated from France's second printing centre at Lyon. This was certainly true of reports of Turkish horrors and atrocities that Lyon acquired via its trade connections with Italy, but also of various other natural disasters and apparitions, comets, floods and strange births. The undisputed master of this sensational literature was the Lyon publisher Benoist Rigaud. The major Parisian printers tended in any case to be more high–minded and they might have had additional political reason to pass over in silence an event which could hardly do credit to an ally of France. For that reason, there was not even any attempt to engage debate about Mary's alleged adulterous affair and subsequent marriage to the man closely linked with Darnley's murder, James Hepburn, Earl of Bothwell. There was not even any mention of Mary's deposition by the Scots and imprisonment on Loch Leven.

In fact, not even Mary's imprisonment by Elizabeth following her flight into England in 1568 convinced French Catholic pamphleteers to take up her cause. As we have seen in chapter one, the diplomatic reaction in France to Mary's imprisonment was cautious, though designed to influence Elizabeth to release Mary. Functioning diplomatic relations with England were, however, immeasurably more important than embarking upon a war over the issue. The French limited their pressure to infrequent threats and to ensuring that Mary was confined with the comfort due to her rank. At least partially, the rapid relaxation of France's diplomatic position regarding Mary was made possible by the lack of any public Catholic outburst to her imprisonment. For France, there is no evidence to support James Phillips's statement that 'Mary's defenders . . . on the continent reacted swiftly and strongly to the propaganda attacks launched against her after she came to England.'[180] In fact, the reality is quite the opposite. More concerned with internal affairs in France, it is telling that not even Mary's Guise relatives made any public protest.

It was to be two years before Mary was mentioned in the French press and even then the references were couched in notably cautious terms. These mentions appeared in two works published in 1570 that related to the northern rebellion of November 1569, led by Sir Thomas Percy, 8th Earl of Northumberland.[181] The revolt had been ignited by the imprisonment of the Duke of Norfolk for his conspiracy against William Cecil and for his intention to marry Mary Queen of Scots without the permission of Elizabeth. This was a particularly sensitive issue given Norfolk's close proximity to the English succession. The rebellion, however, which sought the restoration of Catholicism in England and Mary to the throne, quickly collapsed. This was partly due to the critical failure of the rebels to free her from prison. Loyalist forces had wisely transferred her from Tutbury to the more secure location of Coventry. Despite Mary's desperate pleas to Philip II that 'if he would consent to assist her, then she would be Queen of England in three months, and mass shall be said all over the country', foreign support did not materialise.[182]

Details of the northern rebellion were reported in France in two works, the *Discours des troubles nouvellement advenus au royaume d'Angleterre* which went through two editions and the *Continuation des choses plus célèbres*.[183] Both these pamphlets considerably misrepresented the agenda of the nobility. While the central aim of the revolt – the restoration of the ancient liberties of the Catholic Church – was maintained, other details were altered. The pamphlets made absolutely no mention of the fact that a secondary priority of the rebels had been to place Mary on the throne of England in place of Elizabeth. Rather, they simply conveyed that one of the aims of the rebels had been the advancement of James's right to succeed to the throne of England after Elizabeth's death. Throughout, the rebels were presented not as having treasonous designs but as being 'very faithful subjects of Her Majesty'.[184] More than a passing reference was made to Mary's captivity, though her claim to the English crown was not mentioned once. While there was a certain sympathy for 'the piteous and deplorable state of the Queen of Scotland' there was no direct appeal to the French to intervene.[185] In fact, this text is barren of any of the emotive polemical rhetoric that we might have expected it to have contained. The statement that Elizabeth had imprisoned a legitimate Catholic Queen is quite matter of fact. The *Continuation des choses* even went so far as to describe Mary's confinement in not uncongenial terms. Coventry, where she was then held, was described as one of the most beautiful towns in England.[186]

Writing after the collapse of the revolt and seeking authorisation from Charles IX for the publication of their texts, these pamphleteers would have found it difficult to favour an unsuccessful revolt against a legitimate monarch, particularly in a climate of religious rebellion within France and in a climate of positive though brittle Anglo-French relations. Instead, these texts adopted a rather uneasy stance. While demonstrating sympathy for the aims of the rebels, they neither explicitly condemned nor supported their actions. Various elements might have been introduced into the prose to incite anger in the French audience against the treatment of their co-religionists across the channel. For instance, they could have commented on the particularly brutal way in which the English suppressed the rebellion. Yet, the pamphlets are free from such remarks. Sympathy for the aims of the rebels but distance from the means by which they sought their realisation was a view undoubtedly shared by the French crown. Diplomacy required tact and Catherine de Medici was to show no official support for the Northern rebels. In the same way, in the spring of 1571, after the discovery of the Ridolfi plot, Catherine chose to distance the crown as far as possible from the conspirators and from Mary.

It was not until late December or early January 1573 that any defence of Mary Stuart appeared in French, four years after Mary had been deposed in Scotland by a Protestant faction and imprisoned in England by a Protestant Queen.[187] Without any supporting evidence, it is usually assumed that Mary's ambassador, John Leslie, Bishop of Ross, wrote

L'Innocence de la trèsillustre, très chaste et débonnaire Princesse Madame Marie Roine d'Escosse.[188] But this seems improbable. More likely, the book was composed by a group of Catholic exiles, and, given its anonymous publication in Reims by Jean de Foigny, Guise sponsorship might reasonably be assumed.[189]

L'Innocence was no spontaneous outburst of newly found sympathy for Mary in France. It was published in late December 1572 to influence public and political opinion at a sensitive period in Anglo–French relations. By the fragile Treaty of Blois signed in April 1572 more out of the necessity for solidarity against Spain than goodwill, France and England formulated a commercial and defensive alliance which was to remain valid even if either country was attacked on grounds of religion. Also stipulated in the treaty was that both countries should accept joint responsibility for settling the raging civil conflict in Scotland. While France and England maintained a veneer of neutrality in Scotland in order to respect the Blois accord, both sides intervened to some extent. The pro-Marian forces, who by June 1572, had been reduced to holding Edinburgh castle only, looked to Charles IX for support, and there is some evidence to suggest that they received it.[190] Certainly by November, the French King had begun to send money to support those in the castle. According to one English ambassador, the French played a delicate diplomatic game in order to maintain the party in Scotland until 'they have settled their things at home'.[191] *L'Innocence* was timed, therefore, to coincide with debates within the French court about involvement in Scotland.[192] It is not impossible that the text was published with the court's tacit consent to justify possible future involvement in support of the pro-Marian cause. It is difficult to determine how near the French actually came to dispatching significant support to the Castilians. Perhaps some indication can be gained by the swelling English frustrations at the ambivalent policy of the French crown.[193]

The book was designed as a reply to George Buchanan's attack on Mary that had been published during the negotiations for Blois in April 1572. According to *L'Innocence*, Buchanan's *Histoire* had been designed to vilify both Mary and the Duke of Norfolk in the mind of the French King and therefore frustrate any hopes she had of benefiting from the Blois accord.[194] The *Histoire* was a catalogue of anti-Marian Scottish and English argument that had matured during the conferences of York and Westminster.[195] These arguments were dismissed in *L'Innocence*. Buchanan was personally attacked, characterised as 'the greatest slanderer, impudent liar, coward, ungrateful and detestable atheist on the planet', while Camuz, the translator, was described rather uncharitably as 'a rebel, heretic, fugitive for his conspiracies, troublemaker among the wicked and traitor'.[196]

L'Innocence was carefully crafted for a French audience. Even small details were orientated towards a French readership. For instance, the date given to Buchanan's work was that of the French translation, 17 February 1572, not the date of the English version.[197] More significant was the attempt to manipulate anti-Huguenot sentiment following the massacre of St. Bartholomew's Day a few months earlier. Scottish Protestantism was linked with the Huguenot movement in France, not only by their theological similarity but also by the 'intelligences' of their leaders. The principal objective of *L'Innocence* was to discredit the anti-Marian party in Scotland and it did so for the most part by attacking its previous leader, James, Earl of Moray. Moray was Mary's half-brother and her principal opponent as head of the Protestant faction in Scotland. He was assassinated in January 1570 by the head of the pro–Marian party, James Hamilton, 2nd Earl of Arran, and Duc de Châtellerhaut.[198] In *L'Innocence*, Moray was associated closely with Admiral Coligny, whose assassination in August 1572 had sparked the Paris and provincial massacres in France.[199] At one section in the text, Moray was described thus:

> O abominable bastard and infamous murderer ! O wretched heretic! You who having made war with God and his Saints, polluted sacred things and abused the goods of the crucifix [the benefices of the church], have not feared to attack kings, to conspire against princes, and to be in league with Colligny (the true scourge of France). You have made trouble in your country and caused a bloody civil war between those of your nation![200]

The opening of the *Innocence* has the quality of a sermon, railing against the iniquities of an age of irreligion, where Satan was so far advanced in the world, that knowledge of God was almost completely sidelined. Protestantism had brought to his age, the author narrated, strange things and new inventions which had resulted in seditions of subjects, rebellions, murders, treasons, plots, a reversal of all sanctity and justice and a violation of all good laws and customs.[201] Libertines and followers of Machiavelli were accused of misleading the people. Symptoms of this sickness, the text concluded, could be found in the cases of the illustrious Mary Queen of Scots and the Duke of Norfolk.

L'Innocence narrated the history of Mary's personal reign in Scotland, replying to the accusations of Buchanan who had emphasised her uncontrollable and adulterous passions, her marital problems with Darnley and her involvement in a prolonged and eventually successful campaign to assassinate her husband Lord Darnley. 'If the illustrious Queen of Scotland had harboured a soul as vicious as is alleged here', the authors of *L'Innocence* wrote, 'I pray you, would she not rather have romped about in France, where there is a great deal more freedom than in Scotland?'[202] Never had a single man or woman in France any occasion to speak badly of Mary.[203] Mary's French character was consistently emphasised. For instance, *L'Innocence* refuted the allegation that Mary was more familiar with David Rizzio than honesty would permit, and that therefore his murder by Darnley and the Protestant Lords in front of Mary (pregnant at this point) was justified.[204] There was no denial of the level of access that Rizzio had with Mary, but this was attributed to the 'honest liberty of French ladies'.[205]

The blame for the troubles facing Scotland in the 1560s shifted from Mary to the Protestants, particularly Moray, who was always referred to in the text as 'the bastard'. He was seen as manipulative, greedy and ambitious. Embodying the opposite characteristics, Mary was portrayed as the conciliator, who had done nothing but honour and respect her half–brother throughout the most testing of circumstances.[206] For instance, Mary had chosen to embrace Moray rather than execute him for his part in the assassination of David Rizzio.[207] As for the principal charge against Mary, the assassination of Darnley, this was blamed on Moray and his accomplices.[208] Various depositions were reprinted to witness to Mary's innocence, rebutting the claims of the infamous Casket Letters.[209]

L'Innocence was the most significant Catholic response to the deposition and imprisonment of Mary Queen of Scots, inverting the argument of Buchanan by establishing a portrait of Mary as a good Catholic ruler, brought down by the machinations of Protestant rebels who would do anything to satisfy their own ambitions. Yet it was a work published in only two editions, one part of a very limited and unsuccessful campaign in France to generate public support for the pro-Marian party in Scotland. Despite a degree of flirtation with this cause, the French chose not to commit themselves to a conflict in Scotland and by May 1573, deprived of foreign support, the Castilians relinquished their control over Edinburgh Castle. Relations between France and England normalised and on 26 March 1575, the Treaty of Blois was confirmed in London. Interest in Mary diminished as quickly as it had developed. There was almost no mention of her at all during the rest of the decade, except for brief mentions in general histories such as Sebastien Münster's *Cosmographie* edited and revised substantially for a French audience by François de Belleforest.[210] In this, Belleforest stated only that she had married François II and 'the son of the Count of Lennox' and that Scotland 'was in trouble, governed by regents during the imprisonment of their legitimate Princess'.[211]

Despite the normalisation of diplomatic relations between France and England, there remained signs of antagonistic feeling, albeit measured. Although not encouraged by the French crown, these editions were printed without any known reprisals. Jerome Osorius' *Remonstrance à Madame Elizabeth Royne d'Angleterre touchant les affaires du monde*, which we have discussed in some detail above, was republished. As we have seen, in 1563 this work had received royal approval for four years. However, there is no evidence to suggest that the printers of the 1575 and 1577 editions of the work applied for a renewal of this privilege. Interestingly, the 1575 edition reprinted the 1563 privilege to Nicolas Chesneau, noting the date 22 June, with the year conspicuously absent.[212] 1577, moreover, witnessed the appearance in four editions of the *Histoire merveilleuse et espouvantable advenue en Angleterre*.[213] This unlicensed work concerned the sudden mysterious sickness and death of the judge and many other persons connected with the trial of the Catholic bookseller, Roland Jenks at Oxford in May 1577.[214]

1576 saw the publication of *L'Histoire et discours au vray du siège qui fut mis devant la ville d'Orléans, par les Anglois, le mardy XII. jour d'octobre 1428*.[215] This text, awarded a privilege for six years, recounted the events of the siege of Orléans in 1428 from a manuscript held in the town hall. According to the preface, it was written to explain that the annual procession through Orléans was held to mark the town's deliverance from the English.[216] The victory of Charles VII over the Lancastrian Henry VI of England was attributed to divine vengeance, particularly for the behaviour of the English who engaged in a spree of sacrilegious behaviour during the campaign, including the pillaging of a church, Nostre Dame de Clery.[217] While the English were represented as 'hereditary enemies of this kingdom',[218] the presence of Scotsmen in the ranks of the French army was noted, including Jean Stuart, Constable of Scotland, who had come to France in 1421 at the behest of the Dauphin.[219] *L'Histoire* is revealing of the continuation of historical hostility towards England, at least in Orléans. This hostility was used to incite Catholic outrage. For the text relates the act of the Huguenots in destroying a statue of the saviour of France, Jeanne d'Arc, 'the maid of Orleans'. This was knocked down and smashed to pieces by the Protestants, who then, presumably in an act of symbolic purification, threw it into the Loire.[220] The Huguenots were thus seen as enemies of the French state. Given that processions were often occasions when con-

fessional violence erupted, this text was more than an historical narrative of the origins of this event; it was a polemical pamphlet against
Protestantism.

As we shall see in chapter three, from 1574, Mary became an important symbol in post-St. Bartholomew's Day Huguenot literature. Surprisingly, however, the Catholic presses, while promoting anti-English
feeling, did not respond to Protestant attacks on her reputation. It was
not until 1578 that any edition expressed sympathy for the continued
imprisonment of Mary. This came in a revised edition of Ronsard's
Elegies, Mascarades et Bergeries. A sonnet containing Mary's claims to
England was suppressed, while another sonnet appeared at the beginning of the second book of poems. This favoured a war against England
to liberate Mary Stuart. It asked Elizabeth to mellow in her anger and
to change the composition of her council who were clearly giving her
bad advice.[221]

In January 1579, a short while after the publication of the *Elegies*,
another work appeared which attempted to generate sympathy for
Mary. This was the work of David Chalmers, Lord Ormont.[222] Chalmers
was not only a trained lawyer and churchman, he was also employed
as a diplomat and as a double agent working at different periods on
behalf of Mary Stuart, James VI, France, Spain and England. He was
strongly implicated in the assassination of Lord Darnley;[223] and it was
even suggested that Chalmers had facilitated Bothwell's adulterous affair
with Mary.[224] More significantly for his political survival in Scotland was
his alignment with Mary at the battle of Langside. After her deposition,
Chalmers fled from Scotland, his lands forfeit.[225]

A three volume work by Chalmers was published in French in 1579.
After the first book, the *Histoire abbrégée de tous les roys de France,
Angleterre et Escosse* came *La Recherche des singularitez plus remarquables
concernant l'estat d'Escosse* and *Discours de la légitime succession des
femmes*.[226] The costs of publishing the work were distributed between
three Parisian printers: Jean Fevrier, Michel Gadoulleau and Robert
Coloumbel. Each had a separate issue of the shared edition, which
advertised both their name and location of their shop on the title pages
of the texts. This book is bibliographically complex. Although each
text possessed its own collation and title page, their unity was clearly
signalled by the privilege granted by Henri III in addition to errata
common to all three books which appeared at the end of the *Discours*.[227]
It is unclear why Henri should have granted this privilege at this time.
In terms of foreign policy, perhaps it was an attempt to persuade Elizabeth that consolidating her alliance with France was in her best inter-

est. It is no coincidence that at this moment, his brother, François Duc d'Anjou and Duc d'Alençon was attempting to secure Elizabeth's hand in marriage. Its domestic purpose, however, was probably to keep the concept of the auld alliance fresh in the minds of the French; a renewal of the bond was not impossible under the kingship of James VI.

The first of Chalmers's books was the *Histoire abbrégée*, composed around 1572. It was dedicated to Charles IX in April that year – the same month that negotiations were undertaken with Elizabeth to fashion the Treaty of Blois. No printed edition from this date survives, if it ever existed. More likely, Chalmers's work circulated only in manuscript in 1572, an attempt to persuade Henri to broach the issue of Mary Stuart during the negotiations. The dedication indicated that a copy of the text was presented to the King at this point, though no mention of the work is made in English ambassadorial correspondence, which might suggest that the text enjoyed only a very limited circulation. By 1579, Chalmers had enlarged the *Histoire* to include a history of the Popes and emperors and a dedication to Henri III.[228] Chalmers was clearly attempting to maintain royal favour. The *Histoire* is a tightly structured reference work that moves chronologically and separately through the history of the royal houses of France, England and Scotland and through the Popes and emperors. For each entry, particular comment was made on the moral uprightness of each ruler, their domestic troubles and foreign policy. The text had a double purpose. Firstly, by emphasising the historical continuity of the royal houses of Europe, it sought to reinforce the lineage of Mary Stuart and underline her right to the crown of Scotland and England, though after Elizabeth I. In the dedication to Charles IX, Chalmers proclaimed his desire to see Mary 'restored to her state'.[229] Secondly, the text sought to explore the nature and benefits of the 'auld alliance' to both Scotland and France.

Hector Boëce's *History and Chronicles of Scotland* published in 1527 was the principal source for Chalmers's interpretation of Scottish antiquity and helped enforce the impression, long prevalent on the continent, that the Scottish monarchy was the oldest in Europe.[230] At issue was Scottish patriotism, informed by a strong sense of *ancienneté* and historical identity.[231] The Scots, Chalmers recounted, 'were descended from Scota daughter of Pharoah & Gathelus son of Lecrops founder and first King of Athens'.[232] It was from Scota that Scotland derived its name.[233] Rightful succession and the continuity of the royal line were seen as part of the divine plan. It was within this European and Scottish context, that Mary Stuart was firmly given her place. Mary was held to be 106th in descent to succeed to the crown of Scotland and 57th 'in

direct line to the said Fergus the first King . . . also she was the legitimate heir (following some historiographers) to the kingdom of Great
Britain'.[234] Historical tradition supported Mary's place as Queen of Scotland and her place as heir presumptive to the crown of England after
Elizabeth's death.

Myth and history were woven together in the text to underline Scotland's long and distinguished past and to emphasise the ancient and
particular friendship with France, the auld alliance. The work appealed
to reason, tradition and continuity, exploring this friendship to convince the French to intercede on Mary Stuart's behalf. After all, the
auld alliance against English aggression had allegedly lasted unbroken
for 800 years since the time of Achaius and Charlemagne to the mutual
benefit of both countries; it was to be 'maintained for all time'.[235] By
the terms of the alliance, neither country was able to make peace
or truce with the English without the consent of the other.[236] This, of
course, was a particularly potent point given the French negotiations
with the English at Blois, without the consent of Scotland's lawful ruler.
If any subject either French or Scottish were to 'give aid or assistance
privately or publicly, in arms, council or supplies to the English against
[the will of] either of these two confederates, he will be held guilty
of the crime of lèse majesté by both parties'.[237] In *La Recherche*, the
cultural bond between the two was emphasised. When the French are
in Scotland, Chalmers recounted, they are 'regarded as if they were
natives of that country, and the reverse is also true when the Scots are
in France'.[238]

Throughout the lists of kings, the reciprocal nature of the benefits
of the auld alliance were indicated. A summary of this alliance, with
cross–references to these lists was present in the text entitled 'Brief
Account of the Mutual Assistance given in respect of the Alliance
between France and Scotland.'[239] The strategic advantage of the defensive treaty was explained as well as Scottish loyalty to it. Madeleine,
daughter of François I and wife of James V of Scotland, found that 'the
Scots have never failed or betrayed the French, but have always
remained loyal and faithful, providing excellent assistance in times of
necessity, springing from a pure and complete friendship such as exists
between good and friendly neighbours'.[240]

Chalmers was not willing to countenance French intervention at any
cost. He carefully delineated the parameters of the auld alliance and
even rebuked the French who in the 1550s had sought to represent Scotland as part of their empire. The *Histoire* portrayed the Scots as a proud
nation who would not endure subjection.[241] It was to overstretch the

boundaries of the auld alliance for François II to have called himself King of Scotland, 'pretending to rule over them as subjects, as inhabitants of a French province'. Chalmers went on to observe 'that the majority of the nobility of this kingdom, and especially those who detest the new religion and assist the Queen regent [Mary of Guise], assure themselves that the King of France (only looking to his own particular profit and convenience), desires nothing less than to deprive them of their ancient freedom'.[242]

The second text in the volume *La Recherche des singularitez plus remarquables concernant l'estat d'Escosse* was dedicated to Mary.[243] It was a political handbook to Scotland, outlining various aspects of Scottish society and identity. These included Scottish courageousness, as well as discussions on monarchical government, the state of the church, various social ranks, the law of succession, the laws and customs to be observed and finally the principal way to maintain good relations between monarchy and the people. A portrait of Scotland was drawn that served to distance it from any association with England.[244] The third and final text in the volume was the *Discours de la légitime succession des femmes* which was written in 1573 but not published until 1579.[245] Dedicated to Catherine de Medici, the *Discours* was the most legalistic in style of the three books, taking as its principal theme the succession of women and more particularly the succession of Mary Stuart to the throne of England. The first section dealt with the general question of female succession, the second with female succession to government. The text ended with a plea to Catherine de Medici to intercede on Mary Stuart's behalf.

The publication of Chalmers' *Histoire abbrégée* in January 1579 did not achieve its ostensible object. The French King, now Henri III, was not persuaded to intervene in Mary's favour, nor did the French press rally to defend her cause. There was no mention of her until 1581 and even then she appeared as fleetingly as ever. Guillaume Rouille's *Promptuaire des médailles* referred to François II and Mary Stuart briefly.[246] On each page in this book were two decorative medals on which were portraits of noble figures. The 'medallion' chosen for Mary carried the title 'MARIA D.G. FRANC.ET SCOT.REG' which omitted, as all of the post–1560 literature did, her claim to England. There was a brief biography of François II, followed by an even briefer biography of Mary, which narrated that 'regarded as being very beautiful and virtuous, Mary returned to her country after the death of the King, where she was subject to the vagaries of fortune, and where she is today held prisoner'.

'It is generally put into men's heads that they are only executed in England for conscience and not for treason':[247] Persecution of Catholicism in England and the French Catholic press, 1582–5

In response to the 1570 Papal Bull that excommunicated Elizabeth and freed her Catholic subjects from any obligation to obey her, an act was passed in England which allowed Catholic priests to be charged with treason. It was a tenuous though entirely practical association. Catholic priests were to be regarded as traitors to the English realm. During the 1580s, persecution of England's Catholics developed with growing trenchancy as a response to increased Jesuit missionary activity in the British Isles and the related fear, both real and imagined, of international Catholic conspiracies against the life of Elizabeth. The consequence of this legislation and its enforcement was the execution of a number of priests. This persecution and the wave of martyrs it produced was to have a powerful resonance in France. Swelling numbers of refugees fled to the continent, bringing with them news and tales of the situation at home to generate public sympathy for their plight.[248]

The following section will explore French interest in the Catholic martyrs in England. It is designed to highlight two principal points. The first is that despite significant French attention to the persecution of Catholics in England during the 1580s, Mary as a living victim of this persecution, languishing in prison, received little attention. Secondly, an examination of this body of material will help to create the context for the martyr narratives relating to Mary that would appear after February 1587.

One unambiguous martyr of the English persecution was the Jesuit priest, Edmund Campion.[249] In 1581, he was charged with treason for attempting to coax English subjects away from loyalty to Elizabeth towards obedience to the Catholic Church. While this charge was abandoned, a second charge, undoubtedly fabricated, was brought accusing Campion of involvement in a plot to assassinate the Queen.[250] Campion's arrest was probably the consequence of the general suspicion with which the intelligence service viewed the Jesuit order, combined with the publication of an anti-Protestant work written by Campion. It was no coincidence that Campion was arrested one month after having distributed four hundred copies of his *Rationes Decem*, a work that publicly opposed the Anglican Church.[251]

The persecution of Catholics in England in the period before 1582 had generated only slight attention in the French Catholic press. Nevertheless, the martyrdom of Edmund Campion brought a swift and pronounced reaction in France. A wave of rumours and several published editions concentrated the minds of France's Catholics on the predicament of their co-religionists across the channel.[252]

In 1582, shortly after news of Campion had arrived in France, four printed editions relayed the circumstances of Campion's death.[253] Henri awarded a privilege to two of these editions, ensuring carefully that these did not criticise Elizabeth directly. The execution narrative followed martyrological conventions, consciously evoking parallels between the treatment of Campion and Jesus. Just as Christ had been betrayed, an informer, George Elior, had turned Campion over to the authorities. With obvious biblical parallels, during Campion's journey to London, he was mocked; a placard was placed on his head with an inscription which called him a 'Jesuit seducer'.[254] He was first tempted then tortured in the Tower of London,[255] but despite being close to death, he responded to various disputations with such precision that it seemed to the author that 'no living person could deal with it better'.[256] Many Protestant onlookers admired his modesty, intellect and patience in enduring this practice.[257] An important theme in the narrative was Campion's defence of his book, the *Decem Rationes*. During the torture, he was asked specific questions about who was involved in its publication, but Campion refused to reveal any details, whilst during the disputations, he defended his work intellectually. The emphasis in the narrative on the interrogation focusing on the *Decem Rationes* thus dismissed English allegations that Campion was arrested on the grounds of treason. Another noteworthy aspect of this section which dealt with the torture of Campion, was the way in which the martyr with some discomfort distanced himself from the activities of Mary Stuart. During the interrogation, the Jesuit vehemently denied the English charge that he had involved himself with the Scottish Queen in a plot against the life of Elizabeth; he made no defence of the imprisoned Scottish Queen.[258] After the interrogation, Campion was sentenced to be disembowelled before execution. He was decapitated and his body divided into four parts, a traitor's death.[259]

Another account of the martyrdom, the *Discours des cruautés et tirannyes qu'a faict la Royne d'Angleterre à l'endroict des Catholecques [sic]* followed the text of *L'Histoire*. However, additional details were incorporated into the narrative, including a transcription of Campion's alleged speech before his death where he emphasised that he died solely for his religion, dismissing English charges of treason. A new section was also added containing an account of the martyrdom of Edward Hansius, referred to in the text as 'Edverard Hance'. The *Discours* did not receive a royal privilege and it is easy to see why. While the major-

ity of the text followed *L'Histoire*, the tone of the *Discours* was fundamentally different. Its very title emphasised its hostility to the English
Queen, who was personally blamed for the persecution.

Another work published in 1582 which did receive a privilege was
the *Épistre de la persecution meue en Angleterre contre l'église chrestienne
catholique*, written by the Jesuit Robert Parsons.[260] Parsons, who had
accompanied Campion into England, had in fact been responsible for
setting up the press at East Ham in Essex on which Campion's *Decem
Rationes* had been printed.[261] While the *Épistre* stopped short of vilify-
ing Elizabeth, blaming instead her evil counsellors, it was structured
with the explicit intention of arousing pity in England's neighbours. As
well as general narratives on how Catholics were treated, the author provided accounts of specific martyrs, including Edward Hansius and of
course Edmond Campion.[262] The picture painted of English Catholicism
by the *Épistre* was of a destitute and miserable remnant, deprived of
goods, placed in prisons, emaciated with hunger, diseased, cold and persecuted. Emphasised in particular were the restrictions placed on the
conscience of English Catholics.[263] The text began by explaining the legislation in England, which ensured that the everyday lives of ordinary
Catholics were full of fear and danger. This legislation was listed and
divided into two categories, pecuniary and sanguinary.[264] Examples
of such legislation included the loss of all commodities for anyone
attempting to entice a subject of Elizabeth away from Calvinism to
Catholicism.[265]

Execution was to be applied to Catholics as if they had committed *lèse
majesté*.[266] Capital offences included the affirmation that the Pope was
the leader of the Catholic Church or had any authority whatsoever, carrying Papal Bulls, Agnus Dei or crucifixes into England, or to write or
signify in any way that Elizabeth was a schismatic or a heretic. The
prisons, the author reported, were full of faithful Catholics who, for the
sake of their faith, were forced now to associate with thieves and criminals.[267] The Tower of London became a symbol for the English Inquisition. Once used for traitors, it was now filled with sacred priests who were
to go to their deaths like meek lambs to the slaughter.[268] Particular attention was also given, in order to excite the pity of the reader/listener, to
the macabre stories of how martyrs were put to their deaths.[269] Nevertheless, the text narrated, 'these deaths rendered such Catholics martyrs,
for everyone knew that religion was the sole cause of their deaths'.[270]

Parsons failed at any point in his book on the persecution to mention
the example of Mary Queen of Scots. This seems all the more surprising given his own activities in Normandy in the early 1580s. In co-

operation with Mary's Council in Paris and Father Creighton in Scotland, Parsons was involved in a plan to invade Scotland directed by the Duc de Guise. This had substantial backing by the Pope and Spain because it had a good chance of success. In Scotland, Creighton was in close contact with the Earl of Lennox, a Catholic and cousin of Lord Darnley who in 1580 had been elevated to a key advisory position within the court of James VI, still in his minority. A successful coup in the Scottish court, led by Lord Ruthven, Earl of Gowrie, however, put an end to this particular enterprise in August 1582. Nevertheless, the point is clear. Even Mary's own supporters in France, organising an invasion of Scotland, did not attempt to engage public opinion in her favour.

Interest in the plight of the English Catholics grew. In 1583, a number of images were produced accusing Elizabeth of cruelty, including an unofficial placard which appeared in November which was posted up in various locations around Paris.[271] Elizabeth appeared

> on horseback, her left hand holding the bridle, with her right hand pulling up her clothes; upon her head written La Reine d'Angleterre [the Queen of England]; verses underneath signifying that if any Englishmen passed that way, he could tell what and whose the picture was. Under it was a picture of Monsieur [François Duc d'Anjou], very well drawn, in his best apparel, on his fist a hawk, 'which continually baited and could never make her sit still'.[272]

The significance of this placard is evident; oppositional elements within the populace – the English ambassador suspected English exiles from Rouen – mocked the Duc d'Anjou's unsuccessful attempts to woo the immoral and lascivious Elizabeth. Exiles inflamed native French Catholic hostility against England. While this placard was hastily removed, Henri did, in 1582 and 1583, grant privileges to works that criticised English policy. It seems likely that Henri had to tread a very delicate path between pursuing a foreign policy that maintained Catholic support at home, represented by the ideas contained in this placard and pursuing a pro-English, and in the Netherlands a pro-Calvinist policy. It was, then, perhaps an attempt to pacify his own Catholic conscience and the Catholic majority in France that Henri awarded a privilege in 1582 to *L'Histoire de la mort que le R.P. Edmond Campion* and the *Épistre de la persecution meue en Angleterre contre l'église chrestienne catholique* and in 1583, via a general privilege to the Society of Jesus, to John Hay's *Demandes faictes aux ministres d'Escosse*. In terms of foreign policy, moreover, there was much to be said for gently flexing his muscles over the issue of persecution in England if he wished to signal his disapproval to Elizabeth without resorting to undermining their alliance.

John Hay's *Certaine demandes concerning the Christian Religion*,[273] originally published in Paris for an exile audience and for clandestine distribution in the British Isles, was translated into French and published in two editions in 1583 under the title *Demandes faictes aux ministres d'Escosse*.[274] Hay was a Jesuit and a Scot, who had taken the post of professor of theology at the college of Tournon. His *Demandes* described the cancerous effect of Calvinism on England and Scotland, reporting on the desolation of a once flourishing Scotland. There was no doubt as to the cause of this desolation. The Church of Scotland was to blame, or as the author, displaying marked anti-semitism, described it, the 'new Synagogue of Scotland'.[275] The *Demandes* asked by what authority the confession of faith had been adopted, since it had never been used by any Christian people from the time of the Apostles.[276] It also asked why there was so much emphasis on lay reading of the Bible when there were 'many poor people who do not know how to read, and simple women-folk,[277] who know not their a's or b's, have no way to receive consolation, or to reach their eternal salvation'.[278]

Hay's work was not just an attack on Calvinism in its abstract theological form. It was an attack deeply critical of the way events had turned in France and Scotland. He despaired at the attempts of the Scots to destroy their ancient alliance with France.[279] He railed also against the anti-Marian faction in Scotland, who attempted to portray Mary's half-brother and political foe, James, Earl of Moray, as a martyr.[280] He quipped that this 'Scottish bastard' had not been killed in the defence of Calvinism, but because of a quarrel with one in his own faction.[281] Hay's sympathy was extended also to the plight of the English martyrs. While casting aspersions on the veracity of English Protestant martyrological accounts, principally that of John Foxe, Hay emphasised that Catholics died cruelly in England simply because they would not confess Elizabeth to be the head of their Church.[282]

1583 also saw the appearance of *Mémoires contenante le vray discours*, a text far less reluctant to apportion responsibility to Elizabeth who was vilified for her treatment of the English Catholics.[283] As in the *Épistre de la persécution*, there was an emphasis on describing their tortures in gruesome detail. 'Catholics were hung. The rope was then cut while they were still half alive, their heart still hot and still beating. Their entrails were torn out of their stomach and thrown into the fire and then their bodies were quartered.'[284] The *Mémoires* did not simply accuse Elizabeth of responsibility for the persecution of English Catholics, but also of attempting to bring ruin to all of England's neighbouring states by interfering in their internal affairs.[285] 'One only had to look at Scotland', noted the text, 'to see the fruits of her manipulative activity.' Mary, the legitimate Queen had been deposed and unjustly held captive, while Elizabeth supported the rebel faction to satisfy her own appetite.[286] Likewise, Elizabeth had meddled both in the affairs of the Netherlands and of France, in the latter case assisting the rebels against Henri III, furnishing them with money and munitions and thereby helping to pit brother against brother.[287]

It was probably the circulation of this text which led to Elizabeth's instructions to her ambassador, Edward Stafford.[288] He was to inform Henri III in February 1584 of their good alliance and her anxiety at the allegations that had been lately circulating in France against her, principally of her 'secret practices and intelligences with the King of Navarre'. Elizabeth assured Henri that she did not 'intermeddle in any matter with his subjects that may just be to his dislike . . . For we have always had in remembrance the place we ourselves hold, and that to deliver any counsel to his subjects against him, being an absolute prince, might be a precedent of dangerous consequence to ourselves.' Significantly, she also thanked Henri for his suppression of certain books and pictures produced by Catholic exiles, punishing those responsible. If this was true, then it would suggest not unreasonably that Henri's toleration of hostility towards English policy had strictly defined boundaries.

The period 1584 to 1585 witnessed a relaxation of hostility to England in print. Various circumstances converged to make even limited criticism unwelcome. Pressure from Elizabeth combined with a succession crisis. With the death of Henri's brother the Duc d'Anjou in June 1584, a Protestant, Henri de Navarre, became heir presumptive to the throne of France. John Hay's *Demandes faictes aux ministres d'Escosse*, still under privilege, was republished, while another edition of Pierre de Ronsard's *Elegies, mascarades et bergeries* was issued which had the poem to William Cecil completely removed.[289] But this hardly represented the strength of feeling that had been demonstrated in the preceding two years. The convention of blaming Elizabeth's advisors was continued in the only new work relating to England printed during this time. This was an unofficial dialogue, published without the authority of the crown, in 1585.[290] The text may well have originated in the Netherlands, published to stimulate support for the pro-Spanish cause in France. While it did not openly criticise Elizabeth, it did directly attack her favourite Robert Dudley, Earl of Leicester, whom she sent in that year to command a force of 6,000 troops to assist the Calvinist rebels in the Netherlands in their revolt against Spain. Leicester, so the text narrated, 'excelled Heliogabale in bawdiness, Nero in murders and cruelties, and the apostate Julian in sorceries'.[291] The text invited Elizabeth to take action against him.[292]

In February 1585, Henri III accepted the Order of the Garter from Elizabeth, an honour he had been awarded ten years earlier following the confirmation of the Treaty of Blois in London. Two hundred English Protestant knights stood side by side with knights of the order of Saint-Esprit at the conferral ceremony. This was more than a manifestation of Anglo–French amity. It signalled Henri's commitment to the succession of the Protestant Henri de Navarre to the throne of France, following the death of his brother the Duc d'Anjou a year earlier. It also signalled his commitment to pursue pragmatic religious toleration within France.[293]

Conclusion

The public face of Mary and the British Isles developed in several distinct phases. In the period before the death of François II, Mary was praised in the traditional courtly manner. This anticipated and then celebrated Mary as a dynastic entity, a Queen who would bring with her Scotland and a strong claim to England. Following the death of François, Mary returned to Scotland. The Catholic presses fell still. While this silence was punctured by a number of generally warm references to her in the period 1561–85, there was little significant interest in France's former Queen. The French public did not even rally to defend her reputation after her imprisonment by Elizabeth in 1568. This can be explained by two main factors. Firstly, Mary's chequered career made her a wholly unsuitable Catholic hero. Secondly, in a delicate power game involving Spain, alliance with England was essential to maintain equilibrium.

Given England's stance towards Catholicism, however, there was bound to be some antagonistic response in the French press, particularly given the active involvement of Catholic exiles in drawing attention to their cause. But references to Mary remained, for the most part, peripheral. Outbursts of public sympathy for Catholics persecuted by a Protestant English state were successfully managed by the French crown through the privilege system. Even during fraught periods, acceptable boundaries of criticism were clearly marked; pamphlets were to be directed against Elizabeth's advisors, not Elizabeth herself. While most pamphleteers toed the official line, some adopted a more uncompromising attitude and were vigorously restrained by a crown caught between the Scylla of maintaining Catholic support at home and the Charybdis of pursuing an ever fragile military and trade alliance with England.

3
The Huguenot Image of
Mary Queen of Scots

In the first two chapters of this study, we demonstrated the extent to which Mary was a figure deeply embedded in French Catholic culture. Her French upbringing and her family drew her inevitably into the conflicts that surrounded the ambitions of the Valois and the machinations of the Guise. The inevitable corollary of this was that Mary would be an important figure too for those who attempted to thwart the designs real or imagined of the French crown and the Guise. For Protestants on both sides of the Channel, English, Scottish and Huguenot, Mary would be a powerful polemical presence. But the rush to demonise her, so evident in later Protestant presentations of her career, was not in fact marked in earlier treatments. Protestant writers took an unexpectedly measured view of Mary's actions.

These writings have been little used by historians of Mary's career or indeed in any general considerations of her in polemic. For this reason, it is worth breaking off the narrative at this point to consider specifically the Huguenot image of Mary. We will see that a powerful and predictably negative view of Mary developed. But the first writings were cautious and unexpectedly fair–minded. In fact, the demonisation of Mary Queen of Scots began only when the trend had been established with that other notable 'femme fatale', Catherine de Medici.

The first known Protestant mention of Mary Queen of Scots in print came in 1560.[1] It was commissioned in response to the publication of a protestation made by the Sieur de Seure, the French ambassador to London. De Seure's pamphlet, which had been sanctioned by the French crown, was a justification for military involvement in Scotland in 1559–60.[2] It was a work that criticised Elizabeth sharply for her part in supporting the Scottish rebels. Two days after de Seure's *Protestation* was published in Lyon, Orléans and Tours, Francis Throckmorton, the

English ambassador to France sent William Cecil, Elizabeth's principal advisor and public relations officer, the following letter:

> [Throckmorton] has presently sent to the Queen, the French Ambassador's *Protestation* newly printed here at Tours. Advises him to have the Queen's answer printed in Latin and French, and to join the Ambassador's protestation and his in one volume. He must sort the articles otherwise than they be; viz. the infractions and doleances together as they chanced first, and the rest as it is sorted, and must add some fit short preface. If Cecil sends them in order to him he will try to have them printed in Paris. Thinks Cecil's very well translated, both in French and Latin.[3]

Throckmorton's letter highlights the close attention paid by the English government to opinion relating to England that was circulating in France. Several months earlier, in November 1559, William Cecil invited his ambassadors in France to send him two catalogues of books that had been newly printed there.[4] These catalogues were compiled with the assistance of booksellers and agents of the English crown. Clearly, there was a network in place to supply the English government with this type of information. Stray survivals in the Codrington Library in Oxford provide additional testimony to the interest paid by Cecil in French print. It is fascinating to find that a copy of as influential and popular a book as Claude Gousté's *Traicté de la puissance et authorité des roys* seems to have been in Cecil's possession at this time.[5]

Throckmorton's letter reveals that the English were also fully prepared to actively engage with the debate in France. In this particular case, Throckmorton wanted to reprint de Seure's *Protestation* together with a second protestation penned by Cecil. The objective of such active involvement was not simply to reach out and register support for their co-religionists across the Channel and encourage international Protestant solidarity, which at this point was a stronger consideration than it would subsequently become, but also to serve the security interests of England which would have been well served by exploiting factional conflict in such a powerful neighbour.

William Cecil followed the advice of Throckmorton, and wrote a rebuttal to the *Protestation*, which was appended to the end of the original text. This was printed not in Paris, as Throckmorton had originally suggested, but in London by the Queen's printers, Richard Jugge and John Cawod.[6] While provincial Protestant presses were emerging in France, the rationale behind printing this work in London can best be explained by two considerations. Firstly, it sent a very bold signal to the

French government that they were not the only ones who could attempt to influence opinion in France. Secondly, by printing this in London, Cecil avoided too close an association between English Protestantism and the Huguenot movement. Such connections would have played directly into the hands of Catholic polemicists, who were eager to associate Calvinism with treason and rebellion. Clearly, such an association was particularly dangerous at this time of national conflict, and at a time when the Calvinist congregations were only beginning to set down firm roots and attract large numbers of converts.

Cecil's rebuttal articulated very powerfully why Elizabeth was forced to undertake military action in Scotland. No mention was made of a willingness to aid the Protestant rebellion. Instead, Cecil stressed English anxiety that the security of the realm was being threatened by the French presence to the north of their kingdom, especially given France's recent public assertions in favour of Mary's claim to the crowns of England and Ireland as well as Scotland.[7] Mary as a dynastic entity, backed by French military prowess, posed a clear and present danger to England.[8] Most significantly for our discussion of the image of Mary, however, was that while in the English *Protestation* she was associated with French claims to the English state, she was simultaneously distanced from culpability. French claims to England, Cecil's pamphlet argued, were, to a large extent at least, not Mary's fault. She was a pawn in the ambitious designs of her bellicose French relatives, her uncles, the powerful family Guise.[9] This followed the official line adopted by Elizabeth in diplomatic correspondence, which complained that François and Mary's pretensions to the throne of England were a product of the ambitions of the house of Guise, rather than the wishes of the newly-wed couple, portrayed as being young and naive.[10]

Following the death of François II in December 1560, the political situation in France changed dramatically. During the minority of Charles IX, Catherine de Medici quickly wrested control of the government from the Guises. In domestic politics, Catherine began to pursue a moderate approach to the deepening religious crisis, while in foreign affairs she completely abandoned the belligerent policy of Henri II and François II and pursued an alliance with England to counteract the looming power of Spain. While her policy of pragmatic toleration would generate significant political resistance in France, by 1561 even Catholics who pursued a hard line against Protestantism in France such as François Duc de Guise and Anne de Montmorency, recognised, at least for the time being, the advantages of an English alliance.

The English eagerly exploited this fragile consensus. As we have demonstrated already in the previous chapter, the English complained robustly about specific works published in France which had slandered their sovereign. While such protestations had fallen on deaf ears in the pre-1561 period, after 1561 the French administration had a vested interest in being seen to act on English complaints. The English ambassador in Paris managed to suppress offending sections in such works as Jean Gay's *Histoire des scismes et hérésies des Albigeois.*[11]

At this initial stage in the rapprochement between England and France, however, it is noteworthy that the English, in involving themselves in debate in France, were far more concerned with developing their relationship with the Huguenot party than with shoring up political consensus for the Anglo-French alliance. This strategy is evident in the decision of the English government to publish several editions of a work justifying the prudent philosophy of pragmatic religious toleration favoured by the regent Catherine de Medici. Ostensibly, of course, the *Protestation faicte par la Royne d'Angleterre, par laquelle elle declare les justes & necessaires occasions qui l'ont meuë de prendre la pretection de la cause de Dieu, la defense du roy & de son royaume, contre les autheurs des troubles qui y sont à present* was designed to appeal to Huguenots and moderate Catholics alike. However, the *Protestation* was clearly aimed at rallying support from the former more than the latter. It was designed to encourage the Huguenots to view England as a natural ally in their quest for political recognition. Almost certainly, the work would have alienated more militant Catholic supporters of the alliance. Elizabeth's *Protestation*, undoubtedly moulded by William Cecil, was printed in no fewer than six editions between 1561 and 1562.[12] Four editions were published in Orléans on the Eloy Gibier press. A further two editions appeared with variant titles. One of these editions has been recognised as the work of the Caen printer Pierre Philippe,[13] while the other remains to be identified.[14]

The pamphlet publicised Elizabeth's offer to broker a peace agreement between the Huguenots and Catholics. There was at least a semblance of reality to this offer. Sir Henry Sidney had been dispatched for France at the end of April 1561 with instructions to join Nicholas Throckmorton, the English ambassador in France, in proposing England act as peace-broker. His real agenda, however, was undoubtedly something quite different. 'Although', Elizabeth wrote to Sidney, 'she wishes well to both parties, yet the said ambassadors must be wary how to appear more affectionate to one than the other.'[15] With the collapse of the negotiations before they had begun, Sidney quickly turned his diplomatic talents to his primary objective, strengthening links between England and the Huguenot leaders in France. Since 1560, the English had supplied covert support to the Huguenot party in France. A formal alliance was concluded on the outbreak of the Wars of Religion in 1562, when Louis Prince de Condé, the Huguenot leader, sent an envoy to Elizabeth, appealing for direct intervention and a loan of 100,000 crowns.[16] For English participation, the Huguenot party promised control over Le Havre and Calais.

The language used in this *Protestation*, a propaganda exercise written to accompany Elizabeth's offer, made clear that the English Queen was proposing to bring about 'the peace and tranquillity of religion, and the well-being of the state of the said lord King'.[17] While we might have expected 'la religion' to have referred solely to Protestantism, in fact the pamphlet was proposing something intriguingly different. Elizabeth made it clear that she was offering to bring about peaceful coexistence between Protestantism and Catholicism, in which both sides respected their sovereign and preserved Christianity, understood in broad terms, in peace and tranquillity.[18] Elizabeth's own credentials to act as negotiator were, of course, thoroughly debatable, but in this pamphlet she was portrayed in a positive fashion as having negotiated a comparably thorny settlement in England. Elizabeth was, therefore, well placed to offer advice to her neighbour. Emphasising the tolerant attitude that the English state held towards Catholics was clearly intended to broaden the appeal of this pamphlet to moderate Catholics.

Mary's moment in this pamphlet was brief. Elizabeth's friendship towards her was highlighted, as was her good will towards all of Mary's ministers and friends passing through England. She even extended this benevolence, though no doubt with her tongue firmly embedded in her cheek, to the Guise family, Mary's powerful French relatives.[19] Indeed, the biggest threat to the peaceful state of France identified by this *Protestation*, was what was described as a true tyranny, a tyranny against which Elizabeth offered armed assistance.[20] This tyranny was not Catholicism, but those who attacked peace and the attempts to promote toleration between the faiths, and those who sought to engage in violence by which the French realm was becoming increasingly disfigured.[21] Touching on a particularly sensitive nerve, the pamphlet argued that such disfiguration disturbed commercial relations between England and France. Identified as being primarily responsible for this tyranny were the Guise, as were certain governors and public officers who contravened the will of their monarch by directing violence against Protestants.[22]

This insulation of Mary from criticism continued throughout the 1560s, while vituperative attacks on her relatives the Guises gathered momentum. The image of malignant Guise ambition had matured on the hot Protestant presses of the early 1560s which overflowed with printed polemic defending the Protestant part in the 'Conspiracy' or, as they declared it, the 'Tumult of Amboise' in March 1560. The Protestants argued, in pamphlets that sometimes cost them their lives,[23] that François Duc de Guise and Charles Cardinal de Lorraine – foreigners – had usurped power away from the Council in François II's minority.[24] There was such a flood of pamphlets against the Guise in 1560, that the Cardinal de Lorraine was to remark at a meeting of the notables at Fontainebleau, that 'there are twenty two [pamphlets] on my table at this moment. I preserve them carefully, for it is the greatest honour I shall ever receive to be blamed by such scoundrels. I hope they will form the true eulogy of my life, and make me immortal'.[25]

In one of these pamphlets, the *Epistre envoiée au tigre de la France*, François Hotman demonised the Cardinal de Lorraine, describing him in scarcely flattering terms as, an 'enraged, venomous viper and sepulchre of abomination'.[26] The Guise wished nothing less than the ruin of the kingdom of France and the death of François II. They were warmongers, seeking nothing but the profit of their own house. Religion was simply a mask, a cover for their trade in ecclesiastical offices and a pretext for squashing those who opposed their tyrannous control over government.[27] In another tract by François Hotman, *L'Histoire du tumulte d'Amboise*, the author intimated that the Guise were all too aware that Henri II, before his death, was on the verge of imposing measures of toleration for the new faith.[28] Amboise, then, was no conspiracy against François, but against the ambitious designs of the house of Guise.[29] Elizabeth had entered the war in Scotland, as she protested by her own 'printed writing' not against the King, but against Guise tyranny and corruption – 'they extorted taxes, tributes and intolerable exactions from the poor people'.[30] Clearly Elizabeth's own printed word, Cecil's 1560 *Protestation*, was to have an important resonance in subsequent Huguenot literature in France; it was referred to repeatedly. It interacted with native Huguenot publications and played an important role in the articulation of the image of the Guise and of Mary Stuart.

The next significant mention of Mary in Huguenot literature appeared in Pierre de La Place's *Commentaires de l'estat de la religion*, one of the key works of sixteenth-century French historical writing. It was published in no less than five anonymous editions in 1565.[31] Professor Jean-François Gilmont has managed to identify the place of publication for these editions. They emerged from Caen, Rouen, Orléans, and La Rochelle.[32] One edition was even printed in Paris, possibly on the press of Robert Estienne, printer to Charles IX. Interestingly, however, there were no editions of La Place's *Commentaires* published in two of the principal Protestant centres of printing Lyon or Geneva, as might have been expected.

Pierre de La Place had become attracted to Calvinism around 1560, serving Louis Prince de Condé, the leader of the Huguenot movement. His history covers the period from 1556 to 1561, the period immediately before the outbreak of the Wars of Religion. It is revealing in what it has to say of the Scottish Queen. The timing of Mary's marriage was, La Place intimated, conditioned by the Cardinal de Lorraine's perception that the time was then right to extend the grandeur of his house through his niece.[33] La Place alleged that the Guise had brought inordinate pressure to bear on the Estates of Scotland to consent to the marriage through Henri Clutin, the sieur d'Oisel, and had also pressurised Henri II by goading him with the observation that Charles V, his arch-enemy, had lived to see his son, Philip II, crowned.[34] Therefore, so should Henri II see François crowned King of Scotland during his lifetime. The flagrant display of English armorial bearings, La Place alleged, was the work of the Cardinal de Lorraine and the Duc de Guise. For the Guise, the Scottish campaign was nothing short of an attempt to quell domestic French criticism of their power.[35] Mary was not presented as a monarch in her own right, but as 'their niece'.[36] As for Elizabeth's involvement in Scotland in 1559–60, this had been a consequence of justifiable suspicion at the growing French military presence in Scotland. Yet, involvement had been undertaken only reluctantly after a remonstrance had been issued to the French King, and after the Scots themselves had requested English assistance.[37] La Place made a great deal of the fact that the Scots had preferred to appeal to their old enemies rather than subject themselves to the tyranny of the papacy.

La Place's image of Mary, and also of the Guise, had been forged at least partly under the influence of literature emanating from England. The author cited Elizabeth's diplomatic remonstrances to Henri II directly, and the 1560 *Protestation* that had signalled Guise ambition as the cause of the French military campaign in Scotland.[38] Citing the *Protestation* again, La Place repeated Elizabeth's belief that the titles adopted so detrimentally by the Queen of Scots from November 1558, 'would not have been adopted by her, except that she was moved to do so by the ambitious will of the leading figures of the house of Guise'.[39] La Place criticised the politics of ambition of the Guise family, yet insulated Mary from criticism by emphasising that she was then in her minority and had no control over the direction events had taken:

> The said house of Guise, having no other way to bring about their own particular advancement, except by the aggrandisement and exal-

tation of their niece the Queen of Scotland, used their relationship with her as a pretext to meddle in the affairs of France. In this way, under their own authority, they injuriously and insolently continued, in time of peace, to join their arms and titles to those of the kingdoms of England and Ireland, by means of the Queen their niece.[40]

The dearth of interest in Mary Queen of Scots so evident in Catholic literature of the 1560s was, as has been demonstrated, shared by Protestant public opinion. Mary's career in Scotland attracted almost no attention at all. The French press reported neither her widely reputed involvement in the assassination of her husband Henry Stuart, Lord Darnley, nor her marriage to James Hepburn, fourth Earl of Bothwell. Similarly disregarded were her deposition by the Scots, subsequent defeat at the Battle of Langside in May 1568, her flight to England, and her imprisonment by Elizabeth. This lack of interest even extended to her trials at York and Westminster in October-November 1568 at which the Casket Letters were produced, fortuitously, but not necessarily falsely, proving Mary's complicity in the murder of her husband. There was, it seems, general Protestant ambivalence during her personal reign, which continued into the first four years of her imprisonment.

Several explanations can be put forward to understand this ambivalence. In part, it can be explained by the initial hope that Mary would follow a policy of toleration towards Scottish Protestantism. This hope was undoubtedly overtaken by an uncertainty as to how events would resolve themselves following her imprisonment. It was, we must remember, by no means expected, least of all by Elizabeth's own advisors, that Mary would spend the next eighteen years in captivity. Perhaps more importantly, the primary reason why the Huguenots did not raise the issue of Mary after 1568, was that a Protestant monarch holding a legitimate sovereign prisoner was an extraordinarily thorny issue. Besides, it would have made little sense to rile Catholic public opinion which, left to its own devices, appeared wholly unconcerned with the fate of the Scottish Queen.

While there was no substantial coverage of Mary's career in print, there were a few mentions of the Queen in Huguenot literature, including one anonymous pamphlet published in 1568, the *Advertissement sur le pourparlé, qu'on dit de paix, entre le roy & ses rebelles. Avec son contre-poison.*[41] The author rejoiced towards the end of this text that the Protestant religion had been firmly established in England and Scotland, and remarked on the piteous and tragic consequences for the Queen of Scots, 'and all of it for having been too attached to the side and council of her uncle'.[42] There is evidence here of a subtle change from the predominant Huguenot attitude to Mary in the 1560s. There is a close identification between Mary and her Roman Catholic faith, absent from Protestant accounts before this point which tended to downplay the religious difference between the Queen and her subjects. Moreover, it extended the theme of Guise influence over Mary beyond what might reasonably be classified as her minority. Mary was no longer 'very young', which as we have seen was the way she had been characterised in English diplomatic correspondence eight years previously. In short, her disastrous personal reign, for this author at least, had brought about a slight but pronounced shift in the way in which he viewed the Queen of Scots. Nevertheless, perhaps waiting to see how events developed, the author made no mention of her imprisonment. There remained a marked authorial sympathy for Mary, despite an overwhelming sense of hatred and mistrust of her manipulative Guisard relations.

In the Protestant stronghold of La Rochelle, several editions were published between 1568 and 1570 that mentioned the Queen of Scots. These were subsequently reprinted together in a collection in 1570, entitled *Histoire de nostre temps*.[43] They were printed anonymously on the press of Barthelemy Berton, carrying Berton's distinctive 'Imprimée Nouvellement', 'Newly Printed' on the title page with the date of publication printed beneath in italics. The primary purpose of these editions was to provide a justification for Huguenot resistance,[44] though they were targeted, ostensibly, not only at a specifically Protestant audience, but also at moderate Catholics.[45]

In the prologue to this collection, dated 22 August 1570, the author briefly outlined the history of the 'reformed religion' during the reigns of Henri II, François II and Charles IX to 1568, offering a damning indictment of François Duc de Guise, and Charles Cardinal de Guise.[46] In one tract, the *Petit discours*, the Cardinal de Lorraine was portrayed as having spread fire and fury not just in France, but also in Flanders, England and Scotland.[47] These pamphlets vilified the Guise, portraying them as subversives of the international peace. One pamphlet reproduced a letter, warm in tone, from Jeanne d'Albret to Elizabeth I of England dated 15 October 1568, in which she brought the activities of the Guise firmly to the Queen's attention, and mentioned Guise actions against Albret's own family, in particular against the life of the prince de Condé.[48] In this corpus of works, as in Protestant polemic generally, the Guise were to blame for the failure of the various Edicts of Toleration. They were on the political fringe, acting against royal authority. Their characters were attacked. The Cardinal, for example, was mischievously slandered. The text alleged that his school-friends described his childhood spirit as being 'remuant & malin', 'restless and crafty'.[49] This was, of course, as malicious as it was mischievous: for the French word for 'crafty', 'malin' can also be used in the sense of 'le malin', the devil. The effect of the Guise on the French state was seen as malignant; the Duc de Guise was accused of bringing the country into civil war several times, behaving like Nero.[50] The pamphlet pulled no punches against the hero of intolerant Catholicism.

The *Histoire de nostre temps* exploited the issue of Mary Stuart to publicise the deviousness of the Guise in a fairly tried and tested fashion. The marriage between Mary and François took place simply to expand the house of Guise and was brought about by underhand political manoeuvring which went against the better judgement of Henri II. The reign of François and Mary was, as usual, presented in terms of Guise domination of government. They ruled with tyranny and violence, or, as the author compared it in his work, the rule of the Israelites by the Pharaohs.[51] They were described as foreigners, 'the house of Guyse, foreigners and not natural Frenchmen', who had usurped the function of natural French lords. And it was to foreign princes that the Guise looked to expand their power; they were agents of the Pope, and the King of Spain. It is to the warmongering Guise that the author ascribed the conflict in 1559 and 1560 against England. In order to renew the conflict, while others including the Constable of France had worked towards peace, they pursued Mary's claim to the throne of England in opposition to Elizabeth. By following their advice, Mary had lost her crown and her honour. In fact 'extreme ruin befell all those who allowed themselves to be led by the said advice that has always been accompanied by a cursed and miserable end'.[52]

To this point, although Mary was clearly identified as a member of the opposing political constellation – it could hardly have been otherwise – hostility toward the Queen was muted, and largely impersonal. She was portrayed as an agent, and therefore partly as a victim, of her Guisard relatives. But the 1570s were to witness a significant revolution in the Huguenot portrayal of Mary Queen of Scots. The flare which heralded this change was the publication of George Buchanan's *Histoire de Marie Royne d'Escosse* in 1572.[53] Buchanan's *Histoire* was written primarily to justify the revolt of 1568 to the English, the Scots and the international community.[54] It was in effect the case of the prosecution used against Mary during the Westminster Conference of 1568. It was not published, however, until 1571, when it appeared in an expanded and polished form in Latin, then in English and Scots.[55] Five months after the appearance of these editions, the text was translated into French. The orchestrating force behind the publication of Buchanan's book into Latin, English and French was the English government. The Latin and English editions of the book were published anonymously, but with official approval, on the John Day press in London. Moreover, while the French translation carried a false Edinburgh imprint, it is likely that this too was published in London, albeit with its origin carefully disguised.[56] It was then transported by ship into France.

Buchanan's book was published in 1571 and 1572 as part of Cecil's campaign of 'semi–publicity' against Mary.[57] Elizabeth had adopted an official position of restraint in regard to Mary, while in 'unauthorised' editions, Mary's character was explicitly attacked. The device of anonymity gave the English a degree of plausible deniability, yet allowed them to justify both at home and abroad their policy of the continued imprisonment of the Scottish Queen. But the timing of these editions, shortly after the discovery of the Ridolfi Plot of 1571, suggests that in attacking Mary, Cecil was also attempting to discredit the Duke of Norfolk. Norfolk's intention to marry Mary, and his involvement in the Northern Rebellion of 1569 and the Ridolfi Plot 1571 to place her on the throne of England, had earned him a degree of popularity. There was, moreover, another pressing reason for the publication of Buchanan's text. In Scotland, in April 1571, Marian forces had occupied the capital, Edinburgh. The *Histoire*, then, also served the function of rallying support in England and Scotland against the Marian party.

While such explanations help to explain the publication of Buchanan's text in England and Scotland, three years after it had been written, there still remains the question of why Cecil chose to publish the book in a French translation at the beginning of 1572. The timing of the French edition is curious, published five months after the Latin and English editions. Certainly, Cecil had sanctioned its publication for many of the same reasons that he had commissioned the publication of the Latin and English editions. Yet, the publication of the French translation in March–April 1572, only a few months before negotiations were due to begin at Blois to formalise the Anglo-French alliance seems a bold if not downright dangerous diplomatic decision. After all, Mary had complained to Charles IX about the book from her prison in Sheffield on 22 November 1571, and asked that her friends and relatives in France be allowed to publish a work, 'without reproach', to counter the Latin and English editions of Buchanan's libel.[58] While Charles, at this moment at least, does not appear to have granted Mary's second request,[59] he did remonstrate with Elizabeth about the appearance of the Latin and English editions of the text.[60] On 10 December 1571 Elizabeth responded by pretending that the book had been printed in Scotland, not in England.[61]

Despite these considerations, Cecil had been strongly advised to publish the work by men close to the evolving events in France. In a letter written from Amboise on 9 January, Sir Thomas Smith spoke of the encouraging reception that the Latin version of the *Histoire* was enjoying in France. 'Touching the Scottish matters and the treasons', he wrote, 'they [unnamed] have distributed certain books of Buchanan in Latin which have done no hurt, but made the matter so plain that they be ashamed to defend her that fain would.'[62] A day later, Henry Killegrew repeated Smith's sentiments, emphasising the keen interest in Buchanan's arguments at the French court.[63] In this dispatch, Killegrew seems to have sent a translation of Buchanan's *Histoire* asking that it be published in England and sent back across to France. He reported the comments of one Mr Beale, saying that it was necessary to articulate to the French King the 'greater advantage that France would get by an alliance with England than with Scotland'.[64] As this remark suggests, the critical consideration for the English was the growing interest of the French crown in involvement in Scotland in favour of the pro–Marian faction. This text, therefore, sought to dissuade both French political opinion and, given its publication in French, public opinion more broadly, from favouring a Scottish rather than English alliance.

The decision of William Cecil to print and circulate this work, at this particular moment, seems unduly rash. This is especially true given that Catholic publications from 1561 had been remarkably restrained in discussing the Scottish Queen, and that there is no known evidence to suggest that in early 1572 political opposition to the Franco-English alliance planned to engage public opinion on the issue. Cecil was undoubtedly right to ensure that the publication details of the *Histoire* were so carefully disguised that even modern bibliographers have failed to identify its place of publication. Clearly, he realised the risk he was taking in publishing this particular work.

Buchanan's *Histoire* followed two related lines of argument. The first was an articulation of Mary's unfitness to rule, the second was the espousal of the greatness of James Stewart, 1st Earl of Moray, who had become regent following Mary's deposition in 1568. Buchanan's text was heavily influenced by Cicero. Cicero's rhetorical technique undoubtedly inspired Buchanan's work and informed its character, shaping the way in which the Scottish humanist completely blackened the image of the Scottish Queen. On a purely technical level, Buchanan borrowed many of Cicero's devices. A rhetorical manoeuvre such as the following, 'I should not dare to mention these things, were I not afraid that you have heard more about the man [i.e. Gaius Verres, the notorious Sicilian magistrate] from the conversation of others than from my own speech at court', finds repeated expression in Buchanan's text.[65] Thus everyone in Scotland knew that Mary's unbridled lust led to her conducting an affair with the Earl of Bothwell, wronging Lord Darnley. The concept that Buchanan cannot possibly recount all the misdeeds of the Queen, her keeping bad company, the notion of airing a nation's dirty laundry in the presence of foreigners, are all devices which drew on Ciceronian techniques.

Attributes that were commonly associated with women, such as inconstancy and irrational emotion, were also a dominant theme in Buchanan's text. Mary's decision to marry her cousin Henry Stewart Lord Darnley was rash; and she just as rashly repented of it without offering any rational explanation.[66] This led to an unsubstantiated hatred for her husband, who was treated not even with a basic human courtesy. The underlying thread in Buchanan's narrative was a sinister one – Mary's evolving secret criminal intentions against the life of her husband which, as the jury and readers would have been aware even before they began reading the chronological narrative, reached a climax at Kirk o' Field in February 1567. These intentions are highlighted in the text, even at the point where Mary has just given birth to her child, the future James VI. Any maternal image of the Queen was never allowed to develop. While pregnant, for instance, Mary attempted to persuade Darnley to enjoy the 'company' of the Earl of Moray's wife,

> not that she thought that a lady so virtuous would herself take part in such baseness, but she did wish in the same instant to avenge herself on three of her enemies, the King, the Earl [of Moray] and his wife. Through this, she hoped to have occasion to obtain a divorce and leave the nuptial bed completely barren, so that she could then leave with the Earl of Bothwell. [67]

Moreover, in another section, Buchanan reported Mary's alleged claim that she wished to move from Stirling to Edinburgh in the interests of the health of her son. Stirling Castle was, Mary suggested, 'uncomfortable', adding that the place was 'cold and humid'.[68] Countering this image, Buchanan concluded that this was simply a pretence for altogether ulterior motivations. For Edinburgh was far less healthy than Stirling, and in any case the child aged seven months had to be moved in the middle of winter. In fact, Mary's true intention was to move to

Edinburgh in order to conspire again against the life of Darnley, her previous plot of attempting to poison him having failed.

Developing alongside Mary's burning hatred and homicidal intentions towards Darnley in Buchanan's work, was Mary's adulterous relationship with James Earl of Bothwell, a man who kept terrible company which included pirates. Buchanan here touched the sensitive nerve of reputation. On what precisely Mary got up to at Alloa castle with Bothwell and these rascally sailors, Buchanan, using another great rhetorical technique, simply noted, 'I would prefer that each of you imagines that for themselves, than to hear it from me.'[69] Mary's claim that Bothwell had raped her, then forced her to marry him, was vehemently dismissed in Buchanan's account.[70] Expressions of Mary's unrestrained and uncontrollable passion litter the text, including expressions such as 'unbounded lasciviousness',[71] and 'senseless'.[72] This lack of ability to control herself, for Buchanan, seriously jeopardised her credibility as a monarch. Even foreigners recognised the shamelessness of Mary's behaviour in respecting only twelve of the traditional forty days of mourning for Lord Darnley. Even in France, reported Buchanan, Mary's actions were of ill repute.[73]

In the second part of the *Histoire* is an expansive oration against the Queen following the rhythms of the general outline of Mary's career reported in the first part of the book. Within the discussion in the 'Plaidoyé', Buchanan launched an attack on Mary's upbringing in France, alleging that her vices were plain for all to see even at this early stage of her life. Buchanan spoke of rumours circulating in France that criticised her character and her behaviour towards François, but did not explicitly mention their substance.[74] The text offers a portrait of the young Queen, which emphasised both her own naturally malicious character, in addition to the harmful effect to her development caused by being brought up by her Guisard relatives:

> As it was this young woman was suddenly elevated to a sovereign degree of power, never having seen before with her own eyes the face of a legitimate kingdom, nor heard with her ears, or conceived of it in her mind. Instructed by the insupportable advice of her relatives (who conspired to establish a tyranny in France), she applied herself to realise her fantasy.[75]

It is possible in this text to sense something of the political thought that was laid out in detail in Buchanan's *De Jure Regni apud Scotos*, composed in 1567 to justify Mary's deposition but not published until

1579.[76] In brief, Buchanan advanced the essentially republican argument that kings were appointed by the people and accountable to them.[77] Mary was unable to rule within the established laws of the kingdom of Scotland; through flagrant tyranny, including the murder of her husband Lord Darnley, Mary had broken her contract with the people of Scotland. Her deposition, therefore, was an entirely legitimate action.

Following the expanded oration in the second part of his *Histoire*, Buchanan included a more legalistic section containing some of the evidence against Mary.[78] The Casket Letters were printed, allegedly proving that the Earl of Bothwell had carried on an adulterous relationship with the Queen, and that they had both conspired to assassinate Lord Darnley, Mary's husband. The text discussed details of the marriage contract between Mary and Bothwell, to be activated in the event of Darnley's death. This committed the Earl of Bothwell to divorcing his then current wife, Jane Gordon. Also discussed were Mary's attempts to absolve Bothwell of responsibility of the crime after the fact. The official placards that had been circulated in Edinburgh appealing for the denunciation of those involved in the murder of Darnley were also reprinted, together with the placards posted in response.[79] The latter listed the names of those involved in Darnley's murder. Bothwell was one of the names that appeared on this list.[80]

Unlike the English translation, at the end of the French *Histoire* appeared a short justification for Mary's continued imprisonment in England.[81] She had escaped from her prison in Scotland and had fled to England on her way to France. In England, she was apprehended and detained for her crimes. While in prison there, she conspired against the life of Elizabeth during the Northern Rebellion. The Queen of England had shown clemency to the Duke of Norfolk, one of the leaders of the rebellion, by releasing him from the Tower. Elizabeth had done so, however, relying on the promises of Mary and Norfolk to renounce their intention to marry without the approval of the crown, and to cease their conspiratorial ways. Nevertheless, Mary and Norfolk broke their promises to Elizabeth. At the very end of the text, the trial of Norfolk in January 1572 was reported, as was the sentence of death that was pronounced against him.[82]

For all the English government attempted to engage public as well as political opinion on the issue of Mary, only one edition of Buchanan's *Histoire* was ever published. Moreover, it would be another two years before the change in the representation of Mary signalled in the *Histoire* would be taken up in any significant way in Huguenot polemic. The reason for this pause was partly a consequence of lack of interest in the subject, and partly the consequence of the St. Bartholomew's massacre in late August 1572 which virtually obliterated the Huguenot leadership and led to many Protestants fleeing to the safety of exile. Many more, doubting the viability of the Reformed faith in France, abjured their faith. From publication statistics at least, the movement appears to have been immediately stunned into a disbelieving silence.[83] From a low point in 1573, Huguenot writings only gradually recovered some of the vigour they had exhibited in the 1560s. And it was in this context, in the newly radicalised climate created by the horror of the massacre, that one witnesses the highpoint of Huguenot interest in Mary Queen of Scots.

It was within the womb of the Genevan refuge, that the Huguenot response to the massacres took shape. The results of this, in publication terms, began to appear from 1574, as the French exiles influenced by the Genevan hierarchy, aimed to shape international public opinion on the massacres, painting a portrait of a Europe-wide Catholic plot against Protestantism. From 1574, Mary Stuart became an important symbol in this Huguenot literature for three main reasons. She was closely linked to the champions of Catholicism, the Guise. She was a useful tool in the drive after St. Bartholomew's day to internationalise European interest in the Wars of Religion in France. And, like Catherine de Medici so hated for her part in the massacres of St. Bartholomew's Day, she was an example of the dangers of female rule. No greater example of this can be found than in the 1574–75 *Le Reveille–Matin des françois et de leurs voisins*, pseudonymously published under the name Eusebius Philadelphius, but often attributed to a Protestant refugee by the name of Nicolas Barnaud.[84] It was dedicated to Elizabeth and dated 20 November 1573. The *Reveille–Matin* was published in several stages, the intricate details of which, and the attribution of location of publication, need not detain us for too long here. It is sufficient to indicate that the stated place of publication was given as Edinburgh, perhaps echoing the form used by the English in producing Buchanan's *Histoire*, though again, this was a patent subterfuge. In fact, some if not all of the French editions were probably published in Strasbourg on the press of Bernard Jobin.[85] There were two editions in Latin,[86] two in German,[87] three editions in Dutch,[88] and four in French.[89]

The *Reveille–Matin* was a work particularly critical of Catherine de Medici, who was singled out as being responsible for many of France's problems, having devoured the kingdom rather than governed it.[90] Catherine, a wicked Jezebel, was accused of having usurped her son's authority, and brought Italian perversions to the kingdom. It was she who planned the Parisian massacre. The *Reveille–Matin* argued that peace and moral virtue would return to France only after the hated

Italians were banished, a theme that would be repeated in another daz-
zling publication success, Henri Estienne's *Discours merveilleux de la vie,
actions et deportemens de Catherine de Medicis*, printed in four editions
between 1575 and 1576 and in one edition in 1578.[91]

The *Reveille-Matin* was divided into two dialogues, which related
the history of religion in France from the reign of François I to St
Bartholomew's Day in 1572. The main conversation was reported
through the dramatic character of Alithie or Truth who resided in
Hungary. Apparently, it was better to be a Calvinist under the Turkish
regime than to live in France.[92] Several of Alithie's friends, fleeing the
massacres in France, arrived to see him. One of these friends was called
Historiographe, the Historian, and the second was named Politique, the
Politician. The first dialogue dealt with Historiographe's narration of the
history of Protestantism in France since the arrival of Martin Luther's
ideas.

In this first dialogue, there were only a few brief mentions of Mary.
The most important of these was Historiographe's rather standard reference to Guise domination of government under François II through
their niece the Queen of Scots.[93] The second reference involved a rather
more entertaining story. This was of the Pope who, in 1560, sent the
Cardinal de Guise–Lorraine a painting by Michaelangelo of our Lady of
Grace holding her son between her arms. This he did after hearing about
the successful crushing of the Conspiracy of Amboise.[94] 'As God would
have it', the text narrated, 'the courier who carried this painting fell ill
on the journey', and, fortuitously for the tale, a young Catholic
merchant from Lucca promised he would carry the painting to the
Cardinal for the courier. However, the young man from Lucca was not
quite the good Samaritan he seemed. For he hated Lorraine – who owed
him money – and so plotted to embarrass him by commissioning a sub-
stitute painting, wherein was depicted the Cardinal, his niece Mary
Queen of Scots, Catherine de Medici, and the Duchesse de Guise, all
completely naked, with their arms and legs intertwined with each
other.[95] Needless to say, Barnaud's text takes delight in telling of how
the Cardinal and assembled dignitaries were surprised during the unveil-
ing ceremony. The positive image of the Queen of Scots dominated by
the Guise but who was not all that bad really, underwent a radical shift
towards an image of a Queen whose interests were completely interwoven with those of her relatives. No longer was Mary considered to be
a separate entity from her relations.

It may well have been this story, referred to in Barnaud's text, which
provided the inspiration for one particular section of a Protestant
cave sculpture at Dénézé sous Doué in the Loire valley (see Figure 3.1).

Figure 3.1 Photograph of La Cave aux Sculptures at Dénézé sous Doué in the Loire valley. The four central figures in the sculpture represent the Cardinal de Lorraine (left) and Catherine de Medici (right). On their laps sit Mary Queen of Scots (left) and François II (right). Copyright © René DELON/CASTELET

The importance of this cave was recognised only recently by Andrew Pettegree and detailed research has yet to be carried out on the site. However, the satirical imagery of the Cardinal de Lorraine, Catherine de Medici, Mary Stuart and François II that appears to be represented would place it in keeping with the Huguenot image of Mary of around 1574. The sculpture emphasises the close relationship between Mary and the Cardinal de Guise–Lorraine, on whose lap she sits. While the sexual overtones of Barnaud's story are omitted from the sculpture, there remains a sense of something sinister in this familial setting. Mary's diminutive size represents her youthfulness and frailty, but also emphasises the fact that she is completely dominated by her uncle. This domination can also be seen when we examine the figure of François, his body draped lifelessly across the lap of Catherine and Mary. It is ironic that the climax of Guise power in 1560–1 would be so dependent on such a sickly figure.

The second of Barnaud's dialogues had a good deal more to say about the Queen of Scots. In fact, a considerable portion of this dialogue was devoted to discussing Mary's case. It began indirectly with an extended discussion of the current state of religion in England, displaying a marked puritan influence. Barnaud's work is curious in several respects, but particularly in this emphasis on Puritanism. Certainly, the work was never printed in English. Yet, it does seem odd that the various editions of the work, including those in Latin, would directly criticise Elizabeth and her government, particularly since the ostensible objective of the work was to raise international awareness concerning the plight of the Huguenots. But this is exactly what happens. Historiographe described the situation in England, having been there on a recent visit. Politique agreed with Historiographe, criticising the ambition and insolence of the English bishops, privy councillors and even the Queen.[96] The Church, he said, lacked discipline, and England was currently running the risk that God may exact punishment on its people by permitting the accession of Mary Queen of Scots to the throne.[97]

Therein began an all–out assault on Mary Stuart, punctuated with calls for her execution for her association with the Duke of Norfolk in the Northern Rebellion. The possibility that Mary might succeed to the throne was the greatest threat to the state and religion in England.[98] Nor should she be allowed to flee to France, as Charles IX had, allegedly, attempted to arrange, for then she would become a daily focus for wars against England.[99] This emphasis on Charles IX being responsible for attempting to arrange the release of Mary is another curious aspect of Barnaud's work. The Guise were not even mentioned in this context. Moreover, the text is scarcely critical of the Guise at all. Emphasis is even placed on the role of the Guise family in safely hiding Protestant nobles in the days after the massacre.[100] If they will only embrace the idea of toleration, Barnaud argued, the Huguenots would surely follow them. For all of Barnaud's apparent attempt to reconcile the Guise with the Huguenots, however, there was no mercy shown towards one of the Guise's own – Mary. 'There was nothing more insidious', Politique narrated, 'than to have a successor for Elizabeth embodying those pernicious qualities that are displayed by Mary Queen of Scots'.[101] Her worst crime, according to Politique, was that she was a foreigner in matters of religion.[102] Her execution then would be 'very useful for the greater peace and tranquillity of this kingdom, so that no-one can doubt that it was a great thing for this thorn, which had not ceased to prick and trouble it, to be removed from its side'.[103]

Historiographe, manipulating a dramatic device, then assumed the role of devil's advocate, putting forward four main points.[104] Mary was not a subject and thus neither subject to the law nor an inferior to Elizabeth. Mary was a refugee in England and therefore should be maintained with honour and dignity. Mary was a prisoner, and 'cannot be blamed for looking for a way out by any means possible'.[105] Historiographe warned that if Elizabeth were to execute Mary, then neighbouring monarchs would have an excellent pretext – the dignity of kings – to embark on a war with the Queen of England.[106]

Historiographe's position was then refuted in some detail by Politique. On the first point, he argued that Mary was no longer a true Queen, sovereignty being dependent on location in one's own kingdom. On the second point, a refugee who ungratefully conspires against her protector should be punished with even greater severity. On the third point, Mary pretended that she had been unjustly kept as a prisoner. This was not the case. On the fourth point, the Politician argued that clemency was not an attribute of rule. For as long as Mary was kept alive, she would act as a spur for others, especially the Pope, Philip II and the Duke of Alva, to attempt to invade England.[107] Execution would be a legitimate punishment for Mary, if she were found guilty in a court of law, in order to conserve the life of the Queen and the State of England. Historiographe was, of course, duly and naturally persuaded by Politique's arguments.

The second work to emerge from the period of the Genevan refuge, was Simon Goulart's *Memoires de l'estat de France sous Charles neufiesme*.[108] Goulart had, in fact, left France six years before the massacres, and had come to settle in Geneva where he had been appointed a minister. He enjoyed a privileged position in the Genevan hierarchy, having his marriage blessed in 1570 by no less a figure than Theodore de Bèze. His book is a bibliographically complex work, and therefore the following figures are tentative. But it seems that in French there were seven editions/states published between 1576 and 1579. All seem to have emanated from Geneva and the press of Eustache Vignon, though carried either no imprint at all or the false imprint Henrich Wolf at Meidelbourg (i.e. Middelburg in the Netherlands). This was clearly intended to disguise the Genevan connection.

Professor Robert Kingdon has described Goulart's *Memoires* as 'the most complete single source of our knowledge of the multifaceted reactions to the St Bartholomew's massacres' – not without cause.[109] For Goulart gathered complete and unabridged texts of previously published pamphlets and selected extracts from earlier writings and manuscript sources, translated from English, Latin, German and Italian, which were then arranged in historical order to cover the period from the Edict of St Germain in 1570 until the death of Charles IX in 1574. In his highly popular work, Goulart reprinted George Buchanan's *Histoire*, which was entitled 'Histoire Tragique de la Royne d'Escosse', 'The Tragic Story of the Queen of Scotland'. This was followed by a lengthy section from Nicolas Barnaud's second dialogue of the *Reveille-Matin*, relating to whether the detention of Mary Queen of Scots was legally defensible. Gone from this reprinted account, however, were any criticisms of Elizabeth or the English Church, and the misguided attempts to recruit Guise support for the Huguenot cause.

After the craze of editions published during the second half of the 1570s, Huguenot interest in Mary fell quiet. Only a few works published after this date bothered to mention her at all. When they did, they generally chose to adopt the attitude towards the Queen of Scots that had characterised the 1560s, isolating her from personal responsibility, rather than following the trend of the 1570s which had criticised her directly. One such text was François de La Planche's pseudonymous work *La Legende de Charles, Cardinal de Lorraine, & de ses frères de la maison de Guise*, published in one edition in 1579.[110] A particularly interesting aspect of this work, is the way in which it directly cited many of the sources discussed above. On Guise ambition and domination of Mary Queen of Scots, La Planche drew from and cited Pierre de La Place's *Commentaires* of 1565.[111] On the Guise ambitions in England, he cited Elizabeth's printed *Protestation* of 1560.[112] The story of the tableau given to the Cardinal by the Pope was recounted directly from Nicolas Barnaud's *Reveille-Matin*.[113]

Despite La Planche's bitter attacks on the house of Guise, Mary remained a figure isolated from personal culpability. Nicolas Barnaud's *Le Miroir des françois*, for instance, published in three editions between 1581 and 1582, mentioned Mary only very briefly in connection with her involvement in plots aimed at deposing Elizabeth.[114]

The *Histoire véritable de la conspiration de Guillaume Parry anglois contre la Royne d'Angleterre*, published in La Rochelle by Pierre Haultin in 1585,[115] as with William Cecil's *Exécution de justice*, published the previous year, made much of the international network of conspiracy which threatened the life of the English Queen.[116] Yet they made no direct criticism of Mary Queen of Scots. The *Histoire*, with its firm belief that it was divine providence that was ceaselessly active in preserving the life of the English Queen, attacked William Parry, the Jesuits, and Thomas Morgan, described as an 'English fugitive living in Paris', for their plot to assassinate Elizabeth. Moreover, the text included Parry's alleged deposition, given in the Tower of London on 13 February 1584. Parry admitted coming to Paris and being reconciled to the Roman Church. It was here, according to the text, that English Catholics took an interest in Parry because of his close links with the Elizabethan government. From Paris, Parry journeyed to Lyon and from there to Rome via Milan and Venice.[117] After this visit, Parry was firmly committed to helping his co-religionists in England, and returned to Paris to formulate his treasonous designs. It was in Paris that he met Thomas Morgan, plotted to assassinate Elizabeth and organised a force of twenty to thirty thousand men to invade England 'in support of the Queen of Scotland'.[118] Significantly, however, the text also mentions and even highlights Parry's protestation that the plan to invade England to further Mary's cause was conducted without her knowledge: 'I protest on my conscience that she had no part in it or in any other way gave her consent, that I know of, nor the King her son.'[119]

The general lack of printed comment on the Scottish Queen that had so marked the early 1580s, also marked the Huguenot reaction to her execution. Yet, whereas before 1587, the scarcity of printed editions relating to the Queen of Scots reflected for the most part a general lack of interest, the failure of the Huguenot movement to respond to the death of Mary was primarily the result of embarrassment. Huguenots no less than Catholics were outraged when they learned of Mary's fate in Paris. Edward Stafford, the English ambassador to France wrote to William Cecil describing the public fury, 'I must needs write unto your lordship the truth, that I never saw a thing [more hated by] little, great, old, young and of all religions than the Queen of Scots' death, and especially the manner of it.'[120] It is not surprising, therefore, that while, as we will demonstrate in chapters four and five, the Catholic/Leaguer response to the execution was overwhelming both in print and in other media, in stark contrast only one Protestant edition attempted to justify Elizabeth's decision. This was Maurice Kyffin's anonymous *Apologie ou defense de l'honorable sentence & très–juste exécution de defuncte Marie Steuard [sic]*, published in the Protestant centre of La Rochelle in 1588, a year after the event.[121] The *Apologie* was a translation of the English work published a year earlier under the title, *A Defense of the honourable sentence and execution of the Queene of Scots.*[122]

Kyffin's *Apologie* is indeed a weighty tome. While there was a religious undercurrent to the work, this was kept well below the surface. The text was not vitriolic anti-Catholic sentiment by any means, but a measured legal defence of Elizabeth's decision to execute a monarch. It was based on precedent, dynamically engineered to provide a manual of reasoned arguments justifying Elizabeth's decision to execute Mary. In the opening section, Kyffin presented his readers with an historical analogy between Mary Queen of Scots and Jeanne, Queen of Navarre and of Naples who for the love of the Duc of Tarent had her husband, André King of Naples, strangled; Jeanne subsequently married Tarent.[123] Jeanne had stirred the cauldron of schism in Italy in a period which saw a divided Papacy with two Popes: Urban at Rome and Clement at Avignon. Likewise, Mary Queen of Scots had attempted to introduce schism into the Church of England, by rebelling against the sovereign Queen.[124] Mary did this not only to regain her territory in Scotland, but also to gain power in England.[125] Kyffin then cited several letters to back up these accusations, including letters written by John Leslie dated 26 October 1576, and from Mary to James Beaton, Archbishop of Glasgow, dated 6 November 1577.[126]

Kyffin then progressed to another historical precedent, Constantine's judgement against Licinius. Constantine took Licinius, a persecutor of Christians, as a prisoner of war – Licinius had taken up arms against Constantine over land. However, Constantine showed great generosity to Licinius including arranging a marriage with his sister.[127] Despite such kindness being shown to him, when Licinius was banished to Nicodemia, he renewed his efforts to raise a force against the Emperor. For this, he was sentenced to death. 'No good author', Kyffin observed, has ever reproached Constantine for this act.[128] In a similar way, Mary was accused of breaking the symbiotic relationship which existed in what Kyffin calls the 'the royal state in the island of Great Britain'.[129] Like Licinius, she aspired to the title of 'universal emperor'.[130] The author then listed certain kings and emperors and popes who under certain circumstances condemned princes to death, such as Constantine's condemnation of his wife Maximinia for a conspiracy against his life,[131] or Clements' condemnation of Conradin for his attempt to take the life of Charles of Naples.[132]

The *Apologie* proceeded to offer several rebuttals to what were described as commonly held objections to Elizabeth's decision to execute Mary. Kyffin argued that Mary had been deposed by her subjects and was therefore no longer a monarch, that sovereign authority in any case only applied to the country over which Mary ruled.[133]

Outside her kingdom, she was a private person subject to the laws of that country.[134] Against the accusation that Elizabeth, 'the pearl among Queens',[135] broke the law of hospitality, Kyffin argued that Mary had brought it upon herself, passing into another country where there was no alliance or truce.[136] Moreover, let us not forget that Mary had killed her husband, had pretended to the throne of England and had made entreaties to foreign princes to introduce troops into England.[137] The *Apologie* concluded that the execution of a monarch was legitimate under two circumstances: the first, if the life of a prince was placed in danger: the second, if the ruin of the republic or subversion of the state was plotted.[138]

In conclusion, the importance of the image of Mary Stuart in the polemic of the Huguenot movement developed in three main phases. In the 1560s, she was represented in a number of editions almost solely in terms of her brief period as Queen of France and wife of François II. It was an image that focused on her youthfulness, inexperience, and fragility in the face of malicious Guise ambition. It was also an image that had been moulded largely by the active involvement of the English government in public debate in France. Mary was distanced from her Guise relations, perhaps in the hope that she would become a symbol of religious toleration. The second phase began, rather later than might have been expected given Mary's imprisonment in 1568, in 1572 with the publication of Buchanan's *Histoire*, again placed into the French market by agents of the English regime, and climaxed in the period following the St Bartholomew's Day Massacre. From the safety of the Genevan refuge, Huguenot exiles seized on Mary as a symbol of Catholic perfidy. Drawing on Buchanan, in addition to native authors, French Protestantism blackened Mary's character as another means of attacking her Guisard relations and as a useful way of internationalising the conflict. As a monarch, she was a monstrous woman, unable to control her evil passions and character. The peak of Protestant editions relating to Mary were published in the five years between 1574 and 1579. The third phase was very much one of decline. From 1579 until the end of the century, there were virtually no Protestant editions relating to the imprisoned then executed Queen. Kyffin's lengthy legal defence of Elizabeth's decision to terminate Mary's life was the only edition to puncture this lack of interest and was published, rather tardily, a year after the event itself. For all the Barnaud and Goulart editions published in the wake of the St Bartholomew's Day Massacre in the 1570s, Huguenots were to feel deeply uneasy when, a decade later, they were to get what they had asked for – the execution of Mary Queen of Scots.

4
Spreading News of the Execution: Mary Queen of Scots and the Parisian Catholic League

Two days after Mary Queen of Scots had been beheaded at Fothering-hay on the orders of Elizabeth I, Lord Burghley noted zealously 'the tree of treasons has been cut off'.[1] By 1 March, two weeks later, news of the execution had reached Paris. Henri III was outraged by this decision and responded immediately by severing diplomatic ties with England. The spiritless public interest in Mary that had characterised the period 1561–86 was at once transformed into an energetic and passionate defence of the dead Queen. Nevertheless, the convergence of royal policy and public opinion on this issue was at best transitory and at worst an illusion. News of the death of Mary erupted on to an already fragile political context in which many French Catholics already exhibited signs of hostility towards the King. Successfully exploiting news of the execution and other current affairs, militant Catholic opinion embodied by the Catholic League quickly gained substantial popular support in the capital. When, in May 1587, Henri III healed fractured relations with England, open demonstrations erupted in Paris in defiance of his foreign policy of appeasement towards England and his domestic policy of pragmatic toleration towards the Huguenots.

This chapter will investigate how the League circulated news of the martyrdom of Mary in Paris.[2] During the period 1587–8, the League matured from a clandestine party into a party that enjoyed substantial popular support. The League was founded in 1584 as a direct response to the prospect of a Protestant succession following the death of Henri's brother, the Duc d'Anjou. It existed on two partially interrelated levels: an aristocratic level based on Guise clientage and association with Philip II, and on an urban level.[3] The principal urban League, based in Paris, was established by Charles Hotman, sieur de la Rocheblond, *receveur de l'évêque de Paris* and a member of Mary's Parisian council.[4] Since 1584, this urban League had evolved from its embryonic state of only a few members, gathering supporters in the major arteries of government.

On 7 July 1585 the League, supported by Spain, had pressured Henri III into signing the militantly anti-Protestant Treaty of Nemours, only five months after the King had received the Order of the Garter from Elizabeth and had publicly committed himself to the succession of Navarre, to pragmatic toleration for Protestants and to the alliance with England. The King's subsequent adherence to the spirit of Nemours was, at best, unenthusiastic. While he was prepared to pass harsh legislation against the Huguenots, he only half-heartedly committed his forces to military conflict. The Duke of Parma's victories in the Netherlands, meanwhile, only further served to convince Henri of the absolute necessity of preserving his alliance with Elizabeth. Even Elizabeth's financial support of the Huguenot party from 1586 was not sufficient reason for Henri to alter this strategy. From 1585, Henri's reaction to the enveloping political tensions was to shun the court in favour of interior spiritual reflection, waste money and angrily blame those who had failed to save him without opposing those who had sought his ruin.[5] The political landscape following 1585 was one marked by the disintegration of crown authority.

On 12 May 1588, when Henri III ordered his body of professional Swiss soldiers into Paris, the Leaguer revolution began, ousting the King from his capital. The most striking aspect of the Day of the Barricades was the sheer extent of popular support for the League. Unfortunately, historians do not enjoy the luxury of opinion polls for this period. Any conclusions, therefore, relating to the extent and character of Parisian support (public opinion) either before or after the Barricades have to remain in the realm of conjecture. Elie Barnavi may have provocatively over-interpreted available evidence by portraying the League as the first modern totalitarian party enjoying mass support from 1587.[6] However, it is clear that a significant number of Catholics in Paris who had initially fought to save the monarchy for their faith, turned decisively against the royal leadership that they felt had betrayed them, and that this reaction had been fermenting well before May 1588. As the royalist, though generally reliable, Pierre de L'Estoile noted in his diary, 'the artisan downed his tools, the merchant his wares, the University its books, the *procureurs* their bags, the lawyers their cornets [hats], even the *présidents* and councillors took *hallebards* [an axe like weopan with a long spear handle] into their hands'.[7]

As we will see, the death of Mary was one of the most significant themes of the propaganda of the League in the period of its ascendancy into a popular movement. It has long been recognised that reaction to Mary's death contributed to an atmosphere of fear and anxiety in Paris in the period before and after Henri was expelled from his capital by the Leaguer revolution in May 1588. What has not received sufficient critical attention, however, is the way in which this response was orchestrated by the League in the various media of communication available to it.

The use of the media by the Catholic League is a subject by no means ignored by historians. Charles Labitte in 1841 and more recently Arlette Lebigre in 1980 have both emphasised the roles of radical preachers and *curés* in sustaining popular support for the movement.[8] In addition, two works appeared in the mid-1970s to further our knowledge of the League's use of the printed word. In 1976, Denis Pallier published his impressive bibliographical study *Recherches sur l'Imprimerie à Paris pendant la Ligue*, which recorded details of 870 surviving Leaguer pamphlets for the period 1585–94.[9] Prefacing this bibliography were broadranging and stimulating chapters on the organisation of Leaguer propaganda and the social world of Leaguer printers and booksellers, drawn from the author's considerable archival investigations. However, the logical conclusion of this work, a wide-ranging study of the media rather than simply separate studies of its various components, has not been undertaken.

The dangers of approaching this subject with a very narrow remit are all too obvious. For instance, historians have struggled to come to terms with the disparity in tone between print and other modes of communication in this period. Frederic J. Baumgartner in his monograph *Radical Reactionaries* has noted that 'the Seize and curés of Paris were loudly condemning the King, branding him a tyrant and calling for rebellion but they wrote few of the works attributable to the League before May, 1588. Consequently, a study of the pamphlet literature fails to give a complete account of the political thought of the League, especially in Paris, before the Day of the Barricades'.[10] While admitting that he had only an incomplete picture, Baumgartner stoically defended the parameters of his own work. The printed pamphlets, he argued, were more truly representative of an essentially conservative party in this early period. 'These pamphlets', he wrote, 'could have had only a small part in creating the climate in Paris which led to the defiance of the King's authority in 1588.'[11]

From 1586, the League engaged the Parisian populace to a quite extraordinary degree. It did so with the express intention of radicalising public opinion against the authority of Henri III. The mechanics of how this could be in a population where literacy was so far from general is a question that historians need to address very directly. This chapter is intended to make a very small contribution to this process, and to redressing the balance of studies which have focused on the separate components of the Leaguer media, by examining the interface of published polemic and the other media of public opinion over the issue of the execution of the Queen of Scots. The events which took place in the parish of St Sévérin in 1587 open up many of these issues.

The disturbances at St Sévérin

Only months after the execution of Mary Queen of Scots, Edward Stafford, Elizabeth's resident ambassador in France, complained to Henri III about an unnamed work considered offensive to the English government. The French authorities, in collaboration with Stafford, rapidly identified those responsible. They could do little about the majority of copies which had already been sold. With some effort and no little symbolism, they destroyed those examples that remained – tearing them before setting them alight.[12] This work, and others like it, not only challenged the crown's domestic policy of pragmatic toleration, but also threatened Henri's foreign policy of appeasement towards Elizabeth.

Henri's heavy–handed action against this book catalysed opposition against him. In demonstration against 'that little punishment' as Stafford somewhat mischievously called it, a board was erected in the cloister at the church of St Sévérin as soon as Henry had left the city walls in July 1587.[13] Many suspected that the impetus for the posting of this board, which contained representations of the suffering of English Catholics, had come from Madame de Montpensier, the sister of the Duc de Guise.[14] Montpensier had probably used the images of Richard Rowlands (better known as Verstegan), a man closely linked to the exile community in Paris, the Guises and Spain. In fact, since 1586, Verstegan had received considerable sums of money from Philip II for his activities in France which were serving to destabilise Henri III and gather support for any future invasion of England by Spain.[15] The images were probably drawn from those contained in Rowlands's *Theatrum Crudelitatum Haereticorum Nostri Temporis*, first published in Antwerp in 1587, then in two French translations in 1588.[16] The final engraving in Rowlands's work depicted the last moments of Mary Queen of Scots, her head placed on the executioner's block.[17] Edward Stafford observed that 'not so few as five thousand people a day come to see it, and some English knave priests that be there, they point with a rod and show everything'. While Stafford may well have exaggerated the size of the crowd, the impression of a dangerous groundswell of opinion forming in Paris is striking. To Stafford and to the contemporary diarist Pierre de L'Estoile, the activities of the English priests were focused to the end of animating and stirring them to rebellion.[18]

The English ambassador reported the publication of another book at this time, 'wherein', he remarked,

> is contained as much as in the table [board] set up, with the Queen of Scots' death, whom they will have a martyr, added in the end, and their conclusion to their purpose to mutiny the people, both against Huguenots, the succession of Huguenots, and the Catholics associ-ate that hold their part.[19]

The pamphlet referred to and identified by Stafford was the *Advertisse-ment des Advertissements* of Jean de Caumont, formerly a lawyer from Langres near Troyes in Champagne, who now worked in the Paris Par-lement.[20] Bibliographically anonymous, the text was published no fewer than six times in 1587, suggesting a striking popularity. Stafford com-plained about the book. It was, after all, his duty to do so. Yet he must have recognised that his earlier complaint about a book considered offensive to Elizabeth had been partly to blame for the incident at St Sévérin in July. Perhaps somewhere in his considerations, was the real-isation that to preoccupy Henri with problems at home would serve to hinder any prospect of a renewed Franco–Scottish alliance, a possibility the English took very seriously indeed.

With Henri still absent from Paris, Stafford took his concerns to the *lieutenant civil*, who in turn asked for an audience with the Leaguer curé of St Sévérin, Jean Prévost. It would have been quite clear to the *lieu-tenant civil* that Prévost was responsible for the organisation of the board. Also clear to this royal officer, through the activities of royal agents such as Nicolas Poulain, would have been the close links fostered between the church at St Sévérin and the exile British Catholic com-munity.[21] Prévost, curé at St Sévérin since 1578, provided financial assis-tance to the English college at Reims and patronised exile priests. This parish was also closely associated with some of Mary's closest sup-porters, members of her Paris council such as François Nau and Jean de Champuhon.[22] The church and community also had close links with the Guise and with the League, as Stuart Carroll has recently demonstrated.

But while the demonstration at St Sévérin had been carefully organ-ised by the League undoubtedly in collaboration with members of the exile community and perhaps even Mary's Council, the degree of popular involvement in this demonstration is indisputable. With this support to insulate him against the wrath of the authorities, Prévost stood defiant in front of the *lieutenant civil*, saying that had he known that it was over this issue he had been summoned, he would simply not have bothered turning up. He would not, he said rebelliously, answer to a layman for his actions. The stakes were soon raised again when a secret watch and guard was established to protect the board, while Prévost himself pronounced that whomsoever attempted to pull it down would be excommunicated from the Catholic church. A councillor was sent to discuss the matter with the curé, but he returned 'with such a fear as he dare no more return'.[23] Quite rightly judging the situation explosive, the *lieutenant civil* informed the English ambassador that he could not resolve the complaint himself and that he should speak directly to the King. Henri 'fearing disorder' ordered the Parlement to remove the board at night and 'as secretly and modestly as they could'.[24] The man appointed to carry out the task was carefully chosen – Hiérosme Anroux, a councillor at court with a reputation for zealous Catholicism.[25]

The board was taken down, but not without a further act of opposition. A sonnet was rapidly published against Anroux and those who had engineered the suppression of the Catholic voice.[26] It was posted up in the cemetery at St Sévérin and at various other locations around the city. It called those involved in the removal of the board political foxes who had no concern for the blood of the Catholic innocents martyred in England. It called for action to be taken against the 'heretical sects':

> Leave this painting, O Politiques foxes
> Leave this painting, in which is depicted
> Piteous spectacles and blood stained bodies
> Blood, I say, of very fortunate devout Catholics.

> In the end, your foxy practices will not serve,
> As God, who on high moves the heart of humans,
> Will move people and the heart and the hands,
> To exact vengeance, through Him, against heretical sects.

> And you, Hierosme, and you, to whom was given
> The order to remove this crafted tableau,
> Take good care not to harm this dear work!

> Your father, in his lifetime, in his craft was a builder;
> If you pull this down, you steal the reason,
> Despising, ungrateful son, the craft of your father.[27]

By enlisting Anroux's help, the crown had temporarily defused the situation. Yet only two months later, tensions once more overflowed into open demonstration. A riot broke out in the Rue St Jacques, which runs past the church of St Sévérin, spurred on by rumours and the deliberately inflammatory sermons and actions of the preachers. According to Nicolas Poulain, a lieutenant of the Prévoté and an agent of Henri III, these preachers were deliberately attempting to goad the King into taking action in order to further undermine his authority in the city.[28] On 12 September 1587, Henri ordered the arrest of the curé Jean Prévost. The officer sent to arrest him met with resistance, as the crowds gathered round to protect their man. Men bellowed through the streets, 'to arms, my friends' and 'who is a good Catholic? Now is the time to prove it, for the Huguenots intend to kill preachers and Catholics.'[29] A larger force was sent to resolve the situation. Finally, Henri managed to take several preachers into custody, including Prévost, alleging that they had been too 'bold and too insolent'.[30]

   The unpredictability of the mob was certainly an issue that worried the League, as Nicolas Poulain attested.[31] Yet, it was a calculated risk. The League deliberately exploited popular sympathy for Mary and the predicament of English Catholics to fuel anti-Huguenot feeling in France and encourage defiance against the adopted policies of Henri III. To accomplish this, the League worked through various modes of communication, including preaching, teaching, placards, rumour, public meetings and the printed word. Symptomatic of the developing militancy of the public mood in Paris reflected and exacerbated by this exploitation of the media, was the fact that, at various points in the narrative of events at St Sévérin, crowds of people gathered to defend the right of the League to express its religious agenda. They undoubtedly recognised that both their views, and making their feelings known in this way, was in fundamental opposition to the agenda of the crown. Increasingly synonymous with mainstream Catholic sentiment, from 1587 the League made its shift from a clandestine organisation to a party which attracted considerable popular support.

   We should now examine in more detail the various elements that constituted the media, and the ways in which these were exploited by the League.

Print

The period of Leaguer ascendancy, 1587–9, was an extraordinary moment in the printing history of early modern France. Yet, many historians have failed to appreciate the significance of the printed word for this period or any other in France's ultimately successful defence of Catholicism. Far more alluring, it seems, has been the importance of the book in attracting and sustaining Protestantism.

Before we discuss Table 4.1, some explanation is required of the statistics it represents. They were compiled using the files of the ongoing St Andrews Sixteenth-Century French Vernacular Book Project in conjunction with my own bibliography of works relating to Mary and the British Isles. Each edition was ranked according to its confession and genre. It is a relatively trouble–free task to identify the confessional orientation of a work from its author, title and bibliographical details. However, the identification of whether an edition was Royalist–Politique or Leaguer is far more complicated and requires that the book be read in some detail. Moreover, as we shall see, there are a good number of difficult areas. One such area is the question of what exactly constitutes a Leaguer text? For example, in the context of Paris in 1587, a work sanctioned by the crown outlining the death of Mary, Queen of Scots probably contributed as much (if not more) to generating support for the League as to enhancing the authority of Henri III.

Table 4.1 indicates an explosion in the volume of works over this brief period, from 260 editions in 1586 to 862 editions in 1589.[34] This peak in publications, which declined after 1589, was the consequence of an increase in Catholic polemical editions, usually short unbound octavo pamphlets around sixteen pages in length produced in around 1,200 copies. These unbound pamphlets were sold by printers in their own shops and by colporteurs operating in areas such as the Rue

Table 4.1   Catholic polemical output 1587–9[32]

Total number of editions[33]	% of total publications	% of Catholic polemic
1586 = 272 editions		
1587 = 457 editions	Catholic polemic = 223 editions (49%)	Relative to British Isles = 51 editions (23%)
1588 = 682 editions	Catholic polemic = 416 editions (61%)	Relative to British Isles = 91 editions (22%)
1589 = 1038 editions	Catholic polemic = 830 editions (80%)	Relative to British Isles = 46 editions (5%)
1590 = 525 editions		

Saint–Jacques, in front of the Palais de Justice, at the Louvre and at the Pont–Neuf. The overwhelming number of polemical editions from this period were a direct product of Leaguer propaganda. Moreover, in the complex environment of Paris in 1587–8, with the League the dominant manipulator of communications, even a number of works not consciously orchestrated by the League served Leaguer ends.

The table also highlights the remarkable importance of editions relating to Mary Queen of Scots. In 1587, literature relating to her execution, or more broadly the persecution of Catholics in England, featured in or was the subject of around one quarter of the total polemical output. By 1588, interest in Mary remained pronounced, though the number of editions which dealt significantly with her declined. By 1589, Mary remained a subject of some importance, but references to her tended to be less substantial and more firmly integrated into the broader vitriolic polemic directed against Henri III.

Through a simple reading of these works, it would appear, ostensibly, that Leaguer pamphlets in the period 1587–8 remained remarkably conservative. Certainly, all referred respectfully to Henri III. The main themes of the 1587 polemical editions were the execution of Mary, where there is no open criticism of Henri III's policies, or the double victory of the Duc de Guise over the Protestant *reiters*, where the Duc was nearly always portrayed as acting under the authority of the King. In 1588, presumably after the assumption of power by the League in May, there was an increase in the number of editions that specifically criticised Henri's favourite, Jean–Louis Nogaret de La Valette duc d'Épernon, though the veneer of respect for monarchical authority was scrupulously maintained. The decisive change in the character of Leaguer polemic came only after the assassination of the brothers Guise at Blois in late December 1588. For Henri, this had been a calculated act to decapitate the leadership of the League and recover his authority. Nevertheless, this decision further radicalised public opinion against him. In response to the assassinations, there was an explosion of literature which openly criticised and ridiculed Henri de Valois, as he was derisively referred to from December 1588 onwards.

Nevertheless, it is not sufficient simply to read these texts without understanding the context in which they were published or were understood. A crucial piece of evidence in helping to understand the character of this corpus of works can be gained by an examination of the legality of the publications.

In a letter written by Estienne Pasquier, the author of several anonymous *politique* pamphlets in the 1560s, to Monsieur de Sainte-Marthe, he wrote: 'as for the pen, do not think that in war it is not as formidable as the sword'.[35] While the French crown understood the wisdom of Pasquier's remark, it did not adopt his advice on the necessity of opinion–forming by winning the polemical battle.

The French crown preferred to adopt a moderate religious political philosophy from the 1560s for purely pragmatic reasons. It was confronted with the overwhelming financial and logistical difficulties of attempting to impose its might firstly on a large proportion of its nobility, and from 1572 on an entrenched Calvinist minority.[36] It was not by any means a successful philosophy. Faced by the inability of the faiths to live together, the crown was dragged repeatedly into conflict. As Luc Racaut has recently demonstrated, the French monarchy faced a formidable task in making toleration work.[37] A large part of the problem lay in the inability of the crown to curb inflammatory anti-Protestant sentiment and its failure to ensure the propagation of its alternative *politique* philosophy. Royal printing houses had to be established almost exclusively to print edicts of toleration, so despised were they by the Catholic community.[38]

Henri made sturdy efforts to bring the situation under control. In October 1586, he reiterated the crown's requirements for the regulation of the printing trade, arguing that all presses should be registered at the Prévosté in Paris as should the printer's device (an identificatory woodcut mark) that would be used on all publications. The crown also required that a list of typographical characters be handed over, counter–marked on the reverse with the name of the printer and the printer's device.[39] It was forbidden to sell a book that had not obtained a privilege. A syndicate of four booksellers and printers was elected to act as a self-regulatory body that operated in collaboration with the *lieutenant civil*, to find the printers of 'any defamatory libel or heretical book'.[40] While the judicial records are incomplete for this period, it is clear that substantial efforts were made to enforce the royal regulations. In 1586, for instance, an *avocat* from the court named Le Breton was imprisoned. He was subsequently hanged on 22 November 1586 for having written and put to print a text, though not a religious text, judged offensive to the King, his chancellor and the *Parlement*.[41] Rigorous enquiries were undertaken; copies of the work were seized and the printer Gilles Carroy and his corrector were imprisoned and thereafter banished for nine years.[42] Henri was sending out a clear signal to those who undertook publication of unauthorised editions, particularly those who dared criticise official policy.

Tension arose, however, when Henri attempted to use the privilege system to curb editions seeking to express mainstream Catholic hostil-ity against Protestantism, specifically those editions that threatened France's alliance with England. If since 1561 all parties had agreed to demonstrate restraint in works hostile to Elizabeth, by 1586 the League shattered this agreement in order to rally public opinion against Henri's foreign and domestic policies of religious moderation. By taking steps to maintain his relationship with England and thus prosecuting the authors and printers of works hostile to this position, Henri III played directly into the hands of the League.

Numerous examples testify to the resistance generated in Paris against this decision. There was a fear, in part justified, in part mistaken, that while Catholic works were being condemned, Protestant works were being tolerated. For instance, in a work published in 1588 entitled *Remonstrances très humbles au Roy*, written anonymously by Nicolas Rolland, a *procureur de l'Hôtel de Ville* and member of the embryonic secret council of the League, a complaint was made that abominable and blasphemous works against God and the Church were tolerated, such as those by the two heretic traitors Phillipe du Plessis Mornay and Pierre Belloy. Rolland argued that these were sold publicly without the slightest fear of investigation or punishment. But when it came to Catholic works, such as Louis d'Orléans' *Advertissement des catholiques anglois*, the authorities undertook the most exact investigations in order to suppress them.[43] Rolland was by no means alone in voicing his objections. Nicolas Anroux, a banker and leading member of the inner council of the League, the Sixteen, wrote an unpublished apologia, in which he defended the preachers and rioters at St Séverin.[44] He was, like Rolland, critical of the crown, and reported its alleged attempts to allow the free cir-culation of heretical pamphlets, while it tried to suppress the Catholic voice.

There may in fact have been at least some truth to these broadly shared criticisms of the crown. While it is unlikely that the crown freely sanctioned the publication of Protestant works in the capital, it is possible that specific editions were published with its approval. For instance, it is likely that at least one edition of Pierre de Belloy's *De l'Authorité du Roy et crimes de lèse-majesté* was published in Paris.[45] Moreover, even the royalist Pierre de L'Estoile testified to the ferocity of the crown in attempting to clamp down on militant Catholic/Leaguer editions. L'Estoile remarked that the sonnet at the start of Louis d'Orléans' *Advertissement des catholiques anglois aux français catholiques* was 'enough to send its author to the gallows'.[46]

France, are you astonished if the fury of God
Ceaselessly pursues you, and sickens you, and undermines you?
If war and pale famine,
As a devouring fire consumes you in every place.

The horrible impiety, which against your judgement,
Walks in your land with impunity,
The crime of acquiescing Jezebel your neighbour,
Who mops Christian blood, is destroying you little by little.

You who made a pact with Death who follows you,
The heresy which makes you pale day and night,
You are the Babylon mother of all filth.

Your lily is withering, can you prevent it?
Wafted under the nose of God this impure flower,
Will be trodden underfoot, so will be smelled no more.[47]

Yet there was nothing especially unorthodox about these sentiments. The work had received an approval from the respected Louvain Doctors of Theology. Exactly why the work should have received this particular sanction is difficult to determine. Certainly, it is unlikely that the *Advertissement* was ever published there. More likely, Orléans wished to have his work approved by one of the foremost centres of Catholic orthodoxy. While religiously orthodox, politically, the views expressed in the book – hostility against Elizabeth, against Protestantism and the prospect of a Protestant succession in France – were entirely inconsistent with either the maintenance of the English alliance or with the concept of an autonomous secular reason which Henri believed necessary to bring France to a stable state of civil peace. Later, it would be alleged that Orléans' work was so despised by the authorities that they flogged its printer and the colporteurs that distributed it.[48] While it is difficult to confirm or deny the accuracy of this statement, it is significant that even a sympathetic source such as L'Estoile seems to confirm the accusations of Rolland and other members of the League that the crown attempted to censor the publication and circulation of aggressive Catholic print in the capital.

Henri was all too aware of the dangerous path he was attempting to tread, and on the whole remained sufficiently concerned about possible repercussions to avoid punishing Catholics too severely, or Protestants too lightly. On Friday 10 May 1587, Jean Boucher, Doctor of Theology at Paris, minister of the parish of Saint–Benoist and prolific

Catholic author, burned works printed against the League by the Parisian printer Michel de Roigny.[49] The burning of works reflected the power of the objects as well as of the texts. For this act of defiance, intended to incite popular anger against Protestantism and the *Politique* way, Jean Boucher was summoned before the King at the Louvre and asked to mend his ways. He was, however, to suffer no penalty. Another case was that of David Douceur who was condemned in October for selling prohibited, presumably Protestant books. The penalty was, however, small on the grounds that Douceur appeared to have always been of the Catholic religion.[50]

There were signs, however, that during the course of 1587, Henri's patience was beginning to wear thin. The case of Michel Buffet furnishes an excellent example. A printer of such works as Sixtus V's *Bulle de Reconciliation*[51] which carried a portrait of Mary Stuart, and a *dizain* praising the manner of her death, Buffet was arrested on 25 September 1587, because he was found selling works which did not carry a royal privilege. Substantial interrogations were conducted, including the extraction of a confession under torture, but Buffet was subsequently released on 17 December 1587.[52] It is extremely likely, though not explicitly stated in the legal document, that Michel Buffet was arrested for printing incendiary Catholic editions contrary to the will of the crown. Despite several months of imprisonment, he was released, albeit with a thorny caution threatening that he would be 'hung or strangled' if he continued in his ways.

The publishing community responded to attempts by the crown to silence its voice by using the device of anonymity. Table 4.2 demonstrates the extensive use of Catholic anonymity for editions published in 1587 and its declining use from 1588, presumably after the assumption of power by the League in May. From the general aspect of this body of anonymous texts and the political environment that they address, it seems probable that the majority were printed in Paris. Catholics drew from Protestant experiences in France and Germany. Not

Table 4.2 Place of publication of Catholic editions relating to Mary Queen of Scots and the British Isles 1587–9

	Paris	Lyon	Rouen	Antwerp	Others	Anonymous (or false address)
1587	15	1	2	–	7	29 (56%)
1588	31	10	4	4	6	34 (38%)
1589	26	4	–	2	11	13 (23%)

only did Catholics use the political pamphlet on a massive scale, but they also recognised the value in manipulating the device of anonymity to their own advantage. Protestants had disguised their names and the origin of publication of their works for various reasons. There were, in short, layers of anonymity in the Protestant book world.[53] In Paris where demand for Protestant works was high, but penalties severe, editions exhibited no distinguishing information to reveal the name of a printer. Such editions were printed for the most part by accomplished printers conscious of the fact that the authorities often carried illegal works around print shops, asking those of the profession to identify the guilty persons.[54] However in Caen, Lower Normandy, relations between the confessions were more relaxed. After a brief period of Protestant domination, Caennais society was to remain pragmatically tolerant of the new religion. An important centre of Calvinist printing in the early 1560s, Protestant works continued to be published there throughout the rest of the century. While anonymous, they can clearly be identified as the work of specific printers. This was driven by the need for brand recognition. At stake for the authorities in areas such as Caen was plausible deniability and a token level of anonymity satisfied this need. The municipal authorities wanted to be able to say to the monarch, particularly during periods of clampdown on Protestantism such as in September 1572 following the events of St Bartholomew's Day, that they had no knowledge of illegal printing activities.[55]

For the body of literature printed during the ascendancy of the League in Paris between 1586 and 1588, anonymity became a mark of orthodoxy. Texts were disguised only to the extent that the names of the printer and the place of publication were left off the title pages. A number of obvious clues to who was responsible for their publication were invariably left in the books, including the use of initial letters and ornamental headpieces.

If modern bibliography has so far managed to identify the printers of only a relatively small proportion of these anonymous texts, it is for the lack of systematic study; the Leaguer printers of the period did not go to any great lengths to disguise their works. Figure 4.1, from Renaud de Beaune's *Oraison funèbre*, highlights just how poorly anonymised many of these works actually were.

While the overwhelming number of anonymous editions appeared only as anonymous editions, a small number of works, intriguingly, existed in both semi-legal and illegal states. For instance, John Leslie's *Oraison funèbre sur la mort de la Royne d'Escosse* appeared in one edition

Figure 4.1 Highly decorative woodcut headpiece and ornate initial letter from the opening page of Renaud de Beaune's funeral oration for Mary. Renaud de Beaune's *Oraison Funebre de la très–chrestien, très–illustre, très–constante Marie Royne d'Escosse* ([Paris, Guillaume Bichon], 1588), A2r.

in 1587 with Paris and the name of the printer, Jean Charron, indicated boldly on the title page. It did not signal any privilege.[56] The same printer then produced two other title pages that did not carry his name or place of publication, but used exactly the same printing types for the body of the text. In addition, Charron added the phrase 'with the approbation of the holy faculty of theology at Paris' to the bottom of the title pages of these editions.[57] Another example of this phenomenon is Renaud de Beaune's funeral oration for Mary, which took place at the behest of Henri III in Notre Dame cathedral in Paris. We shall deal in a few moments with the interaction between sermons and the printed word, but relevant to our present discussion is the fact that the first edition of the work was printed in Paris with the printer's details clearly indicated on the title page, while a subsequent edition of the work carried no such visible information.[58]

The most convincing explanation for the Catholic use of anonymity, was that it functioned as a symbolic form of opposition against the policies and authority of the crown.[59] It was a fundamental act of defiance on the part of publishers, printers and consumers. To buy a prohibited book, to hold, read, or be read a prohibited book was to defy the authority of the crown. Parisian Catholics and undoubtedly Catholics in the provinces, bought these pamphlets in their thousands. From 1586, moreover, not only was the phrase 'with privilege' omitted on many works, even on those editions such as Renaud de Beaune's *Oraison funèbre* that we might reasonably assume was actually granted a privilege, but also other phrases began to appear including 'approved by the Louvain Doctors' which could be found on Orléans' notorious *Advertissement des catholiques anglois*. Another phrase 'with permission' also became increasingly used, signifying that it had been approved by the Catholic League. Even before 1589, the League had begun to establish its own system of book regulation.

So far, we have dealt with the book as a physical artefact and explored the issue of anonymity as a mark of religious orthodoxy and as a device of opposition to the authority of the crown. If we are to understand more fully the context in which the Leaguer texts of this period were interpreted, however, it also necessary to examine the way in which print interacted with other media of communication. A particularly revealing remark by the Leaguer Jean de Camont testifies to the necessity of recognising that early modern French society was predominantly oral. He noted that he had written his book to combat 'the pestilent books' which penetrated the 'ear' of 'the simple people'.[60] The ideas contained within books did not stay on the printed page; they interacted with other forms of communication. Published polemic can only be understood in terms of its interface with other media of public opinion.

Placards, images and verse

Placards, that is single sheet broadsheets, had a long history as an official form of communication. They were used by the authorities to publicise edicts and other proclamations. But they were also a formidable tool in the propagation of oppositional ideas. It may indeed have been their physical form, as much as their contents, that so outraged contemporaries, representing as it did the appropriation, or parody, of an official mode of communication. Certainly the most notorious of all, the sacramentarian placards of Antoine Marcourt that had criticised the Mass, stirred François I to anger in a way no previous evangelical publication had. These placards had been posted up in 1534 around Paris and other French cities.[61] But the use of the unofficial placard was not the preserve of Protestantism. As we have seen in chapter 2, in 1583, the exile community in Paris posted up indecent images of Elizabeth and François Duc d'Alençon to generate sympathy for the plight of Catholics in England. In the late 1580s, the Catholic League also turned placards, and specifically placards which combined text and images, to their advantage.

The ephemeral and fragile nature of placards has meant that very few have survived.[62] For the League, however, we are fortunate to have a number of placards collected by Pierre de L'Estoile, consisting in total of 46 folio sheets. The character of the unofficial placards is similar to that of the printed pamphlets. On the surface, the placards appear less than revolutionary before the assassinations of December 1588. Nevertheless, just as we have seen for the printed texts, the political context in which these placards were published made them far more radical than has generally been recognised. Placards lamenting the death of Mary were forms of political action. The timing of when they were posted up and where they were placed, was always engineered for maximum political effect. Noteworthy was the posting of placards lamenting Mary's martyrdom outside Notre Dame cathedral when Renaud de Beaune was due to deliver his funeral oration.[63] These placards, in combination with the text of the sermon which we will discuss shortly, gave the whole event a decidedly different meaning from that intended by Henri III when he organised the solemnities.

Of all the unofficial placards collected by L'Estoile, it is interesting to note that four-fifths were illustrated.[64] Largely on the basis of German evidence, there is a tendency to assume the importance of the image in early-modern print.[65] In France, images were far less significant than is casually assumed, and certainly far less important to the development of the Protestant movement.[66] Very few editions were illustrated. Nevertheless, the visual image seems to have played a disproportionately important role in the dissemination of the ideas of the League both in the form of placards from 1587 and in printed pamphlets of the period, particularly following the assassination of the brothers Guise in December 1588. While evidence is rather thin, and we must of course be careful not to over-interpret a scattering of evidence, it would seem that it was the activity of English exiles that first spurred the League to recognise the potential of the visual image. Both in 1583 and at St Sévérin in 1587, it was the exiles who were responsible for the posting of placards which combined image and text. One English exile explained that 'seeing everything most clearly at one view excites the ardour of devotion more than if we came to know the same things by ear'.[67] Images were expensive to produce, so expensive in fact that they were often reused as late as the nineteenth century.[68] The informer Nicolas Poulain suggested that during the period of the League, many images were crafted on-site at the Hôtel de Guise.[69]

The mixing of text and image did, to some extent, bridge the oral-literate boundary. But images often required a certain amount of decoding if they were to be understood correctly by non–literate viewers. The preachers at St Séverin cemetery pointed to the placards with rods, heightening their impact for all, but making their significance understood particularly for those who were not able to read.

Another aspect of these placards was their use of verse, though clearly verse would also have circulated orally without the need for a written form. Pierre de L'Estoile, and ambassadors such as René de Lucinge who wrote dispatches to Charles Emmanuel, Duke of Savoy, recorded a great number of poetical works produced as placards that one might imagine were committed to memory and then recited, or perhaps even sung.[70] The form of these Latin and French poems varied, including quatrains, sonnets, anagrammatic poems and proposed inscriptions for Mary's tomb:

> To the English Jezebel
>
> Bastard, incestuous and public bawd,
> Perfidious, disloyal and daughter of your sister,
> Which your father discovered his mistake with her,
> Cruel father and husband, he put her to death shamelessly.
>
> From a father so malicious, from a mother so lustful,
> Bitch, you take after who you are, and Hell full of horror
> Placed inside you a serpent in place of a human heart,
> And to direct it, a satanic spirit.
>
> From a furious tiger your body was weaned,
> As from the cradle, there has not been a day
> That against the Christians, you have not vomited some outrage.
>
> Which authority can you use to justify,
> Having gone against all law, made a prisoner and killed
> Her, who, sovereign, excelled your own lineage?[71]

There was an abundant use of poetry, and verses circulating in placard or oral form were often reprinted in Leaguer printed pamphlets and books such as Adam Blackwood's *Martyre de la Reine d'Escosse*, which went through eight editions between 1587 and 1589.[72] These poems, as can be seen from the example above, were often uncompromising in their declamations of Elizabeth's ancestry and conduct.[73] One particularly ubiquitous quatrain described Elizabeth as 'a she–wolf', worse than a million wolves.[74] This image was recalled in numerous printed texts of the League, including the printed version of Jacques Le Bossu's oration to the people of Nantes, in which he stated that the 'she–wolf, the Queen of England, had handed over to the executioner (against all law divine and human), this so virtuous Queen of Scotland'.[75]

Sermons

From the pulpit, the cause of Mary was defended vigorously. L'Estoile recorded that the preachers of Paris canonised Mary daily in their sermons, emphasising that she had not died a traitor, but a martyr for the faith.[76] Preachers openly accused Henri of complicity in Mary Stuart's death.[77] Unlike those authors and printers who did not have congregations to insulate them from the wrath of the authorities, preachers enjoyed a greater freedom in which to raise oppositional ideas. At St Sévérin, preachers and curés explained the unauthorised martyrological images and then stood with absolute defiance in front of the *lieutenant civil*.

In 1841, Charles Labitte undertook a study of the preachers of Paris, based on the evidence of contemporary, largely hostile sources such as L'Estoile.[78] It suggested, though with undoubted hyperbole, that from 1587 there was hardly a single church where a preacher favourable to the Leaguer cause did not preach several times a day. Only a handful of moderate preachers such as René Benoist, Labitte noted with some distaste, prevented the entire region from descending into 'a centre of sedition'.[79] While figures remain difficult to establish accurately, it is clear that even those inhabitants of Paris who were not exposed directly to Leaguer preaching, would have had some contact with congregations who had. Moreover, events and the growing disparity between public opinion and the actions of the crown played directly into the hands of the League. Thus, even in the traditionally more moderate parish of Saint Eustache, the preacher, possibly Mary's former confessor René Benoist, relayed the news of her execution. He was forced to come down from his pulpit and abandon his sermon altogether, so great was the emotion that had 'won over the audience including himself'.[80] While there is clearly an intimate connection between many of the most vitriolic preachers and curés, such as Jean Boucher, Jean Prévost or the exile

Scots nobleman Jean Hamilton,[81] and the organisation of the League, there was clearly also widespread public sympathy for the League's agenda. The strength of the League lay in its articulation of wider Catholic sentiment, and the insensitivity of Henri III to public opinion.

At least one contemporary observer, Pierre de L'Estoile, remarked on the similarity between the polemical pamphlets published during this period and the sermons delivered around Paris.[82] One particularly fine example of the way in which printed sources would have interacted with sermons, lies in the publication of Renaud de Beaune's *Oraison funèbre*. Henri had organised a ceremony for Mary for the 13 March 1587, attended by members of the Parlement, the University and the Sorbonne.[83] When Henri did attempt to display limited sensitivity to the public mood, it backfired. Despite Auguste de Thou's report that Henri was genuinely outraged at Elizabeth's decision to execute Mary in February 1587, and that he suffered mental anxiety in deciding on how to respond to the situation, the Catholic public were unimpressed by his response.[84] The French court did go into mourning; all wore violet. Diplomatic links with England were also suspended for a few months. Henri organised an oration on 13 March at Notre Dame cathedral, where Mary had married the Dauphin François thirty years before. Henri, the Queen, the Princes, the Parlement and the great nobles of the kingdom, all attended. But in spite of these displays, Henri failed to convince an angered Catholic population that he had done enough. At the root of this failure was Henri's need to carry with him the support of the French public without lending weight to the popular cause associated with the Guise and the League.

During the oration on the death of Mary, de Beaune drew from the communal grief and emotion that pervaded the capital. This oration was deeply emotive and praised in particular Mary's Guisard relatives, whom he called 'two great war leaders'.[85] Renaud de Beaune also referred to the Guise as a great and magnificent family, who had done much across every corner of the earth in the defence of Christianity.[86] The oration also called for vengeance against those who carried out this cruelty. So angered was he by this promotion of the Guise and the League, Henri severely reprimanded de Beaune, saying that he had injured his authority and given added weight to those who sought to disturb the public peace. He ordered him to excise the offending remarks. If the published version did get rid of these remarks, as de Thou evidently believed it did, the version that remained was still highly pro–Guise. However, even if the text had not retained this central element of pro–Guise rhetoric, the Parisian readers of these pamphlets would in any case have brought to this text a knowledge of de Beaune's oration. Readers and listeners brought to texts a system of understanding gleaned from hearing sermons several times a week, and informed from a broad range of communications.

Rumour

But perhaps the primary way in which both literate and non–literate sections of French society learned of events was through rumour. A partial reconstruction of the content of these rumours is made possible in this period, because of the sensitivity of ambassadorial correspondence to public opinion and through the extraordinary diary entries of Pierre de L'Estoile. From these sources, we learn that interest in Mary's situation was first aroused when Pomponne de Bellièvre departed on an ambassadorial mission that sought to dissuade Elizabeth from enforcing the sentence of death. The substance of these rumours, which undoubtedly underwent multifarious refractions, was to allege a sinister ulterior motivation to Bellièvre's embassy, that he had been sent by Henri III to conclude some form of Genevan alliance with Elizabeth.[87]

Before Mary was executed, rumours had circulated reporting variously that she had been executed and had been saved by the intervention of Henri III. On 8 February,[88] for example, René de Lucinge, the ambassador to Savoy, wrote in his diary, without any further detail, 'news of the Queen of Scots'.[89] On the 18 February, the actual date of the execution, but before news could possibly have reached Paris, Lucinge posed the question with obvious doubt 'would the Queen of Scots have been poisoned?'[90] Two days later, Guillaume de L'Aubespine, the French ambassador to England, could give no good news about Mary, nor a gentleman who arrived on her behalf to gain an audience with Henry.[91] One rumour reported that Henri had intervened on 25 February, and had succeeded in saving the life of the Scottish Queen,[92] and another that Mary had been broken out of prison, that the City of London had been put to the torch and that many noble Spaniards had been landed successfully in Wales.[93]

The first reliable report of Mary's execution reached Lucinge and L'Estoile at different times. It is clear that Paris was aware of the execution from around 31 February–1 March. L'Estoile wrote in his diary that he was aware of the dreaded event on 1 March, while the first reliable report arrived at the French court on 2 March. Giovanni Dolfin, the Venetian ambassador writing to the Doge and Senate recorded that a special courier only arrived on 2 March to explain *viva voce* to Henri III, Elizabeth's reasons for carrying out the sentence.[94] René de Lucinge, after a conversation with the Cardinal de Bourbon, reported news of the execution to the Duke of Savoy on 4 March, though he talked of earlier rumours of Mary's death.[95] Interpretation of these facts has been further complicated by one simple but often overlooked fact. France had adopted the Gregorian calendar, whereas England was still dating according to the traditional calendar, a difference of ten days. Calendar reform had long been recognised as a necessity given the increasingly obvious discrepancy between the calendar years and true seasons. A papal commission had taken the matter in hand, and after much deliberation advanced the drastic decision to excise ten days from the calendar in October 1582. By papal decree, 5 October 1582 would be followed by 15 October. The reform was dutifully adopted by Catholic nations, but angrily rejected as a papal plot to steal time in Protestant parts of Europe. The impasse continued for almost one hundred and fifty years until the last Protestant power, England, reluctantly fell into line.[96] This calendar confusion has long been a snare for the unwary historian. Thus Mary was executed on 8 February 1587, but on 18 February (New Style) as the Catholic press would express it.

This crucial fact has led virtually all of Mary's biographers to exaggerate the time it took for news of the execution to reach Paris. As a censequence, these scholars have suggested that the news of Mary's execution was somehow deliberately and successfully suppressed in England.[97] In fact, the delay was only thirteen days, often the normal period of time that it took for news to be transported across the channel.[98] As reliable news of Mary's execution spread through a capital already highly charged with anxiety over Mary's fate, the Parisian populace became stunned and outraged. Stafford wrote to Burghley:

> I must needs write unto your lordship the truth, that I never saw a thing [more hated by] little, great, old, young and of all religions than the Queen of Scots' death, and especially the manner of it ... And for my part I do think that it is a happy thing for us that there is a thing of that humour of this King, that no man knoweth and can dissemble [sic] his thoughts; for surely else everybody is so animated against this, that they would put him to the touch with this matter, to sound the bottom of his stomach ... For my part, I think he will not be brought unto it; and that which is happiest for us are the jealousies that the King and they of the League be [in] one another, which is daily continued and augmented; and if, as I have written to Mr. Secretary ... I never saw all so desperately bent against her [Elizabeth] as they are.[99]

On 6 March, Lucinge confirming Stafford's observation, that 'everybody here, from the small to the great, are in an extreme state of grief – all mortally hating the Queen of England who consented to such a cruel and merciless act'.[100] Such shock and outrage could only have been exacerbated by other rumours, such as that corrected by Lucinge on the 12 March, which reported that shortly after the execution, Mary's head had been placed on London Cross.[101] Stafford was still writing worriedly to Burghley of the intensity of feeling against Mary's death on 24 March 1587.[102]

Importantly, rumours of Henri's complicity in Mary's execution, though clearly circulated from before Mary's execution, were not put to print until late December 1588 when Henri had given the order to assassinate the brothers Guise, the popular champions of Catholicism.[103] Then, the pamphleteers opened their attack on Henri III, reiterating rumours of late 1586 and 1587 that Pomponne de Bellièvre had been sent on a diplomatic mission to Elizabeth for reasons other than to save Mary's life.[104] 'The Queen of England', reported one pamphleteer, 'led him [Henri III] by the muffle as with a bull, and made him approve the conspiracy of the death of her sister in law, the Queen of Scotland, that, without his consent, she would never have been so bold as to attempt it'.[105] The author of *Les Considerations sur le meurdre commis en la personne de feu Monsieur le Duc de Guyse*, indicated that Henri had 'secret foreknowledge that Mary would be executed.[106] The work emphasised Henri's friendship with Elizabeth, noting that he had sent his brother, the Duc d'Anjou, to propose marriage to her and to plan a secret league against the Catholics.[107] Henri's ill-will towards Mary could also be seen through the imprisonment of Thomas Morgan, a key member of her Paris–based council, who was place in the Bastille following orders given by the Queen of England.[108]

While recognising the seemingly conservative nature of the printed word before the Blois assassinations, we should also recognise that from the very beginning, even bringing up Mary's name in print had connotations which the authors, readers and listeners would have clearly understood.

Orchestration

There is insufficient evidence to establish whether propaganda reflecting the aims of the League was spontaneous or orchestrated. There are, in fact, few known sources which allow us more than a superficial insight into the Parisian printing industry at this moment.[109] In part, this is due to the survival of materials over time. In part, it is a reflection of the necessarily clandestine nature of a revolutionary organisation, combined with the deliberate destruction of evidence relating to the League by those involved in it. Henri IV on his assumption of power also made a deliberate effort to destroy both Leaguer propaganda and documents relating to the movement.[110]

Almost none of the polemical pamphlets provide any internal evidence of patronage. The frequent use of anonymity would suggest collective action, but to what extent authors were directed by a central, guiding hand remains unknown. Certainly, the picture that emerges from Auguste de Thou and Pierre de L'Estoile, is of a very sophisticated manipulation of the media by the League. Both authors, hostile sources, point to a virtual minister of propaganda, 'the governess of the League in Paris' – Catherine Marie de Lorraine, Duchesse de Montpensier and daughter of François de Guise.[111] From these accounts, Catherine was involved in every aspect of the media. The placard set up at St Sévérin was known as the 'tableau of Madame de Montpensier'.[112] She was also heavily involved in directing the preachers in Paris. After Henri III had arrested several preachers following the riot at St Sévérin, they reported to him that both they and the majority of preachers in Paris, 'preached nothing other than the news contained in the bulletins sent by Madame de Montpensier'.[113] Preaching was an effective tool of communication, not least because of the familiar, direct and passionate opportunity it afforded to influence opinion. Montpensier harnessed its power, ensuring the support of preachers and curates, often by bribery. L'Estoile accused her of offering wages, bishoprics, abbeys and other great beneficies, which was certainly in her power to do.[114] Louis II Cardinal de Lorraine was, after all, the leading prelate in the French Church.[115] L'Estoile also noted her involvement in making 'visual symbols' as trophies for the Duc de Guise, by which she hoped to 'maintain her brothers in the good graces of the Parisians',[116] while Auguste de Thou accused her of having spread many false rumours among the populace.[117] There was probably at least some measure of truth in these allegations. In January 1588, Henri III asked the Duchesse de Montpensier to leave Paris because of her activity against him and France, and remarked that she had done more to advance the Leaguer cause than any army could.[118]

Conclusion

The Day of the Barricades on 12 May 1588 was a bloodless revolution that succeeded in ousting Henri III from his capital. If this was an insurrection that had been minutely planned by the organisation of the League and its influential supporters in the key organs of Parisian government, it was also an insurrection that received an astonishing degree of popular support from all ranks of Parisian society. But while short-term impetuses such as the appearance of Henri's Swiss guards did serve to mobilise an extraordinary number of the inhabitants of Paris into helping form the barricades, the long-term influence of Leaguer exploitation of the media certainly cannot be ignored.

The polemical editions that responded to the execution of Mary Stuart contributed to an increasingly radicalised political climate in Paris during 1587–8. Printed polemic interacted with every other media and a process of cross-fertilisation of ideas took place. Together, all of these forms of communication played a critical role in the process of discrediting Henri III and enhancing the image of the League and of the Guise. However, it is important to keep constantly in mind that polemic neither fully dictated nor reflected public opinion; it contributed to the articulation of general patterns of thinking that were already present. But without the capable and dominant exploitation of current affairs in the media, it is unlikely that the revolution of 12 May 1588 would have been greeted with such widespread popular support. At least partially, the success of the League lay in the failures of Henri III. The crown failed to fashion a coherent political agenda acceptable to the Catholic population. More importantly, the crown failed to dominate systems of communication. It would not be until the first decades of the seventeenth century, under Henri IV, that the crown would be able to take more effective charge of the press. It did this, on the one hand, by introducing a more effective system of censorship. On the other, the crown began to exploit their use of patronage to commission works, in order to overwhelm the political opposition.[119]

5
A Catholic Tragedy: The Radical Image of a Martyred Queen

On 23 November 1586, from her prison in Fotheringhay, Mary wrote a letter to Bernardino de Mendoza, the Spanish ambassador to France. It would have been an exceptionally difficult and emotional moment in which to compose her thoughts, for Mary had just learned that she was to be executed for treason. Underneath the formality of the prose, the letter reveals a tangle of emotions, including disbelief, frustration, apprehension and defiance. Recounting the attitude of her persecutors, Mary exclaimed, 'that I was no more than a dead woman, without any dignity. I think that the work in my room is for the purpose of erecting a scaffold on which I am to perform the last act of the tragedy'.[1] In fact, another three months would pass before Elizabeth gave the final authorisation for the sentence to be carried out. In this interval, in constant expectation of the end, Mary had a good deal of time to contemplate her own mortality and to prepare for her final performance.

In this chapter we will explore how the extraordinarily emotive account of Mary's final moments was reported by the Catholic press in France. Over one fifth of all Catholic polemic in the period 1587–8 referred to Mary's execution, often in the context of the 'English example'. England became a symbol of the evils of Protestantism that profoundly shaped the way in which French Catholics rationalised their present circumstances. It served as a powerful warning at a time when it looked as if the leader of the Huguenots, Henri de Navarre, would certainly succeed to the French throne when Henri III died. The image of Mary as a martyr, together with this cautionary 'English example' was employed by the League to radicalise public opinion against the pragmatic foreign and domestic policies so tenaciously pursued by the crown. Catholics needed to unite in militant action against the Huguenots, otherwise they risked suffering the same fate as their co-religionists across the Channel.

The execution narrative

In his influential 1964 monograph *Images of a Queen*, James Phillips surveyed the evolution of the principal printed accounts of Mary's execution.[2] Phillips' survey, however, is very far from being the definitive account that historians have so casually assumed.[3] The purpose of the following analysis, quite apart from setting the record straight, is to explore the representation of Mary's martyrdom in the printed literature that appeared in French from February 1587.

It is worthwhile to pause for a moment to consider what will be a key theme in this analysis of the execution narratives, the relationship between martyrology and historical reliability. In his seminal monograph, *Salvation at Stake*, Brad Gregory explored this very question.[4] According to Gregory, literary and anthropological hermeneutics have tended to ignore the motivations of those who died for their faith. Instead, 'with arbitrary condescension', they have pigeonholed the past according to contemporary values and assumptions more reflective of the anachronistic and sceptical commitments of scholars than those of the martyr.[5] Traditionally, when historians have discussed martyrology, they have tended to portray martyrological writings as 'worlds away from detached reporting'.[6] In short, the formulaic nature of martyr stories has often aroused scepticism.

In contrast, Gregory draws the conclusion that, contrary to established historical opinion, sixteenth-century martyr narratives were to a very large extent true historical accounts. In support of this contention, he cites the fact that when reports of the same execution survive from opposing confessional groups, sympathetic and hostile, they often differ little in their central narratives.[7]

Gregory's point offers a valuable corrective, if slightly overstated. Previous scholarship, including the work of Jean–François Gilmont on Pierre Masson, and that of David Watson on the printer and martyrologist Jean Crespin, has tended to press the evidence in the opposite direction, emphasising the role of martyrologists in pruning and embellishing the historical evidence.[8] Nevertheless, on the whole, such an approach does not seem to be entirely symptomatic of the reductionist approach to religion that Gregory wishes us to decry, but simply a very practical recognition that a number of factors undoubtedly informed the working practice of the martyrologist, including a firm sense of the purpose of history as a way of understanding God's activity in the world. History was a pedagogical tool with which to nourish the religious life of the community.

Every account should be evaluated as far the historical record allows, and undoubtedly different levels of reliability and embellishment can be found in each. In general, however, the depictions of the behaviour of martyrs should clearly not be dismissed because of the explicit ideological commitments of the author. From the evidence that Gregory has amassed from Protestant, Catholic and Anabaptist martyrdoms which do have surviving corroborating evidence, it is clear that martyrologists, on the whole, tended to use the best information available concerning the executions: 'facts, not fabrication best served propaganda'.[9] But while recognising this general reliability, we should not ignore the specific role played by the martyrologist in reconstructing the theatre of martyrdom in print.

The high profile case of the execution of Mary Queen of Scots offers an interesting case study. Not only do we possess a significant number of martyrological narratives, but also a number of first and second hand accounts. We will demonstrate that despite the fact that Mary had become an important political figure in France from the moment that news of her death arrived there, the League, surprisingly, did not adjust the narrative in any significant way to suit its broader purposes. Though a small portion of the narrative accounts can be attributed to dramatic and pedagogic embellishment, Leaguer martyrologists, on the whole, remained faithful to the way in which Mary chose to conduct herself between the evening of 17 February, when she received confirmation that she was to be executed, and 18 February when she placed her head on the block.

Perhaps the first pamphlet to report the death of Mary, published in no less than six editions, was the *Discours de la mort de très–haute & très–illustre Princesse Madame Marie Stouard, Royne d'Ecosse.*[10] The text followed, almost in every detail, the report written by the French ambassador to London, Guillaume de L'Aubespine, to Henri III in late February.[11] Just how L'Aubespine obtained his information is uncertain, but an interesting aspect of the *Discours de la mort* and the report on which it was based, is the frequent employment of the phrase 'it is said', revealing an honesty when faced with uncertain sources.[12] The L'Aubespine report formed the core of all the accounts that were to follow. An edited translation of this version of Mary's last days is provided below:

> On the evening of Saturday 23 February,[13] Belé [Robert Beale], the brother in law of Walsingham was dispatched with a commission signed by the hand of the Queen of England calling for the decapitation of the Queen of Scots. The commission commanded the

Counts [Earls] of Shrewsbury, of Heut [Kent] and Rutland and a number of other gentlemen who were near Fotheringhay to assist with the execution. Beale took with him an executioner from London, dressed in black velvet. Leaving secretly late on Saturday, Beale arrived on the evening of Monday 15 February.[14] The following day, Beale called a meeting with the Earls and Gentlemen. That day, in the evening, [Amias] Paulet, the custodian of the Queen of Scots, accompanied Beale and the head of the province[15] (the equivalent of a Prevost de Marchans of a bailliage or a criminal judge) and went to find Mary to inform her of the will of the Queen their mistress, who was constrained to execute the sentence of her Parliament.

It is said that the lady remained extraordinarily constant saying that she did not believe that the Queen her sister would have ever wished it to have come to this. Since she had been reduced to such great misery for three months, she welcomed death, and wished to receive it when it pleased God. They wanted to leave her a [Anglican] minister, but she refused.

There was a great room in the castle, wherein was erected a scaffold draped in black cloth, with a velvet cushion upon it. On Wednesday at nine in the morning, the Earls and Mary's guardian came to fetch the said Lady Queen of Scots. Finding her 'fort constante' and dressed, they escorted her to the great room followed by her *maistre d'hostel*, Melvin, her surgeon, her apothecary and one other servant.[16] Mary had also asked that her ladies in waiting might accompany her, a request which had been granted. The rest of her servants had been locked up the night before.

It is said that she ate before leaving the room. She asked Paulet to help her up onto the scaffold as the last service she would ask of him. On her knees, she spoke a long time to her faithful *maistre d'Hôtel*, asking him to go and find her son, to go into his service and that he would recompense him since she could not; she asked him to carry to him her benediction which she made that hour. Then she prayed to God in Latin with her ladies. Not wishing an English bishop to approach her, she protested that she was a Catholic and would die in this religion. After this, she asked of the Sieur Paulet if the Queen her sister had agreed to the will that she had made fifteen days before for her poor servants. Paulet replied that Elizabeth had, and that she would carry out that which she had asked concerning the distribution of money.

Mary spoke of Nau, Curl and Pasquier who were in prison but I have not known the truth of what was said.[17] Then Mary fell again to prayer, asking God to console her ladies who were weeping, while she herself approached death with very great constancy. One of her ladies covered Mary's eyes. Mary then lowered herself onto the block where her head was cut off, an axe being the custom of the country. Her head was then picked up and shown to the audience of around three hundred people or thereabouts from the area who had gathered in the room.

The body was covered in black cloth and taken into her bed-room, where it is said, it was covered and embalmed. The Earl of Shrewsbury then despatched his son that same hour to the Queen of England, to convey the news of this execution. The news was not long concealed. On Thursday the 19th,[18] around three in the after-noon, all the clocks of the city of London began to ring, and fires were lit and there were signs of great joy in all the streets, with feasts and banquets. There was a rumour that the said Lady died insisting that she was innocent and that she had never planned to kill the Queen of England, and that she had prayed to God for her, and that she had charged the said Melvin to say to the King her son that she prayed him to honour the Queen of England as his mother, and never to depart from amity towards her.

Other printed accounts of the execution soon followed, drawing from the well of first and second hand evidence freshly available from England. James Phillips has, however, wrongly attributed the next stage in the development of the narrative to the influence of the Sieur de Gondy, an agent to the French ambassador in London.[19] This version of the execution, an adaptation of the L'Aubespine account, survives in three sources: in a letter from Gondy to James Beaton, Archbishop of Glasgow; in correspondence between Bernardino de Mendoza, Spanish ambassador in Paris, and Philip II; and between Giovanni Dolfin and the Doge and Senate of Venice.[20] The Gondy account was a slightly revised version of the L'Aubespine narrative, which included an empha-sis on Mary's political innocence (despite her justifiable attempts to procure her own liberation). Gondy also added details of how Mary had spent the final night before her execution in prayer. While there is clearly evidence to demonstrate that the Gondy account was being cir-culated in official circles from early March 1587, there is scant evidence that it was adopted by pamphleteers such as John Leslie and Renaud de Beaune, as Phillips has suggested.

Let us deal firstly with the funeral oration of John Leslie, published in three editions in 1587 under two variant titles.[21] Leslie was the Bishop of Ross and Mary's confidant. His poignant oration on her execution was probably delivered to a congregation of Scottish Catholics exiled in Normandy in March 1587.[22] The printed version of the text was translated into French. The oration was less detailed than the *Discours de la mort*, and exhibited factual inconsistencies. For instance, the names of the Earls were not mentioned, Melvin not Paulet was recorded as having helped Mary onto the scaffold, while in the *Oraison*, on the morning of her execution not the evening prior, the Earls offered Mary the services of two Anglican ministers, not one. On a more substantial note, the *Oraison* related that Mary had had the courage to fall asleep for at least part of the evening of 17 February, experiencing neither perturbation nor any inquietude, but rather a tranquility of conscience that only the innocent could experience.[23] This was surely an embellishment, but there also exists the possibility that Leslie drew from a source or sources which remain unknown. In fact, only one tenuous detail links the *Oraison* to the Gondy account. While Mary's parting speech to Melvin is contained in the *Oraison*, emphasising Mary's touching concern and generosity towards her servants, there is no mention of her instruction to Melvin to inform her son, James, that he should regard Elizabeth as if she were his mother.

Reflective of the way in which some of the details of the narrative evolved over the course of 1587–8, was the publication of a revised version of Leslie's *Oraison*, under the title *Harangue funèbre*.[24] The change in the narrative was the consequence both of fresh information of the execution becoming available in France, and of a 'standard' version beginning to take root. Leslie's *Harangue funèbre* contained considerably more detail than the *Oraison*, including for instance the names of the officials who had supervised the execution. It added more details of the speeches. On hearing the news that she was to be executed, for instance, Mary replied that she had never done anything to cause Elizabeth offence, but had only striven for the advancement of Catholicism; death would be a comfort to her. The section where Mary had the courage to go to sleep was completely removed, undoubtedly to enhance the image of the pious Mary spending the evening before her execution in prayer. The name of Paulet now replaced that of Melvin as the man who had helped Mary onto the scaffold.[25] There is evidence that Leslie, if we can assume that he was responsible for the revisions in the *Harangue*, had at least read, but not substantially relied on, the report of the Sieur de Gondy for this single edition. Introduced into the *Harangue*, was the detail that Mary had been given the Eucharist by a disguised priest.[26] Leslie's *Harangue*, published once, was in fact the only printed account to incorporate this portion of the Gondy narrative. In following what he must have regarded as a reliable source, Leslie was clearly attempting to resolve a particularly thorny problem in the martyr story, the validity of Mary's final confession.[27]

The Archbishop of Bourges, Renaud de Beaune, also delivered a funeral oration in honour of Mary on 13 March 1587. This service, held at Notre Dame cathedral where Mary had been married to the dauphin thirty years before, was organised by Henri III and attended by the notables of Paris. The printed version of the *Oraison funèbre*, published a year later in 1588, was highly polished.[28] It is worthwhile to remember that it is unlikely that this text would have been a verbatim transcript of the original oration. The printed *Oraison* was deeply moving and rhetorically impressive, following for the most part the L'Aubespine account of Mary's execution. There were additions, which could, with some stretch of the imagination, be taken as evidence that de Beaune had access to the Gondy source. It emphasised Mary's piety on the evening before her execution and her time spent on her knees in prayer.[29] Also introduced into the narrative was the fact that one of Mary's ladies placed the blindfold over her eyes, after the services of the executioner had been refused.[30] Another detail to be found in Gondy, but not in L'Aubespine, was the omission of the rumour that Mary had commanded James to regard Elizabeth as his mother.[31]

But if de Beaune did have a copy of the Gondy narrative that he had chosen to use, we would have to explain a number of significant omissions. For instance, why did de Beaune make no mention of the two speeches reported in Gondy where Mary announced that she had always solicited the propagation of the Catholic religion in England?[32] Additionally, there was absolutely no mention of the priest being smuggled into Mary's room to conduct the final Mass.[33] More telling, perhaps, than these omissions were the additions to the narrative. Probably for the sake of embellishment, de Beaune mentioned that Mary had prayed with such ardour on the evening of 17 February that she had been taken out of her body and elevated above the things of this world to be united with the angels.[34] This out of body experience allowed Mary the assurance and peace that she would soon be delivered from the hands of her enemies into the hands of God, her creator and saviour. It was this assurance of spiritual victory that she related to her ladies in waiting when they began to cry.

Following the release of Mary's servants from captivity in August 1587, more detailed accounts began to reach pamphleteers in France, particularly of how Mary conducted herself on the evening before her execution. The only surviving eyewitness report from Mary's servants was that of Dominique Bourgoing, Mary's physician.[35] Also circulating

in manuscript was the official English account of the execution, compiled by Robert Wingfield.[36] This latter report is so detailed that Wingfield must have been acting as secretary, noting down verbal exchanges
between Mary and the authorities and her behaviour from the day
before her execution.

Drawing from all available sources, including eyewitness testimony
and the Wingfield report, were two of the most developed martyrological accounts, the *Martyre de la Royne d'Escosse* and *La Mort de la Royne
d'Escosse*.[37] Both texts were written by Adam Blackwood, a Scot who had
benefited from considerable patronage from Mary. With her support,
Blackwood was educated in France. It is surely a mark of how much
trust Mary had in Blackwood that, in 1576, she intended to employ his
services in a particularly sensitive post beside the French ambassador in
London, where he was to deal specifically with her affairs. However, for
undisclosed reasons, this plan came to nothing.[38] By the time of Mary's
execution, Blackwood was working as a counsellor in Poitou, an area
controlled by Mary under the terms of her dowry. A brief overview of
the printing history of these works highlights their extraordinary popularity. His *Martyre de la Royne d'Escosse*, a detailed life of Mary that contained a brief account of the execution, was published in three editions
in 1587, at least three editions in 1588 and one final edition in 1589.
His *La Mort*, a work focusing specifically on Mary's martyrdom, went
through at least two editions in 1588 and one edition in 1589. In
addition, two other editions of the *Martyre* were issued in 1589 under
the title *Histoire et Martyre de la Royne d'Escosse*, to which a variety of
separate editions of *La Mort* were added as supplements.[39] In short,
from 1587 to 1589, Blackwood's *Martyre* and *La Mort* were published in
at least twelve editions.

The principal additions to the execution narrative contained in the
Martyre lay in the incorporation into the text of information on how
Mary had spent the evening before her execution, and how she had conducted herself on the scaffold. Blackwood noted that Mary had passed
the evening of 17 February 'in prayers and orations in the reading of the
passion of Our Lord, and in similar consolations of the soul and holy
meditations'.[40] Blackwood rejected the story that Mary had received the
Eucharist before her death, which had been contained in the Gondy
report and adopted by John Leslie in his *Harangue funèbre*. Instead, Blackwood reprinted a letter from Mary to her priest, to whom she had been
refused direct access, stressing that she continued to remain faithful to
her faith. Also in the letter, Mary confessed her sins, asking that the priest
pray for her that night at the same time as she herself was to be set in
prayer. The priest was asked, given her particular predicament, to send

his absolution and to pardon all her offences. Mary also asked for the advice of the priest on the correct prayers for that evening and for the following morning.[41] Of events on the scaffold, Blackwood added some additional detail, reporting, for instance, that the Earl of Kent had taken an ivory cross away from the Queen, some details of Mary's prayers on the scaffold, and of her final wishes.[42] The execution was described very simply. Blackwood reported that it took three strokes, 'to render the martyr more illustrious', remarking very pointedly 'how much do I know that it is not the punishment, but the cause that makes the martyr'.[43] This last remark, taken from Augustine,[44] was an interesting reflection by Blackwood on the problem of an age in which competing confessional groups claimed that their members, accused of heresy and treason, were in fact martyrs for the true faith.

The second text, published originally in 1588, was *La Mort de la Royne d'Escosse*. This work can best be regarded as the definitive sixteenth–century Catholic account of Mary's execution to appear in French. Blackwood stressed at the outset of the work his commitment, which was more than a rhetorical flourish, to recount 'the pure and sincere truth' of what took place at Fotheringhay for posterity. In the pursuit of this truth, Blackwood claimed that he had sought out reliable witnesses from Scotland, England and France.[45] As with the earlier martyrdom accounts, the emphasis in *La Mort* lay with Elizabeth's decision to execute Mary on the grounds of her religion and Mary's unswerving commitment to the Catholic faith. Where Blackwood differed, however, was in the detail that he was able to include in the narrative, particularly in respect to Mary's speeches. For instance, Blackwood noted that Mary placed her hand on the New Testament and swore 'that she had never plotted, consented nor pursued the death of the Queen of England'.[46] There was also greater emphasis on demonstrating the illegality of the execution and shame of the English officials for having taken part in it.[47] For the evening before her execution, Blackwood drew on information, principally from Bourgoing, that had already been contained in the *Martyre*.[48]

An important addition, however, were new details concerning Mary's speech to Melvin. Blackwood in *La Mort*, drawing directly from Wingfield, reported Mary as saying:

> You know Melvin, all is vanity in this world, full of troubles and miseries; carry this news that I die a Catholic, firm in my religion, a Scottish woman, & true Frenchwoman, and that I hope God will forgive those who have desired my end.[49]

This detail was also incorporated into Robert Guttery's translation of a 1588 work by Robert Turner, rector of the University of Ingolstadt, entitled *L'Histoire et vie de Marie Stuart*.[50] This represents a strengthened emphasis on Mary's French identity. Of course, Mary's French connections were both implicit in *Discours de la mort*, and explicit in earlier accounts such as Leslie and de Beaune. Mary was mentioned as having been Queen of France, and in de Beaune, she was closely associated with the family of Guise–Lorraine. Nevertheless, in Blackwood's *Martyre* and *La Mort*, and in Turner's *L'Histoire et vie*, the stress on Mary's relationship with France was far more vigorous.

Other details testify to the strengthening association made between Mary and France in the martyrological narrative. Perhaps most symbolically, Blackwood publicised one of Mary's final requests, which Elizabeth was not to fulfil, that Bourgoing should take her heart back to France.[51] *La Mort* also included details of Mary's last will and testament, and her final letter to Henri III. Mary wrote both these documents on the morning of her execution. They highlight her connection with the Guise,[52] her close affinity with France, and her trust in Henri III. A full edition of Mary's last will and testament was published in a single edition in 1589.[53] In this will, Mary was to style herself 'Queen of Scotland, dowager of France'. She expressed her wish to have services held at the basilique of St Denis in Paris, and St Pierre in Reims, and gave instructions for the distribution of her dowry. In her final letter to Henri III, reported in Blackwood, Mary referred to the King as her 'brother in law' and 'old ally' and even indicated that she would pray for him at the moment of her execution.[54] We can explain the strengthening of the French connection within accounts of the martyrdom of Mary, principally in terms of access to the Wingfield and eyewitness accounts from late 1587.[55] That these fresh details would tug the sensitivities of an audience already familiar with the rumours that Henri III had been complicit in Mary's execution, and had not taken any significant action against Elizabeth following the act, was fortuitous but for the most part incidental. However, martyrologists were alert to their political environment, and no doubt selected and framed the historical detail for maximum effect. Not least, the title pages of Blackwood and Turner's works, which advertised the text to its potential readers, trumpeted Mary's position as dowager of France.

Significant new details were also available to the readers and audience of *La Mort* and *L'Histoire et vie* of the execution itself. In *La Mort*, the condemned Mary was described elaborately: 'her face was a lively and innocent colour, the eyes set in a steady gaze, without any changes at all, her beauty even more apparent than ever, with a remarkable constancy and her usual majesty'.[56] Mary's performance on the scaffold was also recounted. While the English began to pray, Mary prayed loudly in Latin, particularly the penitential psalms of David.[57] Then Mary prayed in English, so that everyone might understand. The English were moved by pity and regret at this. Mary then said a number of prayers, invoking the Saints, especially St Peter, the first Pope, and St Andrew, the patron saint of Scotland. Then Mary kissed her cross. The presence of the physical symbols of Mary's faith was noted by Blackwood, but were mentioned in greater detail in Turner's *L'Histoire et vie*. Both authors drew their information from the English Wingfield account. Mary went to her death with a wooden cross in one hand, and a book of hours in the other.[58] She also had a cross of gold, which had in its centre, rosary beads.

As well as offering what was probably the most complete contemporary account of the execution, Blackwood also included details of the way in which the English dealt with Mary's servants following her death. The gates to the castle of Fotheringhay were closed and her servants were imprisoned. They were not, Blackwood recounted, even to hold a Mass for Mary's soul. Also described was the funeral service which was held for Mary in August 1587.[59] A silent procession, in which Mary's servants participated, was subject to the verbal abuse of onlookers as it moved towards Peterborough Cathedral. Insults were hurled at the servants in addition to Protestant singing. The sermon was delivered by the Bishop of Lincoln. Blackwood expressed no surprise that Mary should have been given even these modest honours. He suggested that the reason why the English had carried out these solemnities was that those responsible could 'hide their lies and treasons'.[60]

It is clear that there was a generally reliable and efficient transfer of information from Fotheringhay to the printed French martyrological accounts. Certainly, we have to allow for a certain degree of rhetorical embellishment along the information route for dramatic effect and for pedagogical purpose. In composing his *Oraison funèbre*, Leslie stated explicitly that his oration had two aims: to honour God, and to edify those who heard it.[61] Yet, overwhelmingly, the martyrologists followed the historical sources. It is interesting to note that the fabulous detail, mentioned in the Wingfield account, of Mary's terrier lying piteously between her head and body was omitted from the French accounts, presumably since such sensational detail might have aroused scepticism.[62] Nevertheless, while we might have assumed a greater bending of the execution narrative to the broader purposes of the League, in the printed accounts, which were of different degrees of detail, length and complexity, the events were left largely to speak for themselves.

Mary Queen of Scots was overwhelmingly responsible for the construction of her own martyrdom, conducting herself in a manner appropriate to the role of martyr. From the moment in late 1586 that Mary was aware that the sentence of execution had been passed, she had made thorough preparations for her final performance. This role began from the moment that Beale arrived with the news that Elizabeth had given the final authorisation required for her execution. Mary understood the importance of this drama to the Catholic cause. As Brad Gregory has noted, martyrdom was 'more powerful than a thousand sermons'.[63] Not only were martyrs models of Christian virtue and symbols of God's activity on behalf of the true faith, but also during the sixteenth century, as in the Early Church, martyrs were regarded as saints, available to intercede between man and God. While not the official position adopted by the Church, there is evidence that the papacy tacitly supported the veneration of unofficial saints by members of the clergy and laity.[64] But if Catholics had hoped to obtain relics of Mary, as they had of the English priests executed in 1582,[65] they were to be sorely disappointed. Elizabeth had taken great effort, not so much to prevent Mary from becoming a martyr to the cause, for that one might argue was almost inevitable, but rather to ensure a certain damage limitation. All of Mary's belongings were burned or washed to prevent them from being traded as relics. Revealingly, Adam Blackwood turned to Eusebius, the great martyrologist of the Early Church, when discussing Elizabeth's actions, 'all the things of the martyrs they burned, as Eusebius said, and they were spread into Rhodes, so that the memory of those men might also perish with their bodies'.[66]

The lack of relics may indeed have limited to some extent Mary's longer-term status as a saint, yet in the short-term, her memory was to be an extraordinarily powerful force in France. Her execution was offered as a prime example of the malignance of Protestantism and its total disrespect for the order of the world. The martyrdom of Mary, however, also demonstrated the triumph of liberty over the servitude of Satan.[67] In dying for her faith, Mary had imitated Christ. Through crucifixion and resurrection, Christ had overcome worldly strength despite apparent weakness. It was a spiritual victory won through suffering. Mary, therefore, along with other martyrs, upset the purpose of secular punishment by suffering torment and punishment with a constancy that had been granted to them by God. In defying the authorities by refusing consolation from their ministers, Mary had prevented her soul from being destroyed along with her body. Mary's constancy was seen less as a tribute to her own personal devotion, and more as proof of God's presence in the world, and His commitment to sustain those of the true Church. Mary's martyrdom provided a number of models for Christian behaviour, of piety, innocence, forgiveness and benevolence. But above all, as Mary herself was reported to have remarked to her servants before her death, 'take the example of my constancy for the dearest and surest gauge that I can give you of my friendship'.[68]

The image of the martyred Mary within the context of the 'English example'

Leaguer authors saw their own time as a defining moment in history. The urgency in the literature of this period was reflected to some extent in an apocalypticism present in texts such as *Les Quinze signes advenuz és parties d'occident, vers les royaumes d'Escosse & Angleterre*.[69] Fifteen was, of course, an important ecclesiastical number. In particular, it signified the 15 effusions of the blood of Christ, and thus assumed an important place in eschatological thought.[70] Nevertheless, the majority of editions were far less eschatological in their outlook, but no less sure that now was the time to act. Jean de Caumont made a plea to the Catholic community, arguing that if they took no action now, posterity would look back on this period, and blame them for having let the Church of Jesus Christ fall in the kingdom of France at a moment when there was a way to conserve it.[71]

The remedy was not the moderate way. Official recognition of the Huguenot religion would lead, argued one Leaguer polemicist, to little or no religion.[72] Protestants were dissimulators, chameleons who changed their colours as they wished.[73] Above all, Henri de Navarre should not be allowed to succeed to the throne of France. He was an adulterer, a bad husband and a cruel excommunicate. The remedy was unity and militant action against Protestantism. As the author of one pamphlet, the *Exhortation aux catholiques de se réconcilier les uns aux autres, pour se deffendre des hérétiques* argued, 'the citizens are the limbs of the body, and that if the limbs are not in agreement with each other, the body cannot survive. St. Augustin said that just as the human spirit can never give life to the limbs if they are not united, the Holy Spirit cannot give life to us, unless we are united by peace.'[74] The kingdom of God needed to unite against the kingdom of Satan. After all, the Protestants had formed the United Provinces. Just as 'the staff of Moses devoured the staffs of the magicians of Pharaoh, also the Holy Union of Catholics [the League] will devour the impious plots of the heretics'.[75]

Inward renewal was necessary, as was the need to pray for the heretics, but the wicked also required punishment on Earth.[76] One example given was that of a man who had a diseased foot beyond cure.[77] Two doctors examined the problem. One suggested amputation, the other sweet potions. Who, it asked, was the crueller? The text responded emphatically that it was the second doctor. For without acting, the disease would spread.[78]

In order to convince the French public of the dangers of failing to take action at this moment, Leaguer pamphleteers drew heavily on the example of England. In chapter two, we demonstrated the difficulties faced by the crown in pursuing an alliance with England whilst, simultaneously, having to manage Catholic criticisms of the way in which their co-religionists were being mistreated by the English government. Except for a few radical exceptions, the French press from 1561 to 1585 disseminated a robust yet diplomatically sensitive response to events across the Channel. The publication of one text in particular, however, was to mark a fundamental shift in political and popular opinion on England and Elizabeth. This was Louis d'Orléans' *Advertissement des catholiques anglois aux françois catholiques*.[79] It was published, illegally, in at least five editions/states in 1586 alone. In 1587, it appeared in two editions, in 1588 in one, and in 1590 in at least two editions together with a second *Advertissement*.[80] It was a supposed address by the English Catholics to the French Catholics, warning them of the dangers facing them if Navarre should ever succeed to the throne of France. The majority of the book focused on French history since the early 1560s, portraying Protestantism as a subversive force that was violating and polluting the French state. Yet, a prominent theme that ran throughout the book was Elizabeth's mistreatment of England's Catholics. Under a heretic ruler, Orléans argued, atheism had taken root in England.[81] This was his warning to his fellow Catholics in France as they faced the very real possibility that Henri de Navarre would succeed Henri III.

There were two distinctive aspects to the corpus of polemic relating to Mary and the British Isles in the period that followed Orléans' publication. The first was that the corpus of works was far more voluminous and represented over one fifth of the total Catholic polemical output for 1587–8. Secondly, the representation of England and Elizabeth in this body of works was far more radicalised than that which appeared before this date. As the political divide between the League and the crown grew ever deeper following the King's dogged refusal to adhere to the spirit of the Treaty of Nemours, editions that criticised Elizabeth far from being kept on the margins of political opinion, began to form an integral part of the agenda of the League. Moreover, as we have seen in chapter four, through all methods of communication at their disposal, the League succeeded in linking their own agenda with mainstream Catholic sentiment. Previous restraint in dealing with Elizabeth was completely abandoned, consciously fracturing the fragile consensus of restraint and congruence with crown foreign policy that had existed since the early 1560s.

The contours of the image of Mary Queen of Scots and England in Leaguer polemic are worth exploring in some detail. Leaguer literature drew heavily on established ways of negatively stereotyping Protestantism. It was the language of militancy, not of compromise. Common themes included the polemical association between heresy and disease, and the feminisation of heresy. This type of comparison in anti-Protestant polemic of the early 1560s has recently received critical attention from Luc Racaut.[82] Catholics understood the progress of heresy in Europe in terms of the spread of a contagion. It was a metaphor borrowed from the medieval world,[83] and used frequently – at least since the eve of the religious wars. It was not simply a convenient way of describing the progress of Protestantism; it was also the way in which early modern French Catholics rationalised the divided world in which they lived.

England, and to a lesser extent Scotland, stood as examples in Catholic polemic of Protestant states, and as an example of what the French could expect if Protestantism was ever allowed to flourish legitimately in their own country. Robert Turner in his *L'Histoire et vie de Marie Stuart*, described the progress of Calvinism from Geneva into Scotland in terms of 'the fumes and vapours of the Helvetian [Calvinist] plague and contagion'.[84] The spread of Protestantism in England under Elizabeth, according to Jerôme Osorius, whose *Remonstrance* was republished in 1587, was due to the Queen's advisors. The *Remonstrance*, first printed in 1563, followed a pattern of criticising Elizabeth's advisors rather than the Queen. If she chose better advisors, Osorius observed, 'then they would not infect the great courts and places . . . and that the poison would not reach the kings, pervert and trouble their state, and not ruin the public good with contagion and mortal sickness'.[85] Orléans in his *Advertissement*, spoke of a 'violent, evil and contagious sickness, caused by a tumour of the spirit'.[86] Protestantism was spiritual leprosy, affecting the whole of Europe including France, a destructive force even worse than that facing the Early Church.[87] This disease, associated with sexual excess,[88] was a tumour of the spirit which affected the body politic. As with lepers, those who suffered from the disease should be segregated from the wider community.

England was a prime example of the world turned upside down. In an age where rank and social status were of the utmost importance, Protestantism became associated with insurrection and rebellion, an inversion of the natural order. A common theme permeating anti–Protestant polemic was the feminisation of heresy. Protestantism was associated with 'immodest women' and 'whores'. Women could be seen from an idealised perspective, as in the courtly love tradition, but were also seen as rebellious, ignorant, sexual temptresses and thus a potent negative stereotype for Protestantism.[89] The stereotype of sexual temptress of course linked the idea of women with the metaphor of leprosy which the early modern, as the medieval world believed, was sexually transmitted; lepers were believed to have been exceptionally lecherous.[90] The temptation of Eve in the Garden of Eden, of course, formed an important symbolic origin for this portrait. As Jean de Caumont observed, 'I fear that just as the serpent tempted Eve by his cunning, so too your senses are now corrupted and that you are turned from the simplicity of faith in Jesus Christ'.[91] An extension of this concept of the feminisation of heresy was the depiction of Protestant men as effeminate. We find, for instance, that in Richard Verstegan's *Théâtre des cruautez* published in 1588, Henry VIII was described as an 'effeminate, incestuous and miserable Prince'.[92]

We have seen for the period before 1586 that, except for a handful of editions, Elizabeth was distanced from criticism. The outspoken criticisms of authors such as Jean Gay and Gabriel de Sacconay who in 1561 had held Elizabeth primarily responsible for the persecution was, in the interests of foreign policy, marginalised in the thirty years that followed.[93] From 1586, there were editions that continued the conventions of blaming Elizabeth's counsellors rather the Queen herself, and indeed of omitting any mention to Mary Queen of Scots. In this respect, it is interesting to note three texts that had first appeared before 1586 and which were subsequently reprinted. Robert Persons's *Épistre de la persécution*, first published in Latin in 1581 and in French in 1582, was republished in 1586.[94] It had been one of the least incendiary editions to respond to the executions of Edward Hansius and Edmond Campion. Jerôme Osorius' *Remonstrance à Madame Elizabeth Royne d'Angleterre*,[95] had appeared originally in Latin then in French in 1563 and had been appended to Ferdinand I's *Les Graves et sainctes remonstrances de l'Empereur Ferdinand*.[96] Also republished in 1587 was Anne Percy's *Discours des troubles*, which had been published in 1570 in response to the rebellion of the northern earls in 1569.[97] These works had originally received the sanction of the crown. Yet, even with these seemingly lawful editions, all was not what it seemed. Given the impending succession of Navarre to the throne, and the current political climate in which respect for the person and policies of Henri III was fast disintegrating, this literature was far more radical in the context of 1586–9 than it had been when it had first been published. It is important to note that from 1585, no works critical of Elizabeth or England obtained the consent of the King. It is highly likely that the printers of these works were specifically targeting an increasingly militant Parisian market, whilst protecting themselves by producing a work that had at some point carried a privilege.

One of the principal charges against Elizabeth in Leaguer polemic was her illegitimacy, that as a bastard born from incest, she had usurped the thrones of England and Ireland.[98] For instance, in denigrating Elizabeth's mother, Anne Boleyn, as a 'hacquenee d'Angleterre', 'the prostitute [literally a horse kept for hire] of England', physically and spiritually deformed, Adam Blackwood claimed to have found the root of Elizabeth's own unrestrained sexual immorality.[99] It was a theme intimately bound up with the literary construction of the susceptibility of women to Protestantism, and the concept of heresy as disease, in particular leprosy which was associated with unrestrained sexual behaviour. Accusations of conventicles and orgies in which Protestants would gather in an attempt to fulfil their unbounded lusts, had been one that had pervaded Catholic polemic on the eve of the Wars of Religion.[100] While Leaguer literature does not, on the whole, draw on this early stereotype, it is interesting to examine the language that is used of Elizabeth. Consider, for instance, the use of phrases such as, 'see the whore, the bitch of England'.[101] Ubiquitous insults against Elizabeth were those frequently hurled against women, by men or by women. But embedded in these insults were associations with Protestantism that Catholic readers and audiences would have readily understood.

The only concession to Elizabeth's royal position in Leaguer polemic was that she was often compared with other bad rulers, most frequently to Jezebel:

> The horrible impiety, which against your judgement,
> Walks in your land with impunity,
> The crime of acquiescing Jezabel your neighbour,
> Who mops Christian blood, is destroying you little by little.[102]

Jezebel was the archetypal wicked and ruthless female ruler, mentioned in Kings I and II. In the ninth century BC, this Queen, wife of King Ahab of Israel, had introduced the worship of the Tyrian god Baal-

Melkart, and thus abandoned the exclusive worship of God. A woman of ferocious energy, she was responsible for the slaying of a number of prophets; Elijah escaped Jezebel's wrath only by going into exile.[103] It was to this figure that Leaguer pamphleteers turned to a find an historical antecedent for Elizabeth. Jean de Caumont, for instance, argued that the English Queen surpassed Jezebel in her inhumanity.[104] We might have expected such rhetorical comparison between Elizabeth and Jezebel to have interacted with the established theme in Catholic polemic of associating heresy with pandering to women. Yet, misogynistic comment on the nature of female rule seems to have occurred only very indirectly. Certainly, there were frequent references, especially in verse, to Elizabeth as a 'louve', a she–wolf, worse by far than a million wolves:

> English, you say that among you,
> No living wolf can be found?
> No, but you have a she–wolf
> Worse than a million wolves![105]

This image played, in part, on the fact that England was well known to be free of these animals.[106] Moreover, the wolf was also a particularly apt image given its strong religious connotations. Wolves prey on sheep, the flock of Christ. Nevertheless, the dominant direction of Leaguer literature in this period was that it was not Elizabeth's sex, but her illegitimacy and perpetuation of a false religion that disbarred her from the throne.[107]

The fruits of a country ruled by a heretic were plain for all to see, most significantly manifested in Elizabeth's illegal and ungodly persecution of Catholicism. The idea of a liberty of conscience that *politiques* had been calling for in France was completely turned on its head in this literature. In their portrait of England and in other areas where Protestantism had become the dominant religion, Catholic pamphleteers emphasised the tyranny of heresy.[108] As the author of the *Exhortation aux catholiques de se réconcilier les uns aux autres, pour se défendre des hérétiques* put it, 'while the Catholics who live in England are not at war, are they at peace? I would say not. They have lost their freedom, they cannot live as they would like, they are deprived of the sacraments, they are forced to baptise their children as Huguenots and when they are on their death beds, they have no way of being absolved [of their sins] by priests'.[109] Where was the liberty of conscience for English Catholics, forced to abide by the cruel edicts of the Jezebel Elizabeth? In addition to those martyred, Caumont estimated that around ten million had renounced their faith in the face of this persecution to prolong their temporal life; in so doing, they lost their eternal life.[110] The faithful were deprived of their goods, the consolation of priests, they could not even send their children or servants out of the country without a special licence signed by the Queen or her Privy Councillors. Where was the liberty of conscience for these people? 'O kingdom of Jesus Christ! O kingdom of Satan! Antithesis!', cried one pamphleteer:[111]

> Imagine for yourself what we have to go through in England. If you have rosary beads, if you do not pay your respects to the ministers, you will be criminals guilty of lèse majesté. During the day, at night, in all seasons and at all hours, your homes will be searched, your furniture stolen and your money pillaged under the pretence of a search for priests. If you do not go to the sermon, if you do not baptise your children there, if you even celebrate your weddings there, you will incur large fines. Tortures, extraordinary questioning, the straps and gallows are never in short supply. In short, you will think yourselves the most miserable creatures that ever there were.[112]

Accusations levelled against the English and Elizabeth were their contradictory opinions, novelty, inconstancy and their dissimulations.[113] England was a country in which atheism had taken root, a country in which Catholicism had been criminalised and considered treason.[114] The immediacy of the parallel was emphasised continually. Caumont, for instance, remarked that

> The very voice and cry of the poor martyrs can reach our ears, if we but paid attention; and we could see from our shore the erected gallows and the lit fires, where everyday our Catholic brothers are put to their death.[115]

As with earlier Catholic editions which described the persecution in England, such as Robert Persons's *Epistre de la persécution*, Leaguer literature described in some detail the macabre tortures and deaths suffered by England's Catholics. In England, God had been exiled and banished, the Church destroyed, violated and polluted. Priests were hung, drawn and quartered, while 'the gallows, the squares and the gates of the town, were adorned with the heads, arms and legs of our poor Catholic brothers', who, for showing any sign of their religion, were cruelly murdered, tortured and mutilated.[116] England was characterised as 'a prison for Catholics', all the towers and prisoners of the kingdom were full of

Catholics treated as common criminals, destined to die if they did not renounce their Catholicism. Jean de Caumont in his *Advertissement des advertissemens* described the various tortures inflicted on these prisoners. These included being chained up, being plunged into pits of snakes and toads, and the torture of being placed in fire.[117] There was, moreover, also the gruesome execution method most associated with the English penal system. This involved persistent torment in prison followed by a brief hanging – to ensure suffering but not death. The stomach was then cut open, the heart ripped out of the stomach and held up to the victim whose mouth, Caumont recounted, still quivered with life. The heart was then thrown into the fire. Following this the body was, as in cases of treason, cut up into quarters and placed in eminent public locations, so that 'heretics and crows in the sky could feast their eyes upon the parts'.

Perhaps the best example of the way in which the persecution of Catholics in England was represented can be found in the work of Richard Rowlands, better known as Verstegan. The *Théâtre des cruautez des hérétiques de nostre temps* was published in two editions in 1588.[118] According to the prefatory material written by the printer of the work, Adrien Hubert, the text had originally been produced in Latin and put together in Flanders,[119] Germany, Italy and in Spain, while the French edition had been translated from the Flemish.[120] As well as being the author of the *Théâtre des cruautez*, Richard Rowlands was also an engraver; in all, quite remarkably, thirty of his woodcuts accompanied the text. It was almost certainly these images that had been the cause of so much commotion at the cemetery of St Séverin in 1587. The text and the woodcut images outlined very graphically the Protestant butchery of Catholics, predominantly in England but also in France and the Netherlands.

The picture the *Théâtre* painted of the Protestant faith was of inhuman cruelty which had no respect for Catholicism, age, gender or decency. To take a few examples, the English Protestant authorities attacked people as they slept, impaled those who tried to escape burning buildings by throwing themselves out of windows and cut off the limbs of a Catholic sailor whose ship had been seized and threw him overboard. Catholics were made to watch their own feet being burned, priests were thrown into cess pits and shoed like horses. Priests were pinned to crosses and shot. Gloating Protestants played bowls with the heads of Catholics and made barbaric chains to go round their necks made of the ears of those they had slain. Interestingly, however, in the *Théâtre* and many other Leaguer works, the Catholicism of the individual martyrs was something that was largely taken for granted. Of greater interest to the author was the emotive description of the persecution of the martyrs, rather than on using their stories to serve any elaborate didactic purpose.

The life and martyrdom of Mary Queen of Scots was one of the most potent examples of Elizabeth's ungodliness. It fitted into the broader discourse that had seen Catholics die for their religion in a heretic country that disrespected human and divine law. Not content with inflicting an infinity of torments on a multitude of Catholics, Elizabeth had chosen to execute a legitimate Catholic sovereign. Elizabeth's motivation in carrying out this sentence was given as her manifest hatred for Mary and for the Catholic faith. While Mary's political innocence during her Scottish career was defended at some length in Blackwood's *Histoire* and Turner's *Histoire et vie*, authors were noticeably coy about discussing Mary's alleged involvement in plots against the life of the English Queen whilst in prison. In contrast, almost the entire corpus of works relating to Mary focused to some extent on the illegality of the imprisonment and execution. Perhaps the most forceful exponents of this theme were Pomponne de Bellièvre, the French ambassador to Elizabeth, and Jacques La Guesle, procureur to the King. Pomponne de Bellièvre's *Harangue* to Elizabeth which he delivered to Elizabeth in late 1586–early 1587 in order to dissuade the Queen from exacting the death penalty on Mary, was published in two editions in 1588.[121] Similarly, Jacques La Guesle's *Remonstrance à la Royne d'Angleterre*, was published after the execution had actually taken place.[122]

The *Harangue* and the *Remonstrance* did not debate the subject of Mary's guilt or innocence, but rather disputed Elizabeth's jurisdiction in the case. Only God, Bellièvre and La Guesle remarked, could judge kings.[123] Bellièvre agreed that a foreigner who entered a foreign kingdom was liable to the laws of that kingdom. However, he argued that the condition of the lower orders was that of iron and lead, while that of the kings was of gold.[124] This inevitably contributed to the theme of Protestantism turning the world upside down; the English had judged and then executed a legitimate sovereign. Bellièvre and La Guesle denied Elizabeth's jurisdiction over Mary for a number of other reasons. Principal among these was that the Queen of Scots had entered the kingdom with every assurance of Elizabeth's good will, in short as a supplicant.[125]

The initial illegality of her imprisonment in 1568 was a point emphasised in a number of accounts. Elizabeth had abused the ancient code of hospitality, inviting the Queen into England only to imprison her.[126] Breaking this code of hospitality was even more heinous given three other considerations. Firstly, Mary was a legitimate sovereign and all sovereigns called each other 'close relations'.[127] Imprisoning Mary was therefore an abuse of the sanctity of kingship. Secondly, there was the link of consanguinity between Mary and Elizabeth, and this was stressed in most of the accounts, with the use of terms such as 'sister',[128] and 'her closest relative and closest neighbour'.[129] Thirdly, there was the fact that Elizabeth was herself a woman.[130] While the female sex was seen as being more 'infirm and more vulnerable to injuries', it was seen also as 'more full of gentleness and empathy'.[131] Perhaps Jean de Caumont summarised all of these arguments best, when he noted that the imprisonment and execution of Mary was an act committed against all the laws of the world:

> And it is hoped that . . . God will turn His vengeance against this demented person [Elizabeth] who, full of demons and evil spirits, has violated the rights of ordinary people, the right of hospitality, the law of consanguinity and all laws human and divine, who, against her sex has become deranged, who has held the majesty of kings in contempt, likening it to the pleb, answerable to an executioner.[132]

An important way in which the image of Mary Queen of Scots intersected with the English example, and more broadly the image of the progress of the Protestant heresy in the sixteenth century was that of a tragedy. Surprisingly, if we examine the print record alone, we would imagine that there was a very limited interest in classical tragic drama itself during the sixteenth century, either in original languages or in translation.[133] However, classical texts were circulated predominantly in manuscript and dramatised by the colleges. Perhaps more popular than these ancient plays, in print and in performance, were newly composed tragedies based around classical models, such as those of Robert Garnier.[134] The interest in classical dramas and the application of the tragic form in sixteenth–century France owed much to contemporary historical circumstances, spurred by the experiences of a society divided by religion and scarred by civil war. The themes of classical tragedy took on a very immediate significance – the instability of human affairs, human suffering, the reversal of fortune in the lives of the great, and issues such as civil war, rebellious subjects, good government and the powers and obligations of a sovereign. As Robert Garnier, in his dedication to *La Troade* wrote,

I know there is no sort of poetry less pleasing than this one [tragedy], which presents naught save the sad mischances of princes along with the calamities befalling their people. But then the feelings that such themes arouse have become so commonplace that the examples from antiquity ought to serve us as consolation in our own troubles in our own land.[135]

Some fine work has been undertaken on this subject by specialists of French literature, such as Gillian Jondorf, who has explored the theme of political tragedy in the plays of Garnier.[136] What has received less attention, however, is the evocation of the theme of tragedy in the polemical literature of the period. An exploration of the use of tragedy in the corpus of works relating to Mary Queen of Scots and the situation facing Catholics in England is revealing of the way in which contemporaries rationalised the divided world in which they lived.

In *L'Histoire de la mort de Campion*, published in 1582, the final moments of Edmond Campion and his companions were described as the 'last act and catastrophe of their tragedy'.[137] It seems, however, that this sense of the tragic adopted a far more prominent emphasis in the Leaguer literature of the post–85 period, especially but not exclusively in the corpus of works relating to the 'English Inquisition'.[138] This inevitably raises the question of how far the readership or audiences of these texts would have understood frequent references to classical mythology such as the Minotaur,[139] or would have been able to grasp the relationship between literary and historical tragedy. Tragedy, whether as text or performance was largely the domain of the elite. It is likely, however, that there would have been different levels of understanding and awareness amongst other sections of society. The presence of this imagery in Catholic polemic does offer an extraordinarily important caution, however, to viewing the readership or audience as a monolithic entity. In otherwise straightforward polemical language the scattered presence of classical imagery that would have meant more to the elite and educated than to those on the margins of literacy, does indicate that authors had various layers of readership in mind when composing their works. In short, different rhetorical strategies often operated simultaneously, but were focused towards the same purpose.

Various examples of images drawn from classical, especially Greek, myths can be given. The multiple references to the Cyclops in Renaud de Beaune's *Oraison funèbre*, evoked the scattering of devoured human remains in the monster's cave, in order to compare it with Elizabeth's own barbarous treatment of Catholics in England.[140] That Odysseus was eventually triumphant over this one–eyed fiend made this an even more appropriate analogy.

Another comparison, mentioned in at least three texts, was that between the martyred Mary Queen of Scots and Iphigeneia, the daughter of Agamemnon, who had to be sacrificed if the King was to appease the gods in order to lead his allies into a war against Troy.[141] To be sure, a certain Christianisation did take place. The authors who mentioned the Iphigeneian comparison, also indicated that perhaps Mary would be better compared to the virginal St Agnes. That Iphigeneia was mentioned at all, however, suggests that it was meant to be taken seriously. When we examine the Iphigeneian comparison further, it is clear that it was not just a question of rhetorical garnish. There are two main versions of the Iphigeneian myth. In Euripides' *Iphigeneia in Aulis*, Iphigeneia went gloriously to her death as a human sacrifice, but only when she recognised that there was no opportunity for her to escape her fate.[142] At one point in the story, Iphigeneia even remarked that it was better to live ingloriously than to die gloriously.[143] The end of the play, however, in less than tragic convention, saw Artemis save Iphigeneia, substituting a kid in her place. This was clearly not the myth that the polemicists wished its readership and audience to relate to Mary Queen of Scots. The other version of this story, undoubtedly the myth being evoked, was Aeschylus' *Agamemnon*.[144] In this play, the King sacrificed Iphigeneia, but in so doing had made his wife, Clytemnestra, his enemy. While fighting for a period of ten years in Troy, his wife, who remained in Argos, took a lover named Aegisthus son of Thyestes. On Agamemnon's return, in revenge for the killing of her daughter, Clytemnestra killed Agamemnon. The relevance of this tragedy to the sacrifice of Mary Queen of Scots lay not only in Mary and Iphigeneia's innocence, but that their deaths would be avenged.

It does seem, however, that far more important than specific myths, which would have been understood fully by relatively few, was the general mentality that the language of tragedy evoked. In particular, the language is agonistic. Classical 'myths for the most part show men struggling towards some goal, in conflict with one another, or against some force of circumstance or destiny, which is often personified in a god'.[145] Their use against the progress of Protestant persecution was intended to highlight the great conflict against Satan, who acted through figures such as Elizabeth or William of Orange. Of course the adaptation of the Greek model for a Christian world held its own implications. While Mary's execution was tragic, through death she had won spiritual victory. Yet the use of the tragic to describe the evil way the world had turned since the advent of Protestantism was an effective motif. The contemporary world surpassed the Greek tragedies because it was real. For Greek drama, as one martyrologist reported, was simply 'fables and subjects chosen at leisure to move the spectators'.[146]

Mary Queen of Scots herself rationalised her predicament in terms of an unfolding piteous tragedy. Mary was extraordinarily self-conscious that she was being executed for her Catholicism, and that this was to be understood in tragic terms. This can be seen in the quotation in the opening paragraph of this chapter and in other letters, for instance that to the Duc de Guise also written on 23 November 1586, in which she recommended her servants to him saying that they were 'eye witnesses to this my last tragedy'.[147] The polemic published following her death was marked by this same understanding. In the 1587 edition of Orléans' *Advertissement*, for instance, the author inserted a small section on the execution of the Queen of Scots. In discussing Mary's death, he spoke of Elizabeth having 'finished the last act of one of the bloodiest of tragedies'.[148] But perhaps the most developed expression of the use of tragedy to present the contemporary reality of religious conflict, can be found in Richard Rowlands's impressive *Théâtre des cruautez*. In the prologue, Rowlands announced that he had composed his drama, his 'theatre' in order to represent the miserable tragedies practised by heretics in Europe since Luther's 'bloody gospel'.[149] In this theatre, Rowlands staged three tragedies, that of France, England and Flanders. Each tragedy was divided into numerous acts. The English tragedy began by describing Henry VIII's inability to control his sexual passions and compared Anne Boleyn to Helen of Troy, the 'cause of the loss of the country'.[150] The contagion spread, with a brief interlude in the time of Mary Tudor. Elizabeth was described as a 'wicked Jezebel','devouring her own children'.[151] But as William Cecil Lord Burghley noted, the rest of the book was only an 'induction' to the portrait of the Scottish Queen.[152] The execution of Mary Queen of Scots was the primary example of the malignance of Protestantism, and spoke directly to the situation in France. Rowlands described the progress of heresy in France in six acts, seeing the Edicts of Toleration as intermissions.[153] However, the next act of the unfolding drama, according to the League, was still being written.

The images of Mary Queen of Scots and England as radical propaganda

That the League was attempting to unite support for a militant crusade against Protestantism was in itself an act of opposition against the will of the King. But Leaguer literature relating to Mary's death and the English example went beyond advocating alternative courses of action, by incorporating criticisms of the King himself. Before Henri's rash decision to assassinate the brothers Guise in late December 1588, these criticisms remained far more implicit than explicit. Yet even these seemingly covert criticisms would have been far more readily identified and understood by contemporaries than by modern readers.

A number of texts urged the French King not to allow Mary's execution to go unpunished, emphasising Henri's own familial connection with the martyred Queen.[154] There were accusations circulating in rumour and sermon of Henri's complicity in her death. Henri's rapid resumption of diplomatic relations with England only a few months after the execution of Mary, meant that calls for action would adopt an increasingly critical dimension. Some works were republished up to two years after the events at Fotheringhay. It is with the knowledge that texts were read and heard in a world in which Mary had been executed and Henri had failed to take action, that we must view, for example, the publication of Pomponne de Bellièvre's *Harangue* to the English court. To modern eyes, much of Bellièvre's rhetoric appears unexceptional and diplomatic. One might have casually assumed that it was published to illustrate Henri's efforts to have Mary's sentence of execution commuted. Yet, to contemporaries, it would have appeared powerless, grovelling and effeminate. Consider, for instance, the following quotation, 'and I can assure you, Madame, that the King my master, your good brother and good friend, has no other aim in this than the good and interest which he has in common with your Majesty'.[155] The effect of Henri's hollow warnings to Elizabeth would have been equally damaging to his reputation, 'if some Catholic Princes would commit to a move against your kingdom, it will not be to save the Queen of Scotland, but will be for religion'.[156]

One pamphlet, published in no fewer than five editions, two in Paris, and one each in Poitiers, Rouen and Lyon, reported that James VI of Scotland had since 9 November 1587 declared war on Elizabeth and had seized the town of Berwick and burned ten or twelve places in England.[157] This was blatant misinformation. It is difficult to determine the motivations behind the publication of this text, mainly because we do not know precisely when it was published. But given the state of religious turmoil in France, it is likely that the work represented an attempt by the League to urge support in spirit not in substance for action in England in order to shore up both the alleged military effort of James VI, and, although unmentioned in the text, the Armada of Spain launched against England that year. In praising James VI's attempts to exact retribution for the execution of his mother as an outrage committed against Scotland,[158] this would have indirectly reflected on the inactivity of Henri III and his insensitivity, both to the memory of Mary and to public opinion.

A more explicit tone in Leaguer polemic and in the use of the English example to criticise Henri can be discerned from 1588, almost certainly after the Day of the Barricades in May. Nicolas Rolland's *Remonstrances très-humbles au Roy de France* included, amongst its various accusations against Henri III, a criticism of his financial improprieties.[159] Amongst these was a rebuke for Henri's handling of the 'dowry of the late Queen of Scotland, lately deceased'.[160] Undoubtedly this was a tougher engagement with what had previously been far more latent criticisms of the unseemly haste with which Henri had reincorporated Mary's dowry lands back into the fold of the crown, despite her desire stated in her last will and testament that the revenue should be used for several years to pay off her considerable debt. A year earlier, the publication of Henri's *Edict du Roy pour la vente et aliénation* had contained only a very indirect criticism of the King's attitude to Mary's finances.[161]

Alongside a popular distaste for Henri's financial mismanagement was distaste for his political dealings. Verstegan, for instance, described the state of France in 1588 as a 'kingdom of Machiavelli, a cabinet of mignons, a Nogaretan republic, an ant nest of Albigensian survivors,[162] a den of Gascon rats, of excitable effeminates, of women disguised as men'.[163] Perhaps the most prominent example of the more radical line adopted by Leaguer pamphleteers in this respect was the literature relating to one of the King's favourites, Jean Louis Nogaret de La Valette, Duc d'Epernon. Ostensibly, this followed the convention of blaming the King's advisors, rather than the King himself. Yet, in publishing Thomas Walsingham's *Histoire tragique de Pierre de Gaverston* no fewer than nine times, the League manipulated this convention in quite a radical way.[164] The text was given a new dedication to the Duc d'Epernon, and while not explicitly stated, this raised the comparison between Henri's relationship with his favourite, and that between Edward II and Piers Gaverston, a homosexual friendship that, according to Walsingham, was to lead, ultimately, to Edward's death.

While clearly increasingly radical and oppositional, Leaguer literature before December 1588 did not publicly advocate Henri's permanent removal from office. What is more, the Catholic League persisted in portraying itself as 'the sovereign remedy against heresy', operating under the commandment of the King.[165] Following the Blois murders, however, the situation was to change dramatically. Leaguer polemic became openly vitriolic and revolutionary against Henri III, or 'Henry de Valois' as he was thenceforth known. He was accused, amongst other things, of homosexuality, sodomy and sorcery. The subtle allegation of Henri's homosexual relationship with Epernon, became openly commented upon in editions such as *Discours aux françois sur l'admirable accident de la mort de Henry de Valois*.[166] In *Les Considerations sur le meurdre commis en la personne de feu Monsieur le Duc de Guyse*, published without any pretence of anonymity in Paris by Guillaume Bichon in 1589, the author accused Henri of Machiavellianism, a ruler who detested Catholics whom he called Spaniards and Leaguers.[167] Interest in Mary and England may have been partially superseded by interest in the martyrdom of the Guises. Nevertheless, the theme of England and of Mary Queen of Scots remained strong and was incorporated into this openly critical polemic, putting into print accusations that had been circulating in other forms of communication for two years. In one edition which took the form of a dialogue between a Catholic and *Politique*, which was published in Nantes and entitled the *Deux devis*, Jacques Le Bossu, a Doctor of the Sorbonne in Paris and ardent Leaguer, openly accused Henri of trying to reduce the French state to that which could be found in England.[168] Bossu's work stated openly in print what rumours circulating since 1587 had been suggesting – Elizabeth had signed the warrant for Mary's execution with the consent of the French King. This allegation was to find repeated expression, as in for instance *Les Considérations*, where the English Jezebel's hands were soiled with the blood of Catholic martyrs, including the Queen of Scots. Henri, though he made a public show to the contrary after the execution, had 'secret foreknowledge' of the affair.[169] Bossu cited as evidence of his complicity, that he had been 'so lacking in pity towards his family, that he has not granted a single article of what she has asked for in her last will. He saw to it that he himself appropriated her dowry.'[170]

The strong connection between Henri and Elizabeth was also mentioned in other works. Emphasised was Henri's attempts not just to maintain an alliance with Elizabeth, but to make her his strong friend. After all, he had even sent his brother, François Duc d'Anjou to negotiate a marriage with Elizabeth, 'or indeed to plot and make a secret league against the Catholics'.[171] In one edition, *La Trahison decouverte de Henry de Valoys*, the author even accused Henri of selling the town of Boulogne to Elizabeth and of receiving payment to wage war against the Catholics.[172]

Conclusion

How effective was this writing? In one respect, French Catholic writers did not have to embellish accounts of Mary's death – shock at Mary's execution was widespread and genuine. Mary was at this point by far the most elevated casualty of the Religious Wars. Elizabeth's long and genuine hesitation over taking the final step was a recognition that the destruction of Mary was a near unprecedented event; reigning monarchs had been done away with by their own peoples but scarcely, if ever, at the conclusion of a judicial process in another sovereign state.

Yet Henry, in the last resort, had done little beyond sending an embassy to point this out. Nothing could more eloquently demonstrate the qualities that had weakened the loyalties of so many Catholic subjects and prepared the triumph of the Catholic League. Henry was powerless, or worse. In the final instance, he preferred amity with the apostate regicide of England to other Catholic powers.

The martyrdom of Mary Queen of Scots was then, in a very real sense, a Leaguer cause. Not only was Mary tied to the leaders of the Catholic League by multiple connections of kinship and affinity, her destruction was the ultimate symbol of the unbridgeable gulf between Catholics and Protestants that the League clearly acknowledged, and over which Henry hesitated. For the League, and for much moderate French opinion, the death of Mary was the final poof that the friendship with Spain promised in the controversial Treaty of Joinville in 1585 was a surer protection for religion than Henry's fickle diplomacy. For him, therefore, the execution of Mary was an unmitigated disaster from which his reputation could scarcely recover, and this was no less the case because the polemical lessons were left largely implicit. No amount of official mourning could turn back a public opinion convinced that the faith required more ardent protectors. This was the true lesson of the multiple pamphlets celebrating the martyr Queen.

Conclusion

From politics to historical drama

The representation of Mary Queen of Scots in sixteenth–century French polemical literature evolved in several discrete stages. Initially, Mary was praised in a traditional courtly manner in dedications and prefaces that anticipated her marriage to the Dauphin François and the obvious dynastic advantages that would follow from such a union. However, the death of François II not long after he succeeded to the throne of France, brought a rapid end to French public interest in the Queen. When Mary returned to Scotland in 1561, the French presses fell silent. Given that Mary would eventually become such a towering symbol of the Leaguer cause, it is truly remarkable that the Catholic presses from the 1560s until around 1587 chose, for the most part, not to follow her turbulent career. This lack of interest was not just a consequence of a political consensus, which included hard line Catholics, that Elizabeth I should not be antagonised unnecessarily. Alliance with England was, after all, essential if France was to keep the menacing power of Spain at bay. Equally significant was the stark fact that Mary was by no means a natural Catholic hero. Indeed, if anything, Mary's adoption of a moderate religious tone in her management of Scotland, especially during the early 1560s, had begun to earn her the respect of those who favoured a moderate solution to France's religious crisis. The Huguenot portrait of Mary during the 1560s, following the example of editions placed into the French market by agents of the English government, remained restrained but positive, insulating Mary from the brutal criticisms it reserved for her Guise relations. During the later 1560s, however, Mary's notorious governance of Scotland and in particular her alleged complicity in the assassination of her husband, Henry Darnley, would put an end even to this meagre interest.

During the 1570s, in the wake of the massacre of St. Bartholomew's Day, the Huguenot barrage blackening the character of the Queen of Scots began. The Huguenots seized on Mary as a symbol of Catholic perfidy in works that highlighted the plight of Protestantism in France and appealed to the international Protestant community to come to their aid. While the Catholic press did respond to this onslaught against Mary, interest was short–lived. Even when, during the early 1580s, the persecution and suffering of Elizabethan Catholics became an ever more common theme in French polemic, there was seldom any mention of the Queen of Scots – who had, since 1568, languished in an English prison. Even Mary's involvement in sensational high–profile plots to depose Elizabeth and place herself on the throne of England and Scotland provoked little comment in France.

Mary's rehabilitation in French Catholic public opinion was achieved only with her martyrdom. The extraordinary response in print to the execution of Mary on 18 February 1587, on the orders of Elizabeth I, was only partially the consequence of the way in which she conducted herself during her final hours. Mary's execution also coincided with an exceptionally volatile political situation in France in which the author-ity of the King was becoming increasingly eroded by the Catholic League. The polemical response to Mary's execution interacted with the broader theme of the 'English example' and interfaced with all other media to produce a powerful rallying cry for the Catholic League's radical challenge to the weakened and discredited Henri III. Without the explosive environment in which news of Mary's execution was received, it is unlikely whether the French response to her death would have been so strong or so protracted. As it was, the polemic surround-ing the execution represented one fifth of all Catholic polemic over the two–year period 1587–8. It played a fundamental role in forging the popular enthusiasm with which the Day of the Barricades – and the ousting of the King from his own capital – would be greeted in May 1588.

Following 1588, the importance of Mary waned. The overwhelming popular anger at Henri's decision to assassinate the Duc de Guise and his brother the Cardinal de Lorraine at the meeting of the Estates at Blois on 23–24 December 1588, dramatically overtook the theme of Mary Queen of Scots. A number of works published in 1589 still made reference to the martyrdom of Mary, but such mentions were often small and deeply embedded in the discourse lamenting the fate of the brothers. The Guise family were the crusaders of militant Catholicism, the champions of the League and unambiguous martyrs of the Catholic cause. They were also the very direct victims of the despotism of Henri III.

In the 1590s, references to Mary could still be found in, for instance, reprinted editions of Louis d'Orléans' *Advertissement des catholiques anglois* which was published, along with a second *Advertissement*, in Lyon, Toulouse and Paris.[1] Orléans work became staple reading for the League and its supporters. In another text, the *Responce à l'injuste et sanguinaire edict d'Elizabeth*, the tyrant Elizabeth was once again accused of interfering in Scotland as in France, and of bringing about the ruin of Mary Queen of Scots.[2] But public interest in the Queen was hardly considerable after 1589.

By 1600, the image of the martyred Mary had finally completed its transformation from a hot political issue to the stuff of history. As the sixteenth century gave way to the seventeenth, the figure of Mary Queen of Scots was, at various times, to hold a renewed fascination for the French public as a dramatic character. In particular, the fate of the Queen of Scots was, fittingly, to form the basis of tragedies such as Montchrestien's *L'Escossoise/La Reine d'Escosse* (1601), Charles Regnault's *Marie Stuard* (1637), and Boursault's *Marie Stuard* (1691).[3] The enduring portrait of Mary as a tragic Catholic figure was to be the legacy of her own performance on the scaffold at Fotheringhay.

Appendix 1: House of Guise: Lines of Guise, Mayenne and Aumale

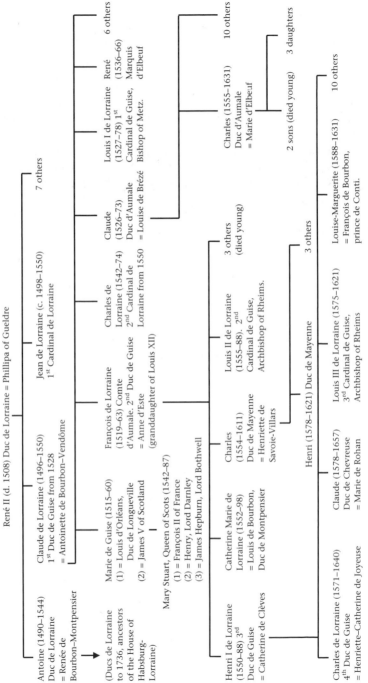

René II (d. 1508) Duc de Lorraine = Phillipa of Gueldre

Antoine (1490–1544)
Duc de Lorraine
= Renée de
Bourbon–Montpensier

Claude de Lorraine (1496–1550)
1st Duc de Guise from 1528
= Antoinette de Bourbon–Vendôme

Jean de Lorraine (c. 1498–1550)
1st Cardinal de Lorraine

7 others

Marie de Guise (1515–60)
(1) = Louis d'Orléans,
Duc de Longueville
(2) = James V of Scotland

François de Lorraine
(1519–63) Comte
d'Aumale. 2nd Duc de Guise
= Anne d'Este
(granddaughter of Louis XII)

Charles de
Lorraine (1542–74)
2nd Cardinal de
Lorraine from 1550

Claude
(1526–73)
Duc d'Aumale
= Louise de Brézé

Louis I de Lorraine
(1527–78) 1st
Cardinal de Guise,
Bishop of Metz.

René
(1536–66)
Marquis
d'Elbeuf

6 others

(Ducs de Lorraine
to 1736, ancestors
of the House of
Habsburg-
Lorraine)

Mary Stuart, Queen of Scots (1542–87)
(1) = François II of France
(2) = Henry, Lord Darnley
(3) = James Hepburn, Lord Bothwell

Charles
(1554–1611)
Duc de Mayenne
= Henriette de
Savoie-Villars

Louis II de Lorraine
(1555–88). 2nd
Cardinal de Guise,
Archbishop of Rheims.

3 others
(died young)

Charles (1555–1631)
Duc d'Aumale
= Marie d'Elbeuf

10 others

2 sons (died young)

3 daughters

Henri I de Lorraine
(1550–88) 3rd
Duc de Guise
= Catherine de Clèves

Catherine Marie de
Lorraine (1552–98)
= Louis de Bourbon,
Duc de Montpensier

Henri (1578–1621) Duc de Mayenne

3 others

Louise-Marguerite (1588–1631)
= François de Bourbon,
prince de Conti.

10 others

Charles de Lorraine (1571–1640)
4th Duc de Guise
= Henriette–Catherine de Joyeuse

Claude (1578–1657)
Duc de Chevreuse
= Marie de Rohan

Louis III de Lorraine (1575–1621)
3rd Cardinal de Guise,
Archbishop of Rheims

Adapted from *Encyclopaedia Britannica* (Chicago, 1993), v. 5, p. 559.

Notes and References

Introduction

1. On the Catholic response to the Reformation in Germany, see Richard A. Crofts, 'Printing, Reform, and the Catholic Reformation in Germany (1521–45)', in *SCJ*, xvi/3 (1985), pp. 369–81.
2. See for instance J.M.H. Salmon, *Society in Crisis: France in the Sixteenth Century* (London, 1975) and Nicola Sutherland, *The French Secretaries of State in the Age of Catherine de Medici* (London, 1962), *The Massacre of St. Bartholomew's Day and the European Conflict* (London, 1973), *The Huguenot Struggle for Recognition* (London, 1980) and *Henri IV and the Politics of Religion, 1572–96* (Bristol, 2002).
3. Jürgen Habermas, *The Structural Transformation of the Public Sphere* (Cambridge, 2003). This seminal work was first published in German in 1962. It was first translated into French in 1978 and then into English only in 1989. Useful critiques of Habermas and his influence on neo-revisionist interpretations of eighteenth–century political culture include Harvey Chisick, 'Public Opinion and Political Culture in France during the second half of the eighteenth century' in *EHR*, cxvii, 470 (2002), pp. 48–76, Jon Cowans, 'Habermas and French History: The Public Sphere and the Problem of Legitimacy', in *French History*, vol. 13, no. 2. (1999), pp. 134–160 and Jeremy Popkin, 'The Concept of Public Opinion in the Historiography of the French Revolution: A Critique', in *Storia della Storiograpfia*, 20 (1991), pp. 77–92.
4. Habermas, *Structural Transformation*, ch iii, sections 8 & 9.
5. Ibid., p. 30.
6. Ibid., p. 54.
7. See Keith Michael Baker, 'Politics and Public Opinion under the Old Regime: Some Reflections' in Jack Censer and Jeremy Popkin (eds.), *Press and Pre–Revolutionary France* (Berkeley and Los Angeles, 1997), p. 246, cited in Chisick, 'Public Opinion', p. 54.
8. Luc Racaut, *Hatred in Print. Catholic Propaganda and Protestant Identity during the French Wars of Religion* (Aldershot, 2002), p. 49.
9. See Yves–Marie Bercé, *Fête et révolte: des mentalités populaires du XVIe au XVIIe siècle* ([Paris], 1976).
10. On sermons see Larissa Taylor (ed.), *Preachers and People in the Reformations and Early Modern Period* (Leiden, 2001) and *Soldiers of Christ. Catholic Preaching in Late Medieval and Reformation France* (New York, 1992). See also Barbara Diefendorf, *Beneath the Cross. Catholics and Huguenots in sixteenth–century Paris* (Oxford, 1991). On the German woodcut see Robert Scribner, *For the Sake of Simple Folk: Popular Propaganda for the German Reformation* (Oxford, 1981, 1994). On English broadsides see Tessa Watt, *Cheap Print and Popular Piety, 1550–1640* (Cambridge, 1991). On song, see Andrew Pettegree, *Huguenot Voices: The Book and the Communication Process during the Protestant Reformation* (Greenville, November 1999).

11. Information from the St Andrews French Vernacular Book Project based on a sample of books published between 1540 and 1559 suggests that around 10 per cent of books, which we know to have existed from reliable bibliographical references, have no surviving copy in any public library.
12. R. A. Houston, *Literacy in Early Modern Europe: Culture and Education 1500–1800* (London, 1988).
13. Peter Matheson, *The Rhetoric of the Reformation* (Edinburgh, 1998), p. 27.
14. One example of the negative attitude towards this literature can be found in Henri Hauser, *Les Sources de l'histoire de France: XVI siècle, 1494–1610* (Paris, 1906–15, reprinted Neudeln, 1967), t. II, pt. 1, p. 22.
15. Barbara Diefendorf, *Beneath the Cross*, Wylie G. Sypher, 'Faisant ce qu'il leur vient a plaisir: The Image of Protestantism in French Catholic polemic on the eve of the Religious Wars', *SCJ*, 9/2 (1980), pp. 59–84; Luc Racaut, *Hatred in Print. Catholic Propaganda and Protestant Identity during the French Wars of Religion* (Aldershot, 2002).
16. Georges Ascoli, *La Grande-Bretagne devant l'Opinion française depuis la Guerre de Cent Ans jusqu'à la fin du XVIe siècle* (Paris, 1927).
17. James E. Phillips, *Images of a Queen. Mary Stuart in Sixteenth–Century Literature* (Berkeley & Los Angeles, 1964).
18. *Short Title Catalogue of Books Printed in England, Scotland and Ireland, and of English Books Printed Abroad, 1475–1640*, ed. A. W. Pollard and G. R. Redgrave (2nd edition, 3 vols., Oxford, 1976–91).
19. The *Répertoire bibliographique des livres imprimés en France au seizième siècle* (32 vols., Baden-Baden, 1958–80) surveys printing on a town by town basis.
20. John Scott, *A Bibliography of Works Relating to Mary Queen of Scots, 1544–1700* (Edinburgh, 1896).
21. *Collection des Manuscrits, Livres, Estampes et Objets d'Art relatifs à Marie Stuart, Reine de France et d'Ecosse* (Paris, 1931).
22. Samuel T. Tannenbaum & Dorothy R. Tannenbaum, *Marie Stuart, Queen of Scots. A Concise Bibliography* (3 vols., New York, 1944).
23. For an introduction to the work of the St Andrews French Vernacular Book Project, see Andrew Pettegree, 'The Sixteenth–Century French Religious Book Project', in A. Pettegree, P. Nelles & P. Conner (eds.), *The Sixteenth–Century French Religious Book* (Aldershot, 2001), pp. 1–17.
24. On the advantages of statistical bibliography, see Jean-Pierre V. M. Hérubel, 'Historical Bibliometrics: Its Purpose and Significance to the History of Disciplines', *Libraries & Culture*, vol. 34, no. 4 (Texas, 1999).
25. This bibliography is contained in the second volume of my thesis, 'Mary Queen of Scots in the Polemical Literature of the French Wars of Religion' (University of St Andrews, 2001).
26. A survey from the files of FVB indicates that for a sample period 1540–59, La Bibliothèque Nationale de France (BNF) holds 30 per cent of all items. A further 16 per cent of items not in the BNF are held in other Paris libraries, which leaves a total of around 50 per cent of all books which are not available in any Paris library. Of these, 23 per cent can be found in a French library outside the capital. However, a full 31 per cent survive solely in a copy outside France.
27. *Apologie contre certaines calomnies mises sus, à la desfaveur & desavantage de l'estat des affaires de ce royaume* (Paris, Pierre Leber, 1562).

1   Mary Queen of Scots: A French Life

1. The exact date of the *entrée* into Angers is not certain. Two letters, one written by the Sieur de Cabassolle du Réal and a second by M. de La Porte, a royal counsellor, present contradictory statements. Both are addressed to the council of Angers and dated 14 September 1548. The first, MS. AAC AA4 (6) indicated that 'la petite reine sera dans quatre ou cinq jours à Angers'. The second, MS. AAC AA4 (4) written by M. de La Porte from Nantes, conveyed information from the governor of Bretagne, M. d'Etampes, reporting that 'elle partira de ceste ville samedi prochain et s'en ira séjourner trois ou quatre jours Ancenis, ainsi on estime qu'elle pourra estre Angiers dedans six ou sept jours'. It is likely that Mary arrived in Angers between 18–21 September 1548.
2. MS. AAC BB24 fol. 207r–v. An ordinance stated that those citizens who refused to display their tapestries were to be fined or placed in prison 'en cas de deffaut'.
3. MS. AAC BB24 fol. 207r.
4. MS. AAC BB24 fol. 205v. Guillaume Lerat was mayor of Angers from 1546–8.
5. MS. AAC BB24 fol. 205v.
6. MS. AAC BB24 fol. 207r.
7. MS. AAC AA4 (3) is a contemporary copy of the original letter sent by Henri II in Montcallier to Monseigneur le duc d'Estampes governor and lieutenant general in Bretagne, dated 25 August 1548.
8. Perhaps the most elaborate sixteenth-century royal *entrée* was that of Henri II into Rouen in 1550, see Michael Wintroub, 'Civilizing the Savage and Making a King: The Royal Entry Festival of Henri II (Rouen, 1550)', in *SCJ* vol. xxix/2 (1998), pp. 465–94.
9. James V was the son of Margaret Tudor, daughter of Henry VII of England.
10. MS. BNF fonds français 17330, 17888, 17889 and 17890; William M. Bryce, 'Mary Stuart's Voyage to France in 1548,' in *EHR* xxii (1907), p. 43. Bryce does not provide folio numbers for these large manuscripts. The name of the suitable marriage partner is not stated.
11. MS. BNF fonds français 20977 f. 144, given in Bryce, 'Mary Stuart's Voyage', p. 43.
12. On the evolution of the use of the phrase 'Rough Wooing', see Marcus Merriman, *The Rough Wooings. Mary Queen of Scots 1542–51* (East Linton, 2000), pp. 7–10.
13. Mary-Noëlle Badouin-Matuszek, 'Henri II et les Expéditions françaises en Écosse', in *Bibliothèque de l'École Des Chartres* 145 (1987), pp. 339–98.
14. Ibid., p. 349. See appendix I for a genealogical tree of the house of Guise.
15. MS. EAL. Balcarres Papers, vol. iii. 18, given in Bryce, 'Mary Stuart's Voyage', p. 44.
16. M.H. Merrimann estimates that this figure may well be too low, see his 'Mary, Queen of France,' in Michael Lynch (ed.), *Mary Stewart. Queen in Three Kingdoms* (Oxford, 1988), p. 39. Badouin–Matuszek, 'Henri II et les Expéditions françaises en Écosse', p. 366 suggests that this figure was spent for 1549 alone.
17. Gordon Donaldson, *James V–James VII* (Edinburgh, 1965, 1994), p. 79.
18. *CSP Spanish, Edward VI*, p. 334, cited in Badouin–Matuszek, 'Henri II et les Éxpeditions françaises en Écosse', p. 334.

19. That Brest was the intended landing site can be confirmed by a letter written by Henri II to Monseigneur le duc d'Estampes from Tourraine dated 21 July 1548, MS. AAC AA4 (2). The details of this voyage from Scotland to France have been traced in minute detail by Bryce, who follows a series of letters which the sieur de Brézé addressed to Marie de Guise between 31 July and 18 August 1548, in 'Mary Stuart's Voyage to France in 1548', pp. 43–50. Portions of the Sieur de Brézé's letters to Marie de Guise can be found reprinted in Bryce, and in Jane T. Stoddart, *The Girlhood of Mary Queen of Scots from her landing in France in August 1548 to her departure from France in August 1561* (London, [1908]).

20. The letters written variously between Henri II, his governor and lieutenant in Bretagne the Duc d'Etampes, La Porte and the mayor and council of Angers, are preserved in the collection MS. AAC AA4. The council minutes from circa 12 September 1548 can be found in MS. AAC BB24 fol. 204v–221r. Short but accurate transcriptions of the letters only can be found in M. Céléstin Port, *Inventaire Analytique des Archives Anciennes de la Maire d'Angers* (Paris & Angers, 1861).

21. Sources exist for at least one other *entrée*, at Nantes, which Mary reached just before her arrival in Angers. Mary was received with similar celebrations. The accounts for this *entrée* were compiled by one 'Jullien Poullain, receveur et miseur des deniers communs' and can be found in MS. NAC AA31. For a partial transcription, see S. de la Nicollière–Teijeiro (ed.), *Inventaire Sommaire des Archives Communales antérieures à 1790. Ville de Nantes* (Nantes, 1888), p. 26.

22. Henri II 'A Noz trèschere et bien amez les maire eschevins bourgeois mamans et habitans de nostre bonne ville d'angiers', from Mascon 23 July 1548, MS. AAC AA4 (1).

23. MS. AAC BB24 fols. 205v–206r.

24. MS. AAC BB24 fol. 205v. Unfortunately the contents of this speech have not survived. Following her reception in Angers, Mary probably spent around six days in the area, as the next recorded mention of her voyage towards Saint–Germain–en–Laye is her arrival in Fontrevaux by the port de Monsoreau on Saturday 29 September 1548 where she was taken to 'la chappel blanche', MS. AAD G.1473. This short note that Mary passed through Fontevraux is contained in an accounts book for the church of the Sainte Croix at Monsoreau 1542–53.

25. *C'est la deduction du Sumptueux ordre plaisantz spectacles et magnifiques theatres, dresées et exhibes par les citoyens de Rouen ville metropolitaine du Pays de Normandie* ([Rouen], on les vend à Rouen par Robert Le Hay Robert & Jean du Gord, 1551).

26. Wintroub, 'Civilising the Savage', pp. 465–94. See also Merriman, 'Mary, Queen of France', pp. 37–40.

27. Merriman, 'Mary, Queen of France', p. 40.

28. The presence of Marie de Guise is noted in *C'est la deduction du Sumptueux ordre plaisantz spectacles et magnifiques theatres, dresees et exhibes par les citoyens de Rouen ville metropolitaine du Pays de Normandie* ([Rouen], on les vend à Rouen par Robert Le Hay Robert & Jean du Gord, 1551), B2v. Given that one of the reasons that Marie de Guise had come from Scotland was to see her daughter, we might assume the presence of Mary Stuart during

this ceremony. Surprisingly however, no indication exists in the account of the *entrée*.

29. Henri II succeeded his father, François I, on 31 March 1547. On the Parisian *entrée*, see Lawrence M. Bryant, *The King and the City in the Parisian Royal Entry Ceremony: Politics, Ritual, and Art in the Renaissance* (Geneva, 1986).

30. Mary's French career has been examined in three main studies. The finest of these is Jane. T. Stoddart's *The Girlhood of Mary Queen of Scots*. The other studies are Alphonse de Ruble, *La Premiere Jeunesse de Marie Stuart* (Paris, 1891) and Joseph Stevenson, *Mary Stuart: A Narrative of the First Eighteen Years of Her Life* (Edinburgh, 1886).

31. Henri II to M. de Humyeres, from Thurin on 24 August 1548, MS BNF fonds français 3134 fol. 12 cited in Georges Guiffrey (ed.), *Lettres inédites de Diane de Poytiers* (Geneva, 1970 a facsimile of the original Paris edition of 1886), pp. 33–4, n. 1.

32. Diane de Poitiers to Mons. de Humyeres, from Tarare on 3 October [1548], in Guiffrey (ed.), *Lettres inédites de Diane de Poytiers*, p. 35. Elizabeth, called 'Ysabal' by Poitiers, was born on 13 April 1545 and married Philip II of Spain on 22 June 1559, aged fourteen.

33. Guiffrey (ed.), *Lettres inédites de Diane de Poytiers*, p. 35. This affection is reported in a number of sources, such as MS. EAL Balcarres Papers iii. 19 where Montmorency remarked when writing to Marie de Guise on 30 March 1549, 'I will assure you that the Dauphin pays her little attentions, and is enamoured of her, from which it is easy to judge that God gave them birth the one for the other'. Cited and translated in Bryce, 'Mary Stuart's Voyage to France', pp. 43–50.

34. MS. BL Add.ch.13955, as cited in Stoddart, *The Girlhood of Mary Queen of Scots*, p. 39.

35. Ibid.

36. Alphonse de Ruble, *La Premiere Jeunesse*, pp. 37–8 and pp. 286–90.

37. MS. BNF fonds français 5898. An inventory drawn up in 1561 by François du Jardin, Pierre Redon and Henry de Baux following the death of François II. It catalogues and estimates the value of Mary's precious stones.

38. The word Marie is of Icelandic origin, meaning virgin or maid. It was an interesting touch that Mary's Maries were all called Mary. Antonia Fraser, *Mary Queen of Scots* (London, 1969), p. 48.

39. Jenny Wormald, *Mary Stuart. A Study in Failure* (London, 1988), pp. 78–9. Indications of rivalries and tensions between Mary's entourage and the royal nursery staff are evident from 1548, see Diane de Poitiers to Mons de Humieres from Chavaigne, 15 October [1548] in Guiffrey (ed.), *Lettres inédites de Diane de Poytiers*, p. 42, n. 2 and Henri II to an unknown recipient, from St André, 17 October 1548, ibid.

40. Frederic J. Baumgartner, *Henry II. King of France 1547–59* (Durham and London, 1988), pp. 95–6.

41. Alphonse de Ruble, *La Premiere Jeunesse*, p. 73.

42. Bryce, 'Mary Stuart's Voyage to France', p. 50.

43. Réné de Bouillé, *Histoire des Ducs de Guise* (Paris, 1850), t. I, p. 206.

44. Cited in Ruble, *Le Premier Jeunesse*, p. 31. Ruble did not identify his source.

45. Alexander Labanoff (ed.), *Lettres, Instructions et Mémoires de Marie Stuart*,

Reine d'Écosse; Publiés sur les originaux et les manuscrits du State Paper Office de Londres et des principales archives et Bibliothèques de l'Europe (London, 1844), t. I, p. 9.

46. Note by Etienne Vaucheret, in his edition of Pierre de Bourdeille (Brantôme), *Recueil des Dames* ([Paris], 1991), pp. 1099–102. On Brantôme, see also Ludovic Lalanne, *Brantôme sa vie et ses Écrits* (Paris, 1896).

47. Brantôme, *Recueil des Dames*, t. iii, p. 74.

48. Ibid., p. 72.

49. Ibid., pp. 72–3.

50. Ibid., p. 72.

51. Ibid., p. 73.

52. Fraser, *Mary Queen of Scots*, p. 54.

53. Estienne Perlin, *Description des royaumes d'Angleterre et d'Escosse* (Paris, François Trepeau, 1558), D7v.

54. M.I. Heyns, *Le Miroir du Monde, reduict premièrement en rithme Brabançonne* (Antwerp, Christopher Plantin pour P. Galle, 1579), B1v. Scots Gaelic was often mistaken for 'Irlandois', see Nicolas d'Arfeville, *Navigation du Roy d'Escosse Iaques Cinquiesme du nom, autour de son Royaume* (Paris, Gilles Beys, 1583), A3v.

55. Sebastian Münster, *Cosmographie*, ed. François de Belleforest (Paris, Michel Sonnius, 1575), e3v, columns 101–2.

56. Jenny Wormald, *Mary Queen of Scots*, p. 86.

57. The secret contract can be found in MS. AN. Trésor des Chartres. Series J. carton 679 no. 59, signed by Mary. The formal wedding contract, dated 19 April 1558, is contained in MS. AN. Tr. des Ch. J. 680, no. 63. Both these documents are summarised by Jean Baptiste Teulet, *Inventaire Chronologique des documents relatifs à l'histoire d'Écosse conservés aux archives du royaume à Paris [AN], suivi d'une indication sommaire des manuscrits de la Bibliothèque Royale [BNF]* (Edinburgh, 1839), pp. 99–103.

58. For the marriage contract between Mary Tudor and the future Philip II, see David Loades, *The Reign of Mary Tudor* (London, 1979), pp. 121–2.

59. *Acts of the Parliaments of Scotland* (12 vols, 1814–75), v. ii, pp. 506–7. The *Parlement* of Paris registered the reciprocal act on 8 July 1558, see Alexandre Teulet, *Relations*, i. pp. 312–17.

60. C. Read, *Mr. Secretary Cecil and Queen Elizabeth* (London, 1955), p. 125.

61. MS. AN. K. 1385, B.11, 182, 24 March 1560, a manifesto written by Elizabeth criticising the pretensions of the Queen of Scotland to the crown of England. The manifesto argued that behind these pretensions lay the ambitious designs of the house of Guise.

62. *Acts of the Parliaments of Scotland*, v. II, 499–500, cited in Gordon Donaldson, *James V–James VII* (Edinburgh, 1965, 1994), p. 87.

63. Jenny Wormald, *Mary Queen of Scots*, p. 85.

64. Ibid., p. 83; see also Marie-Noëlle Baudouin–Matuszek, 'Un ambassadeur en Ecosse au XVIe siècle: Henri Clutin d'Oisel', in *Revue Historique* v. CCLXXXI (1989), pp. 98–9.

65. On the issue of transient motivations in the collaboration of the Scots with the English garrisons, see Gordon Donaldson, *Scotland's History. Approaches and Reflections*, ed. James Kirk (Edinburgh, 1995), see in particular chapter 5, 'Archives and the Historian', pp. 53–64.

66. In a fine recent study, Stuart Carroll has explored the logistical problems of raising and supporting an army from Normandy, the French base of operations for the conflict in Scotland, *Noble Power during the French Wars of Religion. The Guise Affinity and the Catholic Cause in Normandy* (Cambridge, 1998), pp. 96–7.
67. Jenny Wormald, *Mary Stuart*, p. 103.
68. Elizabeth Bonner, 'Scotland's Auld Alliance with France, 1295–1560' in *History* vol. 84 (1999), p. 29.
69. Louis Paris (ed.) *Négociations, lettres et pièces diverses relatives au règne de François II tirées du portefeuille de Sébastien de L'Aubespine évêque de Limoges* (Paris, 1841), pp. 750–4.
70. Brantôme, *Recueil des Dames*, p. 78.
71. Reported in a letter from Cardinal de Sainte-Croix, Papal nuncio in France, 'La regina di Scotia un giorno gli disse che non sarrebe mai altro che figlia di "un mercante". Cited in Adolphe Chéruel, *Marie Stuart et Catherine de Médicis. Étude historique sur les relations de la France et de l'Écosse dans la second moitié du XVIe siècle* (Geneva, 1975, a reprint of the original Paris edition of 1858), p. 17. Chéruel does not state his source. In a manuscript held in the Bibliothèque de Reims, Lacourt also reports Mary as having called Catherine a 'marchande florentine'. An extract is given in Louis Paris (ed.) *Négociations, lettres et pièces diverses relatives au règne de François II tirées du portefeuille de Sébastien de L'Aubespine évêque de Limoges* (Paris, 1841), pp. 755–8.
72. Brantôme, *Recueil des Dames*, p. 82.
73. 'Officiers domestiques de la Reine d'Escosse Mary Stuart du 1er Janvier 1548 (1549) jusques au 31 Décembre 1553' original on parchment MS. BNF fonds français 11207, fol. 128. A transcription is provided by Ruble, *La Premiere Jeunesse*, pp. 281–2.
74. The household list for this period has been transcribed without citing the location of the original source, in Paris (ed.), *Négociations, lettres et pièces diverses*, pp. 744–50. Of particular note on the 1560 list is the presence of no less a figure than Auguste de Thou, Mary's *solliciteur général.*
75. For the *état* of 1566 see Teulet, *Rélations*, t. ii, pp. 268–81; For the 1573 *état* see MS. The Honourable Society of the Inner Temple, London, Misc. 41, no. 90. A transcription of the majority of this list, excluding the list of pensioners, can be found in Andrew Lang, 'The Household of Mary Queen of Scots in 1573', in *SHR* ii, no. 8 (July 1905), pp. 345–55. Note, however, the new classmark for the manuscript.
76. Various spellings include Peguillen, Puyguillen, Pinguillon and Peguillon.
77. Wormald, *Mary Stuart*, p. 119.
78. Andrew Lang, 'The Household of Mary Queen of Scots in 1573', p. 347.
79. Ibid., p. 348.
80. On Benoist, see Emile Pasquier, *Un Curé de Paris pendant les Guerres de Religion, Réné Benoist Le Pape des Halles (1521–1608). Étude Historique et Bibliographique* (Paris & Angers, 1913). Pasquier pays scarce attention to Benoist's time in Edinburgh.
81. In 1577, Nicolas Winzet became abbot of the Schottenkloster at Regensburg and was closely linked with John Leslie. See J.H. Burns, *The True Law of Kingship. Concepts of Monarchy in Early-Modern Scotland* (Oxford, 1996), p. 211.
82. John Durkan, 'The Library of Mary, Queen of Scots', in Michael Lynch (ed.),

Mary Stewart, Queen in Three Kingdoms (Oxford, 1988), pp. 71–4. Durkan does not cite any sources to justify his statement.

83. On the output of the Scottish presses, see H. Aldis (ed.), *A List of Scottish Books Printed in Scotland before 1700 including those printed furth of the Realm for Scottish Booksellers* (Edinburgh, 1904, reprinted in 1970), and A.W. Pollard & G.R. Redgrave (eds.), *A Short Title catalogue of books printed in England, Scotland & Ireland and of English books printed abroad, 1475–1640* (first edition London, 1926, Oxford, 1986).

84. Julian Sharman, *The Library of Mary Queen of Scots* (London, 1889). In her will, Mary left her library to the University of St Andrews. The books never reached their intended destination.

85. This may have been the edition translated by Charles Fontaine, *Les XXI épistres d'Ovide. Les dix premières sont traduites par Charles Fontaine* (Lyon, Jean de Tournes, 1573).

86. This most likely refers to Guillaume Aubert's *Élégie sur le trespas de feu Joachim du Bellay* (Paris, Federic Morel, 1560).

87. This probably refers to Pierre de Ronsard's, *Le Premier [–troisième] livre du Recueil des nouvelles poésies* (Paris, Guillaume Buon, 1564).

88. Pierre de Ronsard, *Discours des miseres de ce temps* (Paris, Guillaume Buon, 1562, 1563 & 1572).

89. This work is difficult to identify from this title. Possible contenders are: [Jacques Grévin], *Response aux calomnies contenues aux discours et suyte du discours sur les misères de ce temps, faits par messire Pierre Ronsard, jadis poëte et maintenant prebstre, la première par A. Zamariel, les deux aultres par B. de Mont-Dieu, où est aussi contenue la métamorphose dudict Ronsard en prebstre* (s.l., 1563), [Florent Chrestien and Jacques Grévin], *Seconde response de F. de La Baronie (Florent Chrestien) à Messire Pierre de Ronsard prestre gentilhomme Vandomois, evesque futur. Plus le Temple de Ronsard où la légende de sa vie est briefvement descrite* ([Orléans], 1563, 1564), or [Florent Chrestien], *Apologie ou deffense d'un homme chrestien (Florent Chrestien) pour imposer silence aux sottes répréhensions de M. Pierre Ronsard, soy disant non seulement poète, mais aussi maistre des poétastres* (s.l., 1563 & 1564).

90. Noted in Claude Binet, *Vie de Ronsard*, cited without page reference in Pierre de Nolhac (ed.), *Ronsard et son Temps* (Paris, 1925).

91. Letter from Thomas Randolph noted in P. Fr. Tytler, *Histoire. d'Écosse*, t. vi, p. 269, cited by Chéruel, *Marie Stuart et Catherine de Médicis*, p. 31, n. 1.

92. Chéruel, *Marie Stuart et Catherine de Médicis*, p. 32.

93. MS. BNF Saint-Germain-Harlay 218, t. I, fol. 63; Chéruel, *Marie Stuart et Catherine de Médicis*, p. 51.

94. MS. AN K. 96, cited in Chéruel, *Marie Stuart et Catherine de Médicis*, p. 57.

95. Ibid.

96. 'Mémoires remis au roi par La Châtre . . .' dated April 1575, reprinted in Chéruel, *Marie Stuart et Catherine de Médici*, pp. 178–88.

97. Mark Greengrass, 'Mary Queen Dowager of France', in Michael Lynch (ed.), *Mary Stewart Queen in Three Kingdoms* (Oxford, 1988), p. 183.

98. Carroll, *Noble Power*, p. 192.

99. This paragraph is based directly on Greengrass, 'Mary, Dowager Queen', pp. 183–4.

100. Ibid., p. 176.

101. Mary Stuart to M. de Mauvissière, 31 March 1586, in Labanoff (ed.), *Lettres*, t. vi, pp. 267–9.
102. Greengrass, 'Mary, Dowager Queen of France', p. 171.
103. On the highly advanced Elizabethan intelligence services see Alison Plowden, *The Elizabethan Secret Service* (Exeter, 1991). Her study, lamentably, fails to footnote her sources.
104. MS. AN J680 no. 63, cited in Jean-Marc Rogier, 'Marie Stuart et Bar-sur-Aube: Les Provisions de Nicolas Bégat (1er août 1586),' in *La vie en Champagne*, no. 267 (juillet 1977), pp. 11–12.
105. Ibid. Eleonor of Austria was sister in law to Charles V, widow of Emmanuel King of Portugal, and subsequently second wife to Francis I. At the death of Francis, Eleonor went to Flanders and then on to Spain where she died on 18 February 1558.
106. MS. BNF fonds français 3335, fols. 74–93.
107. MS. BNF Dupuy 722, fol. 143, cited by Greengrass, 'Mary Dowager Queen of France', p. 173.
108. See, for instance, Mary's declaration on the response made to her chancellor Du Vergier, dated from Sheffield 29 April 1574, where she responded to the pleas of her tenants in Poitou, 'lesquels à tous périls et fortune, mesmes de guerres et troubles, il me semble que je ne suis tenue fayre aucun rabais aux fermiers', in Labanoff (ed.), *Lettres*, t. iv, p. 138.
109. MS. fonds français 5944 fol. 80v, *Acte d'opposition de Marie Stuart, reine d'Écosse, à l'octroi fait au duc d'Alençon du duché de Tourain, pour supplement d'apanage*, undated.
110. *CSP Scot.*, ii. 935 [1582]; cited in Greengrass, 'Mary, Dowager Queen of France', p. 179.
111. Mary Stuart to James Beaton, from Sheffield, 4 September 1574, in Labanoff (ed.), *Lettres* iv, p. 218.
112. Mary Stuart, *Le Testament et derniers propos de la Royne d'Escosse avant son supplice* (Paris, Pierre Marin, 1589), A4v–B1r.
113. Mary to M. de Mauvissiere, from Tutbury 6 February 1585, in Labanoff (ed.), *Lettres*, vi, p. 93.
114. Greengrass, 'Mary, Dowager Queen of France', pp. 180–1. The loan from Arundel was repaid by Philip II following Mary's death.
115. 'Parties deues par le Roy à la deffuncte Royne d'Escosse douairiere de France', in Teulet (ed.), *Relations*, iv, pp. 205–6, cited in Greengrass, 'Mary, Dowager Queen of France', p. 180.
116. MS. AN Y3129 (Registres des insinuations) fol. 323 (12 October 1581), a grant of a pension to George Douglas. Greengrass, 'Mary, Dowager Queen of France', p. 172.
117. Also spelled as Beatoun or Bethune.
118. Declaration of Mary Queen of Scots to the response made to her chancellor the Sieur du Vergier, from Sheffield 29 April 1574, Labanoff (ed.), *Lettres*, iv, pp. 143–4.
119. François de L'Aubespine replaced Yves Rieray on his death, see MS. BNF fonds français 5285, fol. 105. Act of Mary Stuart, undated.
120. This paragraph is based directly on Greengrass, 'Mary, Dowager Queen of France', p. 176.

121. Ibid., p. 177.
122. Mary Stuart to James Beaton, 4 September [1574] in Labanoff (ed.), *Lettres*, iv, pp. 216–17.
123. Greengrass, 'Mary Dowager Queen of France', p. 178.
124. Ibid., p. 177.
125. For instance, *Histoire véritable de la conspiration de Guillaume Parry* (La Rochelle, Pierre Haultin, 1585), passim.
126. DNB entry for Thomas Morgan, died c. 1606.
127. I am grateful to Dr Julian Goodare (University of Edinburgh) who is currently working on an edition of *Chalmers's Dictionary of Scots Law (1566)* for the Stair Society, for generously providing additional biographical information on David Chalmers. His information supports my own suspicions as to Chalmers's role as a double agent.
128. Mary Stuart provided a pension annually for a certain number of youths, while in 1569 James Beaton, possibly using funds allocated by Mary together with one Thomas Winterhop, founded a college for Scottish students in Paris, and bequeathed in his will various monies and a house situated in the rue des Amandiers, close to the Collège des Grassins. See Violette M. Montagu, 'The Scottish College in Paris', in *SHR*, vol. iv (1907), pp. 400–1.
129. W. A. McNeill, 'Documents illustrative of the Scots College, Paris', in the *Innes Review*, xv (1964), p. 67.
130. An edition which exists in three distinct issues with separate title pages for each of the three works, *Histoire abbrégée de tous les roys de France, Angleterre et Escosse, La Recherche des singulartez plus remarquables concernant l'estat d'Escosse and Discours de la legitime succession des femmes* (Paris, variously Jean Fevrier, Michel Gadoulleau, and Robert Coloumbel, 1579).
131. Three letters raise my suspicions as to Chalmers's activities: Henry Killegrew to Lord Burghley, 8 February 1573 in *CSP Foreign 1572–4* (London, 1876) no. 762, pp. 250–1; David Chalmers to Lord Burghley, February 21 1573 in *CSP Foreign 1572–4* (London, 1876), no. 778, pp. 258–9 and Mr. David Chamber of Ormellie to Walsingham from Edinburgh July 4 1584, *CSP Scot. 1584–5* (Edinburgh, 1913), vol. vii, no. 199.
132. 'The names of sundry Englishmen, Papists, presently abiding in Paris', 24 April 1580, in *CSPF 1579–80*, no. 279, pp. 250–2.
133. DNB entry.
134. MS. Cambridge University Library 9462, following the extract given in the *Cambridge University Library Readers' Newsletter*, no. 12, April 1999, p. 2.
135. 'Mémoire de d'Esneval', in Chéruel, *Marie Stuart et Catherine de Médici*, see 'Pieces justificatives'.
136. Evidence relating to this embassy can be found in Teulet (ed.), *Rélations politiques de la France et de l'Espagne avec l'Écosse*, vol. iv, p. 61 et passim. On Bellièvre, see Olivier Poncet, *Pomponne de Bellièvre (1529–1607). Un Homme d'État au Temps des Guerres de Religion* (Paris, 1998).
137. MS. BNF fonds français 5933 fol. 417 records the final offer of Henri III to Elizabeth, also cited by Greengrass, 'Mary, Dowager Queen of France', p. 183.
138. Greengrass, 'Mary, Dowager Queen of France', p. 183.

139. Burnet, *Histoire de mon temps*, t. II, p. 220, reports this letter, though does not cite its source, recorded in Chéruel, *Marie Stuart et Catherine de Médicis*, p. 166.
140. Chéruel, *Marie Stuart et Catherine de Médicis*, p. 156.
141. Ibid.
142. MS. BNF. Supplement français, no. 593(3) fol. 415. Letter dated 24 December 1586.
143. See the collection of correspondence contained in MS. BNF fonds français 15892.
144. Jacques–Auguste de Thou, *Histoire Universelle de Jacques–Auguste de Thou depuis 1543. jusqu'en 1607* (London, 1734), vol. ix, p. 649.
145. The contemporary and modern confusion surrounding the different calendar systems in operation between Britain and the continent will be discussed in chapter 4.
146. Mary Stuart, *Le Testament et dernier propos de la Royne d'Escosse* (Paris, Pierre Marin, 1587), B3v.
147. Ibid., A2r–v.
148. Ibid., B1r.
149. Ibid., A2v.
150. The other three executors mentioned in Mary's will were the Archbishop of Glasgow, James Beaton, the Bishop of Ross, John Leslie, and her chancellor de Ruisseau. Ibid., B2r.
151. *Edict du Roy [Henry III] pour la vente et allienation à faculte de rachapt perpetuel, des parts & portions du domaine de sa Maiesté, dont jouissoit la feu Royne d'Escosse pour son dot & douaire* (Paris, vefue Nicolas Roffet, 1587), A1r.
152. MS. ENL 51.1.1. Given the continued imprisonment of Mary's servants, it is likely that Bourgoing, Mary's physician, delivered the letter seven months after the execution, around August 1587.

2   The Public Face of France's Relationship with the Queen, 1548–85

1. Giovanni Michiel, Venetian ambassador in France to the Doge and Senate, 25 April 1558, in *Calendar of State Papers Venetian, 1557–8* (London, 1884), n. 1216, p. 1487. Michel de L'Hôpital, in his preface to *In Francisci Illustriss. Franciae Delphini, et Mariae Se250 iss. Scotorum Reginae Nuptias, viri cujusdam Ampliss. Carmen* ([Paris], 1558) noted that he wrote his Latin justification for the royal marriage in order to 'quell the scoffers with a statesman's verse', cited and translated by James E. Phillips, *Images of a Queen. Mary Stuart in Sixteenth–Century Literature* (Berkeley & Los Angeles, 1964), p. 13.
2. Pamela Ritchie, *Dynasticism and Diplomacy: The Political career of Marie de Guise in Scotland, 1548–60* (unpublished Ph.D. thesis, University of St Andrews, September 1999), pp. 34–5.
3. Two French galleys reportedly conveyed Stafford and his force from France to England. See MS Lambeth Palace Library, Talbot 3195, f. 31; *Correspondence Politique de Odet de Selve Ambassadeur de France en Angleterre (1546–9)*, ed. G. Lefèvre-Pontalis (Paris, 1888), xiii, fols. 195v–197r; Public Record Office SP31/3/23 fols. 161–2, 172, 179; and *Acts of the Privy Council of England*, ed. J. R. Dasent et al., New Series (46 vols, London, 1890–1964),

vi, p. 80. All of these sources are cited by Ritchie, *Dynasticism and Diplomacy*, p. 231, n.1.

4. Giacomo Soranzo to the Doge and Senate of Venice, from Reims 18 June 1557, in *CSP Venetian 1556–7*, no. 940, pp. 1174–5.

5. See Ritchie, *Dynasticism and Diplomacy*, ch. 7.

6. Ibid., p. 252.

7. Herc. Strozzi to d. de Mantoue from Poissy, 17 December 1557, 'Le fiansaglie di Mons. Smo Delphino con la Mtà della Regina di Scotia, che si doveano fare alla festa dei Re, sono retardate, havendo deliberato S. Mtà per questo effetto fare una dietta, quale deve tenersi per tutto il mese di genaro proximo a Parigi, dove S. Mtà andarà . . . Se intende per certo che S. Mtà hà digià fatto chiamare tutti li principi et ordinato che di tutte le provincie et città et altre terre habbia a venire di ciascun loco un gentilhomo, un ecclesiastico et un cittadino ettutti li presidenti delli suoi parlamenti. Si tene per certo che S. Mtà habbia fatto questa resolutione per rispetto che pochi di sono passo un Spagnuolo che veniva de Fiandra. quale porto lettere a S. Mtà di. M. Illmo contestabile credenciale, dove questo Spagnuolo ragiono con S. Mtà molto longhamente da solo a solo, et si e saputo che Mons. Contestabile ha fatto proponere a S. Mtà il matrimonio di Mons. Smo Delphino con la sorella del Re Catolico et a l'infante di Spagna la prima genita di S. Mtà Chma. Di moto che si vede che, doppo la venuta di questo Spagnuolo, S. Mtà ha sospeso tutto il suo primo disegno . . .', Archives d'État de Mantoue, Francia, confirmed by Alvarotti. Macar to John Calvin, Paris 21 March 1558, *Opera Calvini*, t. xvii, p. 109. All cited in Lucien Romier, *Les Origine Politiques des Guerres de Religion* (2 vols., Geneva, 1974), v. 2, pp. 221–2.

8. For the Angers and Rouen festivities, see chapter one. We should note that the printed account of the Rouen *entrée* does not mention Mary's presence. However, Marie de Guise is recorded as having attended the ceremony and it is likely that her daughter accompanied her, lending legitimacy to the imperial themes projected. See *C'est la deduction du Sumptueux ordre plaisantz spectacles et magnifiques theatres, dresées et exhibés par les citoyens de Rouen ville metropolitqine du pays de Normandie* ([Rouen], on les vend à Rouen par Robert Le Hay et Jean du Gord, 1551). I have not been able to find a contemporary account of the 1554 Paris *entrée* festival. It is, however, mentioned in Melin de Saint Gelais' *Oeuvres Poétiques* (Lyon, 1574). I consulted a modern edition, *Oeuvres Complètes* (Paris, 1873), t. 1, p. 167. Mary Stuart, costumed as the Delphic Oracle, delivered the following lines, no doubt prepared carefully for her: 'Delphica Delphini si mentem oracula tangunt ‖ Britanibus junges regna Britana tuis', 'If Delphic oracles move the mind of the Dauphin ‖ You will join Britain's realms with your Bretons', translation by James Phillips, *Images*, p. 4.

9. Jacques Tahureau, *Les Premieres Poésies* (Poitiers, par les de Marnefz et Bouchetz, freres, 1554). On Tahureau, see Trevor Peach's introduction in Jacques Tahureau, *Poésies Complètes* (Geneva, 1984).

10. The fourteen-line verse 'Avant Mariage de Madame Marie, Royne d'Escosse', is reprinted in Jacques Tahureau, *Poésies Complètes*, ed. Trevor Peach (Geneva, 1984), p. 84.

11. On the marriage between James V and Madeleine, see Edmond Bapst, *Les Mariages de Jacques V* (Paris, 1889), ch. xvii.

12. Ronsard collected a pension of 1,200 *livres* per year – see Antoine d'Artigny, *Nouveaux Mémoires d'histoire*, 7 vols. (Paris, 1749–50), p. 5, 204; MS BNF Dupuy 27, fol. 3; cited in Frederic J. Baumgartner, *Henry II. King of France 1547–59* (Durham and London, 1988), p. 112.

13. Pierre de Ronsard, *Nouvelle Continuation des Amours* (Paris, 1556), reprinted in *Les Amours et Les Folastries (1552–60)* ed. André Gendre (Paris, 1993), pp. 444–5.

14. Ronsard exaggerates. He made two trips to Scotland, from May 1537 to August 1538 and from January to March 1539. See, Pierre de Ronsard, *Les Amours et Les Folastries (1552–60)* ed. André Gendre (Paris, 1993), p. 444, n. 3.

15. Ronsard, *Les Amours*, pp. 444–5.

16. Charles Fontaine, *Odes, Engimes, et Epigrammes adressez pour etreines, au Roy, à la Royne, à Madame Marguerite, & autres Princes & Princesses de France* (Lyon, Jean Citoys, 1557), D5r. The privilege was granted to the author for a period of eight years, signed Declaverie from Villiers Coterets and dated 1 October 1555, A1v. The discrepancy between the date of the privilege and the date of publication may indicate a delay in publication, that an earlier edition not known to me exists (either in French or in Latin) or simply (and this was not uncommon), that there was an error in the date of the privilege itself.

17. Fontaine, *Odes*, D5r.

18. Antoine Fouquelin, *La Rhétorique françoise* (Paris, André Wechel, 1555 & 1557). The privilege was granted on 13 September 1555, A1v.

19. From 1555 to 1559, the publisher of *La Rhétorique*, André Wechel, also published the works of some of the shining stars of the French Renaissance, including Ronsard and Antoine de Baif. See Geneviève Guilleminot, 'André Wechel et la Pléiade (1555–9)' in *Australian Journal of French Studies*, xvii/1 (1980), pp. 65–72. See also Roy. E. Leak, 'Antoine Fouquelin and the Pléiade', in *BHR* xxxII (1970).

20. Ibid., A3r. In François G. de La Croix-du-Maine's *Premier Volume de la Bibliotheque. Qui est un catalogue generale de toutes sortes d'autheurs, qui ont escrit en François depuis cinq cent ans & plus, iusques à ce iourd'huy* (Paris, Abel L'Angelier, 1583), he included Mary Queen of Scots within his list of French authors. He noted Fouquelin's dedication, and observed that Mary's oration in front of Henri II had since been translated into French, 'mais elle ne sont encores en lumiere, non plus que ses poésies françoises', Cc6r.

21. Jean Le Féron, *Le Symbol armorial des armoires de France, & d'Escosse, & de Lorraine* (Paris, Maurice Menier, 1555).

22. Ibid., A3v.

23. Ibid., B1r.

24. Ian de Beaugué, *L'Histoire de la Guerre d'Escosse traitant comme le royaume fut assailly, & grãd partie occupé par les Anglois, & depuis rendu paisible à sa Reyne, & reduit en son ancien estat & dignité* (Paris, Benoist Prevost pour Estienne Groulleau; pour Charles L'Angelier; pour Vincent Sertenas; pour Gilles Corrozet, 1556). There was clearly an expectation that de Beaugué's history would be something of a success. The privilege was granted at Paris by De Courlay to Gilles Corrozet on 6 September 1556, *Histoire*, a1v but was printed as a shared edition by Benoist Prévost in Paris for an association of three publishers. Each issue carried a separate title page, so that the pub-

lishers (for advertising purposes) could receive copies of the edition which carried their respective details. In this case, the standard print run of circa 1,250 copies would probably have been increased.

25. François had been appointed lieutenant-general of the Île de France that year.
26. Ibid., d2v–d3v.
27. Ibid.
28. Ibid.
29. Five main sources provide accounts of this festival. The first is a report contained in the municipal registers of Paris, which can be found in the *Histoire Générale de Paris. Registres des Délibérations du Bureau de la Ville de Paris*, Paris, 1888), v. 4, pp. 538–9 for 24 April 1558 (fol. 284r). The second, a fragment, offers an eyewitness account from a Scot attending the ceremony. The account was discovered in the binding of a 1559 edition of the poems of David Lindsay; see Douglas Hamer, 'The Marriage of the Queen of Scots to the Dauphin: a Scottish Printed Fragment' *The Library* (March 1932), pp. 420–8. The third is a letter from Julio Avarotto, the Ferraran ambassador in France, to Ercole II, fourth Duke of Ferrara, Modena, and Reggio, dated 25 April 1558, held in the Archivio di Stato Modena, 'cancellaria marchionale poi ducale estensi dispacci degli ambasciatori estensi dalla Francia', reprinted and translated in Herbert van Scoy & Bernerd C. Weber, 'Documents. The Marriage of Mary Queen of Scots and the Dauphin', in *SHR*, xxxi (1952), pp. 43–8. The fourth account can be found in John Leslie, *The Historie of Scotland wrytten in Latin by Jhone Leslie and translated in Scottish by James Dalrymple, ed. E.G. Codie* (3 vols., Edinburgh-London, 1885–90), pp. 264–5.
30. The fifth is the printed account of the ceremony noted below, *Discours du grand et magnifique triumphe, fait au mariage de tresnoble & magnifique Prince François de Vallois Roy Dauphin & Princesse, madame Marie d'Estreuart, Royne d'Escosse* (Paris, Annet Briere, 1558). The Briere edition, the only to carry a privilege, exists in two variant states. The other two editions are (Rouen, Jaspar de Rémortier & Raulin Boulenc, 1558) and (Lyon, Jean Brotot, 1558).
31. On the festival literature of Renaissance *entrées*, see W.M. Allister-Johnson, 'Essai de critique interne des livres d'entrée français au XVIe siècle', in *Fêtes de la Renaissance* (3 vols., Paris, 1975), vol. 3, pp. 187–200.
32. Roy Strong, *Art and Power. Renaissance Festivals, 1450–1650* (Berkley and Los Angeles, 1973, 1984), p. 97. Strong misdates Mary's wedding festivities to 1559 [sic for 1558], appendix I, p. 177.
33. Christian Jouhaud, 'Printing the Event: From La Rochelle to Paris', in Roger Chartier and Lydia G. Cochrane (eds.), *The Culture of Print. Power and the Uses of Print in Early Modern Europe* (first edition 1987, Oxford, 1989), p. 326.
34. *Discours du grand et magnifique triumphe* (Paris, A. Briere, 1558), A2v.
35. Ibid., A3r.
36. Ibid., A3v.
37. Ibid., A4r.
38. Ibid., A4r–v.
39. Ibid., B1r. This orb was described by the Ferraran ambassador Julio Alvarotto as 'l'uovo di Napoli' the egg of Naples, Alvarotto to Ercole II, Paris 25 April

1558, transcribed with a translation in Herbert Scoy and Bernerd C. Weber, 'Documents. The Marriage of Mary Queen of Scots and the Dauphin', pp. 41–8.

40. *Discours du grand*, B2r and B3r.
41. Ibid., C1r.
42. Ibid., C1r–v.
43. Ibid., C1v.
44. Ibid., C2v.
45. Giovanni Michiel to the Doge and Senate, in *Calendar of State Papers Venetian, 1557–8* (London, 1884), p. 1488.
46. For example, there is no mention of the seven revolving planets, including Mercury and Mars, which are noted in the municipal registers – surely a show-piece of the event, see *Histoire Générale de Paris*, v. 4, p. 536.
47. The printed fragment records that the 'Quenis grace ‖ [also comman] did that all Scottismen of ‖ [rank, quhaso]euer they vvar, suld haue en- ‖ [trance withthi]s wwaitche vvurde *Brede and . . .*' that not only the high-ranking Scots but large numbers of gatecrashers, of many nationalties, viewed the event, see Hamer, 'The Marriage of Mary Queen of Scots' p. 426, cited in Graham Runnalls and Sarah Carpenter, 'The entertainments at the marriage of Mary Queen of Scots' a forthcoming article.
48. Jacques Grévin *Hymne à Monseigneur le Dauphin, sur le mariage dudict Seigneur, et de Madame Marie d'Esteuart, Royne d'Escosse* (Paris, Martin L'Homme, 1558). For an analysis of this verse, see Lucien Pinvert, *Jacques Grévin (1538–70). Sa Vie, ses Écrits, ses Amis. Étude Biographique et Littéraire* (Paris, 1898), pp. 206–11.
49. Ovid, *Metamorphoses*, trans. A.D. Melville, ed. E.J. Kenney (Oxford, 1986), bk IX, v. 244, pp. 256–7.
50. This chariot is mentioned in Julio Avarotto's letter to Ercole II, in Scoy and Weber, 'Documents', pp. 44 & 47.
51. The privilege was granted to Martin L'Homme, and dated 18 April 1557 [sic for 1558], Grévin, *Hymne à Monseigneur le Dauphin*, D4v.
52. Joachim du Bellay, *Hymne au Roy sur la Prinse de Callais* [sic] (Paris, Federic Morel, 1558). References are, however, taken from the 1559 edition from the same press.
53. Ibid., A2r–A4v.
54. Ibid., A2r–v.
55. Ibid., A3r–v.
56. Ibid., A6r.
57. Jean Antoine de Baïf, *Chant de joie du jour des espousailles de François, roidaufin, et de Marie Roine d'Ecosse* (Paris, André Wechel, 1558), A3v–A4r.
58. Ibid., A2v.
59. Jean de La Tapie d'Aurillac, *Chantz royaulx sur les triumphes du mariage du Roy Dauphin, & la Royne Daulphine* (Paris, Olivier de Harsy, 1558), A2r
60. Ibid., B1v.
61. Ibid., C1v.
62. Jehan de la Maison neufue-Berruyer, *L'Adieu des Neuf Muses, aux roys, Princes, et Princesses de France, à leur departement du festin nuptial de Françoys de Valoys*

Roy Dauphin, & Marie d'Estouart Royne d'Escosse (Paris, Martin l'Homme, 1558), A2r.

63. Ibid., A2v.
64. Ibid., A3r–v.
65. Ibid., A3v–A4r.
66. Ibid., B1r–v.
67. Ibid., B1r–v.
68. Ibid., B2r–v.
69. Ibid., A4r–v.
70. Ibid., A4r.
71. Ibid., A4v.
72. Estienne Perlin, *Description des royaulmes d'Angleterre et d'Escosse* (Paris, François Trepeau, 1558). The work is dedicated to the Duchesse de Berry, only sister to Henri II.
73. Ibid., A2r.
74. Ibid., A7v.
75. Ibid., A8v.
76. Ibid., A7r.
77. Ibid., A5v.
78. See chapter 1, p. 25.
79. Ibid., D4r.
80. Ibid., D6v.
81. *Description*, D6v.
82. *Registrum Magni Sigilli Regum Scotorum*, ed. J.M. Thomson et al. (1882–1914), i. 1272. See also *Registrum Secreti Sigilli Regum Scotorum*, ed. M. Livingstone et al. (1908), v. 109, 568, 597, 601–2, 608, 611, 623. Both cited in M.H. Merriman, 'Mary, Queen of France', in Michael Lynch (ed.), *Mary Stewart. Queen in Three Kingdoms* (Oxford, 1988), p. 42.
83. P.F. Purvey, *Coins and Tokens of Scotland* (1972), p. 6, no. 66; cited in Merriman, 'Mary, Queen of France', p. 42.
84. *Acts of the Parliaments of Scotland* (12 vols., 1814–75), ii., pp. 506–7. Henri III proscribed a reciprocal act in France in June 1588. The *parlement* of Paris registered this act on 8 July 1558, see Teulet (ed.), *Relations politiques de la France et de l'Espagne*, i. pp. 312–17.
85. Frederic J. Baumgartner, *Henry II King of France 1547–59* (Durham and London, 1988), p. 224.
86. J. Lestocquoy et al. (eds.), *Acta Nuntiaturae Gallicae* (16 vols., Rome, 1962–85), vol. 14, p. 168, as cited in Baumgartner, *Henri II*, p. 224.
87. Giovanni Michiel to the Doge and Senate of Venice, Paris 6 February 1559, *CSP Venetian 1558–80*, no. 20, pp. 28–9.
88. *CSP Scot*, i. 156, cited in Merriman, 'Mary, Queen of France', p. 45.
89. Nicholas Throckmorton to Elizabeth I, 19 September 1559, in *CSPF 1558–9*, no. 1355, p. 559.
90. *La Paix faicte entre Princes Henry II. de ce nom, Philippe Roy d'Espagne, les Roy & Royne d'Escosse, & la Royne d'Angleterre* (Lyon, Nicolas Edoard & Jean Petit du Mully, 1559), A3r–v.
91. *Discours Moral de la Paix faicte entre Henry, Philippes et Françoys, & Marie Roy, & Royne d'Escosse, Daulphins de France, et Elizabeth Royne d'Angleterre* (Paris, Barbe Regnault, 1559), B3v.

92. Benoist Troncy, *Le Discours du Grand Triomphe fait en la ville de Lyon pour la Paix* (Lyon, Jean Saugrain, 1559) and *La Paix faicte entre*, B3r–v.

93. *La Paix faicte*, B1r.

94. Ibid., B1v–B2v.

95. Ibid., B3r.

96. Ibid., B3r–v.

97. Ibid., B3r–v.

98. Two marriages cemented the Treaty of Cateau Cambresis: one between Philibert Emmanuel Duc de Savoye and Marguerite, Duchesse de Berry and a second between Princess Elisabeth and Philip II, recently widowed following the death of Mary Tudor in November 1558. The first marriage was celebrated in print by Joachim du Bellay, *Epithalame sur le mariage de tresillustre Prince Philibert Emanuel, Duc de Savoye et Princesse Marguerite de France, soeur unique du Roy, et Duchesse de Berry* (Paris, Federic Morel, 1559 & 1561), B2r [B1r, 1561 ed.].

99. Jerome de La Rouere, *Les Deux Sermo[n]s funèbres es obsèques & enterrement du feu Roy trèschrestien Henri deuxieme de ce nom, faicts & prononcez par Messire Ierome de la Rouere* (Paris, Robert Estienne, 1559).

100. La Rouere, *Les Deux sermons*, C4r–v.

101. Joachim du Bellay, *Hymne au Roy sur la prinse de Calais* (Paris, Federic Morel, 1559).

102. Joachim du Bellay, *Tumulus Henrici Secundi Gallorum Regis Christianiss* (Paris, Federic Morel, 1561). The text is in Latin (on the left) and in French (on the right).

103. Ibid., B2v–B4r.

104. Throckmorton to Elizabeth I, 19 September 1559, in *CSPF 1558–9*, no. 1355, p. 561. For an account of the coronation, see Louis Paris (ed.), *Négociations, lettres et pièces diverses relatives au règne de François II tirées du portefeuille de Sébastien de L'Aubespine évêque de Limoges* (Paris, 1841), pp. 112–26.

105. Michel de Castelneau, in J.A.C. Buchon (ed.), *Choix de Chroniques et Mémoires sur l'Histoire de France* (Paris, 1836), p. 110. Castelneau was to accompany Mary back to Scotland in 1561 and act as French ambassador to Scotland.

106. See the account by Killegrew and Jones to Elizabeth, dated from Blois, 29 November 1559, in *CSPF 1559–60*, no. 337, pp. 145–8.

107. See in particular, 'A Memorial for the Queen' dated 5 May 1560, in *CSPF 1559–60*, no. 32, pp. 17–18 which emphasises Mary's actions against her, and Killegrew & Jones to Elizabeth, November 1559, Ibid., no. 256, p. 110, Throckmorton to Elizabeth, from Amboise, 6 April 1560, Ibid., no. 952, p. 506, & Throckmorton to Elizabeth, from Amboise 28 April 1560, Ibid., no. 1083, p. 598.

108. This is reported in William Cecil's rebuttal to a work by the French ambassador, the Sieur de Seure. The rebuttal was printed at the end of the original text, *Protestation faicte de la part du roy trèschrestien, par son ambassadeur resident pres la Royne d'Angleterre, à sa Majesté, aux Seigneurs de son Conseil* (London, Richard Jugge & John Cawod, 1560), D2r.

109. William Cecil, 5 May 1560, wrote 'The French King has also dated his commissions, "Anno Regni nostri Angliae et Hiberniae primo". All these things have been continually used this last year, and increased after complaints

made. And even since it was declared by de Sevre and the Bishop of Valence that these innovations should be redressed, triumphs have been made at Tours and Chenonceau since Easter' in *CSPF 1560–1*, no. 32, pp. 17–18.

110. *Les Triomphes faictz à l'entrée du Roy à Chenonceau, le dymanche dernier iour de mars MDLIX* (Paris, J. Techner, 1857). The original edition was published in Tours by Guillaume Bouregat in 1559.

111. *Les Ordres tenuz à la reception et entrée du Roy tréschrestien François II. & de la Roine, en la ville d'Orléans* (Paris, Guillaume Nyverd, [1560]), C2v.

112. Ibid., C3v.

113. Ibid., D1v.

114. Ibid., D3v.

115. Ibid., D1r.

116. Caroll, *Noble Power*, pp. 96–7.

117. I have not been able to identify any printed form of Elizabeth's protestation, in English or in French. Its existence is suggested by the following phrase, 'qu'elle [Elizbaeth] à assez declairé vouloir faire par une proclamation de sa volonté qu'elle a fait imprimer', Sieur de Seure, *Protestation faicte de la part du roy [François II] par son ambassadeur resident pres la Royne d'Angleterre, & aux Seigneurs de son Conseil* (Lyon, Benoist Rigaud, 1560), b1v. However, it was undoubtedly a printed form of her proclamation dated 24 March 1560 from Westminster, entitled 'Maintaining Peace with France and Scotland', see P.L. Hughes and J.F. Larkin, *Tudor Royal Proclamations* (Yale, 1964, 1969), vol. II, pp. 141–4.

118. I have not been able to inspect the Tours edition. Details of the date of printing have been inferred from Nicholas Throckmorton to Cecil, from Amboise, 22 May 1560 in *CSPF 1560–1*, no. 116, p. 71, in addition to details contained in the colophon of the printed texts. In the Lyon edition, the colophon is followed by the fleur de lys.

119. Seure, *Protestation* (Lyon, Rigaud, 1560), a2v–a3r.

120. Ibid., a2r.

121. Ibid., a3r.

122. Ibid., a2v.

123. Ibid., a2r.

124. Ibid., b1v.

125. He brought his oration 'en lumiere, que ce qui m'estoit commandé faire', Claude d'Espence, *Oraison funèbre es obsèques de Princesse Marie [de Guise] par la grace de Dieu Royne douairiere d'Escoce* (Paris, Michel de Vascosan, 1561), A2r.

126. Ibid., A2r–B1r. The dedication is dated 21 January 1560 [sic for 1561], B1r.

127. Ibid., G1r–G7v.

128. Ibid., C6v–C7r.

129. Ibid., D7r.

130. *Brief discours de la tempeste et fouldre advenue en la cité de Londres en Angleterre, sur le grand temple et clocher nomé de sainct Paul, le quatriesme Iuin, 1561 (Paris, Guillaume Nyverd, 1561)* and (Paris, pour Christofle Royer, [1561]); *Recit veritable du grand temple et clocher de la Cité de Londres, nommé S. Paul, ruiné par la foudre* (Lyon, Jean Saugrain, 1561). E. Picot would disagree with the identification of these texts as Catholic works. In his *Catalogue des Livres composant la bibliothèque de feu M. le baron James de Rothschild* (5 vols., Paris,

1884–7), t. III, p. 160, he saw in the interpretation of the significance of the bolt of lightning hitting St Paul's cathedral and the addition of Psalm 104 from the Marot translation, the mark of a Protestant translator. The text was, after all, a translation of *The True Report of the burnyng of the Steple and Churche of Paules in London* (London, W. Seres, 1561); cited in *Geneviève Guilleminot, Religion et politique à la veille des guerres civiles: Recherches sur les impressions françaises de l'année 1561* (unpublished Thèse d'Ecole des Chartres, 1977), bibliographic appendix no. 56. Given the specific environment in which this piece was published, however, it is difficult to see how those responsible for its publication in France could have expected anything less than that an anti-Protestant label would be attached to it, at least by the majority of those who came into contact with this work.

131. Jean Gay, *Histoire des scismes et hérésies des Albigeois conforme à celle du present: par laquelle appert que plusieurs grands princes, & seigneurs sont tombez en extremes desolations & ruynes, pour avoir favorisé aux heretiques* (Paris, Pierre Gaultier, 1561). Geneviève Guilleminot, *Religion et politique*, p. 109 highlights that this work was undoubtedly written before the death of Henri II.

132. See Linda C. Taber, 'Royal Policy and Religious dissent within the parlement of Paris, 1559–63' (unpublished Ph.D thesis, University of Stanford, 1982), chapter iv.

133. Throckmorton to Elizabeth I, Paris 24 January 1562, *CSPF 1561–2*, no. 833, p. 503.

134. For instance, Nicolas Throckmorton, the English ambassador to France, reported on 9 October 1561 that Catherine had ordered the lieutenant general of Paris to seize any copies of a work by Gabriel de Sacconay (see below). 'The ordinance is so severe', he wrote, 'that whosoever sells any of the books shall have his goods confiscated, and be imprisoned', in *CSPF 1561–2*, no. 595, p. 361.

135. *Regis Angliae Henrici huius nominis octavi assertio septem sacramentorum adversus Martin Lutherum* (Lyon, Guillaume Rouillé, 1561).

136. This debate is fantastically well documented, see *CSPF 1561–2*, nos. 496, 498, 510, 511, 516, 532, 538, 568, 592, 593, 595, 659 and 682.

137. Geneviève Guilleminot, *Religion et politique*, no. 295.

138. E. Droz, 'Antoine Vincent. La propagande protestante par le psautier', in *Aspects de la propagande religieuse* (Geneva, 1957), pp. 280–5, cited in Geneviève Guilleminot, *Religion et politique*, p. iii.

139. [Jean de Monluc], *Apologie contre certaines Calomnies mises sus à la desfaueur & desvantage de l'Estat des affaires de ce Roiaume* (s.l., 1562), E1v.

140. A history of the use of privilege in the second half of the sixteenth century is a study that remains to be written. For its use at the beginning of the century, see Elizabeth Armstrong, *Before Copyright. The French Book Privilege System 1498–1526* (Cambridge, 1990).

141. Geneviève Guilleminot, *Religion et politique*, t. I, p. 11. The Parlement ignored this legislation and continue to award privileges. On the critical role of the Catholic press in opposing toleration, see Luc Racaut, 'The cultural obstacles to religious pluralism in the polemic of the French Wars of Religion' in K. Cameron, M. Greengrass, and P. Roberts eds, *The Adventure of Religious Pluralism in Early–Modern France* (Berne, 2000), pp. 115–27.

142. William Cecil to Thomas Smith, November 1563, cited in Conyers Read,

'William Cecil and Elizabethan Public Relations' in S.T. Bindoff, J. Hurstfield & C.H. Williams (eds.), *Elizabethan Government and Society. Essays presented to Sir John Neale* (London, 1961), p. 26.

143. Ferdinand I, *Exemplar literarum Ferdinandi, Romanorum imperatoris, ad Pium IIII, pontificem maximum, quibus quidem in literis . . . agit de sarciendis tandemque aliquando diffiniendis hisce rebus, quae in publicam venere concilii deliberationem, nec enim pati conditionem temporum, rem amplius extrahi. Ejusdem imperatoris in eam ipsam rem ad cardinalem Lotharingum admonitio. Epistola etiam cujusdam docti hominis, natione Lusitani [J. Osorii], ad Elizabetam, reginam Angliae, in qua disseritur de ratione reipublicae optime administrandae, tum de constituenda, ex veterum patrum sententia, religione. Quarum literarum adsuetur quoque ad calcem gallica interpretatio* (Parisiis, apud N. Chesneau, 1563). The French translation was entitled *Les Graves et sainctes remonstrances de l'Empereur Ferdinand, à nostre sainct pere le Pape, Pie, quatriesle de ce nom sur le faict du Concil de Trente* (Paris, Nicolas Chesneau, 1563).

144. Osorius, *Les Graves*, A1v 'Extraict du priuilege du Roy' to Nicolas Chesneau for one or two impressions of two books, one entitled 'Exemplum Literarul inuictissimi Caesaris ad Summum Pontificem, and the other Hieronymi Osorii ad Serenissimam Elizabetham Angliae Regnam, for a period of four years from the date of first impression, signed De Courlat from Paris, 22 June 1563.

145. Osorius, *Les Graves*, D3v.

146. Ibid., K2r.

147. Ibid., K3v.

148. Ibid., Y1v.

149. Ibid., F1v.

150. Ibid., I3v.

151. *Proclamation de la Paix faicte entre les roy de France . . . Charles IX de ce nom, & Elizabeth Roine d'Angleterre* (Paris, Robert Estienne, 1564), A2r.

152. Ibid., A2v.

153. *Registres des Délibérations du Bureau de la Ville de Paris 1558–67* (Paris, 1892), pp. 463–71.

154. Ibid., p. 464.

155. Ibid., p. 471.

156. F.A. Mignet, *The History of Mary Queen of Scots* (2 vols., London, 1851), vol. 2, appendix D, signals the dispatches of Paul de Foix on this issue. William Cecil had severe objections concerning this.

157. Pierre de Ronsard, *Elegies, Mascarades, et Bergeries* (Paris, Gabriel Buon, 1565) reprinted in Paul Laumonier (ed.), *Pierre de Ronsard, Oeuvres Complètes*, (Paris, 1948), t. XIII, pp. 30–264. On Ronsard's *Elegies*, see Malcolm C. Smith, 'Ronsard and Queen Elizabeth I' in *Bibliothèque d'Humanisme et Renaissance*, 29 (1967), pp. 93–119, republished in *Renaissance Studies and Articles 1966–94*, ed. Ruth Calder (Geneva, 1999), pp. 10–36.

158. Ronsard, *Oeuvres*, t. XIII, p. 36.

159. Ibid., p. 44.

160. Ibid., t. XIII, pp. 118–9; t. XIV, pp. 152–9.

161. The dedicatory letter was entitled 'A la Majesté de la Royne d'Angleterre', Ronsard, *Oeuvres*, t. XIII, pp. 33–6, the three poems were entitled 'Elegie à la majesté de la Royne d'Angleterre', t. XIII, pp. 39–62, 'Elegie à mylord Du-

Dle conte de l'Encestre', t. XIII, pp. 63–74, and 'Au seigneur Cecille Secretaire de la Royne d'Angleterre', t. XIII, pp. 159–70.

162. Ibid., t. XIV, pp. 177–80.

163. Ibid., t. XIV, p. 178.

164. The pension is noted in Mary's personnel account for 1566–7, in Alexandre Teulet (ed.), *Papiers d'état, piéces et documents inédits ou peu connus, relatifs a l'histoire de l'Écosse au XVIe siècle, tirés des bibliothèques et des archives de France* (3 vols., Paris, 1852), t. 1, p. 133.

165. Pierre de Ronsard, *Elégie sur le despart de la royne Marie* (Lyon, Benoist Rigaud, 1561)

166. Mary Stuart, *La Harangue de trèsnoble et trèsvertueuse Dame, Madame Marie d'Estuart, Royne d'Escosse, douairiere de France, faite en l'assemblée des Estats de son royaume, tenuz au moys de May dernier passé* (Lyon, Benoist Rigaud, 1563; Reims, Jean de Foigny, 1563); the Reims edition also contained Bernard Dominici's *Sermon funèbre faict à Nancy, aux obsèques & funerailles de feu Monseigneur Monsieur François de Lorraine, Duc de Guyse*, and indicated that the work was put on sale in Paris by Nicolas Chesneau. There was possibly a third edition of the *Harangue* published in Reims by Foigny. Its presence is certainly signalled on the title page of the *Sermon funèbre*. However, the one copy I examined contains only a recomposition of the *Sermon funèbre* – the *Harangue* was absent.

167. Mary Stuart, *La Harangue de trèsnoble et trèsvertueuse dame*, A1v.

168. Ibid., A2r–A3v.

169. Ibid.

170. Ibid., A2r–v.

171. Ibid., A2v.

172. Ibid., A3r.

173. Ibid., A3v–A4r.

174. René Benoist, *Traité du sacrifice Evangélique. Où est manifestement prouvé, que le saincte Messe est le sacrifice eternel de la nouvelle Loy* (Paris, Nicolas Chesneau, 1564). The dedication is dated 8 April.

175. Ibid., Aã7v. It is interesting to note Benoist's pride in asserting that his *Le Triomphe et excellente victoire de la foy, par le moyen de la véritable et toutepuissante parole de Dieu ou est monstré la moyen certain et facile de pacifier les troubles presens. Le tout dédié au Roy, a la Royne et aux catholiques Princes et Seigneurs* (Paris, Nicolas Chesneau, 1566 and 1568) was written at the court of Mary Stuart. Noted in Émile Pasquier, *Un Curé de Paris pendant les Guerres de Religion. Réné Benoist. Le Pape des Halles (1521–1608)*, p. 325, no. 18.

176. Benoist, *Traité du sacrifice*, Aã8r. For an alternative interpretation of the reasons that lay behind Benoist's departure, see chapter 1.

177. Ibid.

178. Ibid., Aã8r–v.

179. Joachim du Bellay, *Epithalame sur le mariage de trèsillustre Philibert Emmanuel duc de Savoye* (Paris, Federic Morel, 1569), Michel de l'Hôpital, *Hymne au Roy [François II]* (Paris, Féderic Morel, 1569), Joachim du Bellay, *Les Oeuvres françoises de Joachim du Bellay, gentilhomme angevin, et poete excellent de ce temps* (Paris, Federic Morel, 1569) and Michel de l'Hôpital, *Hymne au Roy [François II]* (Paris, Féderic Morel, 1570).

180. Phillips, *Images*, p. 85.
181. See on the rebellion, Sir Cuthbert Sharp (ed.), *The Rising in the North. The Rebellion. Being a reprint of the Memorials of the Rebellion of the Earls of Northumberland and Westmoreland edited by Sir Cuthbert Sharp 1840* (1840, reprinted Shotton, 1975).
182. Mary was kept in close confinement and this plea was conveyed to the Spanish ambassador in London, Guerau de Spes, via one of Mary's servants. It is reported in a dispatch from de Spes to Philip II, dated London 8 January 1569, Martin Hume (ed.), *CSP Spanish 1568–79* (London, 1894), no. 70, p. 97.
183. *Discours des troubles nouvellement advenus au royaume d'Angleterre. Avec une déclaration faicte par le Comte de Northumberland & autres grands Seigneurs d'Angleterre* (Lyon, Michel Jove, 1570) and (Paris, Nicholas Chesneau, 1570); *Continuation des choses plus célèbres & mémorables advenues en Angleterre, Escosse & Irlande, depuis le moys d'Octobre M.D.LXIX jusques au XXV. jour de Decembre ensuyant & dernier passé* (Lyon, Michel Jove, 1570). For a dated and incomplete analysis of the literature relating to the Northern Rebellion, see James K. Lowers, *Mirrors for Rebels. A study of the Polemical Literature relating to the Northern Rebellion 1569* (Berkeley and Los Angeles, 1953).
184. *Discours des troubles nouvellement advenus au royaume d'Angleterre. Avec une déclaration faicte par le Comte de Northumberland & autres grands Seigneurs d'Angleterre* (Paris, pour Laurent du Coudret, [1587]), B4r.
185. James Phillips is in error on this point, *Images of a Queen*, p. 93; Malcolm C. Smith has also noted Phillips' mistake, 'Ronsard and Queen Elizabeth I' first published in *Bibliothèque d'Humanisme et Renaissance*, 29 (1967) pp. 93–119, reprinted in *Renaissance Studies. Articles 1966–94*, Ruth Calder (ed.), p. 23 n. 74.
186. *Continuation des choses plus celebres*, D3r.
187. Francis Walsingham to Lord Burghley, Paris 20 January 1573, in *CSPF 1572–74*, no. 725, p. 232. Given the outburst of English anger at the publication of *L'Innocence* from 20 January, December or early January would seem a likely date of publication.
188. *L'Innocence de la trèsillustre, très-chaste, et débonnaire Princesse Madame Marie Royne d'Escosse. Où sont amplement refutées les calomnies faulces, & impositions iniques, publiées par un livre secrettement divulgué en France, l'an 1572* ([Reims], [Jean de Foigny], 1572) and (Lyon, Jean de Tournes, 1572). Keith Cameron has identified Reims as the place of publication, 'La polémique, la mort de Marie Stuart et l'assassinat de Henri III' in Robert Sauzet (ed.), *Henri III et son temps* (Paris, 1992). The probable explanation for the anonymity of the Reims editions, not mentioned by Cameron, was that it served to disguise other works printed from this location destined for the British Catholic market. It gave the crown the option of plausible deniability. I have used the copy reprinted in Samuel Jebb (ed.), *Histoire de Marie Stuart, Reine d'Escosse et Douairiere de France: Où Recueil de Toutes les Pieces qui ont été Publiées au sujet de cette Princesse; Contenant l'Histoire secrette d'Angleterre, de France & d'Escosse* (2 vols., London, 1725).
189. The authorship of *L'Innocence* is uncertain. James Phillips, *Images*, p. 96 states 'two of the three parts of the work are literal translations of the Trea-

tise of Treasons'. This is erroneous. At most, we might say that the author(s) were certainly aware of, and had direct access to, *A Treatise of Treasons against Q. Elizabeth, and the Croune of England, diuided into two Partes: whereof, The first parte answereth certaine Treasons pretended, that never were intended: And the second, discouereth greater Treasons committed, that are by few perceiued: as more largely appeareth in the page following* (January 1572) and Morgan Phillips [pseudonym for John Leslie], *A Treatise concerning the defence of the honour of the right high, mightie and noble Princesse, Marie Queene of Scotland, and Dowager of France, with a Declaration, as wel of her Right, Title and Interest to the Succession of the Croune of England: as that the Regiment of women is comfortable to the lawe of God and Nature* (Leodii, 1571). Francis Walsingham indicated in a letter to William Cecil, Lord Burghley, that the book had multiple authors, Francis Walsingham to Lord Burghley, Paris 20 January 1573, in which Walsingham writes that he perceives that Burghley has not yet received his letter of 12 January, which included a parcel of letters and books from a servant who left on 2 January, wherein was contained a book in 'defence of the Queen of Scots, compiled by those whom he named in his last letter', in *CSPF 1572–4*, no. 725, p. 232. Frustratingly, the previous letter in which he names these does not appear to have survived. Alexander Gordon to Alexander Hay, 27 February 1573, *CSP Scot.*, iv, 505 and Francis Walsingham to Lord Burghley, 25 February 1573, *CSPF 1572–4*, no. 789, p. 264, also discuss the question of authorship of a work which is presumably *L'Innocence* though the title is not explicitly stated. Gordon may have participated in the composition of the work, but he admitted only to knowing the identity of the author. If he had written it, he said, it would have displayed a greater mark of learning. David Chalmers, Lord Ormont, was also suspected by the English of authorship, though he denied all knowledge of the work to Walsingham in February 1573 – see Killegrew to Burghley, 8 February 1573 (2 letters) *CSP Scot.*, iv, 487–8.

190. Certainly Lord Hunsdon had strong reason to suspect that Du Croc, the French ambassador to Scotland, may have played on 'both hands' [i.e. neutrality and pro-Marian], Lord Hunsdon to Lord Burghley, Berwick 27 June 1572, *CSPF 1572–4*, no. 443, pp. 138–9.

191. Walsingham to Randolph, Paris 26 November 1572, *CSPF 1572–4*, no. 649, p. 208.

192. Secret plans had even been formulated between the Cardinal de Lorraine and Catherine de Medici to send a French force led by the Marquis de Mayenne to reinforce the Castilians. The choice of a landing site on the west coast of Scotland was probably decided upon to avoid the main part of the English fleet that patrolled the North Sea. In order to preserve a semblance of respect for the Blois accord, Charles IX would disavow any knowledge of de Mayenne's forces. See Walsingham to Burghley, Paris 24 January 1572, *CSPF 1572–4*, no. 729, pp. 235–6.

193. It is likely that it is the *Innocence* that is referred to on 10 February, in a letter between Francis Walsingham and William Cecil, in which the former reported that he had complained to Charles IX regarding its publication and asked to have it suppressed. Intriguingly, he indicated that he believed that the crown's capacity to enforce such legislation was slender indeed. Francis Walsingham to Lord Burghley, Paris 10 February 1573, 'For sup-

pressing of the book he knows of they [sic] were determined to have forbidden the sale by edict, wherein he opposed himself, saying that it would
rather do harm than good, considering how little their edicts are weighed;
for by the edicts men['s] understanding of such a book would be the more
curious to have it', in *CSPF 1572–4*, no. 767, p. 253. Given the overwhelming success in the 1560s of the Elizabethan government in having
the French crown censor works judged offensive to the realm, Walsingham's
remarks possibly reveals less about the climate of respect for the crown's
authority in France, and more about the ambassador's own sense of frustration at the ambivalent policy of the French crown towards England.

194. *L'Innocence*, p. 425.
195. On [George Buchanan], *Histoire de Marie Royne d'Escosse, touchant la conjuration faicte contre le Roy, & l'adultere commis avec le Comte de Bothwel, histoire vrayement tragique* (Edinburgh [London?], Thomas Waltem [?], 1572),
see chapter three.
196. *L'Innocence*, p. 443
197. *A Treatise of Treasons against Q. Elizabeth*, ã6r dates Buchanan's work to 13
October 1571.
198. James Hamilton, 2nd Earl of Arran, and Duc de Châtellerhaut, was heir presumptive to the throne after the accession of Mary Stuart in 1542, and
therefore the lawful regent of Scotland in James's minority. Although not
one of Mary's constant supporters during the 1560s, from 1569 he lobbied
both the French and Spanish to support Mary's claim in Scotland. In April
1570, he sent David Chalmers to 'procure [the] support of France according to the old bond and solicit for [the] help of Spain'. Hamilton's motivations are quite clear. Although Chalmers was instructed to deny Mary's
involvement in the assassination of Henry, Lord Darnley, if she were not
found worthy to broke the crown [or if she could not be secured from
English hands], then Hamilton advocated that he should act as regent, see
'Instructions given to Mr. Chambers [sics] sent by the Duke of Châtelher-
ault to the French King and the Duke of Alva, [July] 1570, *CSP Scot. v.III
1569–71*, no. 333, p. 247.
199. There is truth in this allegation. On 15 May 1567, Don Frances de Alava
wrote to Philip II from the French court, 'El conde de Mure, hermano bas-
tardo de la Reyna de Escocia, despues de haver estado con Bessa [Beza] dos
dias en Orliens [Orléans], fue á ver al principe de Conde [Louis Prince de
Condé] y al Amirante [Admiral Coligny], con losquales ha tenido largas
platicas, de que ha puesto en esta corte harta sospecha, y tiró luego por la
posta á Geneva; adonde havia ydo antes que el Montgomeri [Gabriel,
Comte de Montgomery], y otros siete ó ocho capitanes los mas bravos de
la parte herege', MS. AN Fonds de Simancas, Liasse B. 21, no. 194. A transcription is given in Alexandre Teulet, *Papiers d'état*, t. 3, p. 30. On Moray's
connection with the Huguenots, see also Ibid., t. 2, pp. 231–2 'Mémoire de
la Royne d'Escosse, douairière de France, apporté par le sieur de Duglas pour
estre interpreté au Roy' 26 June 1568. The original manuscript can be found
in BNF St Germain-Harlay no. 222, t. 1, no. 86.
200. *L'Innocence*, p. 487.
201. Ibid., p. 424.
202. Ibid., p. 444.
203. Ibid., p. 445.

204. Ibid., p. 457.
205. Ibid., p. 457.
206. Ibid., p. 447.
207. Ibid., pp. 459–60.
208. Ibid., p. 517.
209. Ibid., p. 475.
210. Sebastien Münster, *Cosmographie*, ed. François de Belleforest (2 vols., Paris, Cherreaut Sonnius, 1575). The bibliography Samuel T Tannenbaum & Dorothy R. Tannenbaum, *Marie Stuart, Queen of Scots. A Concise Bibliography* (3 vols., New York, 1944) notes the publication of two editions relating to Mary in the early 1570s, *Copie d'une lettre de Mariae . . . à ses fidels serviteurs bannis à Angleterre, à leur depart en France* (Paris, 1572) and *Méditation faicte par la royne d'Escoce* (Paris, 1574). I can find no trace of either of these editions.
211. Münster, *Cosmographie*, e6v.
212. Jêrome Osorius, *Remonstrance à Madame Elizabeth Royne d'Angleterre* (Paris, Jean Poupy, 1575), A1v 'Extraict du priuilege du Roy' granted to Nicolas Chesneau for four years. Given at Paris and dated 22 June [1563].
213. *Histoire Merveilleuse et espouvantable advenue en Angleterre . . .* (Paris, Jean Poupy, [1577]), (Paris, Pierre Courant, [1577]), (Paris, Gilles de S. Gilles, [1577]) and (Rouen, Pierre Courant, [1577]) though no known copy of the latter is known.
214. I have not yet been able to consult this work. The description of its content is from A.F. Allison & D.M. Rogers, *Contemporary Printed Literature of the English Counter-Reformation between 1558–1640. An annotated Bibliography* (Brookfield, 1989–94), no. 687.
215. *L'Histoire et discours au vray du siège qui fut mis devant la ville d'Orléans, par les Anglois, le Mardy XII. iour d'Octobre 1428* (Orleans, Saturnin Hotot, 1576).
216. *L'Histoire et Discours*, B2r–v.
217. Ibid., A3v.
218. Ibid., ã2v.
219. Ibid., C4r. He was repaid by the Dauphin not by 2000 livres tournois as promised, but rather was given the castle and town of Concressault near Sancerre, with revenues. See also Jacques Soyer (ed.), *Donation par Charles VII à Jean Stuart Seigneur de Derneley, Connétable de l'armée d'Écosse des Terres de Concressault & D'Aubigny–sur–Nère (21 avril 1421, 26 mars 1423, 3 décembre 1425)* (Bourges, 1899).
220. *L'Histoire et Discours*, B2v.
221. Ronsard, *Oeuvres*, XVII, pp. 378–9. Malcolm Smith discusses this verse briefly, 'Ronsard and Queen Elizabeth I', pp. 109–10.
222. I am grateful to Dr. Julian Goodare for allowing me access to his excellent unpublished biography of the life of David Chalmers.
223. Trial of the Earl of Bothwell, April 12 1567, no. 488 at the Justiciary court, in *CSP Scot. vII 1563–69*, no. 488. This accusation was never to disappear, see for example, *CSP Scot.iv 1571–4* (Edinburgh, 1905), no. 226.
224. The Book of Articles, November 1568, in *CSP Scot. vII 1561–9* (Edinburgh, 1900), no. 902. This text was an explicit attempt to blacken Mary's name by George Buchanan. See also the more developed *Detectio Mariae reginae Scotorum* ([London, John Day], 1572).
225. Chalmers's name assumes a prominent position in the act that resulted

in his forfeiture, see 'Acts of the Scottish Parliament', Edinburgh 16 August 1568, in *CSP Scot. vII 1561–9* (Edinburgh, 1900), no. 766. He was only to regain royal favour in September 1583, where he was given a guarded pacification – a pacification that specifically excluded those involved in the murder of Darnley. However, Chalmers was never to be tried of this crime. *Acts of the Parliament of Scotland*, iii, 314–5, c.73, ratification of May 1584. The restoration of David Chalmers was followed with some interest by the English, see for example Robert Bowes and William Davison to Walsingham, from Edinburgh 18 March 1583, in *CSP Scot. vol. vi 1581–3*, no. 356, pp. 335–8, and William Davison to Walsingham, from Edinburgh 27 May 1584 in *CSP Scot. vol vii 1584–5*, no. 146, p. 155.

226. *Histoire Abbrégée de tous les roys de France, Angleterre et Escosse* (Paris, variously Jean Fevrier, Michel Gadoulleau, and Robert Coloumbel, 1579).

227. *Discours de la Legitime Succession des Femmes* (Paris, Jean Fevrier, 1579). The privilege E4r was granted by the King for nine years to David Chalmers and to the printer-publishers Fevrier, Gadoulleau and Coloumbel. It is dated 10 January 1579. The errata can be found on E4v.

228. There is no known surviving manuscript copy of the 1572 edition of the *Histoire abbrégée*.

229. Chalmers, *Histoire abbrégée*, ã3v.

230. Elizabeth Bonner, 'Scotland's 'Auld Alliance' with France, 1295–1560' in *History* vol. 84, no. 273, January 1999, pp. 5–30. See also Roger Mason, 'Scotching the Brut: Politics, History and National Myth in Sixteenth–Century Britain,' Roger Mason (ed.), *Scotland and England, 1286–1816* (Edinburgh, 1987), p. 60.

231. Arthur H. Williamson, *Scottish National Consciousness in the Age of James VI: The Apocalypse, the Union and the Shaping of Scotland's Public Culture* (Edinburgh, 1979), chapter 6, p. 118.

232. *Histoire Abbrégée*, é6r.

233. France was originally called Semnothé after their first King, and was called Gaul after Galothee the second King of this territory, *Histoire Abbrégée*, é3r.

234. Ibid., D5v.

235. Ibid., m7v.

236. Ibid., under sub–section, 'La Tenevr de l'Alliance entre la France et l'Escosse extraicte des registres & livres dessus mentionnez', m7v–m8v.

237. Ibid., m8r

238. *La Recherche*, D8v.

239. *Histoire abbrégée*, F4v.

240. Ibid., C7r.

241. Ibid.

242. Ibid., G3v.

243. The dedication, 'A très–auguste et très–clemente princesse Marie Royne, d'Escosse, doüairiere de France, ma souveraine', can be found in *La Recherche*, é2r.

244. See the excellent discussion of this text by Arthur H. Williamson, *Scottish National Consciousness*, pp. 118–9.

245. *Discours abbrégée*, ã3r.

246. [Guillaume Rouillé], *Promptuaire des medailles des plus renommees personnes*

qui ont esté depuis le commencement du monde : Avec briefve description de leurs vies & faits, recueillie des bons auteurs (Lyon, Guillaume Roville, 1581), ss5v.

247. Walsingham to Stafford, 18 Jan 1584, *CSPF 1583–4*, no. 376, p. 317.

248. There were 343 refugees named in 'The names of sundry Englishmen, Papists, presently abiding in Paris', 24 April 1580, in *CSPF 1579–80*, no. 279, pp. 250–2.

249. Some of the literature, particularly English literature relating to Edmond Campion is discussed by Brad Gregory, *Salvation at Stake. Christian Martyrdom in Early Modern Europe* (Cambridge Mass. & London, 1999), pp.19–20, pp. 281–5, p. 288, p. 294 & p. 302.

250. Evelyn Waugh, *Edmond Campion humaniste et martyr (1540–81)* (Paris, 1989), p. 166.

251. Edmund Campion, *Rationes decem; quibus fretus, certamen adversarijs obtulit in causa fidei* ([Stonor, Park, Henley-on-Thames, Greenstreet House Press, 1581])'.

252. The rumours are noted in *Épistre de la persecution meue en Angleterre contre l'Eglise Chrestienne Catholique & Apostolique, & fideles membres d'icelle* (Paris, Thomas Brumen, 1583, 1586), A1r. References are to the 1586 edition.

253. *L'Histoire de la mort que le R.P. Edmond Campion prestre de la compagnie du nom de Iesus, & autres ont souffert en Angleterre pour la foy Catholique & Romaine le premier iour de Decembre, 1581* (Paris, Guillaume Chaudiere, 1582) and (Lyon, Jean Pillehotte, [1582]), *Bref discours du P. Edmond Campian contenant dix points & fondemens principaux de l'Eglise Catholique, Apostolique, Romaine contre les heresies de Luther, Calvin, Beze, et autres de la religion pretendue reformée.* (Douay, Jean Bogard, 1582), and *Discours des cruautes et tirannyes qu à faict la Royne d'Angleterre à l'endroict des Catholecques [sic], Anglois, Espagnolz, François, & prestres Catholicques [sic], qui soutenoient la foy & le tourmant qui l'ont soufert avec les noms & surnons d'iceux. Plus y est adiousté la mort d'Edouard Hance Prestre Anglois & le Martyre qui la soufert* (Paris, [1582]). The text from A2r-C3r is identical to *L'Histoire de la mort*, while C3r–C4r provides additional details of the behaviour of Campion and his companions before execution. C4r-v gives an account of the martyrdom of Edouard Hance, an English priest, also in 1581.

254. *L'Histoire de la Mort* (Paris, Guillaume Chaudiere, 1582), A4r.

255. Ibid., A4v.

256. Ibid., B2v.

257. Ibid., B2v–B3r.

258. Ibid., C2v.

259. Ibid., D2r.

260. It was first published in Latin in 1581, appearing a year later with revisions in French [Robert Persons], *De persecutione Anglicana, epistola. Qua explicantur afflictiones, aerumnae, & calamitates gravissimae, cruciatus etiam & tormenta, & acerbissima martyria, quae catholici nunc Angli, ob fidem patiuntur* (Bononiae apud Jo. Baptistam Algazarium. 1581 [sic for Rouen, George L'Oyselet]). *Épistre de la persecution meue en Angleterre contre l'Eglise Chrestienne Catholique & Apostolique, & fideles membres d'icelle* (Paris, Thomas Brumen, 1582, 1586). References are to the 1586 edition. The *Épistre* received its privilege on 7 June 1582, Pi2r from Matthieu de Launoy who would in subsequent years become a pillar of the Catholic League.

261. DNB entry.
262. Ibid., B7v–B7r; C3r–C6v.
263. Ibid., A4v.
264. Ibid., A5v–A6r.
265. Ibid., A7r; A8v.
266. Ibid., B2r.
267. Ibid., C1v.
268. Ibid., C2r.
269. Ibid., D2r.
270. Ibid., B2v.
271. The presence of other images besides the placard is noted in Elizabeth to Stafford, 7 February 1584, *CSPF July 1583 – July 1584* (London, 1914), no. 409, p. 344.
272. Stafford to Walsingham, Paris 17 November 1583, in *CSPF July 1583–July 1584* (London, 1914), no. 246, p. 218.
273. John Hay, *Certaine demandes concerning the Christian Religion proponed to the ministers of the new pretended kirk of Scotla[n]d* (Paris, T. Brumen, 1580).
274. John Hay, *Demandes faicts aux ministres d'Escosse touchant la religion Chrestienne* (Verdun, J. Wapius, 1583) & (Lyon, Jean Pillehotte, 1583). All references are to the Lyon edition.
275. John Hay, *Demandes*, A2r. The association between Calvinism and Judaism can found on C5r.
276. Ibid., A6v.
277. On the use of the image of 'femmellettes' in Catholic polemic, see Luc Racaut, *Hatred in Print*, chapter 6.
278. Hay, *Demandes*, B4r.
279. Ibid., K8r.
280. Ibid., F8v–G1r.
281. In fact, this was only partly true. While reconciled to the Protestants in 1573, James Hamilton Earl of Moray, was an extraordinarily inconstant figure. He had moved between the Protestant and Catholic camps seamlessly.
282. Ibid., C6r.
283. *Memoires contenante le vray discours des affaires du Pays Bas, & choses plus secrettes qui y sont advenues cette année 1583. de quoy chascun pourra apprendre l'estat muable, & inconsta|n]t de toutes choses pour en faire son profit* ([Cologne], 1583).
284. Ibid., d2r.
285. Ibid., a3v.
286. Ibid., a4r.
287. Ibid., a4v.
288. Elizabeth to Stafford, 7 February 1584, *CSPF 1583–4*, no. 409, pp. 343–5.
289. John Hay, *Demandes faicte aux ministres d'Escosse. Touchant la Religion Chrestienne* (Lyon, Jean Pillehotte, 1584).
290. *Discours de la vie abominable, ruses, trahisons, meurtres, impostures, empoisonnements, paillardises, Atheisme, & autres très-iniques conversations, desquelles a usé & use journellement le my Lorde de Lecestre Machiaveliste, contre l'honneur de Dieu, la Majesté de la Royne d'Angleterre sa Princesse, & toute la république chrestienne* (s.l., 1585).

291. Ibid., a2r.
292. Ibid., a5v.
293. Stuart Carroll, 'The Revolt of Paris, 1588: Aristocratic Insurgency and the Mobilization of Popular Support', in *French Historical Studies*, 23/2 (2000), p. 312.

3 The Huguenot Image of Mary Queen of Scots

1. As noted in chapter two, it is likely that Elizabeth had published a pamphlet justifying military involvement in Scotland, which stimulated the French crown to respond by commissioning the Sieur de Seure's *Protestation faicte de la part du roy [François II] par son ambassadeur résident près la Royne d'Angleterre, & aux seigneurs de son conseil* (Lyon, Benoist Rigaud, 1560), (Orléans, Eloy Gibier, 1560) & (Tours, Jean Rousset, 1560). This is suggested by the following remark in de Seure's text, 'qu'elle [Elizbaeth] à assez declairé vouloir faire par une proclamation de sa volonté qu'elle a fait imprimer', b1v. If true, I can find no extant example of this work.
2. See chapter 2.
3. Nicholas Throckmorton to William Cecil, from Amboise, 22 May 1560, in *CSPF 1560–1*, no. 116, p. 71.
4. The titles of the dispatches were 'Memoire delivres nouveau imprime [sic] depuis deulx et trois an [sic] jusque à ce present an, 1559', and 'livres nouveaux depuis l'an 1558, lesquelz sont imprimes à Paris', see Jones to Cecil from Blois, 29 November 1559, in *CSPF 1559–60*, no. 343, pp. 148–9 & no. 345, p. 149.
5. Claude Gousté, *Traicté de la puissance et authorité des roys* ([Paris], 1561). The provenance on the copy in Oxford, All Souls SR.56.b.2.1 reads 'Guillaum Cecilis, 1562'. With thanks to Andrew Pettegree for this reference. Later in the sixteenth century, key works of continental political thought were translated for an English public on Cecil's initiative, see Lisa F. Parmelee, *Good Newes from Fraunce. French Anti–League Propaganda in Late Elizabethan England* (New York, 1996), p. 164.
6. Sieur de Seure [& William Cecil], *Protestation faicte de la part du Roy très-chrestien par son ambassadeur resident pres la Royne d'Angleterre* (London, Richard Jugge & John Cawod, 1560).
7. Ibid., A3r et passim.
8. Ibid., B3r.
9. Ibid., A5-r–v et passim.
10. 'Proclamation of Queen Elizabeth concerning peace with France and Scotland', given at Westminster, 24 March 1560, reported in the dispatches of the Venetian ambassador, *CSP Venetian 1558–60*, no. 139, pp. 167–9.
11. Jean Gay, *Histoire des scismes et hérésies des Albigeois conforme à celle du présent* (Paris, Pierre Gaultier, 1561). For the complaints about this text, see chapter 2.
12. [Elizabeth I], *Protestation faicte par la Royne d'Angleterre, par laquelle elle declare les iustes & necessaires occasions qui l'ont meüe de prendre la pretection de la cause de Dieu, la defense du Roy & de son Royaume, contre les autheurs des troubles qui y sont à present* ([Orléans, Eloy Gibier,] 1561, 1562).
13. [Elizabeth I], *Copie de la Protestation faicte par la Royne d'Angleterre pour le*

secours envoyé en France, afin de conserver le sceptre & couronne du Roy durant sa minorité, ([Caen, Pierre Phillippe], 1562).

14. [Elizabeth I], *Protestation faite et publiée de par la Roine d'Angleterre sur la resolution qu'elle a prinse de subvenir aux troubles du royaume de France, tant pour maintenir le Roy en son estat & dignité contre la violence & tyranie de la maison de Guise que pour soulager les poures Eglises des iniques & cruelles oppressions qui leur sont faites par ceux qui ont conspiré a ruiner la Chrestienté, sil peuvent* (s.l., s.n., 1562).

15. 'Instructions for Sir Henry Sidney', 28 [April] 1561, in *CSPF 1561–2*, no. 1063, pp. 636–7.

16. Only one edition celebrating the union between Condé and Elizabeth was published, *Contract d'alliance entre la Royne d'Angleterre & le Prince de Condé, sur le faict du secours envoyé en France par ladite Royne pour la defence de la religion chrestienne,* (s.l., [1562]).

17. *Protestation faicte par la Royne d'Angleterre,* B1r.

18. Ibid., A3r.

19. Ibid., A4r.

20. Ibid., A4r.

21. Ibid., A2v.

22. Ibid., B2v.

23. Such was the case with Martin L'Homme, the printer of [François Hotman's], *Epistre envoiée au tigre de la France,* (s.l., [1560]). He was to pay dearly for his involvement in this polemic. He was sought out, and condemned to be hanged by an arrêt of the Parlement of Paris, dated 18 July 1560.

24. *L'Histoire du tumulte d'Amboise advenu au moys de Mars, M.D.LX. Ensemble, un avertissement & une complainte au peuple françois* (s.l., 1560), A2v.

25. Cardinal of Lorraine during the meeting of the Notables at Fontainbleau, August 1560, cited in Jane. T. Stoddart, *The Girlhood of Mary Queen of Scots from her landing in France in August 1548 to her departure from France in August 1561* (London, [1908]), p. 267.

26. [Hotman], *Epistre envoiée au tigre de la France,* A2r.

27. Ibid., A5v.

28. *L'Histoire du Tumulte d'Amboise,* B2r.

29. Ibid., B3r.

30. Ibid., D1v, which also contains accusations of Guisard embezzlement.

31. Pierre de La Place, *Commentaires de l'estat de la religion et république soubs les Rois Henry & François seconds, & Charles neufieme* ([Caen, Pierre Le Chandelier; La Rochelle, Barthélemy Berton; Orléans, Eloy Gibier; Paris, Robert Estienne; Rouen, Abel Clemence], 1565).

32. See Jean François Gilmont's excellent bibliographic study, 'Les premières éditions des ouvrages historiques de La Place et de La Popelinière', in *Revue française d'histoire du livre,* v. 50., 1986, pp. 119–52.

33. La Place, *Commentaires,* ([Orléans, Eloy Gibier,] 1565), B4r.

34. Ibid., B4r–v.

35. La Place, *Commentaires,* K6v.

36. Ibid., K6v–K7r.

37. Ibid., K6r–K7r.

38. Ibid., K6r.

39. Ibid., K7r.
40. Ibid., K7r–v.
41. *Advertissement sur le pourparlé, qu'on dit de paix, entre le Roy & ses rebelles. Avec son contrepoison* (s.l., 1568).
42. Ibid., L2v.
43. *Histoire de nostre temps, contenant un recueil des choses memorables passées & publiées pour le faict de la Religion & estat de la France, depuis l'Edict de Pacification du 23 jour de Mars 1568 jusques au jour present* ([La Rochelle], 1570).
44. Jeanne d'Albret, *Lettres de trèshaute, trèsvertueuse & trèschrestienne Princesse, Jane Royne de Navarre, au Roy, à la Royne Mere, à Monsieur frère du Roy, à Monsieur le Cardinal de Bourbon son beau frère, & à la Royne d'Angleterre* ([La Rochelle, Barthelemy Berton], 1568), A4r.
45. Ibid.
46. *Histoire de nostre temps, contenant un recueil des choses memorables passées & publiées pour le faict de la religion, & estat de la France, despuis l'Edict de Pacification [sic] du 23. iour de Mars, 1568. iusques au jour présent* ([La Rochelle, Barthelemy Berton], 1570).
47. *Petit discours sur une lettre responsive de l'Empereur Maximilian au Roy, 1568. Plus une copie de la conspiration de deux Contes d'Angleterre contre leur Royne* ([La Rochelle, Barthelemy Bérton], 1570), A2r. The account of the conspiracy is not contained in the copy held in the Bibliothèque Nationale, Paris.
48. Jeanne d'Albret, *Lettres*, B4r-C1v.
49. *Histoire de nostre temps*, B2r.
50. Ibid. & *Petit discours sur une lettre responsive de l'Empereur Maximilian au Roy, 1568. Plus une copie de la conspiration de deux Contes d'Angleterre contre leur Royne* ([La Rochelle], 1570), A2r.
51. *Histoire de nostre temps*, B1r and B2r.
52. Ibid., B4r.
53. [George Buchanan], *Histoire de Marie Royne d'Escosse, touchant la conjuration faicte contre le Roy, & l'adultère commis avec le Comte de Bothwel, histoire vrayement tragique, traduicte de Latin en François* (Edinburgh [London], Thomas Waltem, 1572).
54. Robert M. Kingdon, 'The Use of Clandestine Printings by the Government of Elizabeth I in its French Policy, 1570–90', in Frank McGregor and Nicholas Wright (eds.), *European History and Its Historians* (Adelaide, 1977), pp. 47–57.
55. George Buchanan, *De Maria Scotorum Regina, totaque eius contra Regem conjuratione, soedo cum Bothuelio adulterio* ([London, John Day, 1571]); *Ane Detectioun of the duinges of Marie Quene of Scottes* ([London, John Day], 1571); *Ane Detectioun of the doingis Marie Quene of Scottis* (St Andrews, Robert Lespreuk, 1572).
56. The accepted place of publication for this book is La Rochelle. Nevertheless, no real evidence has been advanced to support this assertion. In favour of London, we have a statement in the Catholic text that responded to Buchanan in addition to ambassadorial correspondence. *L'Innocence de la très-illustre, très-chaste, & débonnaire Princesse Madame Marie Royne d'Escosse. Où sont amplement réfutées les calomnies faulces, & impositions iniques, publiées par un livre secretement divulgué en France, l'an 1572, touchant tant la mort du Seigneur d'Arley son espoux, que autres crimes, dont elle est faulcement*

accusée. Plus un autre discours auquel son descouuertes plusieurs trahisons, tant manifestes, que iusques icy cachees, perpetrees par les mesmes calomniateurs (1572); ed. Samuel Jebb, *Histoire de Marie Stuart Reine d'Escosse et Douairiere de France. Où Recueil de toutes les pièces qui ont été publiées au sujet de cette Princesse* (2 vols., London, 1725), I, p. 425; Henry Killegrew, French ambassador to London, in a letter to Cecil, from Amboise 10 January 1572, reported that he sent a 'French copy (sic) enclosed to be printed in England, and sent over here secretly', *CSPF 1572–4*, no. 27, p. 14.

57. Phillips, *Images*, ch. 3.
58. Mary Stuart to M. de la Mothe Fénélon (French ambassador to England), Sheffield 22 November 1571, in Labanoff (ed.), *Lettres*, iv, pp. 3–5.
59. While John Leslie's *A Treatise concerning the Defence of the Honour of the Right High, Mightie and Noble Princesse Marie Queene of Scotland*, had been printed on the Guise sponsored Foigny press in Reims for distribution in England and amongst the exile community in 1569, there is little evidence to suggest that Charles IX followed Mary's advice and sanctioned the publication of any similar works in 1571. In fact, it would not be until late December 1572 or early January 1573 that a work defending the reputation of Mary appeared, *L'Innocence de la Royne de la trèsillustre Marie Royne d'Escosse* (Lyon, Jean de Tournes, 1572) and ([Reims], 1572).
60. *Correspondance diplomatique de Bertrand de Salignac de la Mothe Fénélon*, (Paris and London, 1840), t.iv., p. 301; R.H Mahon, *The Indictment of Mary Queen of Scots* (Cambridge, 1923), p. 25.
61. This is noted in Labanoff (ed.), *Lettres*, iv, p. 9.
62. Sir Thomas Smith to Cecil, 9 January 1572, in *CSPF 1572–4*, no. 23, p. 13.
63. Henry Killegrew to Cecil, 3 December 1571 in Allan Crosby (ed.), *CSPF 1569–71*, no. 2158, p. 570. It is highly likely that the text referred to was Buchanan's, but is referred to in this section of the letter simply as 'one of the Latin books lately set forth against the Scottish Queen'. Buchanan is mentioned subsequently in Mr. Bele's recommendation to Killegrew that Buchanan's 'little Latin books' be presented to Charles IX and his court; Henry Killegrew to Cecil, 29 December 1571 from Amboise, indicated that he had given 'one of Buchanan's Latin books to the Ambassador of Venice', *CSPF 1569–71*, no. 2196, p. 582. Interest in the book is also reported in Sir Thomas Smith to Lord Burghley from Amboise, 9 January 1572, *CSPF 1572–4*, no. 23, p. 13, and Henry Killegrew to Lord Burghley, 10 January 1572, *CSPF 1572–4*, no. 27, p. 14.
64. This was the recommendation of Mr. Bele to Henry Killegrew, reported in Killegrew's dispatch to Lord Burghley, 3 December 1571, *CSPF 1569–71*, no. 2159, p. 570.
65. Cicero, *The Verrine Orations*, trans. L.H.G. Greenwood (Cambridge Mass. & London, 1888), II.iv.25, vol. 2, p. 349.
66. [Buchanan], *Histoire de Marie Royne d'Escosse*, A3v.
67. Ibid., B1r.
68. Ibid., C3r.
69. Ibid., B1v.
70. Ibid., B3r.
71. Ibid., B4r.
72. Ibid., B3v.

73. Ibid., E1v.
74. Ibid., H3r.
75. Ibid., H3v.
76. George Buchanan, *De iure regni apud Scotos, dialogus, authore Georgio Buchanano Scoto* ([Edinburgh, John Ross], 1579).
77. On Buchanan's political thought, see Roger Mason, *Kingship and the Commonweal. Political Thought in Renaissance and Reformation Scotland* (East Linton, 1998), ch. 7, and Roger Mason, 'Rex Stoicus: George Buchanan, James VI and the Scottish Polity', in John Dwyer et al. (eds.), *New Perspectives on the Politics and Culture of Early Modern Scotland* (Edinburgh, 1982), pp. 9–33.
78. Ibid., N1r–X1r.
79. Ibid., V1r–V3r.
80. Ibid., V1r–V3r.
81. Ibid., X1r–Y4v.
82. Ibid., Y4r.
83. Andrew Pettegree, 'Religious Printing in 16th-Century France. The St Andrews Project' in *Proceedings of the Huguenot Society*, vol. xxvi/5, 1997, p. 654.
84. Nicolas Barnaud under pseudonymn Eusebius Philadelphius, *Le Reveille–Matin des françois et de leurs voisins* (Edinburgh, Jacques James [sic for Basle, Jaques Jobin], 1574).
85. Robert Kingdon, *Myths about the St Bartholomew's Day Massacres 1572–6* (Cambridge Mass. & London, 1988), pp. 70–2.
86. Eusebius Philadelphius [Nicolas Barnaud], *Dialogi ab Eusebio Philadelpho cosmopolita, in Gallorum et caeterarum nationum gratiam compositi, quorum primus ab ipso auctore recognitus et auctus, alter vero in lucem nunc primum editus fuit* ([Heidelberg, Schirat], 1573 (first dialogue only) & (Edinburgh, Jacques James [Strasbourg, Jacques Jobin, 1574).
87. Eusebius Philadelphius [Nicolas Barnaud], *Réveille-Matin, oder Wacht frü auf, das ist sumarischer und warhafter Bericht von den verschenenen auch gegenwärtigen beschwärlichen Händeln in Frankreich . . . gesprächweis gestellet und verfasset durch Eusebium Philadelphum cosmopolitam [H. Donellum]. Izunder aber aus dem Französischen ins Teutsch gebracht, durch Emericum Lebusium* (Edinburgh, Jacques James [= Strasbourg, Jacques James], 1575 (first dialogue only) & 1593 (both dialogues].
88. Eusebius Philadelphius [Nicolas Barnaud], *Der Francoysen en haerder nagebueren morghenwecker* (Dordrecht [Canin], 1574, 1574–5 & 1588).
89. The first dialogue only appeared under the title Eusebius Philadelphius [Nicolas Barnaud], *Dialogue auquel sont traitées plusieurs choses avenues aux Luthériens et Huguenots de la France, ensemble certains poincts et advis nécessaires* (Basle [La Rochelle, Barthelemy Berton], 1573), while subsequent editions contained both dialogues under the different title *Le Reveille–Matin des françois et de leurs voisins* (Edinburgh, Jacques James [sic for Basle, Jaques Jobin], 1574 (3 editions)).
90. See Kingdon's discussion of this text, *Myths*, pp. 70–87.
91. [Henri Estienne], *Discours merveilleux de la vie, actions et deportemens de Catherine de Medicis*, ([Geneva, Henri Estienne], 1575), (s.l., 1576) & (s.l., 1578).

92. [Barnaud], *Le Reveille–Matin*, c3r.
93. Ibid., A4v.
94. Ibid., A5r–A6v.
95. Ibid., A5r–A6v.
96. Ibid., a5r–v.
97. Ibid.
98. Ibid., a7–a8v.
99. Ibid., a8r.
100. Ibid., b3v–b7v.
101. Ibid., a8r.
102. Ibid., a8r–v.
103. Ibid., a8v.
104. Ibid., b2r–b6r.
105. Ibid., b5r.
106. Ibid., b6r.
107. Ibid., c4r.
108. [Simon Goulart], *Memoires de l'Estat de France sous Charles neufiesme* (Meidelbourg [= Geneva], Heinrich Wolf, 1576, 1577, 1578 (4 editions) & 1579).
109. Robert Kingdon, *Myths about the St Bartholomew's Day Massacres 1572–6*, (Cambridge Mass. & London, 1988), p. 2.
110. François de L'Isle [= François de La Planche], *La Legende de Charles, Cardinal de Lorraine, & de ses frères de la maison de Guise* (Reims [Geneva], Jaques Martin, 1579).
111. Ibid., B4r–v.
112. Ibid., D3v.
113. Ibid., E2r.
114. Nicolas de Montand [Nicolas Barnaud,] *Le Miroir des françois, comprise en trois livres* (s.l., 1581 (copy consulted), 1582) & ([Geneva, Laimaire], 1582), A7v.
115. *Histoire véritable de la conspiration de Guillaume Parry* (La Rochelle, Pierre Haultin, 1585).
116. [William Cecil], *L'Exécution de justice faicte en Angleterre pour maintenir la paix* ([London], Thomas Vautrollier, 1584).
117. *Histoire véritable de la conspiration*, C8v.
118. Ibid., D1r–D3r.
119. Ibid., D3r.
120. Edward Stafford to William Cecil, 5 March 1586 [sic for 1587], from Paris 5 March 1586, *CSPF 1586–8*, p. 236.
121. [Maurice Kyffin], *Apologie ou défense de l'honorable sentence & très-juste exécution de defuncte Marie Steuard dernière Royne d'Ecosse* ([La Rochelle], 1588).
122. [Maurice Kyffin], *A Defense of the Honourable sentence and execution of the Queene of Scots* (London, John Lindet, [1587]).
123. [Kyffin], *Apologie*, B1r.
124. Ibid., B3r.
125. Ibid., B4r.
126. Ibid., B3r.
127. Ibid., C3r–v.
128. Ibid., C1v.

129. Ibid., C2v.
130. Ibid., C4r.
131. Ibid., C7v.
132. Ibid., D5r.
133. Ibid., F4v.
134. Ibid., G4r.
135. Ibid., T8r.
136. Ibid., G4r.
137. Ibid., G4v–C5r.
138. Ibid., I8r.

4 Spreading News of the Execution: Mary Queen of Scots and the Parisian Catholic League

1. William Cecil, 10 [= 20 following Gregorian calendar] February 1587, in *CSPF Holland and Flanders 1586–7*, p. 358.
2. Paris was chosen as the exclusive focus of this chapter principally because the weight of ambassadorial and journal evidence favoured a study of the capital. That reaction to Mary's death appears to have been almost exclusively a Parisian phenomenon, however, is probably the consequence of a paucity of information for the provinces.
3. On the role of the nobility in the League, see in particular, Stuart Carroll 'The revolt of Paris, 1588: Aristocratic insurgency and the mobilization of popular support', *FHS*, 23/2 (2000), pp. 301–37, and the work of J.M. Constant, *Les Guise* (Paris, 1984), and 'La Noblesse seconde et la Ligue', in *Bulletin de la Société d'histoire moderne*, 2, (1988), pp. 11–20. On the urban League, see in particular Robert Descimon, *Qui étaient les Seize? Mythes et réalités de la Ligue parisienne (1585–94)* (Paris, 1983) and J.H.M. Salmon, 'The Paris Sixteen 1584–94: the social analysis of a revolutionary movement', in *Renassance and Revolt. Essays in the Intellectual and Social History of early modern Europe* (Cambridge, 1987), pp. 243–4.
4. Charles Hotman had powerful connections, including his cousin Antoine at this point a magistrate in the *chambre des comptes*. He would later become *avocat–général* in the Parlement of Paris under the League. His nephew, Philippe, was a judge at the Châtelet and an *échevin* of the city – see J. H. M. Salmon, 'The Paris Sixteen 1584–94', p. 242.
5. N.M. Sutherland, 'Henri III, the Guises and the Huguenots', in Keith Cameron (ed.), *From Valois to Bourbon. Dynasty, State and Society in Early Modern France* (Exeter, 1989), pp. 21–34; see also N. M. Sutherland, *The French Secretaries of State in the Age of Catherine de Medici* (London, 1962), ch. xvi.
6. Elie Barnavi, *Le Parti de Dieu. Étude sociale et politique des chefs de la Ligue parisienne 1585–94* (Brussells and Louvain, 1980), ch. 10.
7. Pierre de L'Estoile, *Mémoires Journaux de Pierre de L'Estoile*, ed. M. Brunet, A. Champoillon, E. Halphen, P. LaCroix, C. Reid, T. de Larroque & E. Tricotel, (Paris, 1876), t. III, p. 139.
8. Charles Labitte, *De la Démocratie chez les prédicateurs de la Ligue* (Geneva, 1841, 1971); Arlette Lebigre, *La Révolution des curés. Paris 1588–94* (Paris, 1980).

9. Denis Pallier, *Recherches sur l'Imprimerie à Paris pendant la Ligue, 1585–94* (Geneva, 1976).

10. Frederic J. Baumgartner, *Radical Reactionaries: the political thought of the French Catholic League* (Geneva, 1975–6), p. 80.

11. Ibid., p. 81.

12. 'I made at Mr. Wade's departure a complaint of a book which he brought you over with him, found out them that had it printed, the printer and the place where the rest of the books were. Some fled, some were put in guard, and the books, which were very few in respect of the great number printed, were torn and burnt, and such commandment given that those in the town are kept very secret', Edward Stafford to Francis Walsingham from Paris 22 June [sic for 1 July] 1587 in *CSPF 1586–8*, pp. 315–7.

13. Edward Stafford to Francis Walsignham from Paris 22 June [sic for 1 July] 1587 in *CSPF 1586–8*, p. 316.

14. Ibid. Madame de Montpensier's involvement in orchestrating the propaganda of the League will be discussed below.

15. MS. AS CMC 2a/42. From 1 February 1586, Verstegan received 20 *escudos* per month, which rose to 25 per month after 17 September 1588 and to 30 by 30 March 1594. Between 1586 and 1596, the wage book records that Verstegan had received a grand total of 2,288 escudos from Spain. On 1 0 November 1596, he was to receive an additional 712 escudos. With grateful thanks to Geoffrey Parker for drawing my attention to this document.

16. Verstegan [Richard Rowlands], *Theatrum Crudelitatum* (Antwerp, 1587); *Théâtre des cruautez des hereticques de nostre temps* (Antwerp, Adrien Hubert, 1588).

17. Verstegan, *Théâtre des cruautez*, L3r.

18. Stafford to Walsingham, Paris 22 June 1587, *CSPF 1586–8*, p. 316; L'Estoile, *Mémoires*, t. III, pp. 53–4.

19. Stafford to Walsingham, 22 June 1587 in *CSPF 1586–8*, p. 316.

20. Jean de Caumont, *Advertissement des advertissements. Au Peuple trèschrestien* (1587)

21. Stuart Carroll, 'The Revolt of Paris', pp. 316–21.

22. Ibid., p. 317.

23. Stafford to Walsingham, from Paris 22 June 1587, *CSPF 1586–8*, p. 316.

24. L'Estoile, *Mémoires*, t. III, pp. 53–4.

25. Anroux's cousin, Nicolas was a banker and Nicolas's nephew, Barthélemy, was a leading member of the Sixteen, Carroll, 'The Revolt of Paris', p. 319.

26. It is unknown whether this sonnet was printed or in manuscript.

27. L'Estoile, *Mémoires*, t. III, pp. 54–5.

28. Nicolas Poulain, 'Procès–Verbal', in Cimber and Danjou (eds.), *Archives curieuses de l'Histoire de France*, t. XI (Paris, 1826), p. 308; cited in Baumgartner, *Radical Reactionaries*, p. 44.

29. 2 September 1587 6.00pm, L'Estoile, *Mémoires*, t. III, p. 63.

30. Poulain, 'Procès-Verbal', p. 308 mentions only this priest [Prévost], but Pierre de L'Éstoile, *Mémoires*, III. 63 includes Jean Boucher and a theologian from the Sorbonne; cited in Baumgartner, *Radical Reactionaries*, p. 44.

31. Nicolas Poulain in *Mémoires relatifs à l'histoire de France*, ed. Claude-Bernard Petitot (Paris, 1825), p. 419, cited in Salmon, 'The Paris Sixteen', p. 244.

32. This data has been extracted from the files of the St Andrews Sixteenth–Century French Book Project in addition to my own bibliography of works relating to Mary.

33. Total number of French editions contained in the files of the St Andrews Book Project.

34. This tentative conclusion suggests that Denis Pallier's figure of 870 Leaguer editions for the period 1585–94 will need to be substantially revised upwards.

35. Estienne Pasquier to M. de Sainte-Marthe, in *Letters*, XVI, 7 cited in D. Thickett, 'Estienne Pasquier and his part in the Struggle for Tolerance', in *Aspects de la Propagande Religieuse*, G. Berthoud et al. (eds.), (Geneva, 1957), pp. 377–402.

36. On the military difficulties faced by the crown in imposing their will, see James Wood, *The King's army: warfare, soldiers, and society during the wars of religion in France, 1562–76* (Cambridge, 1996). The political philosophy of pragmatic religious toleration was based on the ideas of Michel de L'Hôpital, who in a speech on 3 January 1562, put forward a bold political theory to defend the Edict of Pacification. He distinguished between the *christianus du civis* and the *constituenda religione* of the *constituenda respublica*, a theme developed in the writings of Pierre de Beloy, Bernard de Girard, and Louis Le Roy. On this, see Philippe Papin, 'L'Image des "Politiques" durant la Ligue', in *Revue d'Histoire Moderne et Contemporaine* 38 (1991), p. 3.

37. Luc Racaut, 'The cultural obstacles to religious pluralism in the polemic of the French Wars of Religion', in K. Cameron, M. Greengrass and P. Roberts (eds.), *The Adventure of Religious Pluralism in Early-Modern France* (Berne, 2000), pp. 115–27.

38. Denis Pallier, 'Les réponses catholiques', in Roger Chartier and Henri-Jean Martin (eds.), *Histoire de l'Édition Française* (3 vols., Paris, 1983), t. I, p. 340, cited in Racaut, 'The cultural obstacles to religious pluralism'.

39. 'Nul cy après ne pourra dresser aucune imprimerie . . . qu'au prèalable il n'ait faict enregistrer au gresse de la Prévosté de Paris le nombre de presses qu'il entend dresser, l'enseigne qu'entend prendre au devant de ses livres, et que pareillement il n'ait baillé et laissé audit greffe son essay et espreuve de toutes les sortes et espèces de charactères desquels il s'entendra ayder en son art d'impression, contre-marquez au dos de sa marque particulière, avec son nom'. MS. BN fr.22065 (1) Lettres Patentes 12 October 1586; cited in Denis Pallier's *Recherches*, p. 39.

40. MS. BN nouv.acq. fr.3651 fol. 247, which is a declaration of Henri III regulating the exercise of the profession of printing and bookselling dated 12 October 1586 from Saint–Germain–en–Laye; cited in Alexandre Tuetey (ed.), *Inventaire Analytique des Livres de Couleur et Bannières du Châtelet de Paris* (Paris, Imprimerie Nationale, 1899) n. 4560, pp. 148–9. See also Denis Pallier, *Recherches*, p. 40.

41. Pierre Fayet, *Journal Historique de Pierre Fayet sur les Troubles de La Ligue*, ed. Victor Luzarche (Tours, 1852), p. 33.

42. Palma Cayet, *Chronologie Nouvenaire*, p.32, cited in Denis Pallier, *Recherches*, p. 64. For details of the trial, from 23 October 1586 to his condemnation on 22 November 1586, see Philippe Renouard, *Documents sur les imprimeurs, libraires, cartiers, graviers, fondeurs de lettres, relieurs, doreurs de livres, faiseurs*

de fermoires en lumineurs, parcheminiers et papetiers ayant exercé à Paris de 1450 à 1600. Recueillis aux Archives Nationales et au Département des Manuscrits de la Bibliothèque Nationale (Paris, 1901), t. I, pp. 48–9.

43. [Nicolas Rolland.,] *Remonstrances très humbles au Roy de France et de Pologne Henry et misères de ce royaume,* ([Paris] 1588); cited in Denis Pallier, *Recherches,* p. 230.

44. Bibliothèque de l'Institut de France, MS fonds Godefroy 288. fol. 35. The manuscript was discovered recently by Stuart Carroll 'Revolt of Paris'.

45. Pierre de Belloy, *De l'Authorité du Roy, et crimes de lèze majesté, qui se commetent par ligues, designation du successeur, et libelles escrits contre la personne et dignité du Prince* ([Paris], 1587). An editions of his *Examen du discours publié contre la maison royalle de Paris* ([Paris], 1587) may also have been published in the capital.

46. Pierre de L'Estoile, cited in A. Lebigre, *La Révolution des curés,* p. 20.

47. [Louis d'Orléans], *Premier et second advertissements des catholiques anglois aux françois catholiques* (Lyon, Jean Pillehotte, 1590), A1v.

48. The fact that the colporteurs and printer were flogged is noted in a later partisan account, *Les Considerations sur le meurdre commis en la personne de feu Monsieur le Duc de Guyse* (Paris, Guillaume Bichon, 1589), B2v.

49. MS BNF Fonds Français 10270, fol. 1r. 'Nicolas Poulain, Lieutenant de la Prevosté de l'Isle de France, L'Histoire de la Ligue, depuis le second Janvier 1585, jusques au jour des Barricades, escheues le douze May 1588'.

50. MS. AN X2b 153, 8 October 1587, no foliation.

51. Sixtus V, *Bulle de Reconciliation pour ceux de la nouvelle religion* ([Paris, Michel Buffet], 1587).

52. The date of Michel Buffet's original imprisonment is noted in Pref. Pol. AB.10. fol. 112v; as cited in Denis Pallier, *Recherches,* p. 495. MS. AN. X/2b/ 154 is the *Arrêt du Parlement* releasing Michel Buffet, dated 17 December 1587.

53. Andrew Pettegree, 'Levels of Anonymity. Clandestine and disguised printing in the Protestant Book World', unpublished paper presented at the Sixteenth Century Studies Conference, St Louis, 28 October 1999.

54. Ibid.

55. Interesting in this respect is a document I discovered in the Caen Archives Départementales. It is an official account of the action taken by the authorities against three prominent Caennais Protestant printers on Friday 11 September 1572: Pierre Philippe, Etienne Thomas and Pierre Le Chandelier. The account contains two lists of books seized during the raid. Despite Le Chandelier's activity in printing controversial polemical works, these are not listed in the official account which confines itself to listing large theological tomes. Le Chandelier resumed his printing activities by 1574. Perhaps reflective of the political climate, we do not have any evidence for any surreptitious printing activity by Le Chandelier until 1578, MS. ADC. 1B3. fols. 150–3.

56. [John Leslie], *Oraison funèbre sur la mort de la Royne d'Escosse* (Paris, Jean Charron, 1587).

57. [John Leslie], *Oraison funèbre sur la mort de très-heureuse mémoire Marie Stuard Royne d'Escosse* ([Paris, Jean Charron], 1587).

58. Renaud de Beaune, *Oraison funèbre de la très-chrestienne, très-illustre et très-constante, Marie Royne d'Escosse* (Paris, Guillaume Bichon, 1588).

59. Paris was the principal printing hub for Catholic works in France. To some extent, the use of anonymity also disguised the fact that these books emanated from Paris, remaining sensitive to provincial anti-Parisian concerns. See also Elie Barnavi, *Le Parti de Dieu : étude sociale et politique des chefs de la Ligue Parisienne 1585–94* (Louvain, 1980), p. 265 for provincial fears against the centralising influence of Paris under the League.

60. Jean de Caumont, *Advertissement des advertissemens au peuple très–crestien* (1587), a[sic for A]2r. This pamphlet was published no less than eight times in 1587.

61. R. Hari, 'Les placards de 1534' in G. Berthoud et al., *Aspects de la propagande religieuse* (Geneva, 1957), pp. 79–142.

62. A systematic study of placards requires to be undertaken. Any such study would need to survey surviving materials not only in libraries, but also in French communal and departmental archives, where ephemeral pamphlets and placards are often to be found bound with manuscripts.

63. L'Estoile, *Mémoires*, t. III, p. 14.

64. Jouhaud, 'Readability and Persuasion', p. 241. L'Estoile's manuscript collection contains 142 items, 76 of which are illustrated by at least one engraving. 15 other manuscript copies or notes in L'Estoile's hand allude to images. 51 contain no pictoral material. 2/3 of this 51 are official proclamations of the King, Parlement and various official ordinances of the League. In all, 4/5ths of all unofficial placards are illustrated.

65. On Germany, see Robert Scribner, *For the Sake of Simple Folk: Popular Propaganda for the German Reformation* (Oxford, 1981, 1994).

66. With thanks to Andrew Pettegree for this observation.

67. P. Renold (ed.), 'Letters of William Allen and Richard Barret, 1572–90', *Catholic Record Society*, 58 (1959), p. xxxix; cited in Carroll, 'Revolt of Paris', p. 319.

68. See Jean-Pierre Seguin, 'L'Illustration des feuilles d'actualité non périodiques en France aux XVe et XVIe siècles' in *Gazette des Beaux–Arts*, July 1958; see also Jean–Pierre Seguin., *L'Information en France avant la périodique, 517 canards imprimés entre 1529 et 1631* (Paris, [1964]).

69. Jean-Marie Constant, *La Ligue* (Paris, 1996), p. 120 mentions this, without citing any source.

70. 'J'envoye aussi l'Epitaphe de la Royne d'Escosse composée par Ponthus de Thyart, évesque de Chaslon, que V.A goustera paraventure', René de Lucinge, *Lettres de 1587. L'Année des Reîtres*, ed. James Supple (Geneva, 1994), p. 240.

71. L'Estoile, *Mémoires*, t. III, p. 17.

72. On Adam Blackwood's *Martyre de la Royne d'Escosse, douariere de France. Contenant le vray discours des traisons à elle faictes à la suscitation d'Elizabet Angloise, par lequel les mesnonges, calomnier & faulses accusations dressées contre ceste trèsvertueuse, très catholique & trèsillustre princesse sont esclarcies & son innocence avérée* (Edinburgh [Paris], Jean Nafield [false], 1587), see chapter 5. Among the verses contained in Blackwood's book is the Latin 'Monumentum Mariae & Monumentum Regale' on ã5r–ã6v, also noted in L'Estoile, *Mémoires*, t. III, p. 16, as well as a number of other poems not contained in L'Estoile's collection, including several sonnets, 'Les Vertus de Jesabel Angloise', ã7r, 'Aux Anglois affligez par la religion catholique' ã7r,

'comparison de Londres à Rome' ã8r and at the end of the book, 'Epitaphium Elisabethae Titherae Anglae' HH7r.

73. See also James Phillips, *Images*, pp. 162–9 for a detailed discussion of this poetry.
74. Pierre de L'Estoile, *Mémoires–Journaux de Pierre de L'Estoile* (Paris, 1982 – reprint of the Paris edition of 1876), p. 18.
75. Jacques Le Bossu, *Deux devis, d'un catholique et d'un politique, sur l'exhortation faicte au peuple de Nantes, en la grande Eglise de sainct Pierre, pour iurer l'union des Catholiques, le huictiesme iour de juin, mil cinq cens quatres vingts & neuf*, (Nantes, Nicolas des Marestz & François Fauerye, 1589), F1v–F2r. The quatrain itself also appeared, along with numerous other verses, in several other printed books, including *Coppie de la requeste presentée au Turc par l'agent de la Royne d'Angleterre* (Verdun, Jacques Eldreton, 1589), poem IV.
76. L'Estoile, *Mémoires*, t. III, p. 14.
77. Charles Labitte, *De la Démocratie chez les Prédicateurs de la Ligue* (Geneva, 1971 original edition 1841), p. 108.
78. Ibid.
79. Ibid., p. 77.
80. Alexandre Teulet (ed.), *Papiers d'état, piéces et documents inédits ou peu connus, relatifs a l'histoire de l'Écosse au XVIe siècle, tirés dés bibliothèques et des archives de France* (3 vols., Paris, 1852), t. II, p. 157. See also Francisque-Michel, *Les Écossais en France. Les Français en Écosse* (2 vols., London, 1862), t. II, p. 106, n.2 and Bernardino de Mendoza to Philip II, 6 March 1587, *CSP Spanish 1587–1603*, no. 32, p. 31.
81. Labitte, *De la Démocratie*, passim and Constant, *La Ligue* (Paris, 1996), p. 238. Hamilton worked in the Parish of Saint Cosme, and was involved in the writing and financing of Catholic editions destined for the British Isles.
82. L'Estoile, *Mémoires*, t. III, 279.
83. *Registres du Parlement* (Copie de la Bibliotheque de la ville de Paris), t. XXII, 11 cited in Labitte, *De la Démocratie*, p.32.
84. Jacques-Auguste de Thou, *Histoire Universelle de Jacques–Auguste de Thou depuis 1543. jusqu'en 1607* (16 vols., London, 1734), vol. 9, pp. 648–9.
85. Ibid., p. 649. See also Jehan de La Fosse, *Journal d'un Curé Ligueur de Paris sous les trois dernières Valois suivi du Journal du Secrétaire de Philippe du Bec, Archêveque de Reims, de 1588 à 1605*, ed. Edouard de Barthélemy, (Paris, 1866), p. 204.
86. Renaud de Beaune, *Oraison funèbre de la très-chrestienne, très-illustre, Marie Royne d'Escosse, morte pour la foy, le 18. Febrier 1587 par la cruauté des Anglois hérétiques, ennemys de Dieu* ([Paris, Guillaume Bichon], 1588), A4v.
87. Henri de Guise notes this in a letter to Bernardin de Mendoza (10 Nov. 1586), now held in the Archives de l'Empire, Papiers de Simancas, B.57 (290). This was followed a few days later by a letter written from the head of the League [Charles Hotman] to the Spanish ambassador, dated 25 November 1586. On 22 December 1586, Bernardino de Mendoza wrote to Alexandre Farnese that the deliverance of Mary Stuart was the 'moindre souci de la cour de France'. All these sources are cited in Adolphe Chéruel, *Marie Stuart et Catherine de Médicis. Étude historique sur les relations de la France et de l'Écosse dans la second moitié du XVIe siècle* (Geneva, 1975). This is a reprint of the original Paris edition of 1858, p. 156. René de Lucinge

noted in his diary that 'car la ligue se doubte que le Roy ne s'entende avec ceste méchante royne'. Lucinge, *Lettres*, p. 82. See also L'Estoile, *Mémoires*, t. II, p. 234–5 where L'Estoile comments on Bellièvre's mission.

88. 29th January old style.
89. Lucinge, *Lettres*, p. 41.
90. Ibid., p. 56.
91. 20 February 1587. Ibid., p. 62
92. Ibid., p. 67.
93. Walsingham to Stafford, 9 March 1587, *CSPF 1586–8*, p. 241.
94. Giovanni Dolfin to the Doge and Senate, 2 March 1587, in *CSP Venetien, 1581–91*, no. 477, p. 249. In fact, the French King may have been informed by Pomponne de Bellièvre on 3 March. In a letter from Stafford to the secretaries, 22 February [4 March] 1587, he wrote 'I am even now advertised that the King for a certainty was yesterday told of this [i.e. the execution of Mary] by M. Bellièver [sic]; that he took it very evil, and said that he might easily perceive how little account the Queen made of him in this', in *CSPF 1586–8*, p. 227.
95. Lucinge, *Lettres*, p. 78.
96. On this, see David E. Duncan, *Calendar. Humanity's Epic Struggle to Determine a True and Accurate Year* (New York, 1998).
97. For instance, Antonia Fraser, *Mary Queen of Scots* (Bungay, 1976) originally published 1969, p. 590 has written, 'as the gates of Fotheringhay were locked, so were the English ports closed immediately after the death of the queen of Scots. It was three weeks before the French ambassador Châteauneuf could write back to his master in Paris with tidings of the calamity'.
98. The time taken to transport news from London to Paris varied according to weather conditions on the Channel. Ships would not sail without wind.
99. Edward Stafford to William Cecil, 5 March 1586 [sic for 1587], from Paris 5 March 1586, *CSPF 1586–8*, p. 236.
100. Lucinge, *Lettres*, p. 81.
101. Ibid., pp. 88–9.
102. Stafford to Burghley, from Paris 24 March 1587, in *CSPF 1586–8*, p. 252.
103. In a printed copy of the letter addressed to Sixtus V by the League to demand the deposition of Henri III, it stated 'Constans in vulgo de prodita ad mortem Scotorum regina rumor', Jean Boucher, *De justa Henrici III abdicatione* (Paris, Nicolas Nivelle, 1589), p. 247v; cited in Chéruel, *Marie Stuart*, p. 156.
104. *Les Meurs, humeurs et comportemens de Henry de Valois* (Paris, Antoine le Riche, 1589), cited in Chéruel, *Marie Stuart*, p. 156.
105. Ibid., p. 157.
106. *Les Considerations sur le meurdre commis en la personne de feu Monsieur le Duc de Guyse* (Paris, Guillaume Bichon, 1589), B2r.
107. Ibid., B1v.
108. Ibid., B2r.
109. See Philippe Renouard, *Documents sur les Imprimeurs*.
110. MS. ADSM. B. Parlement, Registres Secrets, Rouen entrée of 19 July 1593, cited in Philip Benedict, *Rouen during the Wars of Religion* (Cambridge, 1981), p. 168, n. 2. In Rouen, Leaguers were taking steps as early as 1593 to prevent sensitive material falling into hostile hands.

111. L'Estoile, *Mémoires*, t. III, p. 66.
112. Ibid., pp. 53–4.
113. Ibid., p. 63.
114. Ibid., pp. 118–9.
115. Carroll, 'Revolt of Paris', p. 315.
116. L'Estoile, *Mémoires*, III, p. 66.
117. Auguste de Thou, *Histoire Universelle*, 10:26. See also Carroll, 'Revolt of Paris', p. 337.
118. L'Estoile, *Mémoires*, III, pp. 118–9.
119. Jeffrey K. Sawyer, *Printed Poison. Pamphlet propaganda, faction politics, and the public sphere in early seventeenth century France* (Oxford, 1990), p. 134.

5   A Catholic Tragedy: The Radical Image of a Martyred Queen

1. Mary Queen of Scots to Bernardino de Mendoza, from Fotheringhay 23 November [1586], in Alexander Labanoff (ed.), *Lettres, Instructions et Mémoires de Marie Stuart, Reine d'Escosse* (London, 1844), t. vi, p. 459. The strict conditions of Mary's confinement, and the continued imprisonment of her servants months after her execution, meant that this letter was only delivered to Mendoza in Paris on 15 October 1587, almost a year after it had been written.
2. James Phillips, *Images of a Queen. Mary Stuart in Sixteenth-Century Literature* (Berkeley and Los Angeles, 1964), chapter 6.
3. See for instance Joanne Mosley, 'Did Mary Stuart die a "Fidele Françoise"? Mary Stuart's parting speach to Melville', in *Bibliothèque d'Humanisme et Renaissance*, LII 1990 no. 3, pp. 623–5.
4. Brad S. Gregory, *Salvation at Stake. Christian Martyrdom in Early Modern Europe* (Cambridge Mass. & London, 1999).
5. Gregory, *Salvation at Stake*, p. 14.
6. Ibid, p. 16.
7. Ibid, pp. 16–26.
8. Jean-François Gilmont, 'Le Pseudo-Martyre du Vaudois Pierre Masson', *Bollettino della Societa di Studi Valdes*, 13 (1973), p. 44, and David Watson, 'The Martyrology of Jean Crespin and the Early French Evangelical Movement, 1523–55', (unpublished Ph.D thesis, University of St Andrews, 1997), ch. 2 'The reliability of the Histoire des vray tesmoins as a historical source'.
9. Gregory, *Salvation at Stake*, p. 21.
10. This anonymous account appeared in six editions under two similar but variant titles: *Discours de l'exécution de mort. Faicte par la Royne d'Angleterre, sur la personne de très-haute et très-illustre Princesse Madame Marie Stouard, Royne d'Escosse. Facite le dixhuictiesme jour de février, mil cinq-cens quatre-vingts sept. Ensemble les derniers propos tenuz par ladicte Dame* (Paris, Jehan Poitevin, 1587), and *Discours de la mort de tréshaute & très illustre princesse Madame Marie Stouard* (s.l., variously [1587] & 1587).
11. Guillaume de L'Aubespine's report can be found in Alexandre Teulet (ed), *Relations Politiques de la France et de l'Espagne avec l'Écosse au XVIe siècle* (5 vols., Paris, 1862), vol. iv, pp. 169–78. Phillips wrongly identifies Chasteuneuf as Claude de L'Aubespine, *Images*, p. 319. In fact, it was his son, Guillaume.

12. In fact the open admission of uncertainty was not at all unusual in martyological narratives. See Gregory, *Salvation at Stake*, p. 170 who notes similar admissions on behalf of Protestant martyrologists such as Adriaen van Haemstede and Jean Crespin and that such remarks essentially solicited additional information from their audiences. See also Watson, 'The Martyrology of Jean Crespin', p. 20.
13. An error for 14 February.
14. An error for 16 February.
15. Mr. Andrews provost of Northampton.
16. In fact, six people in Mary's service were permitted to witness her execution. These were [Andrew] Melvin, her *maistre d'hostel*, Pierre Gorjon, her apothecary, Jacques Gervais, her surgeon, and Dominique Bourgoin, her doctor, and two ladies, Jane Kennedy and Elizabeth Curle, the sister of her Scottish secretary.
17. Claude Nau, Gilbert Curl and Etienne Pasquier were Mary's secretaries.
18. This date is correct.
19. Phillips, *Images*, p. 152.
20. The letter from Sieur [Jérome] de Gondi to James Beaton can be found transcribed and translated by Walter R. Humphries, 'The Execution of Mary, Queen of Scots', in *Aberdeen University Review*, xxx (1943), pp. 20–5. See also Bernardino Mendoza to Philip II, 7 March 1587, *CSP Spanish 1587–1603*, no. 35, pp. 34–6, and Giovanni Dolfin to the Doge and Senate of Venice, 13 March 1587, *CSP Venetian 1581–91*, no. 484, pp. 256–8.
21. [John Leslie], *Oraison funèbre sur la mort de la Royne d'Escosse. Traduicte d'Escossois en nostre langue Françoise* (Paris, Jean Charron, 1587) and *Oraison funèbre sur la mort de très-heureuse mémoire, Marie Stuard, Royne d'Escosse, de son vivant fille, femme & mère de Roy* (s.l., 1587). Phillips seems to be unaware of this initial version of the oration, *Images*, pp. 152–3.
22. Deprived of being able to fulfill his traditional duties as Bishop of Ross, in 1587 Leslie served as suffragan and vicar general in Rouen. According to information on the title page of the book, Leslie originally delivered his oration in Scots.
23. [Leslie], *Oraison funèbre*, B1v.
24. [John Leslie], *Harangue funèbre sur la mort de la Royne d'Escosse* ([Paris, Jean Charron, 1587–1588]).
25. [Leslie], *Oraison funèbre*, B2r.
26. [Leslie], *Harangue funèbre*, B2r.
27. The issue of Mary's final confession was raised, indirectly, in the dedication to Roch Mamerot's *Bref discours sur la sainte confession nécessaire à un chacun Chrestien, presentée à très-haute & très-illustre Princesse (de bonne mémoire) Marie Stouard . . .* (Paris, 1587)
28. Renaud de Beaune, *Oraison funèbre de la très-chrestienne, très-illustre, très-constante, Marie Royne d'Escosse, morte pour la foy, le 18. febrier, 1587. par la cruauté des Anglois hérétiques* (s.l., 1588).
29. Beaune, *Oraison funèbre*, E1r–E3r; Gondy, 'Execution', p. 22.
30. Beaune, *Oraison funèbre*, E3v; Gondy, 'Execution', p. 24.
31. Beaune, *Oraison funèbre*, E3r; Gondy, 'Execution', p. 23; c.f. *Discours de la mort*, A4v.
32. Gondy, 'Execution', p. 21 and p. 23.

33. Ibid, p. 22.
34. Beaune, *Oraison funèbre*, E1v–E2r.
35. Bourgoing returned from Fotheringhay after a long detainment late in October 1587 with Pierre Gorion, her surgeon, Elizabeth Curle and Jane Kennedy, Mary's ladies in waiting. Bourgoing provided fresh material, particularly relating to the night before the execution, see 'Journal de Dominique Bourgoin Medecin de Marie Stuart' published from the original manuscript by M.R. Chantelauze in *Marie Stuart son procès et son exécution* (Paris, 1876). There is another sympathetic account of the execution, an anonymous manuscript entitled 'Le vray rapport de l'éxecution faicte sur la personne de la Reyne d'Escosse' held in the BNF Fonds de StGerm. Harl. no. 222 t. XI, fol. 31, reprinted in Alexandre Teulet (ed.), *Relations Politiques de la France et de l'Espagne avec l'Écosse au XVIe siècle* (5 vols., Paris, 1862), vol. iv, pp. 153–64. However there is no evidence that the details contained in this source, which include information relating to a supernatural event days before the execution, were known to contemporary propagandists.
36. The Wingfield account can be found in British Museum. MSS. Calig. C.IX, fol. 589 to 599 written to William Cecil a few days after the execution. I consulted the text reprinted in *The Trial of Mary Queen of Scots*, ed. A. Francis Steuart (Edinburgh and London, 1922), pp. 173–85.
37. [Adam Blackwood], *Martyre de la Royne d'Escosse douairiere de France. Contenant le vray discours des traisons à elle faictes à la suscitation d'Elizabet Angloise, par lequel les mensonges, calomnies & faulses accusations dresées contre ceste trèsvertueuse, trèscatholique & trèsillustre Princesse sont esclarcies & son innocence averée* (Edinburgh [Paris], Jean Nafield, 1587), (Edinburgh [Paris], Jean Nafield, 1588), (Antwerp, Gaspar Fleysben, 1588) & (Edinburgh [Paris], Jean Nafield, 1589); [Adam Blackwood], *La Mort de la Royne d'Escosse, douairiere de France. Où est contenu le vray discours de la procedure des Anglois à l'Execution d'icelle, la constante & royalle resolution de sa majesté defunte: ses vertueux depportements & dernier propos, ses funerailles & enterrement, d'ou on peut cognoistre la traistre cruauté de l'hérétique Angloys à l'encontre d'une Royne soveraine très chrestienne & catholique innocente* (s.l, 1588), (s.l., 1589).
38. Mary Stuart to James Beaton, 16 July 1576, in Labanoff (ed), *Lettres de Marie Stuart*, t. iv, p. 329, see also t. viii, p. 7.
39. [Adam Blackwood], *Histoire et martyre de la Royne d'Escosse, douairiere de France, proche héritière de la Royne d'Angleterre. Contenant les trahisons à elle faict es par Elisabet Anglois, pour ou on cognoist les mensonges, calomnies & faulses accusations envers ceste bonne Princesse innocente* (Paris, Guillaume Bichon, 1588).
40. [Blackwood], *Martyre de la Royne d'Escosse* (Antwerp, Gaspar Fleysben, 1588), Dd2r.
41. Ibid, DD1r–DD2v.
42. Ibid, DD5v–DD6r.
43. Ibid, DD6r.
44. 'Non facit martyrem poena, sed causa', Augustine, *S. Aurellii Augustini Hipponensis Episcopi Sermones ad Populum omnes classibus quatuor nunc primum comprehensi. Prima Classe continentur Sermones de Scriptures veteris et Novi Testamenti. Secunda, Sermones de Tempore. Tertia, Sermones de Sanctis. Quarta, Sermones de Diversis*, classis III, 'Sermo CCCXXVII', col. 1451.
45. [Blackwood], *La Mort*, a2r–a3r.

46. Ibid, b4v.
47. Ibid, c1r–v, d4v.
48. Ibid, e1r.
49. Ibid, e6v–e7r. The phrasing in Wingfield was, 'But I praie thee (said she) carrie this message from me, That I doe die a true woman to my religion and like a true woman of Scotland and ffraunce [sic]', in *Trial of Mary Queen of Scots*, ed. A.F. Steuart (Edinburgh, 1922), p. 175. Joanne Mosley, Did Mary Stuart die a "Fidele Françoise"? Mary Stuart's parting speach to Melville,' in *Bibliothèque d'Humanisme et Renaissance* (1990), LII/no.3, pp. 623–5, has argued, unconvincingly, that the reason why the injection of the French element, embodied in the speech to Melvin, did not take place before 1588, was that it might detract from the central message of the argument – that Mary died for her faith. In fact, it was simply a question of availability of information.
50. Obert Barnestapolius [sic for Robert Turner], *Maria Stuarta, regina Scotiae, dotaria Franciae, haeres Angliae et Hyberniae, martyr Ecclesiae, innocens a caede Darleana* (Ingolstadt, ex officina W. Ederi, 1588). The translation was entitled *L'Histoire et vie de Marie Stuart, Royne d'Escosse d'oiriere de France, héritière d'Angleterre & d'Ibernye, en laquelle est clairement justifiée de la mort du Prince d'Arlay [sic] son mary* (Paris, chez Guillaume Julien, 1589). Mary's speech to Melvin can be found on I5r. The principal sources used by Turner, *L'Histoire et vie*, were the L'Aubespine and Wingfield accounts, as well as anonymous 'Le vray rapport de l'éxecution faicte sur la personne de la Reyne d'Escosse le VIIIe février, le mercredy . . .' MS. BNF Fonds de StGerm. Harl. no. 222 t. XI, fol. 31, reprinted in *Relations Politiques de la France et de l'Espagne avec l'Écosse au XVIe siècle*, ed. Alexandre Teulet, (5 vols., Paris, 1862), vol. iv, pp. 153–64. Turner also drew from Renaud de Beaune, *Oraison funèbre*, for instance in the wording on H12r of the desirable accusation of being called a Catholic c.f. de Beaune, D1v, and most particularly on I7v where Turner copied almost word for word de Beaune's comparison of Mary to St Agnes, I7v c.f. de Beaune, E3v.
51. [Blackwood], *La Mort*, f6v.
52. The Duc de Guise was to act as principal executor to her will.
53. Mary Stuart, *Le Testament et derniers propos de la Royne d'Escosse avant son supplice. Ensemble les legs qu'elle à laissé aux officiers de sa maison* (Paris, pour Pierre Marin, 1589).
54. [Blackwood], *La Mort*, d6v–d7r.
55. For a contrasting interpretation see Mosley, 'Did Mary Stuart die a "Fidele Françoise"?', pp. 623–5.
56. [Blackwood], *La Mort*, e8v.
57. Ibid, f2v.
58. Turner, *L'Histoire et vie*, I5v–I6r.
59. [Blackwood], *La Mort*, h7v.
60. Ibid, *La Mort*, i6r.
61. John Leslie, *Oraison funèbre*, A3r–v.
62. Robert Wingfield, Brit. Mus. MSS. Calig. C.IX, fol. 589 to 599, a report written to Willian Cecil dated 11 [21 New Style] February 1586 [sic for 1587], reprinted in *The Trial of Mary Queen of Scots*, ed. A. Francis Steuart (Edinburgh and London, 1922), pp. 173–85.
63. Gregory, *Salvation at Stake*, pp. 134–5.

64. Ibid, p. 494, n. 248.
65. Ibid, p. 298.
66. 'All the things that were of the martyrs they burned, as Eusebius said, and the ashes spread into Rhodes, so that the memory of those men might also perish with their bodies' [Blackwood], *Martyre de la Royne d'Escosse*, Ee1r.
67. John Leslie, *Oraison*, A4v.
68. Beaune, *Oraison funèbre*, E2v.
69. A.D. [Artus Desiré], *Les Quinze signes advenuz és parties d'occident, vers les royaumes d'Escosse & Angleterre* (Paris, Michel Buffet, 1587), & A.D. [Artus Desiré], *Figure des signes merveilleux veuz & apparus vers les royaumes d'Escosse & Angleterre* (Paris, Michel Buffet, 1587). The importance of eschatological thought in the polemic of the Wars of Religion has been grossly exaggerated by Denis Crouzet, *Les Guerriers de Dieu. La violence au temps des troubles de Religion vers 1525–vers 1610* (Paris, 1990).
70. See for instance, *Les Quinze effusions du sang de nostre sauveur Jesu-christ* (Troyes, Jean Le Coq, s.d.).
71. Caumont, *Advertissement*, E2r.
72. Orléans, *Advertissement*, B4v.
73. Ibid., E5r.
74. *Exhortation aux catholiques de se réconcilier les uns aux autres, pour se défendre des hérétiques* (1587), A4r.
75. Caumont, *Advertissement*, F1v–F2r.
76. *Exhortation aux catholiques*, C3v.
77. Ibid, C3v–C4r.
78. Ibid.
79. [Louis d'Orléans], *Advertissement des catholiques anglois aux françois catholiques, du danger où ils sont de perdre leur Religion, & d'experimenter, comme en Angleterre, la cruauté des Ministres s'ils reçoivent à la couronne un Roy qui soit hérétique* (s.l., 1586).
80. [Louis d'Orléans], *Premier et second advertissement des catholiques anglois aux françois catholiques* (Paris, Guillaume Bichon, 1590).
81. [Orléans], *Advertissement des catholiques anglois*, A3r.
82. Luc Racaut, *Hatred in Print. Catholic Propaganda and Protestant Identity during the French Wars of Religion* (Aldershot, 2002). See also See Wylie G. Sypher, '"Faisant ce qu'il leur vient a plaisir": The Image of Protestantism in French Catholic polemic on the eve of the Religious Wars', *SCJ*, 9/2 (1980), pp. 59–84.
83. R.I. Moore, 'Heresy as Disease', in D.W. Lourdeaux and D. Verhelst (eds.), *The Concept of Heresy in the Middle Ages* (Louvain, 1976), pp. 1–11.
84. Obert Barnestapolius [Robert Turner], *L'Histoire et vie de Marie Stuart, Royne d'Escosse, d'oiriere [douairiere] de France, héritière d'Angleterre & d'Ibernye, en laquelle elle est clairement justifiée de la mort du Prince d'Arlay son mary* (Paris, Guillaume Julien, 1589), H7v.
85. Hierosme Osorius, *Remonstrance à madame Elizabeth Royne d'Angleterre, & d'Irlande touchant les affaires du monde, gouvernement politique des royaumes, républiques & empires & rétablissement de l'ancienne catholique religion selon la doctrine des anciens pères & docteurs de l'Église Catholique Apostolique & Romaine* (Paris, Michel Roigny, 1587), a4v.
86. Orléans, A3v.

87. Richard Verstegan [Richard Rowlands], *Théâtre des cruautez des héréticques de nostre temps* (Antwerp, Adrien Hubert, 1588), A2r.

88. P. Jonin, *Les Personnages féminins dans les romains français de Tristan au XIIe siècle. Étude des influences contemporaines* (Gap, 1958), cited in Moore, 'Heresy as Disease', p. 5. Syphilis was one of the diseases which fell under the term 'lepra'.

89. Racaut, *Hatred in Print*, chapter 6.

90. Moore, 'Heresy as Disease', p. 5.

91. Jean de Caumont, *Advertissement des advertissemens*, a2v.

92. Verstegan, *Théâre des cruautez*, B4r.

93. Jean Gay, *Histoire des scismes et hérésies des Albigeois conforme à celle du present: par laquelle appert que plusieurs grands princes, & seigneurs sont tombez en extremes desolations & ruynes, pour avoir favorisé aux hérétiques* (Paris, Pierre Gaultier, 1561); Gabriel de Sacconay, *Regis Angliae Henrici huius nominis octavi assertio septem sacramentorum adversus Martin Lutherum* (Lyon, Guillaume Rouillé, 1561).

94. [Robert Persons], *Epistre de la persecution meue en Angleterre contre l'Eglise Chrestienne, Catholique & Apostolique, & fideles membres d'icelle. Où sont déclarez les très–grandes afflictions, misères & calamitez, les tourmens très cruelz & martyres admirables, que les fidèles chrestiens anglois y souffrent pour leur foy & religion* (Paris, Thomas Brumen, 1586).

95. Jerôme Osorius, *Remonstrance à Madame Elizabeth royne d'Angleterre touchant les affaires du monde* (Lyon, C. Tantillon, 1587) & (Paris, 1587).

96. Ferdinand I, *Exemplar literarum Ferdinandi, Romanorum imperatoris, ad Pium IIII, pontificem maximum, quibus quidem in literis . . . agit de sarciendis tandemque aliquando diffiniendis hisce rebus, quae in publicam venere concilii deliberationem, nec enim pati conditionem temporum, rem amplius extrahi. Ejusdem imperatoris in eam ipsam rem ad cardinalem Lotharingum admonitio. Epistola etiam cujusdam docti hominis, natione Lusitani [J. Osorii], ad Elizabetam, reginam Angliae, in qua disseritur de ratione reipublicae optime administrandae, tum de constituenda, ex veterum patrum sententia, religione. Quarum literarum adsuetur quoque ad calcem gallica interpretatio* (Parisiis, apud N. Chesneau, 1563). The French translation was entitled *Les graves et sainctes remonstrances de l'Empereur Ferdinand, à nostre sainct pere le Pape, Pie, quatriesle de ce nom sur le faict du Concil de Trente* (Paris, Nicolas Chesneau, 1563).

97. [Anne Percy], *Discours des troubles nouvellement advenus au royaume d'Angleterre. Avec une déclaration, faicte par le Comte de Northumberland & autres seigneurs d'Angleterre* (Paris, Laurent du Coudret, [1587], (Paris, Jacques Blochet, 1587) [2 editions] & (Rouen, P. L'Aignel, 1587).

98. Nicholas Sanders, *Origine ac progressu schismatis anglicani libri tres, quibus historia continetur, maxime ecclesiastica, annorum circiter sexaginta . . . nimirum ab anno 21 regni Henrici octavi . . . usque ad hunc vigesimum octavum Elisabethae . . . aucti per Edouardum Rishtonum et impressi primum in Germania . . .* (Rheims, 1585), (Rome, B. Bonsaldini, 1586). The Reims edition is noted in Phillips, *Images*, p. 274 n. 82. The French translation was entitled *Les Trois livres du docteur Nicolas Sanders, contenans l'origine & progrez du scisme d'Angleterre . . . Augmentez par Edouart Rishton, premièrement imprimez en Latin, en Allemaigne, & depuis plus correctement à Rome* ([Louvain], 1587), (Augsbourg, Hans Mark, 1587) & (s.l., 1587).

99. [Blackwood], *Martyre de la Royne d'Escosse*, A4v–A5r.

100. For instance Antoine de Mouchy, *Responce a quelque apologie que les hérétiques ces jours passés ont mis en avant sous ce titre: Apologie ou deffence des bons chrestiens contre les ennemis de l'Église catholique* (Paris, Claude Frémy, 1558), F4r–v; see Racaut, *Hatred in Print*.

101. *Le Testament de Henry de Valoys, recommandé à son amy Jean d'Espernon* ([Paris], Jacques Varengles, 1589) & ([Paris], Jacques Varangles & Denis Binet, 1589), B1r.

102. Orléans, *Advertissement*, verse 2 of the sonnet contained on A1v.

103. Kings 18:19–19:3.

104. Caumont, *Advertissement*, D1v.

105. Pierre de L'Estoile, *Mémoires-Journaux de Pierre de L'Estoile* (Paris, 1982 – reprint Paris, 1876), vol. III, p. 18. The use of 'louve' was not the exclusive domain of verse, as in for instance, Jacques Le Bossu, Frere, Religieux à Sainct Denys en France, & Docteur en la faculté de Theologie à Paris, *Deux Devis, D'un Catholique et d'un Politique, sur l'exhortation faicte au peuple de Nantes, en la grande Eglise de sainct Pierre, pour iurer l'Vnion des Catholiques, le huictiesme iour de Iuin, mil cinq cens quatres vingts & neuf*, (Nantes, Nicolas des Marestz & François Fauerye, 1589), 'louue la Royne d'Angleterre' F1v–F2r. See also Richard Verstegan, *Théâtre des cruautez*, C1r.

106. For instance, Jean de Marconville remarked, 'Il se trouve quelque pays ou les bestes venimeuses ne sçauroient vivre, comme en Crete ou Candie, & en Angleterre n'y a aucuns loups', *La Manière de bien policer la république chrestienne (selon Dieu, raison & vertu) contenant l'estat et office des magistrats* (Paris, Nicolas du Chemin pour Jean Dallier, 1562), Q1v.

107. There were some curious inconsistencies, however. For instance Caumont likened Elizabeth to a Jezebel and considered Elizabeth an usurper to the throne of England, yet Mary was still described as 'Royne envor vraye & legitime heritiere du Royaume d'Angleterre'. See Caumont, *Advertissement des advertissemens*, D3r.

108. [Louis d'Orléans], *Responce des vrays catholiques françois à l'advertissement des catholiques anglois* (s.l., 1588), A2r.

109. *Exhortation aux catholiques de se réconcilier les uns aux autres, pour se déffendre des hérétiques* (1587), C1v–C2r.

110. Caumont, *Advertissement des advertissemens*, C1r–v.

111. [Orléans], *Responce des vrays catholiques françois*, B7r–v.

112. [Louis d'Orléans], *Advertissement des catholiques anglois aux françois catholiques, du danger où ils sont de perdre leur religion, & d'experimenter, comme en Angleterre, la cruauté des ministres s'ils reçoivent à la couronne un Roy qui soit hérétique* (s.l., 1586), C7v.

113. For instance, see [Robert Persons], *Epistre de la persécution meue en Angleterre contre l'Église Chrestienne* (Paris, Thomas Burmen, 1586), C4v–C5r.

114. In fact, this was exactly what had taken place in Catholic France; of course this irony was lost on the contemporary Catholic population, see David Nicholls, 'The Theatre of Martyrdom in the French Reformation' in *Past & Present*, 121 (1988), pp. 49–73.

115. Caumont, *Advertissement des advertissemens*, D2r.

116. Ibid C4r–v & [Orléans], *Advertissement des catholiques anglois*, A3v.

117. Caumont, *Advertissement*, C4v–D1v.
118. Verstegan, *Théâtre des cruautez des hérétiques de nostre temps* (Antwerp, Adrien Hubert, 1588).
119. This at least can be confirmed. Richard Verstegan, *Theatrum crudelitatum haereticorum nostri temporis* (Antverpiae, apud A. Huberti, 1587, 1588 & 1592).
120. Ibid, Pi 2r.
121. [Pomponne de Bellièvre], *La Harangue faicte à la Royne d'Angleterre pour la desmouvoir de n'entreprendre aucune jurisdiction sur la Royne d'Escosse* (1588).
122. Jacques La Guesle, *Remonstrance faite à la Royne d'Angleterre pour la Royne d'Escosse* ([1587])
123. [Bellièvre], *Harangue*, A3v, La Guesle, *Remonstrance*, A2r–v.
124. [Bellièvre], *Harangue*, A4v.
125. [Bellièvre], *Harangue*, B2v ; La Guesle, *Remonstrance*, A2v–A3r.
126. For instance, John Leslie, *Oraison funèbre* A6v, [Blackwood], *La Mort*, e8v and Renaud de Beaune, *Oraison funèbre*, B4v.
127. Renaud de Beaune, *Oraison funèbre*, C1r.
128. Guillaume de L'Aubespine, *Discours de la Mort*, passim.
129. Renaud de Beaune, *Oraison funèbre*, B4v.
130. Ibid, C1r.
131. Ibid.
132. Caumont, *Advertissement des advertissemens*, D4r.
133. R. Bolgar, *The Classical Heritage* (Cambridge, 1954), pp. 494–504; see also appendix II, 'Translations of Greek Authors in the Vernacular before 1600', pp. 508–38. FVB has expanded our knowledge of translations of classical tragedy into the vernacular. However, the total number of printed editions is still very small.
134. Gillian Jondorf, *Robert Garnier and the Themes of Political Tragedy in the Sixteenth Century* (Cambridge, 1969). See also Gillian Jondorf, *French Renaissance Tragedy: the Dramatic Word* (Cambridge 1990).
135. Robert Garnier, *La Troade, Antigone*, ed. R. Lebègue (Paris, 1952), p. 9 cited and translated in William D. Howarth, *French Theatre in the neo–classical era, 1550–1789* (Cambridge, 1997), p. 37.
136. Gillian Jondorf, *Robert Garnier and the Themes of Political Tragedy in the Sixteenth Century* (Cambridge, 1969).
137. *L'Histoire de la mort que le R.P. Edmond Campion prestre de la compagnie du nom de Jesus, & autres ont souffert en Angleterre pour la foy Catholique & Romaine le premier iour de Decembre, 1581* (Paris, Guillaume Chaudiere, 1582), B4v.
138. A phrase used in Caumont, *Advertissement des advertissemens*, D2v and Verstegan, *Théâtre des cruautez*, F4v.
139. Jean de Caumont, *Advertissement des advertissemens*, D2r; Renaud de Beaune, *Oraison funèbre*, C3r.
140. Reanuld de Beaune, *Oraison funèbre*, C3r and 'o barbares Cyclopes, qui sont publiees vos loix & dressez vos pretoires', D1v. On the Cyclops, see Homer, *The Odyssey*, trans. Martin Hammond, (London, 2000), Book 9, pp. 83–94.
141. Renaud de Beaune, *Oraison funèbre*, E3v; Robert Turner, *Histoire et Vie*, I7v; Verstegan, *Théâtre des cruautez*, B2r.
142. Euripides, *Iphigeneia at Aulis of Euripides*.

143. H.D.F. Kitto, *Greek Tragedy. A Literary Study* (London, 1939, reprinted 1961), p. 363.
144. Aeschylus, *Agamemnon*.
145. C. Collard, 'Formal Debates in Euripides' Drama', in Ian McAuslan and Peter Walcot (eds.), *Greek Tragedy* (Oxford, 1993), p. 153.
146. Verstegan, *Théâtre des cruautez*, B1v.
147. Mary Queen of Scots to the Duc de Guise, from Fotheringhay 23 November 1586, in Labanoff (ed.), *Lettres*, t. vi, p. 463.
148. [Louis d'Orléans], *Advertissement des catholiques anglois aux françois catholiques* (s.l., 1587) , R3v.
149. Verstegan, *Théâtre des cruautez*, A1r.
150. Ibid, B3v.
151. Ibid, C1r.
152. MS BL. 290, fol. 215 cited in Phillips, *Images*, p. 182 & p. 297 note 23.
153. Verstegan, *Théâtre des cruautez*, A3r–B1r.
154. For example [John Leslie], *Oraison funèbre sur la mort de la Royne d'Escosse* (Paris, Jean Charron, 1587), dedication to Mary, A2r–v ; *Ode sur la mort de la très-Chrestienne, très-illustre, très-constante, Marie Royne d'Escosse, morte pour la Foy, le 18. Feburier, 1587* (Paris, Guillaume Bichon, 1588).
155. Bellièvre, *La Harangue faicte a la Royne d'Angleterre* (s.l., 1588), C4r.
156. Ibid.
157. *Discours de la guerre ouverte entre le Roy d'Escosse & la Royne d'Angleterre. Et la prinse de la ville de Barruic [Berwick] & ruine par luy faicte en plusieurs endroicts d'Angleterre* (Paris, Hubert Velu, 1588), A2r.
158. *Discours de la Guerre ouverte*, A4r.
159. [Nicolas Rolland], *Remonstrances très–humbles au Roy de France et de Pologne Henry troisiesme de ce nom, par un sien fidelle officier & subject, sur les desordres & misères de ce royaume, causes d'icelles, & moyens d'y pourvoir à la gloire de Dieu & repos universel de cet estat* ([Paris], 1588), C1r.
160. Ibid.
161. Henri III, *Edict du Roy pour la vente et allienation à faculte de rachapt perpetuel des parts & portions du domaine de sa Majesté dont jouissoit la feue Royne d'Escosse pour son dot & douaire* (Paris, veuve Nicolas Roffet, 1587). The publication in 1589 of Mary Stuart's *Le Testament et derniers propos de la Royne d'Escosse* (Paris, Pierre Marin, 1589), in addition to satisfying popular curiosity, would again engage with criticisms of Henri III's unseemly handling of Mary's financial affairs.
162. On the use of the image of Albigensian heresy, see Luc Racaut, *Hatred in Print*, chapter 7. This image does not appear to have been drawn upon to any extent in the literature relating to Mary or Leaguer literature more generally.
163. Verstegan, *Théâtre des cruautez*, A4v.
164. *Histoire tragique et memorable de Pierre de Gaverston, Gentilhomme gascon, mignon d'Edward II Roy d'Angleterre tirée des Chroniques de Thomas Walsingham* (s.l., 1588) & (Paris [Brussels, Rutgerus Velpius], 1588).
165. [Louis d'Orléans], *Responce des vrays catholiques françois, a l'avertissement des catholiques anglois, pour l'exclusion du Roy de Navarre de la couronne de France* (1588).

166. *Discours aux françois sur l'admirable accident de la mort de Henry de Valois* (Paris, 1589).

167. *Les Considerations sur le meurdre commis en la personne de feu Monsieur le Duc de Guyse* (Paris, Guillaume Bichon, 1589), B1v.

168. Jacques Le Bossu, *Deux devis, d'un catholique et d'un politique, sur l'exhortation faicte au peuple de Nantes, en la grande ëglise de Sainct Pierre, pour jurer l'union des catholiques, le huictiesme jour de juin, mil cinq cens quatres vingts & neuf,* (Nantes, Nicolas des Marestz & François Fauerye, 1589), ã3r.

169. *Les Considerations*, B2r.

170. Ibid, F1v–F2r.

171. For example, *Les Considerations*, B1v and *Le Faux-Visage, descouvert du fin renard de la France. A tous catholiques unis & sainctement liguez pour la défence, & tuition de l'Église Apostolique & Romaine, contre l'ennemy de Dieu ouvert & couvert* (1589), C1v.

172. *Trahison descouverte de Henry de Valois, sur la vendition de la ville de Bologne à Jezabel Royne d'Angleterre. Avec le nombre des vaisseaux pleins d'or & d'argent prins par ceux de la ville de Bologne, envoyez par Jezabel audit de Valois* (Paris, Michel Joüin, 1589). Elizabeth's expansionist aims were also reported in *Coppie de la réqueste presentée au Turc par l'Agent de la Royne d'Angleterre, le 9. de Novembre 1587. Traduicte sur la coppie imprimée en Allemand en la ville d'Ingolstadt* (Verdun, Jacques Eldreton, 1589).

Conclusion

1. *Premier et second advertissemens des catholiques anglois aux françois catholiques* (Lyon, Jean Pillehotte, 1590 & 1591) (Paris, Guillaume Bichon, 1590), (s.l. [Paris, Guillaume Bichon], 1590) and (Toulouse, Edouard Ancelin, 1590 & 1591).

2. *Responce à l'injuste et sanguinaire edict d'Elizabeth Royne d'Angleterre, contre les catholiques de son royaume publié à Londres le 29. Novembre 1591* (Lyon, Jean Pillehotte, 1593).

3. An excellent discussion of these tragedies can be found in Jane Conroy, *Terres tragiques. L'Angleterre et l'Ecosse dans la tragédie française du XVIIe siècle* (Tübingen, 1999), pp. 39–206.

Bibliography

Works of bibliographical reference and inventories

Adams, H.M., *Catalogue of Books Printed on the Continent of Europe, 1501–1600, in Cambridge Libraries* (2 vols., Cambridge, 1967).

Allison, A.F., & Rogers, D.M., *Contemporary Printed Literature of the English Counter-Reformation between 1558–1640. An Annotated Bibliography* (Brookfield, 1989–94).

Baudrier, H.L., & Baudrier, J., *Bibliographie Lyonnaise. Recherches sur les imprimeurs, libraires, relieurs et fondeurs de lettres de Lyon au XVIe siècle* (12 vols., Lyon, 1895–1921).

Bibliothèque Nationale, *Collection des manuscrits, livres, estampes et objets d'art relatifs à Marie Stuart, Reine de France et d'Ecosse* (Paris, 1931).

Cartier, Alfred, *Bibliographie des Éditions des Des Tournes Imprimeurs Lyonnais* (1938).

Chaix, P., Dufour, A., & Moelckli, G., *Les Livres Imprimés à Genève de 1550 à 1600* (Geneva, 1966).

Durkan, John, *Bibliography of George Buchanan* (Glasgow, 1994).

Higman, Francis, *Piety and the People: Religious Printing in French 1511–51* (Aldershot, 1996).

Inventaire Analytique des Archives Anciennes de la Maire d'Angers, ed. M. Célestin Port (Paris & Angers, 1861).

Inventaire Analytique des Livres de Couleur et Bannières du Châtelet de Paris, ed. Alexandre Teutey (Paris, 1899).

Inventaire Chronologique des Documents relatifs à l'Histoire d'Écosse conservés aux Archives du Royaume à Paris [Archives Nationales], suivi d'une indication sommaire des manuscrits de la Bibliothèque Royale [Bibliothèque Nationale de France], ed. Jean–Baptiste Teulet (Edinburgh, 1839).

Inventaire Sommaire des Archives Communales antérieures à 1790. Ville de Nantes, ed. S. de La Nicollière–Teijero (Nantes, 1888).

Pallier, Denis, *Recherches sur l'Imprimerie à Paris pendant la Ligue, 1585–94* (Geneva, 1976).

Pasquier, Emile, *Un curé de Paris pendant les Guerres de Religion. René Benoist Le Pape des Halles (1521–1608). Étude Historique et Bibliographique* (Paris & Angers, 1913).

Peach, Trevor, *Catalogue Descriptif des Éditions Françaises, Néo–Latines et autres 1501–1600 de la Bibliothèque Municipale de Poitiers* (Geneva, 2000).

Pettegree, Andrew, *A Short Title Catalogue of Books Published in French before 1601 (The St Andrews Book Project)*, in progress.

Répertoire Bibliographique des Livres Imprimés en France au Seizième Siècle (32 vols., Baden-Baden, 1968–1980).

Scott, John, *A Bibliography of Works Relating to Mary, Queen of Scots 1544–1700* (Edinburgh, 1896).

A Short Title Catalogue of Books Printed in England, Scotland & Ireland and of English

Books Printed Abroad, 1475–1640, ed. A.W. Pollard & G.R. Redgrave (first edition London, 1926, Oxford, 1986).
Tannebaum, Samuel T., & Tannebaum, Dorothy R., *Marie Stuart, Queen of Scots. A Concise Bibliography* (3 vols., New York, 1944).

Archival sources

Angers Archives Départementales de Maine–et–Loire
G. 1473 [29 September 1548].
Angers Archives Communales
AA4 (1–8) [July–September 1548].
BB24 fol. 204v–217v [12 September 1548].
The Honourable Society of the Inner Temple, London
Misc. MS 41 no. 90 [1573] Personnel in the employ of Mary Queen of Scots.
Paris – Archives Nationales
K.1385, B.11, 182 'Manifeste d'Elisabeth' dated 24 March 1560.
Trésor des Chartres series J, carton 679 no. 59. 'secret' marriage contract signed by Mary.
Trésor des Chartres series J, carton 680 no. 63 formal wedding contract between François and Mary, dated 19 April 1558.
X/2b/154 'criminel september-october' for 8 December 1587 noting the arrest of David Dansseau, a bookseller. This carton also contains the arrêt of the Parlement of Paris releasing the printer Michel Buffet, dated 17 December 1587 (un foliated).
Paris – Bibliothèque Nationale de France
Fonds français 3335 fol. 74–93. Initial evaluation of Mary's dowry lands, dated 1561.
Fonds français 5898 fol. 1–6. Inventory drawn up in 1561 by François du Jardin, Pierre Redon and Henry de Baux following the death of François II, which catalogues and estimates the value of Mary's precious stones.
Fonds français 5944 fol. 80v, *Acte d'opposition de Marie Stuart, reine d'Écosse, à l'octoi fait au duc d'Alençon du duché de Tourain, pour supplement d'apanage*, undated.
Fonds français 11207 fol. 128, *Officiers domestiques de la Reine d'Escosse Mary Stuart du 1er janvier 1548 [1549] jusques au 31 décembre 1553*.

Primary sources – sixteenth-century editions

Advis sur ce qui est à faire contre les catholiques simulez, que les ennemis ouverts de l'église catholique apostolique & romaine (Paris, Nicolas Nivelle & Rolin Thierry, 1589).
Albret, Jeanne D', *Lettres de trèshaute, trèsvertueuse & trèschrestienne Princesse, Jane Royne de Navarre, au Roy, à la Royne Mere, à Monsieur frère du Roy, à Monsieur le Cardinal de Bourbon son beau frère, & à la Royne d'Angleterre* ([La Rochelle], 1568).
Arfeville, Nicolay D', *La Navigation du Roy d'Escosse Jaques cinquiesme du nom, autour de son royaume, & Isles Hebrides & Orchades, soubz la conduicte d'Alexandre Lyndsay* (Paris, Gilles Beys, 1583).

L'Atheisme de Henry de Valoys. Où est monstré le vray but de ses dissimulations & cruautez (Paris, pour Pierre des Hayes, 1589).

Barnaud, Nicolas [under pseudonym Eusebius Philadelphius], *Le Reveille–Matin des François et de leurs voisins* (Edinburgh, Jacques James [sic for Basle, Jacques James], 1574).

Barnaud, Nicolas [under pseudonym Nicolas de Montand], *Le Miroir des françois compris en trois livres. Contenant l'estat et maniement des affaires de France* (1581).

Barnestapolius, Obert see under Robert Turner

Bauffremont, Claude De, *Remerciement faict au nom de la noblesse de France, par le Baron de Senecey* (Lyon, Benoist Rigaud [imp par Pierre Roussin], 1588).

Beaugué, Ian De, *L'Histoire de la guerre d'Escosse, traitant comme le royaume fut assailly, & en grand partie occupé par les anglois* (Paris, pour Vincent Sertenas, 1556).

Beaune, Renaud De, *Oraison funèbre de la trèschrestienne, trèsillustre, très-constante, Marie Royne d'Escosse Mort pour la foy le 18. Febvrier 1587 par la cruauté des anglois* ([Paris, Guillaume Bichon], 1587).

Bellay, Joachim Du, *Entreprise du Roy–Dauphin pour le tournoy soubz le nom des chevaliers advanteureux* (Paris, Federic Morel, 1559).

Bellay, Joachim Du, *Epithalame sur le mariage de trèsillustre Prince Philibert Emanuel, Duc de Savoye et trèsillustre Princesse Marguerite de France, soeur unique du Roy et Duchesse de Berry* (Paris, Federic Morel, 1559) and (Paris, Federic Morel, 1561).

Bellay, Joachim Du, *Hymne au Roy sur la prinse de Calais. Avec quelques autres oeuvres du mesme Autheur, sur le mesme subject* (Paris, Federic Morel, 1559).

Bellay, Joachim Du, *Les Oeuvres françoises de Joachim du Bellay gentilhomme Angevin, et Poete Excellent de ce Temps* (Paris, Federic Morel, 1569) and (Paris, Abel L'Angelier, Pierre Le Vorrier & Jean Houzé, 1584).

Bellay, Joachim Du, *Tumulus Henri Secundi Gallorum Regis Christaniss* (Paris, Federic Morel, 1561).

[Bellièvre, Pomponne De], *La Harangue faicte à la Royne d'Angleterre pour la desmouvoir de n'entreprendre aucune jurisdiction sur la Royne d'Escosse* ([Paris], 1588).

Bernard, Jean, *Discours des plus memorables faicts des roys et grands seigneurs d'Angleterre depuis cinq cens ans. Avec les genealogies des Roynes d'Angleterre, & d'Ecosse* (Paris, Gervais Mallot, 1579).

Blackwood, Adam, *Martyre de la Royne d'Escosse, Douairiere de France* (Edinburgh [false imprint], Jean Nafield, 1587).

Boaistuau, Pierre, *Brief discours de l'excellence et dignité de l'homme* (Paris, Jean Longis & Robert Le Mangnyer, 1559).

Boaistuau, Pierre, *Le Théâtre du monde où il est faut un ample discours des miseres humaines* (Paris, Jean Longis & Robert Le Mangnyer, 1559).

Bref discours de ce qui est advenu sur la mer entre l'armée du Roy, & les anglois venuz pour secourir ceux de La Rochelle (Lyon, Jean Pillehotte, 1588).

[Buchanan, George], *Histoire de Marie Royne d'Escosse touchant la conjuration faicte contre le Roy, & l'adultere commis avec le Comte de Bothwel, histoire vrayement tragique* (Edinburgh [often attributed to La Rochelle, perhaps London?], Thomas Waltem, 1572).

Les Considerations sur le meurdre commis en la personne de feu Monsieur le Duc de Guyse (Paris, Guillaume Bichon, 1589).

Caumont, Jean De, *Advertissement des advertissements au peuple très-chrestien* (1587).

[Cecil, William], *La Copie d'une lettre envoyée d'Angleterre à Dom Bernardin de Mendoze Ambassadeur en France pour le Roy d'Espagne* ([La Rochelle], 1588).

C'est la deduction du sumptueux ordre plaisantz spectacles et magnifiques théâtres, dresées et exhibes par les citoyens de Rouen ville metropolitqine du pays de Normandie ([Rouen], on les vend à Rouen par Robert Le Hay et Jean du Gord, 1551).

Chalmers, David, *Histoire abbrégée de tous les Roys de France, Angleterre et Escosse* (Paris, Jean Fevrier, R. Coulombel & M. Gadoulleau, 1579).

Chalmers, David, *La Recherche des singularitez plus remarquables concernant l'Estat d'Escosse* (Paris, Jean Fevrier, R. Coulombel & M. Gadoulleau, 1579).

Chalmers, David, *Discours de la legitime succession des femmes aux possessions de leurs parens, & du gouvernment des princesses aux empires & royaumes* (Paris, Jean Fevrier, R. Coulombel & M. Gadoulleau, 1579).

Congratulation à la France sur les victoires obtenu par le Roy contre les étrangers (Lyon, Benoist Rigaud, 1588).

Continuation des choses plus celebres & memorables advenues en Angleterre, Escosse & Irlande, depuis le moys d'Octobre M.D.LXIX jusques au XXV jour de Decembre ensuyant & dernier passé (Lyon, Michel Jove, 1570).

Coppie de la requeste presentée au Turc par l'agent de la Royne d'Angleterre, le 9. de Novembre 1587 (Verdun, Jacques Eldreton, 1589).

Cronique abrégée ou recueil des faits, gestes, & vies illustres des roys de France. Contenant les choses plus memorables advenues de leur temps: commençant à Pharamond premier Roy, jusques à Henry troisiesme de ce nom (Paris, Simon Calvarin, 1579).

Cruauté plus que barbare infidelement perpetrée par Henry de Valois, ennemy des catholiques du royaume de France, en la personne de Monsieur l'illustrissime Cardinal de Guise, Archevesque, Duc de Reims, dedié & consacré à Dieu ([Paris, 1589]).

D., A., *Figure des signez merveilleux veuz & apparus vers les royaumes d'Escosse & Angleterre, significatifz de la ruine, fin & perte du monde* (Paris, pour Michel Buffet, 1587).

[D., A.], *Les Quinze signes advenus és parties d'occident, vers les royaumes d'Escosse & Angleterre, significatif de la ruine, fin, & consommation du monde* (Paris, Michel Buffet, 1587).

[Dagoneau, Jean], *Legende de Domp Claude de Guyse, Abbé de Cluny. Contenant ses faits & gestes, depuis la nativité jusques à la mort du Cardinal de Lorraine: & des moyens tenus pour faire mourir le Roy Charles Neufieme, ensemble plusieurs princes, grands seigneurs & autres, durant ledit temps* (1581).

Declaration des causes qui ont esmeu le Royne d'Angleterre à donner secours pour la defence du peuple affligé & oppressé es Païs Bas (London, Christopher Barker, 1585).

Discours de ce qu'à faict en France le heraut d'Angleterre, & de la response que luy à faict le Roy (Paris, Annet Briere, 1557).

Discours de la defaicte de trois cornettes de cavallerie du Vicomte de Thuraine, & prinse de Saincte Foy en Guyenne, par Monsieur le Mareschal de Matignon, le neufiesme jour de Decembre (Lyon, Benoist Rigaud, 1588).

Discours de la guerre ouverte entre le Roy d'Escosse, & la Royne d'Angleterre. Et la prinse de la ville de Barruic [Berwick], & ruine par luy faicte en plusieurs endroicts d'Angleterre (Paris, Hubert Velu, 1588) and (Lyon, Benoist Rigaud, 1588).

Discours de la prinse de deux grandes navires envoyées de la part de la Royne d'Angleterre au Roy de Navarre (Paris, pour la veufve de F. Plumion, [1589]).

Discours de la prinse et route des navires envoyes par la Royne d'Angleterre à Diepe [sic for Dieppe], pour le secours du Roy de Navarre (Paris, Hubert Velu, 1589).

Discours de la vie abominable, ruses, trahisons, meurtres, impostures, emposionnements, paillardises, atheisme, & autres très-iniques conversations, desquelles à usé & usé jour-

nellment le my Lorde de Lecestre Machiavelliste, contre l'honneur de Dieu, la Majesté de la Royne d'Angleterre sa Princesse, & toute la république chrestienne (1585).

Discours des cruautes et tirannyes qu'à faict la Royne d'Angleterre, à l'endroict des catholecques [sic], anglois, espagnolz, françois, & prestres catholicques, qui soutenoient la foy & le tourmant qui l'ont souffert avec les noms & surnons d'iceux (Paris, [1582]).

Discours du grand et magnifique triumphe faict au mariage de trèsnoble & magnifique Prince François de Vallois Roy Dauphin . . . & Princesse Marie d'Esteuart (Paris, Annet Briere, 1558), and (Rouen, George L'Oyselet chez Jaspar de Rémortier & Raulin Boulenc, 1558).

Discours trèsample et trèsveritable contenant plus particulierement l'entiere desroutte & deffaicte de l'armée des Huguenots. Faicte par le trèschrestien Roy Henry Troisiesme de ce nom, & les Prince & Seigneurs Catholiques au mois de Novembre dernier (Lyon, Jean Pillehotte, 1588).

Discours veritable de la desfaicte des reistres Protestans à Aulneau, par les armes de Monseigneur le Duc de Guyse, prinses & conduictes par le commandement & soubs l'auctorité du Roy, le mardy xxiiii Novembre 1587 (Paris, chez Guillaume Bichon, 1587).

Dominici, Bernard, *La Harangue de trèsnoble et trèsverteueuse Dame, Madame Marie d'Estuart, Royne d'Escosse . . . faite en l'assamblée [sic] des Estats de son Royaume* (Rheims, Jean de Foigny, et se vendant à Paris chez Nicolas Chesneau, 1563).

Dominici, Bernard, *Sermon funèbre fait à Nancy, aux obseques & funerailles de feu Monseigneur François de Lorraine* (Rheims, Jean de Foigny, et se vendant à Paris chez Nicolas Chesneau, 1563).

Elizabeth I, *Protestation faicte par la Royne d'Angleterre, par laquelle elle declare les justes & necessaires occasions qui l'ont meuë de prendre la pretection de la cause de Dieu . . . contre les autheurs des troubles qui y sont à present* (1562).

Epistre de la persecution meue en Angleterre contre l'église chrestienne, catholique & apostolique, & fideles membres d'icelle (Paris, Thomas Brumen, 1586).

[Espence, Claude De], *Oraison funèbre es obseques de très-haute, très-puissante, & très-vertueuse Princesse, Marie par la Grace de Dieu Royne Douairiere d'Escoce* (Paris, M. de Vascosan, 1561).

Este, Anne D', *Remonstrance faicte par Madame de Nemours à Henry de Valloys avec la response de Henry de Valloys. Ensemble les regrets & lamentations faites par Madame de Guyse, sur le trespas de Feu Monseigneur de Guyse son espoux* (Paris, Jean de Nois, 1589).

[Estienne, Henri], *Discours merveilleux de la vie, actions & deportemens de Catherine de Medici Royne Mere. Auquel sont recitez les moyens qu'elle à tenu pour usurper le gouvernement du royaume de France, & ruiner l'Estat d'iceluy* ([Geneva, Henri Estienne], 1575).

De l'Execution faicte du Duc de Nortomberlan. Avec la confession qu'il fit sur l'escharfaut avant sa mort, envoyée au Roy d'Escosse par son ambassadeur estant en Angleterre (Paris, Jacques Gregoire, s.d.).

Discours de l'ordre tenu par les habitans de la ville de Rouen, à l'entrée du Roy nostre Sire (Lyon, Pillehotte, 1588).

Exhortation aux catholiques de se réconcilier les uns aux autres, pour se deffendre des hérétiques (1587).

Le Faux-visage descouvert du fin renard de la France à tous catholiques unis, & sainctement liguez pour la defence, & tuition de l'église apostolique & romaine, contre l'ennemy de Dieu ouvert & couvert ([Paris], Jacques de Varangles, 1589).

Ferrier, Augier, *Advertissemens à Jean Bodin sur le quatriesme livre de sa république* (Toulouse, chez Arnaud & Jacques Colomies freres, 1580).

Fouquelin, Antoine, *La Rhétorique françoise* (Paris, André Wechel, 1557).

Gallars, Nicolas De, *Forme de police ecclesiastique instituée à Londres en l'église des françois* (1561).

[Goulart, Simon (ed.)], *Memoires de l'Estat de France sous Charles Neufiesme* (Middelbourg [Geneva], Heinrich Wolf [Eustache Vignon], 1578).

[Goulart, Simon (ed.)], *Recueil contenant les choses plus memorables soubz la Ligue* (1587).

[Goulart, Simon (ed.)], *Le Second recueil contenant l'histoire des choses plus memorables advenues sous la Ligue* (1590).

Le Grand diablerie de Jean Vallette dit de Nogaret par la grace du Roy Duc d'Espernon, grand animal de France ([Paris], 1589).

Grévin, Jaques, *Hymne à Monseigneur le Dauphin, sur le mariage dudict Seigneur, et de Madame Marie d'Esteuart, Royne d'Escosse* (Paris, Martin L'Homme, 1558).

Harangue au Roy très-chrestien faite à Chartres, par Dom Barnardin de Mendoça (Lyon, Benoist Rigaud, 1588).

Hay, John, *Demandes faictes aux ministres d'Escosse touchant la religion chrestienne, par M. Jean Hay Escossois, de la compagnie de Jesus, Professeur en Theologie, en l'Université de Tournon* (Lyon, Jean Pillehotte, 1583).

Henri III, *Articles accordez au nom du Roy* (Lyon, Jean Pillehotte, 1588).

Henri III, *Edict du Roy pour la vente et allienation à faculte de rachapt perpetuel, des parts & portions du domaine de sa Majesté, dont jouissoit la feu Royne d'Escosse pour son dot & douaire* (Paris, pour la vefve Nicolas Roffet, 1587).

Henri III, *Response du Roy au articles presentez par messieurs les cardinaux, princes, seigneurs* (Lyon, Jean Pillehotte, [1588]).

Heyns, M.I., *Le Miroir du monde, reduict premierement en rithme Brabançonne* (Antwerp, Christopher Plantin pour P. Galle, 1579).

Histoire au vay meurtre et assassinat proditoirement commis en la personne de Monsieur le Duc de Guyse, protecteur & deffenseur de l'église catholique & du royaume de France (1589).

Histoire contenant les plus memorables faits advenus en l'an 1587 tant en l'armée comandée par Monsieur le Duc de Guyse, qu'en celle des huguenots, conduite par le Duc de Bouillon (Paris, Didier Millot, 1588).

L'Histoire de la mort que le R.P. Edmond Campion prestre de la compagnie du nom de Jesus, & autres ont souffert en Angleterre pour la foy catholique & romaine le premier jour de Décembre 1581 (Paris, Guillaume Chaudiere, 1582).

Histoire de nostre temps contenant un recueil des choses memorables passées & publiées pour le faict de la religion & Estat de la France, depuis l'Edict de Paciffication [sic] du 23. jour de Mars 1568 jusques au jour present (1570).

L'Histoire du Tumulte d'Amboise advenu au moys de Mars M.D.L.X. Ensemble un avertissement & une complainte au peuple françois (1560).

Histoire veritable de la conspiration de Guillaume Parry Anglois contre la Royne d'Angleterre depuis l'an mil cinq cens quatre vingts quatre (La Rochelle, Pierre Haultin, 1585).

[Hotman, François], *Epistre envoiée au tigre de la France* ([1560]).

[Kyffin, Maurice], *Apologie où defense de l'honorable sentence & très-juste exécution de defuncte Marie Steuard dernière Royne d'Escosse* (1588).

[L'Aubespine, Guillaume De], *Discours de la mort de très-haute & très-illustre Princesse Madame Marie Stouart, Royne d'Escosse* ([1587]) & (Paris, Pierre Marin, 1589).

La Guesle, Jacques De, *Remonstrance faite à la Royne d'Angeleterre pour la Royne d'Escosse* ([Paris, 1586–1587]).

La Planche, François De [under the pseudonym François de L'Isle], *La Legende de Charles, Cardinal de Lorraine, & de ses frères, de la maison de Guyse* (Rheims [Geneva], Pierre Martin, 1579).

La Rouere, Jerome De, *Les Deux sermons funèbres es obsèques & enterrement du feu Roy trèschrestien Henri Deuxieme de ce nom, faicts & prononcez par Messire Jerome de La Rouere* (Paris, Robert Estienne, 1559).

La Serre, Michel Sieur De, *Remonstrance au Roy par la Sieur de la Serre, sur les pernicieux discours contenus au livre de la république de Bodin* (Paris, Federic Morel, 1579).

Le Bossu, Jacques, *Deux devis d'un catholique et d'un politique sur l'exhortation faicte au Peuple de Nantes* (Nantes, Nicolas de Marestz & François Faverye, 1589).

Le Bossu, Jacques, *Traité sur le defense d'adherer aux hérétiques & excommunication des politiques* (Nantes, Nicolas de Marestz & François Faverye, 1592).

Le Féron, Jean, *Le Symbol armorial des armoiries de France et d'Escoce et de Lorraine* (Paris, Maurice Menier, 1555).

[Leslie, John under pseudonym M.I.S], *Oraison funèbre sur la mort de la Royne d'Escosse* (Paris, Jean Charron, 1587) Four editions of this text are known for 1587, one under the slightly altered title *Harangue funèbre sur la mort de la Royne d'Escosse* ([Paris, Jean Charron, 1587]).

[Leslie, John] under the pseudonym Morgan Phillips, *A Treatise Concerning the Defence of the Honour of the Right High, Mightie and Noble Princesse, Marie Queene of Scotland, and Dowager of France, with a Declaration, as wel of her Right, Title and Interest to the Succession of the Croune of England: as that the Regiment of women is comfortable to the lawe of God and Nature* (Leodii [Louvain], [J. Fowler], 1571).

[Leslie, John?], *A Treatise of Treasons against Q. Elizabeth, and the Croune of England, diuided into two Partes: whereof, The First Parte Answereth Certaine Treasons Pretended, that neuer were Intended: and the Second, Discouereth Greater Treasons Committed, that are by few Perceiued: as more largely appeareth in the page following* (January 1572).

L'Hôpital, Michel De, *Discours sur le sacre du trèschrestien Roy Francoys II avec la forme de bien regner accommodée aux moeurs de ce royaume* (Paris, Federic Morel, 1560).

M., M., *Responce aux principaux articles & chapitres de l'apologie de Belloy, faulsement & à faux tiltre inscrite apologie catholique, pour la succession de Henry Roy de Navarre à la couronne de France* (1588).

Mamerot, Roch, *Bref discours sur la saincte confession necessaire à un chacun chrestien, presentée à très-haute & très-illustre Princesse (de bonne memoire) Marie Stouard* (Paris, 1587).

Memoires contenante le vray discours des affaires du Pays Bas, & choses plus secrettes qui y sont advenues cette année 1583 ([Cologne], 1583).

Mendoza, Bernardino De, *Harangue au Roy très-chrestien faite à Chartres, par Dom Bernardin de Mendoça* (Lyon, Benoist Rigaud, 1588).

Les Meurs, humeurs et comportemens de Henry de Valois (Paris, Antoine Le Riche, 1589).

[Mornay, Philippe De], *Lettre d'un gentilhomme catholique françois, contenant breve response aux calomnies d'un certain pretendu anglois* (1587).

Neufve-Berruyer, Jehan De La Maison, *L'Adieu des neuf Muses aux roys, princes, et princesses de France, à leur departement du festin nuptial de Françoys de Valoys Roy Dauphin, & Marie d'Estouart Royne d'Escosse* (Paris, Martin L'Homme, 1558).

La Nouvelle deffaicte des reistres par Monseigneur le Duc de Guise (Paris, Didier Millot, 1587).

Ode sur la mort de la très-chrestienne, très-illustre, très-constante Marie Royne d'Escosse, morte pour la foy, le 18 Febvrier 1587 (Paris, Guillaume Bichon, 1587).

Ongoys, Jean D', *Le Promptuaire de tout ce qui est advenu plus digne de memoire, depuis la creation du monde jusques à present. Auquel est adjoustez (à ceste seconde edition) les cathologues des papes, empereurs & roys de France, avec trois genealogies & descentes des roys d'Angleterre, Espagne & Portugal* (Paris, Jean de Bordeaux, 1579).

Les Ordres tenuz à la réception et entrée du Roy trèschrestien François II & de la Roine en la ville d'Orléans (Paris, Guillaume Nyverd, [1560]).

[Orléans, Louis D'], *Advertissement des catholiques anglois aux françois catholiques, du danger où ils sont de perdre leur religion & d'expermineter, comme en Angleterre, la cruauté des ministres s'ils reçevoient à la couronne un roy qui soit hérétique* (1586).

[Orléans, Louis D'], *Premier et second advertissement des catholiques anglois aux françois catholiques* (Lyon, Jean Pillehotte, 1590).

[Orléans, Louis D'], *Réplique pour le catholique anglois, contre le catholique associé des huguenots* (1588).

Osorio, Hierosme, *Remonstrance à Madame Elizabeth Royne d'Angleterre, & d'Irlande touchant les affaires du monde, gouvernement politique des royaumes, républiques, & empires; & restablissement de l'ancienne catholique religion* (Paris, Michel de Roigny, 1587).

La Paix faict entre tèshaults & trèspuissants Princes Henry II. de ce nom, trèschrestien Roy de France, & Philippe Roy d'Espagne . . . les Roy & Royne d'Escosse Daulphin & la Royne d'Angleterre (Lyon, Nicolas Edouard, 1559).

Paradin, Guillaume, *Continuation de l'histoire de nostre temps, depuis l'an mil cinq cens cinquante, jusques à l'an mil cinq cense cinquante six* (Paris, Jean Poupy & Nicolas Chesneau, 1575).

Paradin, Guillaume, *Memoires de l'histoire de Lyon* (Lyon, Anthoine Gryphius, 1573).

Perlin, Estienne, *Description des royaumes d'Angleterre et d'Escosse* (Paris, François Trepeau, 1558).

[Percy, Anne], *Discours des troubles nouvellement advenus au royaume d'Angleterre* (Paris, pour Laurent du Coudret, 1570).

Petit discours sur une lettre responsive de l'Empereur Maximilian au Roy, 1568. Plus une copie de la conspiration de deux Comtes d'Angleterre contre leur Royne ([La Rochelle], 1570).

Philopatre, André, *Responce à l'injuste et sanguinaire edict d'Elizabeth Royne d'Angleterre contre les catholiques de son royaume* (Lyon, Jean Pillehotte, 1593).

Proclamation de la paix faicte entre les Roy de France . . . Charles IX, Elizabeth Roine d'Angleterre (Paris, Robert Estienne, 1564).

Propos tenus au roy à presentation de la requeste des princes (Lyon, Jean Pillehotte, 1588).

Rabel, Jean, *Les Antiquitez et singularitez de Paris. Livre second. De la Sepulture des roys & roynes de France, princes, princesses & autres personnes illustres* (Paris, Nicolas Bonfons, 1588).

La Recompence du tyran de la France et port-banniere d'Angleterre, Henry de Valois, envers nosseigneurs les Cardinal & Duc de Guyse, pour les bons services (Paris, Michel Jovin, 1589).

Remonstrance faite à Monsieur d'Espernon, entrant en l'Eglise Cathedrale de Rouen le 3. de May 1588 par le penitentier dudit lieu (Lyon, Benoist Riguad, 1588) & (Paris, Jean Richer, 1588).

Remonstrance très–docte envoyée aux catholiques françois par un catholique anglois (Paris, Anthoine du Brüeil, 1589).

Requeste presentée au Roy par messieurs les cardinaux, princes, seigneurs et deputez de la ville de Paris, (Rouen, 1588).

Response à un ligueur masqué du nom de catholique anglois ([La Rochelle], 1587).

Responce à un livre de Belloy plein de faulsetez et calomnies, de Guise souz cet excellent & beau titre de l'authorité du Roy (Paris, Guillaume Bichon, 1588).

Responce aux Justifications prétendues par Henry de Valoys 3. du nom sur les Meurtres & Assasinats de feu Messeigneurs le Cardinal & Duc de Guyse. Contenues en sa Déclaration par luy faite, contre Messeigneurs le Duc de Mayenne, Duc & Chevalier d'Aumale (Paris, 1589).

Response d'un gentilhomme françois à l'advertissement des catholiques anglois en laquelle il traitté la question, si pour chasser l'hérésie il faut tuer les héréticques & leur faire la guerre (1587).

Response des vrays catholiques françoys à l'advertissement de catholiques anglois pour l'exclusion du Roy de Navarre, couronne de France ([Montauban has been put forward as a possible place of publication, but this is highly unlikely], 1588).

[Rolland, Nicolas], *Remonstrances très–humbles au roy de France et de Pologne* (1588).

[Rouille, Guillaume], *Promptuaire des medailles des plus renommées personnes qui ont esté depuis le commencement du monde. Avec briefve description de leurs vies & faits, recueillie des bon auteurs* (Lyon, Guillaume Roville, 1581).

Seure, Sieur De [and William Cecil], *Protestation faicte de la part du Roy, par son ambassadeur, resident pres la Royne d'Angleterre, à sa Majesté, & aux seigneurs de son conseil, xx April* (London, Jugge and Cawod, 1560).

Sixtus V, *Bulle de reconciliation pour ceux de la nouvelle religion* (1587).

[Stuart, Mary], *Le Testament et dernier propos de la Royne d'Escosse* ([1587]).

La suite de remonstrances et articles presentez au roy depuis la dernière requeste de messieurs les cardinaux & princes catholiques (Rouen, 1588).

Surius, Laurens, *Histoire où commentaires de toutes choses mémorables advenues depuis 70 ans en ça par toutes les parties du monde*, Jacques Estourneau Xinctongeois (trans.), (Paris, Guillaume Chaudiere, 1573).

Le Testament de Henry de Valoys, recommandé à son amy Jean d'Espernon ([Paris], pour Jacques Varengles et Denis Binet, 1589).

Tillet, Jean Du, *Les Memoires et recherches de Jean du Tillet gressier de la Court de Parlement à Paris contenans plusieurs choses memorables pour l'intelligence de l'estat des affaires de France* (Troyes, pour Philippe des Chams, 1578).

Trahison descouverte de Henry de Valois sur la rendition de la ville de Boulogne à Jezabel Royne d'Angleterre (Paris, chez Michel Joüin, 1589).

Tremblement de terre advenu à Lyon le mardy vingtiesme jour de May mil cinq cens septantehuict, peu avant les quatre heurs du soir (Lyon, Benoist Rigaud, 1588).

Troncy, Benoist, *Le Discours du grand triomphe fait en la ville de Lyon pour le faite & accordee entre Henry second, Roy de France trèschrestien, & Philippe Roy d'Espagne, & leur aliez* (Lyon, Jean Saugrain, 1559).

Turner, Robert [under pseudonym Obert Barnestapolius], *L'Histoire et vie de Marie Stuart, Royne d'Escosse, d'oiriere de France, héritière d'Angleterre & d'Ibernye, en laquelle elle est clairement iustifiee de la mort du Prince d'Arlay son mary* (Paris, chez Guillaume Julien, 1589).

Vallence, Sieur De, *Remonstrances faictes par le Sieur de Vallence aux villes et dioceses d'Uzes, Nîmes & Montpellier & aux Estats Generaux de Languedoc, tenus à Beziers au mois d'Apvril [sic] mil cinq cens soixante dixhuict* (Paris, pour Abel L'Angelier, 1578).

Verstegan, Richard [Richard Rowlands], *Théâtre des cruautez des héréticques de nostre temps* (Antwerp, Adrien Hubert, 1588).

La Vie et faits notables de Henry de Valois. Maintenant tout au Long, sans rien requnerir [sic] ([Paris], chez Didier Millot, 1589).

Le Vray discours contenant au vray le progres, conduite et exécution de la victoire obtenue par Monsieur de La Valette en Dauphiné, contre les suisses protestans, qui y esoient entrez pour les huguenots (Paris, Jamet Mettayer, 1587).

[Walsingham, Francis], *Traduction d'une lettre envoyée à la Royne d'Angleterre par son ambassadeur surprise pres de Moüy par la garnison du Havre de Grace* (Lyon, Jean Pillehotte, 1591).

Reprinted primary sources

Adam, R.J., *History of Mary Queen of Scots: A Fragment; Translated from the Original French of Adam Blackwood* (Edinburgh, 1834).

Alvarotto, Julio, transcribed and translated in Herbert van Scoy and Bernderd C. Weber (eds.), 'Documents. The Marriage of Mary Queen of Scots and the Dauphin', in *SHR* xxxi (1952), pp. 41–8.

Bourdeille, Pierre De (Brântome), *Recueil des Dames. Poésies et Tombeaux*, ed. Etienne Vaucheret (Paris, 1991).

Buchanan, George, *The Tyrannous Reign of Mary Stewart*, ed. & trans. W.A. Gatherer (Edinburgh, 1958).

Calendars of State Papers, Foreign Series, of the Reign of Elizabeth (London, 1863–1950).

Calendars of State Papers Relating to Scotland and Mary Queen of Scots, 1547–1603, ed. R. Lemon (1868).

Calendars of State Papers Venetian, ed. R. Brown et al, (9 vols., London, 1864–98).

Choix de Chroniques et Mémoires sur l'Histoire de France, ed. J.A.C. Buchon (Paris, 1836).

Donation par Charles VII à Jean Start Seigneur de Derneley, connétable de l'armée d'Écosse des terres de Concressault & d'Aubigny-sur-Nére (21 avril 1421, 26 mars 1423, 3 décembre 1425), ed. Jacques Soyer (Bourges, 1899).

Eusebius, *The History of the Church from Christ to Constantine*, trans. G.A. Williamson (London, 1989).

Fayet, Pierre, *Journal Historique de Pierre Fayet sur les troubles de la Ligue*, ed. Victor Luzarche (Tours, 1852).

Gondy, Sieur De, Account of the execution of Mary Queen of Scots written to Archbishop James Beaton, translated from a Latin document held in Blairs College, Aberdeen by Walter R. Humphries, 'The Execution of Mary, Queen of Scots', in *Aberdeen University Review*, xxx (1943), pp. 20–5.

La Fosse, Jehan De, *Journal d'un curé Ligueur de Paris sur les trois derniers Valois suivi du journal du Secrétaire de Philippe du Bec, Archêveque de Reims de 1558 à 1605*, ed. Edouard de Barthélemy (Paris, 1866).

Lang, A., 'The Household of Mary Queen of Scots in 1573', in *SHR* 8 (July 1905), pp. 345–55.

L'Aubespine, Sébastien, *Négociations, lettres et pièces diverses relatives au règne de François II tirées du portefeuille de Sébastien de L'Aubespine évêque de Limoges*, ed. Louis Paris (Paris, 1841).

Law, Thomas Graves (ed.), 'Documents Illustrating Catholic Policy in the Reign of James VI', in *Miscellany of the Scottish History Society*, 15 (Edinburgh, 1893).

[Leslie, John], *L'Innocence de la très-illustre, très-chaste, & debonnaire Princesse Madame Marie Royne d'Escosse. Où sont amplement refutées les calomnies faulces, & impositions iniques, publiées par un livre secrettement diuulgué en France, l'an 1572*, ed. Samuel Jebb, *Histoire de Marie Stuart Reine d'Escosse et Douairiere de France. Ou Recueil de toutes les pieces qui ont été publiées au sujet de cette Princesse* (2 vols., London, 1725), t. I, pp. 423–606.

L'Estoile, Pierre De, *Mémoires Journaux de Pierre de L'Estoile*, ed. M. Brunet, A. Champoillon, E. Halphen, P. LaCroix, C. Reid, T. de Larroque & E. Tricotel (Paris, 1876).

L'Estoile, Pierre De, *The Paris of Henry of Navarre as seen by Pierre de L'Estoile. Selections from his Mémoires-Journaux*, ed. & trans. Nancy Lyman Roelker (Cambridge, 1958).

L'Estoile, Pierre De, *Registre-Journal du Regne de Henri III 1574–81* (3 vols., Geneva, 1992, 1996, 1997).

Lorraine, Charles Cardinal De, *Lettres du Cardinal Charles de Lorraine (1552–74)*, ed. Daniel Cuisiat (Geneva, 1998).

Lucinge, René De, *Lettres de 1587. L'Année des Reîtres*, ed. James Supple (Geneva, 1994).

Poytiers, Dianne De, *Dianne de Poytiers. Lettres Inédites publiées d'apres les manuscrits de la Bibliothèque Impériale (i.e. BNF)*, ed. Georges Guyffrey (Geneva, 1970). This edition is a facsimile of the original Paris edition of 1866.

Registres des délibérations du bureau de la ville de Paris (vols. 4 & 5, Paris, 1888, 1892).

Renouard, Phillipe, *Documents sur les imprimeurs, libraires, cartiers, graviers, fondeurs de lettres, relieurs, doreurs de livres, faiseurs de fermoires en lumineurs, parcheminiers et papetiers ayant exercé à Paris de 1450 à 1600. Recueillis aux Archives Nationales et au Département des Manuscrits de la Bibliothèque Nationale* (Paris, 1901).

Ronsard, Pierre De, *Les Amours et les Folastries 1552–60*, ed. André Gendre (Paris, 1993).

Ronsard, Pierre De, (ed.) Paul Laumonier, *Oeuvres complètes de Ronsard* ([Paris], 1950).

Saint-Gelais, Melin De, (ed.) P. Blanchemain, *Oeuvres Complètes* (Paris, 1873).

Stuart, Mary, *The Casket Letters and Mary Queen of Scots*, ed. T.F. Henderson (Edinburgh, 1889). This work on the casket letters alleged to have been written by Mary, contains in appendix C the documents in their Scots, English, French and Latin translations.

Stuart, Mary, *Letters of Mary Queen of Scots, and documents connected with her personal history*, ed. Prince Alexandre Labanoff & trans. Agnes Strickland (2 vols., London, 1842).

Stuart, Mary, *Lettres, Instructions et Mémoires de Marie Stuart, Reine d'Écosse publiées sur les originaux et les manuscrits du State Paper Office de Londres et des principales archives et bibliothèques de l'Europe*, ed. Prince Alexandre Labanoff (7 vols., London, 1844).

Teulet, Alexandre (ed.), *Papiers d'État, Piéces et Documents Inédits ou peu connus, Relatifs a l'Histoire de l'Écosse au XVIe siècle, tirés des Bibliothèques et des Archives de France* (3 vols., Paris, 1852).

Teulet, Alexandre (ed.), *Relations Politiques de la France et de l'Espagne avec l'Écosse au XVIe siècle* (5 vols., Paris, 1862), 'Le vray rapport de l'éxecution faicte sur la personne de la Reyne d'Escosse', vol. iv, pp. 153–64 while Guillaume de L'Aubespine's account of the execution may be found in vol. iv, pp. 169–78.

Thou, Jacques-Auguste De, *Histoire Universelle de Jacques-Auguste de Thou depuis 1543 jusqu'en 1607* (16 vols., London, 1734).

Tillet, Jean Du, *Jean du Tillet and the French Wars of Religion. Five Tracts, 1562–69*, ed. A.R. Brown (New York, 1994).

Les Triomphes faictz à l'entrée du Roy à Chenonceau, le dymanche dernier jour de mars MDLIX (Paris, 1857). This 19th century edition was a copy of the original published in quarto in Tours by Guillaume Bourgeat in 1559. I have been unable to find any trace of the Bourgeat edition.

Wingfield, Robert, Account of the execution of Mary dated 11 February 1586 [sic for 1587], in *The Trial of Mary Queen of Scots*, ed. A. Francis Steuart (Edinburgh and London, 1922), pp. 173–85.

Secondary sources

Anderson, William, *The Scottish Nation or the Surnames, Families, Literature, Honours and Biographical History of the People of Scotland* (3 vols., Edinburgh, 1869).

Armstrong, Elizabeth, *Before Copyright. The French Book Privilege System 1498–1526* (Cambridge, 1990).

Ascoli, Georges, *La Grande-Bretagne devant l'opinion française depuis la Guerre de Cent Ans jusqu'à la fin du XVIe siècle* (Geneva, 1971). This is a reprint of the original Paris edition of 1927.

Ascoli, Georges, *La Grande-Bretagne devant l'Opinion française au XVIIe siècle* (Paris, 1930).

Bannerman, Edith, *Les Influences françaises en Écosse au temps de Marie Stuart. Thèse présentée pour le doctorat d'Université à la faculté des lettres de Besançon* (Besançon, 1929).

Barnavi, Elie, *Le Parti de Dieu: étude sociale et politique des chefs de la Ligue Parisienne 1585–94* (Louvain, 1980).

Baudouin-Matuszek, Marie-Noëlle, 'Henri II et les expéditions françaises en Écosse', *Bibliothèque de l'École des Chartres*, 145 (1987), 339–98.

Baumgartner, Frederic, *France in the Sixteenth Century* (New York, 1995).

Baumgartner, Frederic, *Henry II, King of France 1547–59* (Durham & London, 1988).

Baumgartner, Frederic, *Radical Reactionaries. The political thought of the French Catholic League* (Geneva, 1975).

Bax, Clifford, *The Silver Casket being Love-Letters and Love-Poems attributed to Mary Stuart, Queen of Scots now modernised or translated, with an introduction* (London, 1946).

Bell, David A., 'Unmasking a King: The political uses of popular literature under the French Catholic League, 1588–9' *SCJ*, 20/3 (1989), pp. 371–86.

Benedict, Philip, 'The Catholic Response to Protestantism. Church activity and popular piety in Rouen, 1560–1600', in James Obelkevitch (ed.), *Religion and the People 800–1700* (Chapel Hill, 1979), pp. 168–90.

Benedict, Philip, *Rouen during the Wars of Religion* (Cambridge, 1981).

Bingham, Caroline, *Darnley. A Life of Henry Stuart, Lord Darnley consort of Mary Queen of Scots* (London, 1995).

Bingham, Caroline, *James VI of Scotland* (London, 1979).

Bonner, Elizabeth, 'The Genesis of Henry VIII's "Rough Wooing" of the Scots', *Northern History*, 33 (1997), pp. 36–53.

Bonner, Elizabeth, 'The Recovery of St Andrews Castle in 1546: French naval policy and diplomacy in the British Isles' *EHR*, 111/442 (1996), pp. 576–98.

Bonner, Elizabeth, 'Scotland's "Auld Alliance" with France, 1295–1560' *History*, 84/273 (1999), pp. 5–30.

Bordier, Henri, *La Saint-Barthélemy et la critique moderne* (Geneva & Paris, 1879).

Bossy, John, 'Leagues and associations in sixteenth century French Catholicism', in W.J. Shiels and Diana Wood (eds.), *Voluntary Religion* (London, 1986), pp. 171–89.

Bossy, John, *Under the Molehill. An Elizabethan Spy Story* (New Haven & London, 2001).

Bouillé, René De, *Histoire des Ducs de Guise* (Paris, 1850).

Britnell, Richard introduction, in Jennifer Britnell and Richard Britnell (eds.), *Vernacular Literature and Current Affairs in the Early Sixteenth Century: France, England and Scotland* (Aldershot, 2000), pp. xiv–xxv.

Bryant, Lawrence M., *The King and the city in the Parisian royal entry ceremony: politics, ritual and art in the Renaissance* (Geneva, 1986).

Bryce, William M., 'Mary Stuart's voyage to France in 1548' *EHR*, 22 (1907), pp. 43–50.

Burns, J.H., 'Three Scots Critics of George Buchanan' *The Innes Review*, 6 (1950), pp. 92–109.

Burns, J.H., *The True law of Kingship. Concepts of monarchy in early–modern Scotland* (Oxford, 1996).

Cameron, Keith (ed.), *From Valois to Bourbon. Dynasty, state and society in early–modern France* (Exeter, 1989).

Cameron, Keith, 'La Polémique, la mort de Marie Stuart et l'assassinat de Henri III', in Robert Sauzet (ed.), *Henri III et son Temps* (Paris, 1992), pp. 185–94.

Carroll, Stuart, 'The Guise affinity and popular protest during the Wars of Religion' *FH*, 9 (1995), pp. 125–52.

Carroll, Stuart, *Noble Power during the French Wars of Religion. The Guise Affinity and the Catholic Cause in Normandy* (Cambridge, 1998).

Carroll, Stuart, 'The revolt of Paris, 1588: Aristocratic insurgency and the mobilization of popular support', *FHS*, 23/2 (2000), pp. 301–37.

Chalambert, Victor De, *Histoire de la Ligue sous les règnes de Henri III et Henri IV ou quinze années de l'histoire de France* (Geneva, 1974). This is a reprint of the original Paris edition of 1898.

Chartier, Jean-Luc A., *Le Duc d'Épernon 1554–1642* (2 vols., Paris, 1999).

Chartier, Roger, *Recherches de R. Chartier sur les origines culturelles de la Révolution françaises* (Paris, 1990).

Charter, Roger, 'Texts, printings, readings' in Lynn Hunt (ed.), *The New Cultural History* (London, 1989).

Chéruel, Adolphe, *Marie Stuart et Catherine de Médicis. Étude historique sur les Relations de la France et de l'Écosse dans la Second Moitié du XVIe siècle* (Geneva, 1975). This is a reprint of the original Paris edition of 1858.

Chisick, Harvey, 'Public Opinion and Political Culture in France during the second half of the eighteenth century' in *EHR*, cxvii, 470 (2002), pp. 48–76.

Chrisman, Miriam U., *Conflicting Visions of Reform. German lay propaganda pamphlets, 1519–30* (New Jersey, 1996).

Chrisman, Miriam U., *Lay Culture and Learned Culture. Books and Social Change in Strasbourg, 1480–1599* (London, 1982).

Christin, Olivier, *La Paix de Religion. L'Autonomisation de la Raison Politique au XVIe siècle* (Paris, 1997).

Conroy, Jane, *Terres Tragiques. L'Angleterre et l'Ecosse dans la Tragédie Française du XVIIe siècle* (Tübingen, 1999).

Constant, Jean-Marie, *La Ligue* (Paris, 1996).

Cowan, Ian B., *The Enigma of Mary Stuart* (London, 1971).

Cowan, Samuel, *Mary Queen of Scots and who wrote the Casket Letters?* (2 vols., London, 1901).

Cowans, Jon, 'Habermas and French History: The Public Sphere and the Problem of Legitimacy', in *French History*, vol. 13, no. 2. (1999), pp. 134–60.

Crofts, R., 'Printing, reform and the Catholic Reformation in Germany (1521–45)', *SCJ* (1985), pp. 369–81.

Crouzet, Denis, *Les Guerriers de Dieu. La violence au temps des troubles de religion (vers 1525 – vers 1610)* (2 vols., Paris, 1990).

Crowson, P.S., *Tudor Foreign Policy* (New York, 1973).

Currey, Kate, 'Themes of power and identity in the court festivals of ducal Lorraine, 1563–1624' in Berthrand Taithe and Tim Thornton (eds.), *Propaganda: Political rhetoric and identity 1300–2000* (Thrupp, 1999), pp. 61–73.

Davis, Natalie Z., *Society and Culture in Early Modern France – Eight Essays* (Stanford, 1975).

Delumeau, Jean, *Le Catholicisme entre Luther et Voltaire* (Paris, 1971).

Diefendorf, Barbara, *Beneath the Cross. Catholics and Huguenots in Sixteenth-Century Paris* (Oxford, 1991).

Diefendorf, Barbara, 'The Catholic League: Social Crisis or Apocalypse Now?' *FHS* (1987), pp. 333–44.

Donaldson, Gordon, *James V–James VII* (Edinburgh, 1965, 1994).

Donaldson, Gordon, *Scotland's History. Approaches and Reflections*, ed. James Kirk (Edinburgh, 1996).

Dosse, F., *New History in France – The Triumph of the Annales* (Urbana and Chicago, 1994).

Duchein, Michel, *Élisabeth Ire d'Angleterre* (Paris, 1992).

Duchein, Michel, *Marie Stuart. La femme et le mythe* (Paris, 1987).

Durkan, John, 'George Buchanan: Some French Connections' *The Bibliotheck*, 4 (1964), pp. 66–72.

Durkan, John, 'The library of Mary, Queen of Scots', in Michael Lynch (ed.), *Mary Stewart. Queen in Three Kingdoms* (Oxford, 1988).

Edwards, Mark, *Printing, Propaganda and Martin Luther* (Berkely, 1994).

Edwards, Mark, 'Statistics on sixteenth-century printing', in Philip N. Bebb and Sherrin Marshall (eds.), *The Process of Change in Early-Modern Europe* (Athens, 1988), pp. 149–63.

Ellul, Jacques, *Propaganda. The Formation of Men's Attitudes* (New York, 1969). The work was first published in French in 1957.

Estebe, H., 'Debate: The Rites of Violence: Religious riot in sixteenth century France – a comment' and Natalie Z. Davis, 'A rejoinder', *P&P* (1975), pp. 127–35.

Fabre, Féderic, 'The English Catholic College at Eu 1582–92' *CHR* (1951), pp. 257–80.

Farrow, Kenneth D., 'The substance and style of Hector Boece's Scotorum Historiae' *Scottish Literary Journal*, 25/1 (1998), pp. 5–25.

Fazy, Henri, *La Saint-Barthélemy et Genève. Étude historique* (Geneva, 1879).

Finley-Crosswhite, Annette, S., *Henri IV and the Towns. The Pursuit of Legitimacy in French urban society, 1589–1610* (Cambridge, 1999).

Fleming, David H., *Mary Queen of Scots from her birth to her flight into England: A brief biography with critical notes, a few documents hitherto unpublished, and an itinerary* (London, 1897).

Fontaine, Marie–Madeleine, 'Dédicaces Lyonnaises aux Guise-Lorraines', in Yvonne Bellenger (ed.), *Le Mecenat et l'influence des Guises. Actes du Colloque 1994* (Paris, 1997), pp. 39–79.

Francisque-Michel, *Les Écossais en France. Les Français en Écosse* (2 vols., London, 1862).

Fraser, Antonia, *Mary Queen of Scots* (London, 1969).

Gilmont, Jean-François, 'Les premières éditions des ouvrages historiques de La Place et de La Popelinière', in *Revue Française d'Histoire du Livre*, 50 (1986), pp. 119–52.

Gilmont, Jean-François, *La Réforme et le Livre – l'Europe de l'imprimé (1517 – v. 1570)* (Paris, 1990).

Gore-Brown, R., *Lord Bothwell* (London, 1937).

Gregory, Brad S., *Salvation at Stake. Christian Martyrdom in Early Modern Europe* (Cambridge Mass. and London, 1999).

Greengrass, Mark, *France in the Age of Henry IV* (London, 1984).

Greengrass, Mark, *The French Reformation* (Oxford, 1987).

Greengrass, Mark, 'Mary, Dowager Queen of France' in Michael Lynch (ed.), *Mary Stewart Queen in Three Kingdoms* (Oxford, 1988), pp. 171–94.

Guerdan, René, *Marie Stuart Reine de France et d'Ecosse* (Paris, 1986).

Guilday, Peter, *The English Catholic refugees on the continent, 1558–1795* (London, 1914).

Guilleminot-Genevieve, *Religion et politique à la veille des guerres civiles: Recherches sur les impressions françaises de l'année 1561* (unpublished Thèse d'Ecole des Chartres, 1977).

Guilleminot-Chrétien, G., 'Le contrôle de l'édition en France dans les années 1560: la genèse de l'édit de Moulins', in P. Aquillon & H.J. Martin (eds.), *Le Livre dans l'Europe de la Renaissance. Actes du XXVIIIe colloque international d'études humanistes de Tours* (Nantes, 1988), pp. 378–85.

Habermas, Jûrgen, *The Structural Transformation of the Public Sphere* (Cambridge, 2003), first published in German in 1962.

Harding, Robert, 'The mobilization of confraternities against the Reformation in France', *SCJ*, 11 (1980), pp. 85–106.

Harding, Robert, 'Revolution and reform in the Holy League: Angers, Rennes, Nantes', *JMH*, 53 (1981), pp. 379–416.

Hay, Camilla H., 'George Buchanan et Adam Blackwood', *BHR*, 8 (1946), pp. 156–71.

Haynes, Alan, *The White Bear. Robert Dudley, the Elizabethan Earl of Leicester* (London, 1987).

Higman, Francis, *Censorship and the Sorbonne. A bibliographical study of books in French censured by the Faculty of Theology of the University of Paris 1520–51* (Geneva, 1979).

Higman, Francis, 'Le Domaine français 1520–62', in Jean Gilmont (ed.), *La Réforme et le Livre – L'Europe de l'imprimé (1517 – v. 1570)* (Paris, 1990), pp. 105–54.

Higman, Francis, 'Ronsard's political and polemical poetry', in Terence Cave (ed.), *Ronsard the Poet* (London, 1973), pp. 241–85.

Higman, Francis, 'Theology in French. Religious pamphlets in the Counter–Reformation', *RMS*, 23 (1979), pp. 128–46.

Holmes, P.J., 'Mary Stewart in England', in Michael Lynch (ed.), *Mary Stewart Queen of Three Kingdoms* (Oxford, 1988), pp. 195–218.

Howarth, William D., *French Theatre in the neo–classical era, 1550–1789* (Cambridge, 1997).

Hume-Brown, P., *George Buchanan. Humanist and Reformer* (Edinburgh, 1890).

Johnson, W. McAllister, 'Essai de critique interne des livres d'entrées français au XVIe siécle', in *Les Fêtes de la Renaissance* (3 vols., [Paris], 1975), t. 3, pp. 182–200.

Jondorf, Gillian, *Robert Garnier and the Themes of Political Tragedy in the Sixteenth Century* (Cambridge, 1969).

Jouanna, Arlette, 'Faveur et favoris. L'exemple des mignons de Henri III', in Robert Sauzet (ed.), *Henri III et son temps* (Paris, 1992), pp. 155–65.

Jouhaud, Christian, 'Printing the event from La Rochelle to Paris', in Roger Chartier & Lydia G. Cochrane (eds.), *The Culture of Print. Power and uses of print in early–modern Europe* (Oxford, 1987, 1989), pp. 290–333.

Jouhaud, Christian, 'Readability and Persuasion: Political Handbills', in Roger Chartier & Lydia G. Cochrane (eds.), *The Culture of Print. Power and uses of print in early–modern Europe* (Oxford, 1987, 1989), pp. 235–60.

Kelley, Donald R., *The Beginning of Ideology. Consciousness and society in the French Reformation* (Cambridge, London, New York, New Rochelle, Melbourne, Sydney, 1981).

Kim, S.H., *Michel de L'Hôpital: The Visions of a Reformist Chancellor during the French Religious Wars* (Kirksville, 1997).

Kingdon, Robert, *Myths about the St Bartholomew's Day Massacres 1572–6* (Cambridge Mass. & London, 1988).

Kingdon, Robert, 'Pamphlet Literature of the French Reformation' in Stephen Ozment (ed.), *Reformation Europe. A Guide to Research* (St. Louis, 1982).

Kingdon, Robert, 'The use of clandestine printings by the government of Elizabeth I in its French policy, 1570–90', in Frank McGregor and Nicholas Wright (eds.), *European History and its Historians* (Adelaide, 1977), pp. 47–57.

Labitte, Charles, *De la Démocratie chez les Prédicateurs de la Ligue* (Geneva, 1841, 1971).

Lalanne, Ludovic, *Brantôme. Sa vie et ses Écrits* (Paris, 1896).

Law, Thomas Graves, 'Father William Crichton, S.J.', *Ecclesiastical Historical Review*, 8 (1893), pp. 697–703.

Leake, Roy E., 'Antoine Fouquelin and the Pléiade', *BHR*, 32 (1970).

Lebigre, Arlette, *La Révolution des curés. Paris 1588–94* (Paris, 1980).

Lebvre, Lucien & Martin, Henri-Jean., *The Coming of the Book – the impact of printing 1450–1800* (Norfolk, 1984). The first French edition of this work was published in 1958.

Lewis, Jayne Elizabeth, *Mary Queen of Scots. Romance and Nation* (London, 1998).

Littleton, Charles, 'The French Church of London in European Protestantism, 1574–1611', *Proceedings of the Huguenot Society*, 26/1 (1994), pp. 45–57.

Loades, David, *The Reign of Mary Tudor* (London, 1979, 1981).

Lockie, D., 'The political career of the Bishop of Ross, 1568–80', *University of Birmingham Historical Journal*, 4 (1953–4), pp. 98–145.

Lowers, James K., *Mirrors for Rebels. A study of the polemical literature relating to the Northern Rebellion 1569* (Berkeley and Los Angeles, 1953).

Lynch, Michael, *Edinburgh and the Reformation* (Edinburgh, 1981).

Lynch, Michael, *Mary Stewart. Queen in Three Kingdoms* (Oxford, 1988).

Lynch, Michael, *Scotland. A New History* (London, 1991, 1994).

Mahon, R.H., *The Indictment of Mary Queen of Scots* (Cambridge, 1923).

McFarlane, I.D., 'George Buchanan and France', in J.C. Ireson, I.P. McFarlane & Garnet Rees (eds.), *Studies in French Literature* (New York & Manchester, 1968), pp. 223–45.

McNeill, W.A., 'Documents illustrative of the Scots College, Paris', *Innes Review*, 15 (1964).

Martin, A. Lynn, *Henry III and the Jesuit Politicians* (Geneva, 1973).

Mason, Roger, *Kingship and the Commonweal. Political Thought in Renaissance and Reformation Scotland* (East Linton, 1998).

Matheson, Peter, *The Rhetoric of the Reformation* (Edinburgh, 1998).

Mattingly, Garrett, 'William Allen and Catholic Propaganda in England', in G. Berthoud et al. (eds.), *Aspects de la Propagande Religieuse* (Geneva, 1957), pp. 325–39.

Merriman, Marcus, 'Mary, Queen of France', in Michael Lynch (ed.), *Mary Stewart, Queen in Three Kingdoms* (Oxford, 1988), pp. 30–52.

Merriman, Marcus, *The Rough Wooings. Mary Queen of Scots 1542–51* (East Linton, 2000).

Mignet, F.A., *The History of Mary, Queen of Scots* (2 vols., London, 1851). The first edition of this work was printed in Paris in 1851.

Montagu, Violette M., 'The Scottish College in Paris', *SHR*, 4 (1907), pp. 399–416.

Mosley, Joanne, 'Did Mary Stuart die a "fidele françoise?" Mary Stuart's parting speech to Melville', *BHR*, 52/3 (1990), pp. 623–5.

Mueller, Martin, *Children of Oedipus and other Essays on the Imitation of Greek Tragedy, 1550–1800* (Toronto, Buffalo, London, 1980).

N, J.F., *Mary Stuart and the Casket Letters with introductory note by Henry Glassford Bell* (Edinburgh, 1870).

Neale, J.E., *Queen Elizabeth I* (Chicago, 1992). It was first published in 1934.

Nolhac, Pierre De (ed.), *Ronsard et son temps* (Paris, 1925). An exhibition catalogue made for an 'Exposition des amis de la Bibliothèque Nationale'.

Pallier, Denis, *Recherches sur l'Imprimerie à Paris pendant la Ligue, 1585–94* (Geneva, 1976).

Pallier, Denis, 'Les Réponses catholiques', in Henri–Jean Martin & Roger Chartier (eds.), *L'Histoire de l'édition française* (3 vols., Paris, 1982), pp. 327–47.

Papin, Philippe, 'Les Images des « politiques » durant La Ligue', *Revue d'Histoire Moderne et Contemporaine*, 38 (1991), pp. 3–21.

Parent, Annie, *Les Métiers du livre à Paris au XVIe siècle (1535–60)* (Geneva, 1974).

Parent, Annie, 'Le Monde de l'imprimerie humaniste: Paris', in Henri-Jean Martin & Roger Chartier (eds.), *Histoire de l'édition française* (3 vols., Paris, 1982), pp. 237–53.

Parmelee, Lisa Ferraro, *Good Newes from Fraunce. French Anti–League Propaganda in Late Elizabethan England* (New York, 1996).

Pasquier, Emile, *Un Curé de Paris pendant les Guerres de Religion. René Benoist Le Pape des Halles (1521–1608). Étude historique et bibliographique* (Paris & Angers, 1913).

Pettegree, Andrew, 'Religious Printing in sixteenth century France: the St Andrews Project', *Proceedings of the Huguenot Society*, 26 (1997), pp. 650–9.

Pettegree, Andrew, 'Levels of Anonymity. Clandestine and disguised printing in the Protestant Book World', unpublished paper, presented at the Sixteenth Century Studies Conference, St. Louis, 28 October 1999.

Phillips, James Emerson, *Images of a Queen. Mary Stuart in Sixteenth–Century Literature* (Berkeley & Los Angeles, 1964).

Pinvert, Lucien, *Jacques Grévin (1538–70). Sa Vie, ses écrits, ses amis. Étude biographique et littéraire* (Paris, 1898).

Poncet, Olivier, *Pomponne de Bellièvre (1529–1607). Un homme d'état au temps des Guerres de Religion* (Paris, 1998).

Popkin, Jeremy, 'The Concept of Public Opinion in the Historiography of the French Revolution: A Critique', in *Storia della Storiograpfia*, 20 (1991), pp. 77–92.

Potter, David, 'The duc de Guise and the fall of Calais, 1557–8', *EHR*, 98 (1983), pp. 481–512.

Potter, David, 'French intrigue in Ireland during the reign of Henri II, 1547–59', *The International History Review*, 5/2 (1983), pp. 159–80.

Racaut, Luc, 'The cultural obstacles to religious pluralism in the polemic of the French Wars of Religion' in K. Cameron, M. Greengrass, and P. Roberts (eds.), *The Adventure of Religious Pluralism in Early–Modern France* (Berne, 2000), pp. 115–27.

Racaut, Luc, *Hatred in Print: Aspects of Anti-Protestant polemic in the French Wars of Religion* (unpublished Ph.D. thesis, University of St Andrews, March 1999).

Racaut, Luc, *Hatred in Print. Catholic Propaganda and Protestant Identity during the French Wars of Religion* (Aldershot, 2002).

Ramsay, G.D., 'The Foreign Policy of Elizabeth I', in Christopher Haigh (ed.), *The Reign of Elizabeth I* (London, 1984).

Read, Conyers, *Mr. Secretary Cecil and Queen Elizabeth* (London, 1955).

Read, Conyers, 'William Cecil and Elizabethan Public Relations', in S.T. Bindoff, J. Hurstfield & C.H. Williams (eds.), *Elizabethan Government and Society. Essays presented to Sir John Neale* (London, 1961), pp. 21–55.

Richards, Judith M., 'To promote a woman to beare rule: talking of Queens in mid-Tudor England', *SCJ*, 28/1 (1997), pp. 101–21.

Ritchie, Pamela, *Dynasticism and Diplomacy: The Political Career of Marie de Guise in Scotland, 1548–60* (unpublished Ph.D thesis, University of St Andrews, September 1999).

Roelker, Nancy L., *One King, One Faith. The Parlement of Paris and the Religious Reformations of the Sixteenth Century* (Berkeley, Los Angeles, London, 1996).

Rogier, Jean-Marc, 'Marie Stuart et Bar-sur-Aube: les provisions de Nicolas Bégat (1er août 1586)', *La Vie de Champagne*, 267 (1977), pp. 8–16.

Romier, Lucien, *Les Origines Politiques des Guerres de Religion* (2 vols., Geneva, 1974).

Ruble, Alphonse De, *La Première Jeunesse de Marie Stuart* (Paris, 1891).

Runnals, Graham A. & Carpenter, Sarah, 'The entertainments at the marriage of Mary Queen of Scots and the French dauphin François, 1558: Paris and Edinburgh', a forthcoming article.

Salmon, J.H.M., 'The Paris Sixteen 1584–94: the social analysis of a revolutionary movement', JMH, 44 (1972), 540–76. This essay is reprinted in *Renassance and Revolt. Essays in the Intellectual and Social History of early modern Europe* (Cambridge, 1987), pp. 235–66.

Salmon, J.H.M., *Society in Crisis. France in the Sixteenth Century* (London, 1983).

Saupin, Guy, *Nantes au temps de l'Edict* ([Paris], 1997).

Sawyer, Jeffrey K., *Printed Poison. Pamphlet propaganda, faction politics, and the public sphere in early seventeenth century France* (Oxford, 1990).

Scribner, Robert, *For the Sake of Simple Folk: Popular Propaganda for the German Reformation* (Oxford, 1981, 1994).

Seguin, Jean-Pierre, 'L'Illustration des feuilles d'actualité non périodiques en France aux XVe et XVIe siècles', *Gazette des Beaux–Arts*, (July 1958).

Seguin, Jean-Pierre, *L'Information en France avant la périodique, 517 canards imprimés entre 1529 et 1631* (Paris, [1964]).

Sharman, Julian, *The Library of Mary Queen of Scots* (London, 1889).

Smith, Malcolm, 'Ronsard and Queen Elizabeth I', in *Renaissance Studies and Articles 1966–94* (Geneva, 1997).

Stevenson, Joseph, *Mary Stuart. A narrative of the first eighteen years of her life* (Edinburgh, 1886).

Stoddart, Jane T., *The Girlhood of Mary Queen of Scots from her landing in France in August 1548 to her departure from France in August 1561* (London, [1908]).

Strong, Roy, *Art and Power. Renaissance Festivals, 1450–1650* (Berkeley & Los Angeles, 1973, 1984).

Sypher, Wylie G., 'Faisant ce qu'il leur vient a plaisir: The Image of Protestantism in French Catholic polemic on the eve of the Religious Wars', *SCJ*, 9/2 (1980), pp. 59–84.

Taithe, Bertrand & Thornton, Jim, 'Propaganda: A Misnomer of Rhetoric and Persuasion?' in their *Propaganda: Political Rhetoric and Identity 1300–2000* (Thrupp, 1999).

Taylor, Philip M., *Munitions of the Mind: A History of Propaganda from the ancient world to the present era* (Manchester, 1994). This study was originally published in 1990.

Thickett, D., 'Estienne Pasquier and his part in the struggle for tolerance', in G. Berthoud et al. (eds.), *Aspects de la Propagande Religeuse* (Geneva, 1957), pp. 377–402.

Thysell, Carol, 'Gendered virtue, vernacular theology, and the nature of authority in the Heptameron', *SCJ*, 29/1 (1998), pp. 39–53.

Trinquet, Roger, 'L'Allégorie politique dans la peinture frnçise au XVIe siècle: Les Dames au Bain', *Bulletin de la Société de l'histoire de l'art français*, (1967–8), pp. 99–119, pp. 7–25.

Valois, Charles (ed.), *Histoire de La Ligue, oeuvre d'un contemporain* (Paris, 1914).

Voss, Paul J., 'Books for sale: Advertising and patronage in late Elizabethan England', *SCJ*, 29/3 (1998), pp. 733–56.

Wardropper, Ian, 'Le Mécénat des Guises. Art, religion et politique au milieu du XVIe siècle', in *Revue de l'Art*, 94 (1991), pp. 27–44.

Warner, Michael, 'Publication and the Public Sphere', in Carol Ambruster (ed.), *Publishing and Readership in Revolutionary France and America* (Westport, London, 1993), pp. 167–74.

Watson, David, *The Martyrology of Jean Crespin and the Early French Evangelical Movement, 1523–55* (Unpublished Ph.D. thesis, University of St Andrews, 1997).

Waugh, Evelyn, *Edmond Campion Humaniste et Martyr (1540–81)* (Paris, 1989).

Wernham, R.B., *The Making of Elizabethan Foreign Policy, 1558–1603* (London, 1980).

Wiggishoff, J.C., *Notes pour servir à l'Histoire du Livre en France. Imprimeurs et libraires Parisiens Correcteurs, Graveurs et Fondeurs. Particularités oubliées ou peu connues de 1470 à 1600* (Paris, 1900).

Williamson, Arthur, *Scottish National Consciousness in the age of James VI: The Apocalypse, the Union and the Shaping of Scotland's Public Culture* (Edinburgh, 1979).

Wintroub, Michael, 'Civilizing the savage and the making of a King: The Royal entry festival of Henri II (Rouen, 1550) in *SCJ*, 29/2 (1998), pp. 465–94.

Wolfe, Michael, *The Conversion of Henry IV. Politics, Power and Religious Belief in Early Modern France* (London, 1993).

Wormald, Jenny, *Mary Queen of Scots: A Study in Failure* (London, 1988).

Zermer, Henri, *L'Art de la Renaissance en France. L'Invention du Classicisme* (Paris, 1996).

Index

Note: publications mentioned in the main text have been included in this index.